HIROAKI

3

SAMURA

LISTEN
TO ME!

S T O R Y & C A S T

Sapporo, Hokkaido. One night at a bar, Minare Koda has her heartbroken ramblings secretly recorded by a local FM radio station director, Mato, who then airs the audio the following day. Minare storms into the station in a burst of fury, only to be duped by Mato into doing an impromptu talk show explaining her severe remarks. The segment turns out to be a big hit, leading Mato to make Minare an official offer to have her own show. The first broadcast—a "real-time fiction" radio drama in which she kills the ex-boyfriend who ran off with her money—was well-received. Now it's the continuation of the second broadcast: "The Late-Night Burial."

Minare Koda

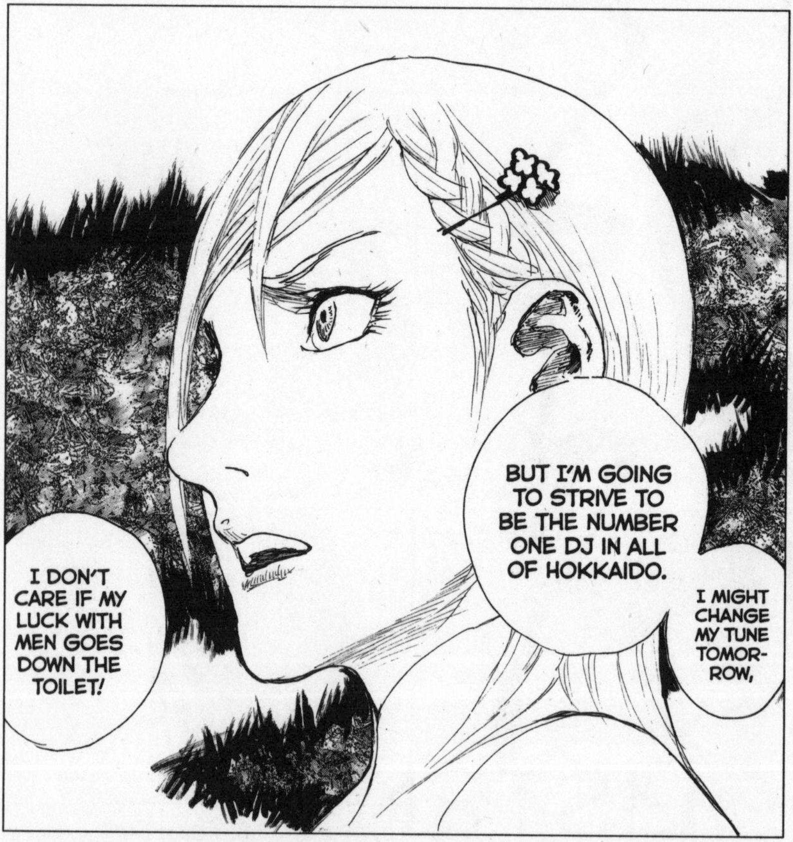
I MIGHT CHANGE MY TUNE TOMOR-ROW,
BUT I'M GOING TO STRIVE TO BE THE NUMBER ONE DJ IN ALL OF HOKKAIDO.
I DON'T CARE IF MY LUCK WITH MEN GOES DOWN THE TOILET!

The protagonist. Lives in Sapporo, a bustling city on Japan's chilly, northern island of Hokkaido. Born and raised in the coastal city of Kushiro. Currently 25 and single. Her day job as a waitress at the soup curry restaurant VOYAGER is in jeopardy, so she's scrambling to make a living as a radio DJ instead.

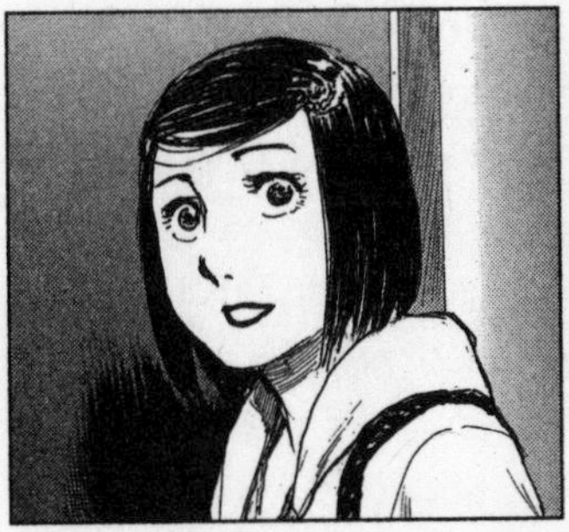

Mizuho Nanba

Assistant director at MRS. Currently letting Minare stay with her after Minare was kicked out of her apartment. Virgin.

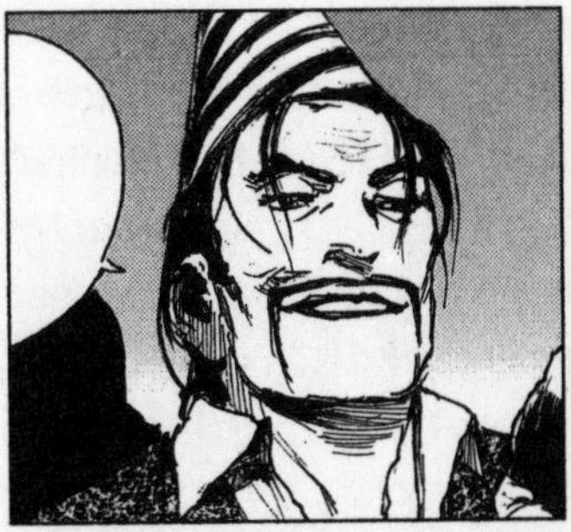

Kanetsugu Mato

A director at the FM station Moiwayama Radio (MRS). Saw potential in Minare's conversational ability and scouted her for the radio business.

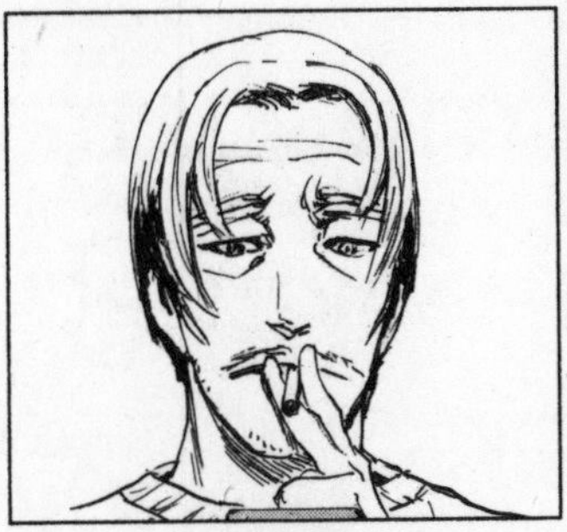

Katsumi Kureko

A scriptwriter for MRS and a veteran of the industry. Supposedly goes way back with Mato.

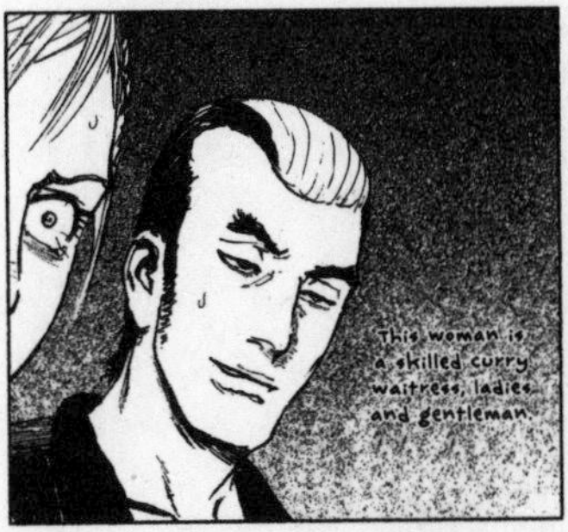
This woman is a skilled curry waitress, ladies and gentleman.

Chuuya Nakahara

An employee at VOYAGER. Supposedly in love with Minare, but invited Makie to stay at his place.

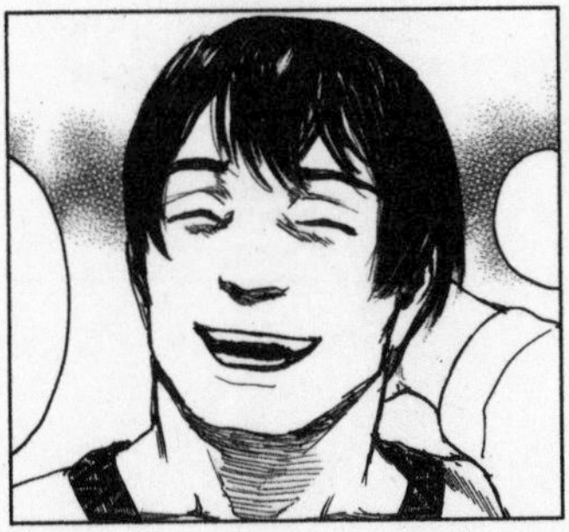

Mitsuo

Minare's audacious ex-boyfriend who swindled her out of 500,000 yen before vanishing without a trace. Recently contacted Minare again to try to patch things up. Born far to the balmy south, in Fukuoka.

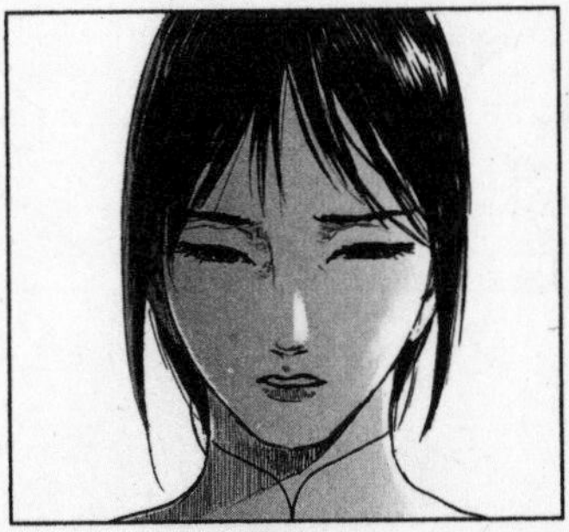

Makie Tachibana

A beautiful woman working at VOYAGER to help pay for the car accident caused by her brother. Not the most skilled swordsperson in this manga, nor a prostitute.

Chapter 17 ◊ "ANAEROBES FEAR NOTHING." 005

Chapter 18 ◊ "IT'S MY DUTY." 029

Chapter 19 ◊ "I WANT TO WARM YOU UP." 049

Chapter 20 ◊ "THEY DON'T EXIST." 069

Chapter 21 ◊ "STEAM IS UNCONCEALABLE." 091

Chapter 22 ◊ "I WANT TO CRY." 107

Chapter 23 ◊ "I WANT TO SUPPORT YOU." 129

Chapter 24 ◊ "DON'T MESS WITH YAKITORI." 151

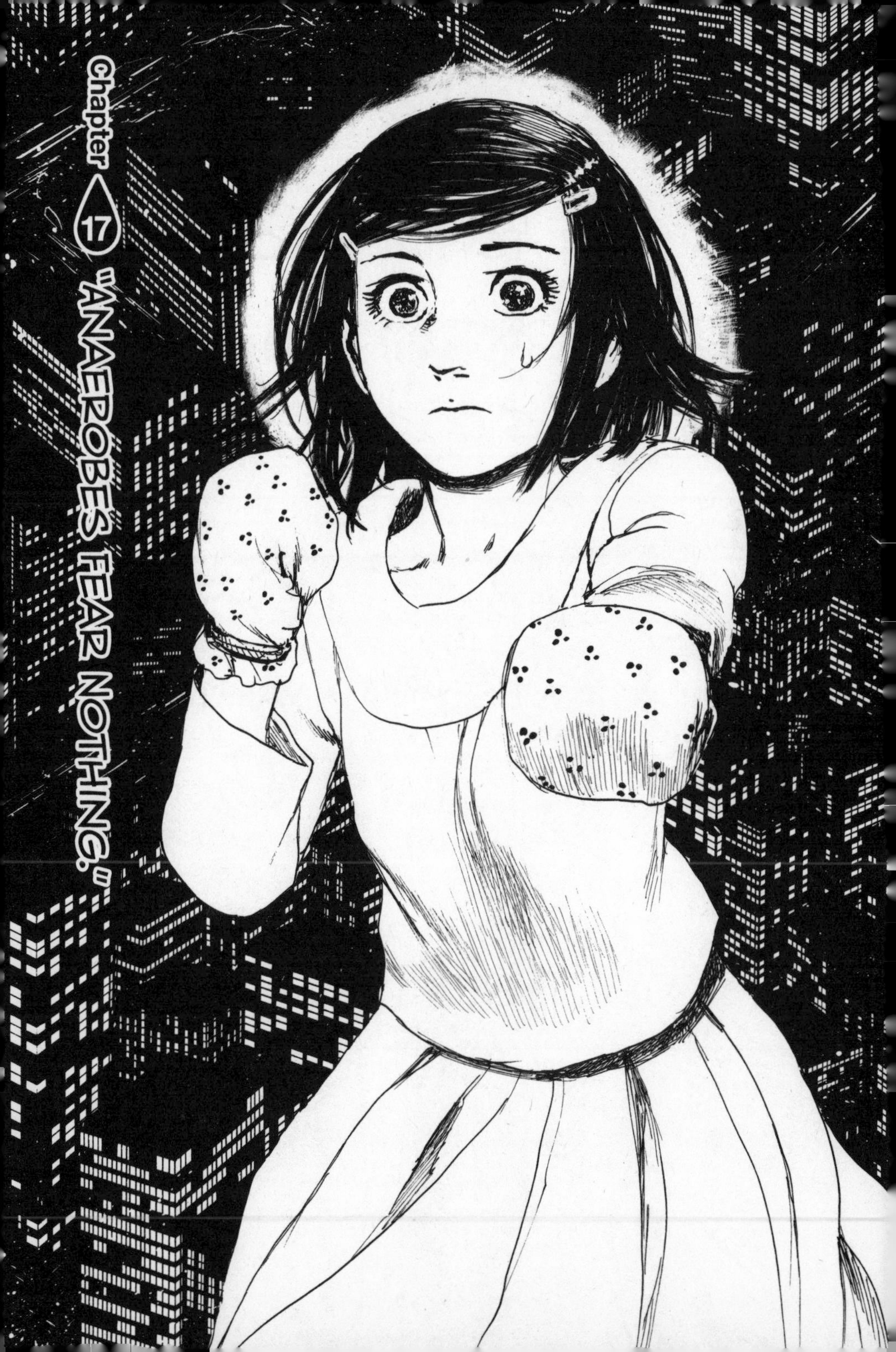
Chapter 17 "ANAEROBES FEAR NOTHING."

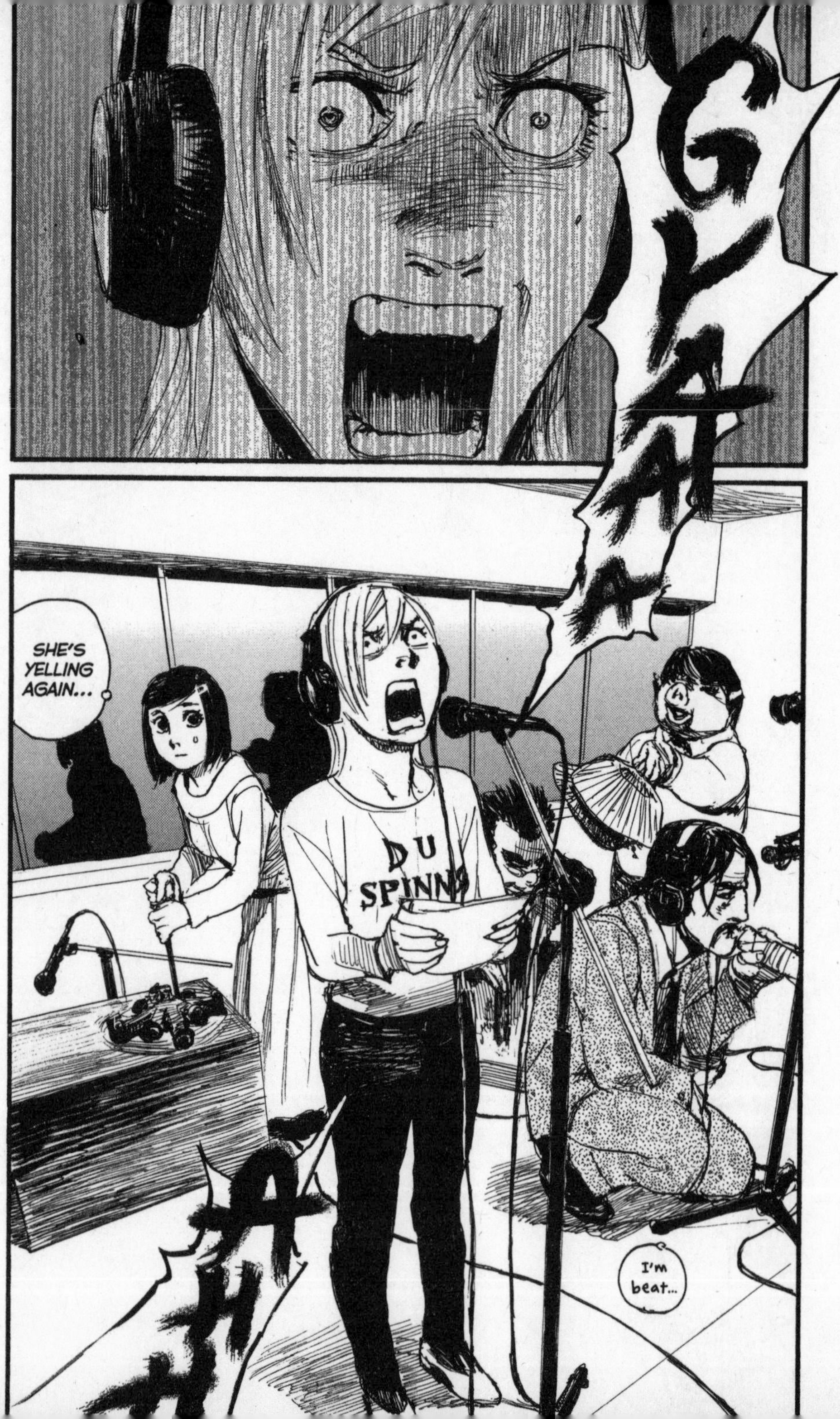
GYAAA
SHE'S YELLING AGAIN...
I'm beat...
AH

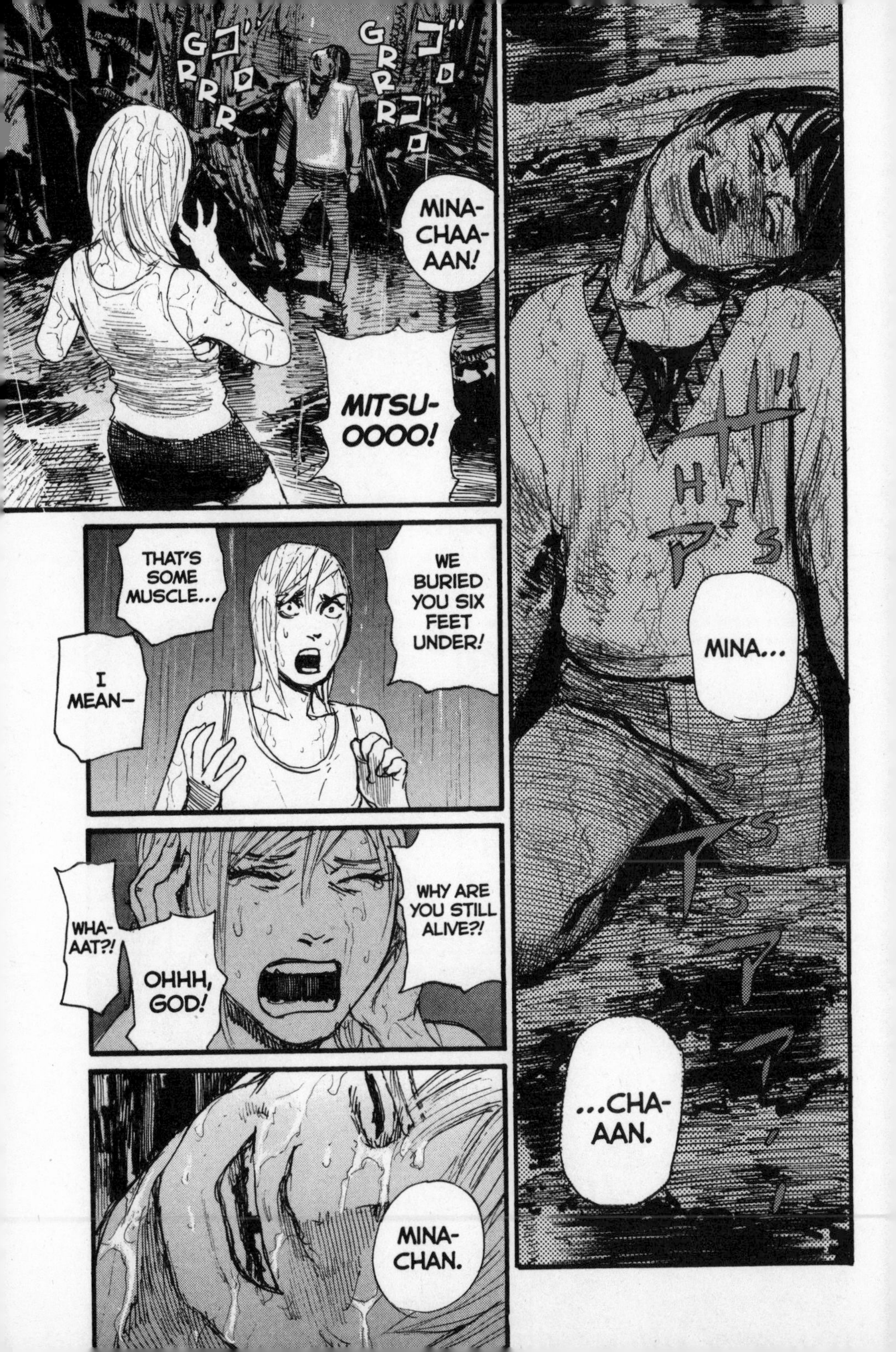
H
I
S
MINA...
S
S
S
...CHA-AAN.
GRRRR
GRRRR
MINA-CHAAA-AAN!
MITSU-OOOO!
WE BURIED YOU SIX FEET UNDER!
THAT'S SOME MUSCLE...
I MEAN—
WHY ARE YOU STILL ALIVE?!
WHA-AAT?!
OHHH, GOD!
MINA-CHAN.

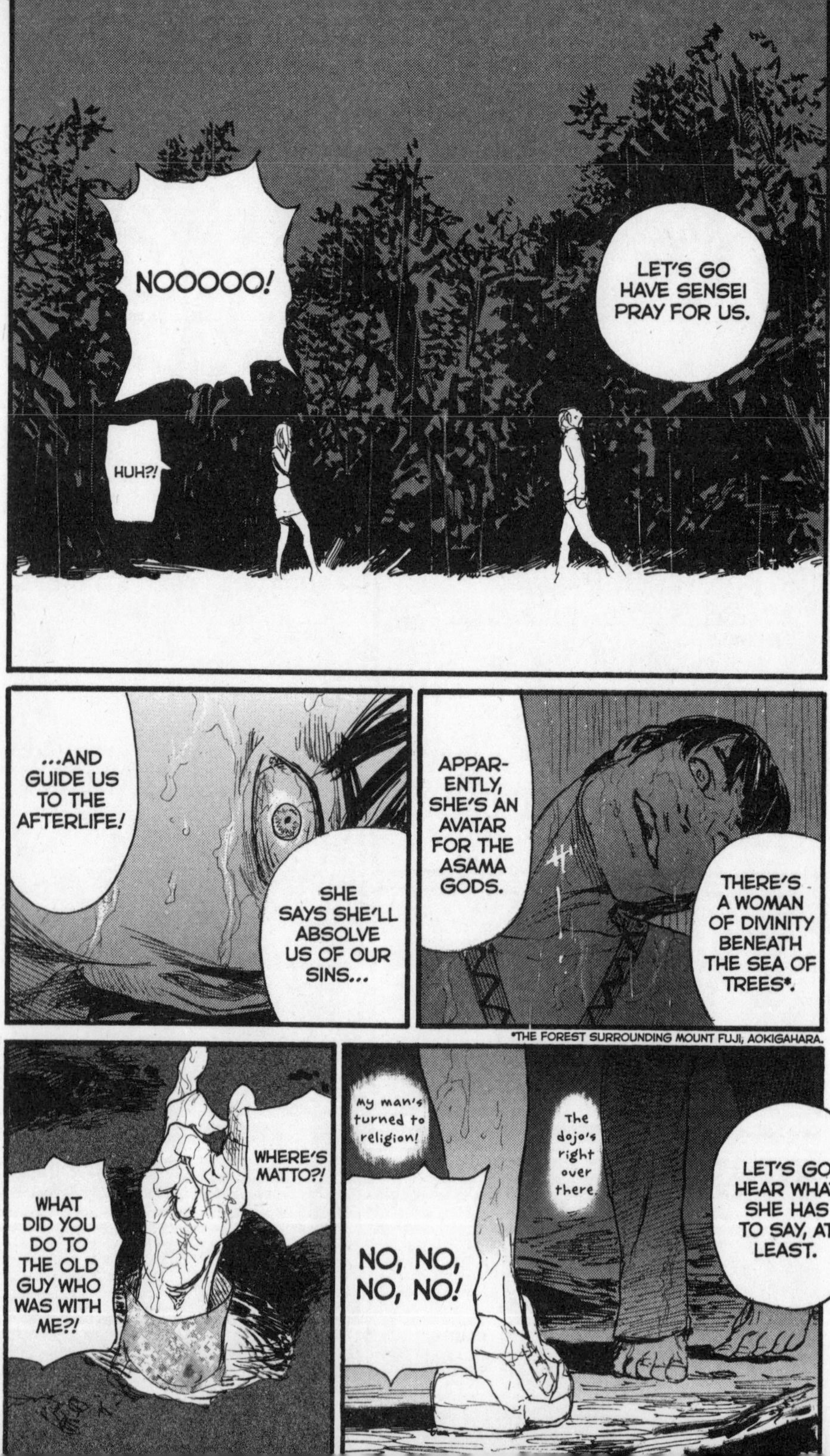
LET'S GO HAVE SENSEI PRAY FOR US.
NOOOOO!
HUH?!
THERE'S A WOMAN OF DIVINITY BENEATH THE SEA OF TREES*.
APPARENTLY, SHE'S AN AVATAR FOR THE ASAMA GODS.
SHE SAYS SHE'LL ABSOLVE US OF OUR SINS...
...AND GUIDE US TO THE AFTERLIFE!
LET'S GO HEAR WHAT SHE HAS TO SAY, AT LEAST.
The dojo's right over there.
My man's turned to religion!
NO, NO, NO, NO!
WHERE'S MATTO?!
WHAT DID YOU DO TO THE OLD GUY WHO WAS WITH ME?!

*THE FOREST SURROUNDING MOUNT FUJI, AOKIGAHARA.

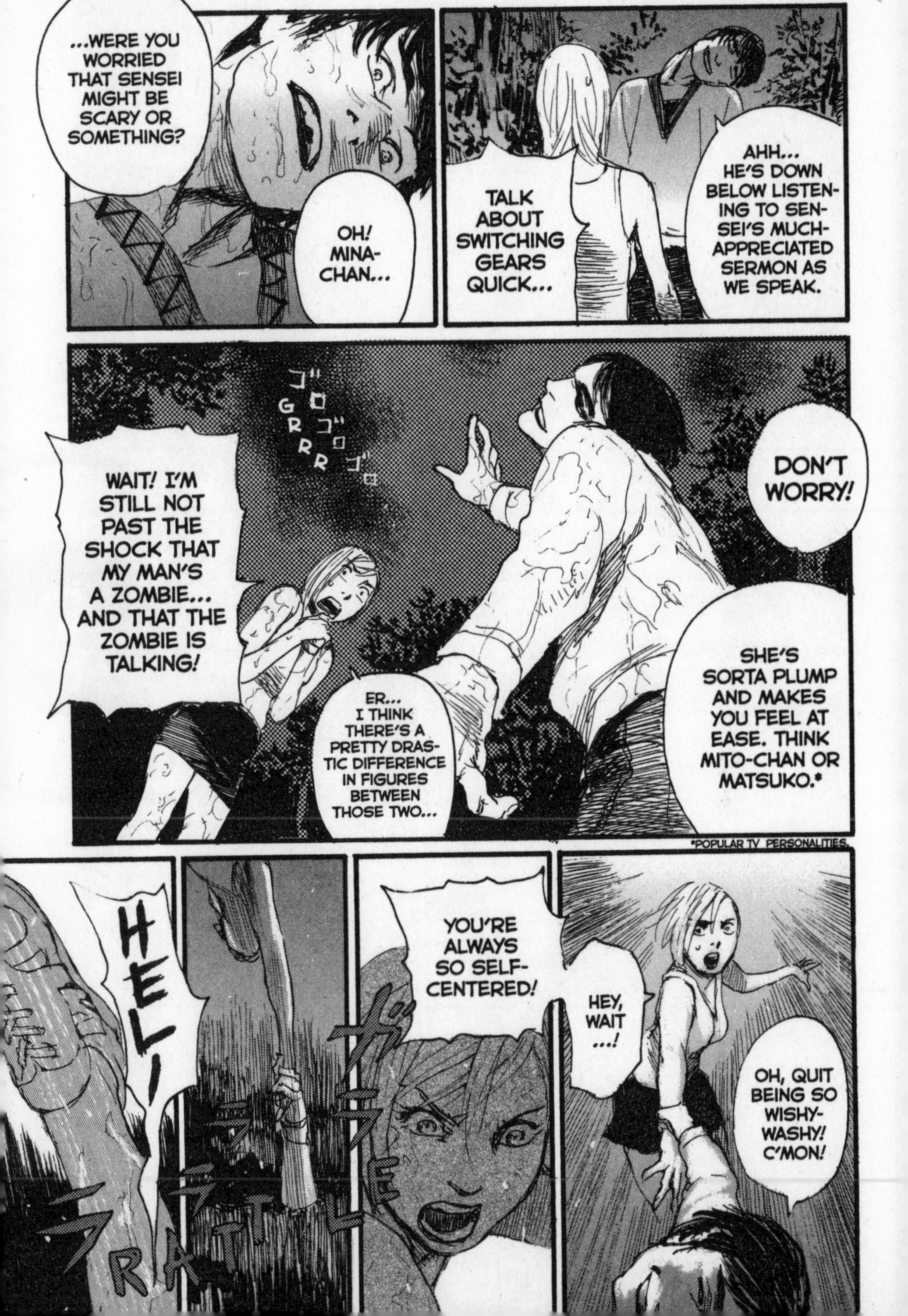
AHH... HE'S DOWN BELOW LISTEN-ING TO SEN-SEI'S MUCH-APPRECIATED SERMON AS WE SPEAK.
TALK ABOUT SWITCHING GEARS QUICK...
...WERE YOU WORRIED THAT SENSEI MIGHT BE SCARY OR SOMETHING?
OH! MINA-CHAN...
DON'T WORRY!
SHE'S SORTA PLUMP AND MAKES YOU FEEL AT EASE. THINK MITO-CHAN OR MATSUKO.*
GRRR
ER... I THINK THERE'S A PRETTY DRAS-TIC DIFFERENCE IN FIGURES BETWEEN THOSE TWO...
WAIT! I'M STILL NOT PAST THE SHOCK THAT MY MAN'S A ZOMBIE... AND THAT THE ZOMBIE IS TALKING!
*POPULAR TV PERSONALITIES.
OH, QUIT BEING SO WISHY-WASHY! C'MON!
HEY, WAIT ...!
YOU'RE ALWAYS SO SELF-CENTERED!
HELL
RATTLE

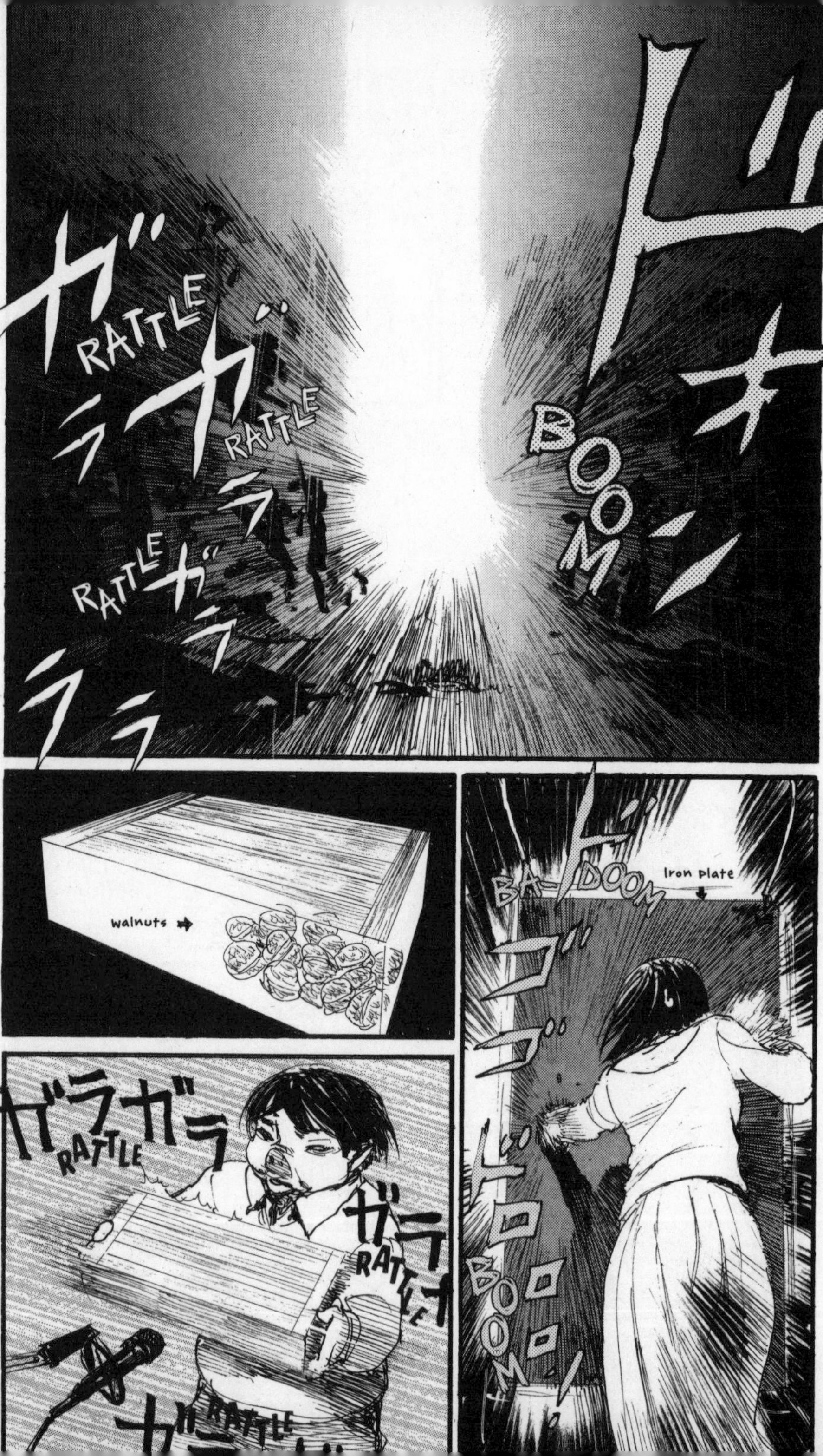

ドオン
BOOM
ガラガラガラガラ
RATTLE
RATTLE
RATTLE
ド
BA-DOOM
Iron plate
ゴゴ
ドロロロ
BOOOM
walnuts
ガラガラ
RATTLE
ガラ
RATTLE
RATTLE...

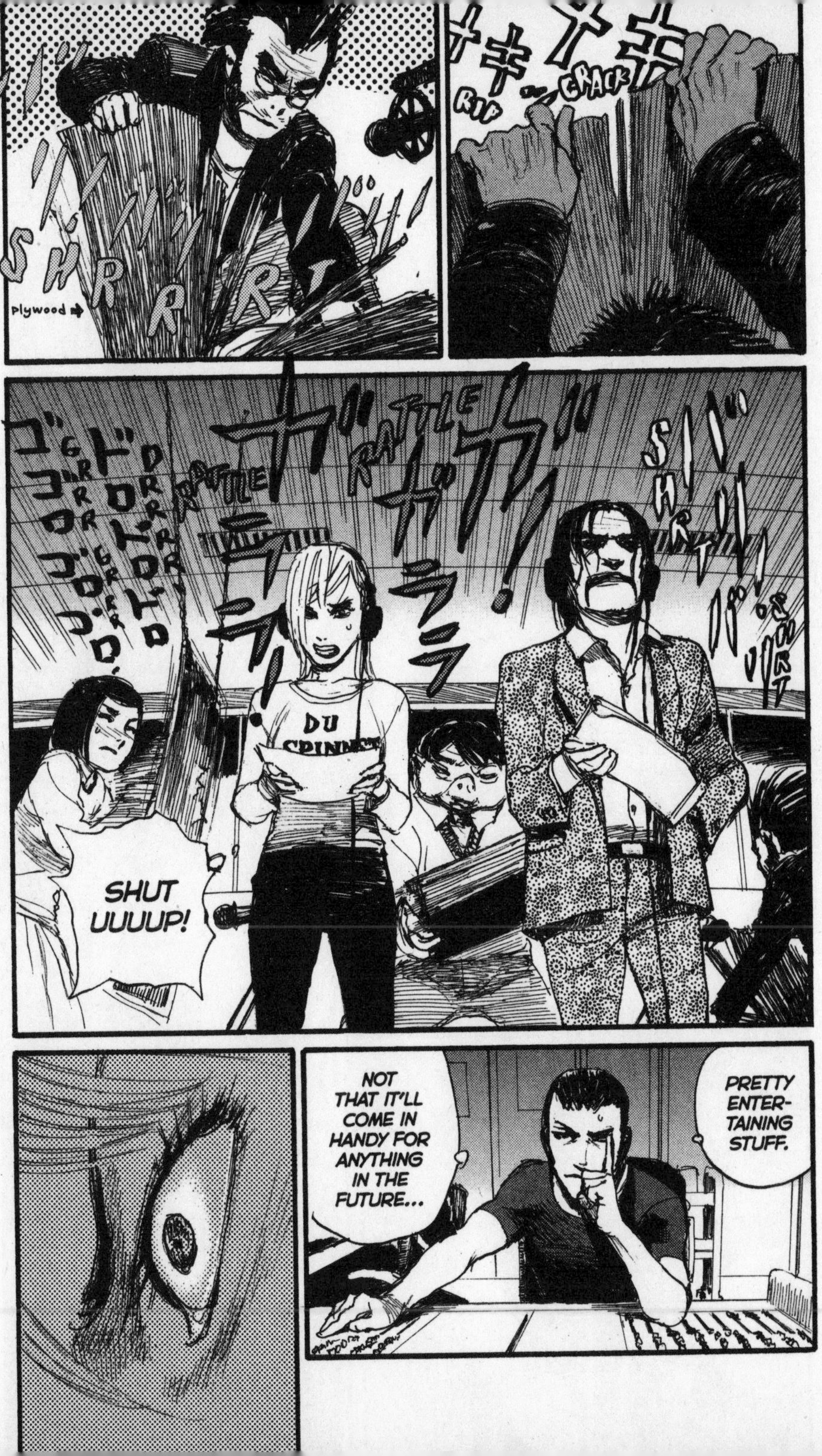
RIP
CRACK
SHRRRRI
plywood
RATTLE
RATTLE
SHRT
SHUT UUUUP!
PRETTY ENTER-TAINING STUFF.
NOT THAT IT'LL COME IN HANDY FOR ANYTHING IN THE FUTURE...

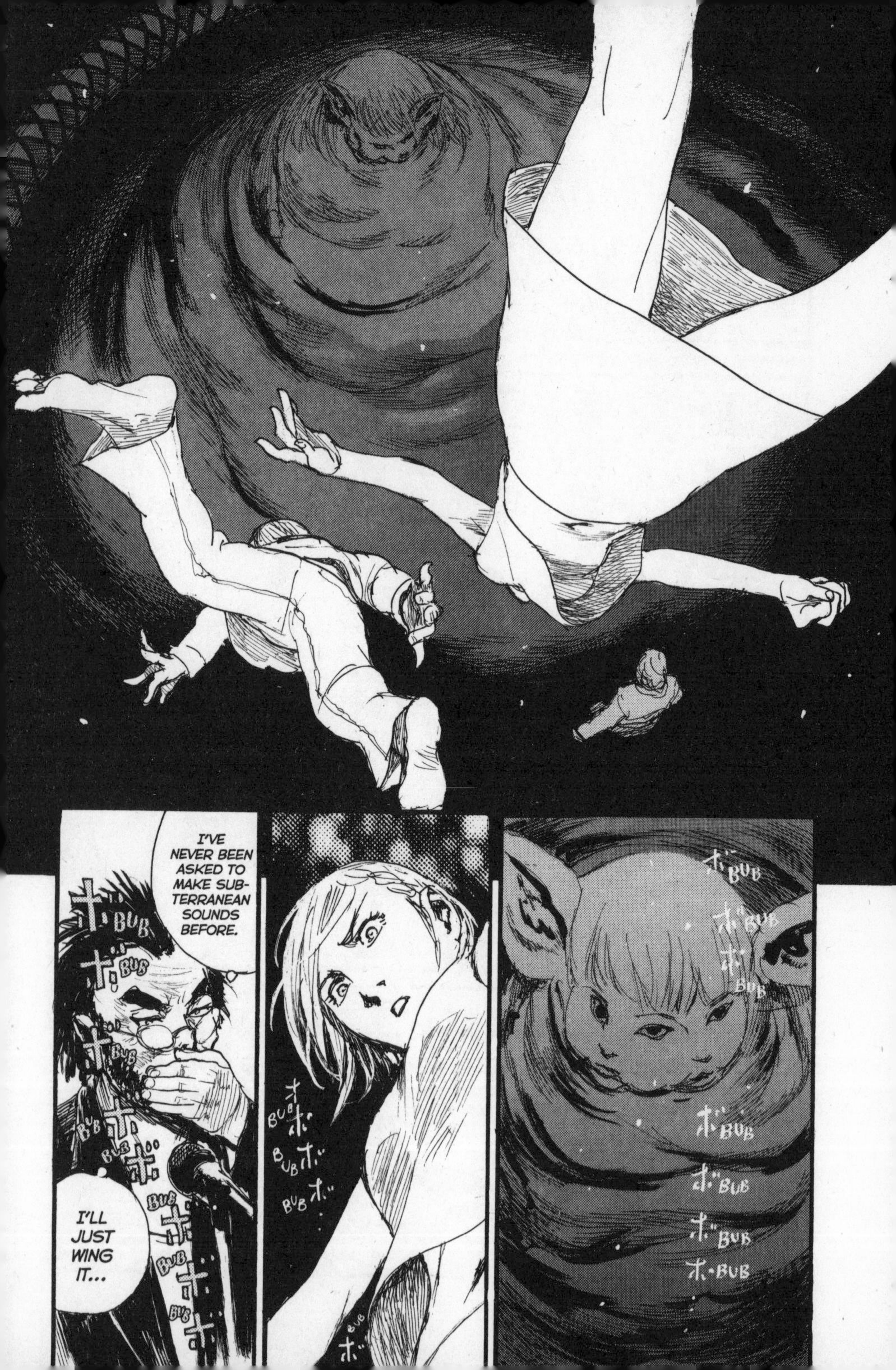
ボBUB
ボBUB
ボBUB
ボBUB
ボBUB
ボBUB
ホ・BUB
BUB ボ
BUB ボ
BUB ボ
BUB ボ
I'VE NEVER BEEN ASKED TO MAKE SUB-TERRANEAN SOUNDS BEFORE.
ホBUB
ホBUB
ホBUB
BUB ホ
BUB ホ
I'LL JUST WING IT...
BUB ホ
BUB ホ
BUB ホ

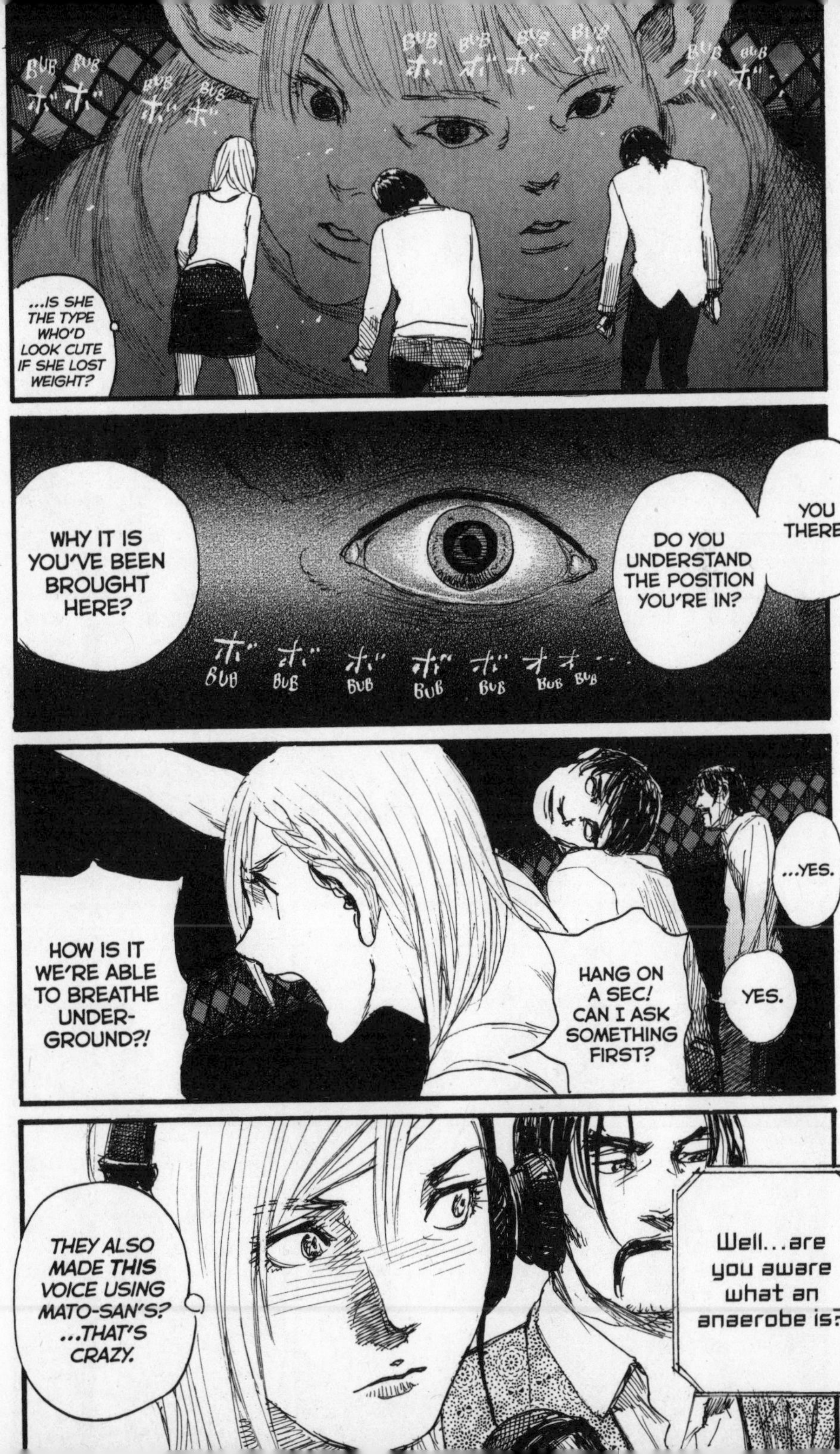
BUB BUB BUB BUB BUB BUB BUB BUB
...IS SHE THE TYPE WHO'D LOOK CUTE IF SHE LOST WEIGHT?
YOU THERE.
DO YOU UNDERSTAND THE POSITION YOU'RE IN?
WHY IT IS YOU'VE BEEN BROUGHT HERE?
BUB BUB BUB BUB BUB BUB BUB
...YES.
YES.
HANG ON A SEC! CAN I ASK SOMETHING FIRST?
HOW IS IT WE'RE ABLE TO BREATHE UNDER-GROUND?!
Well...are you aware what an anaerobe is?
THEY ALSO MADE THIS VOICE USING MATO-SAN'S? ...THAT'S CRAZY.

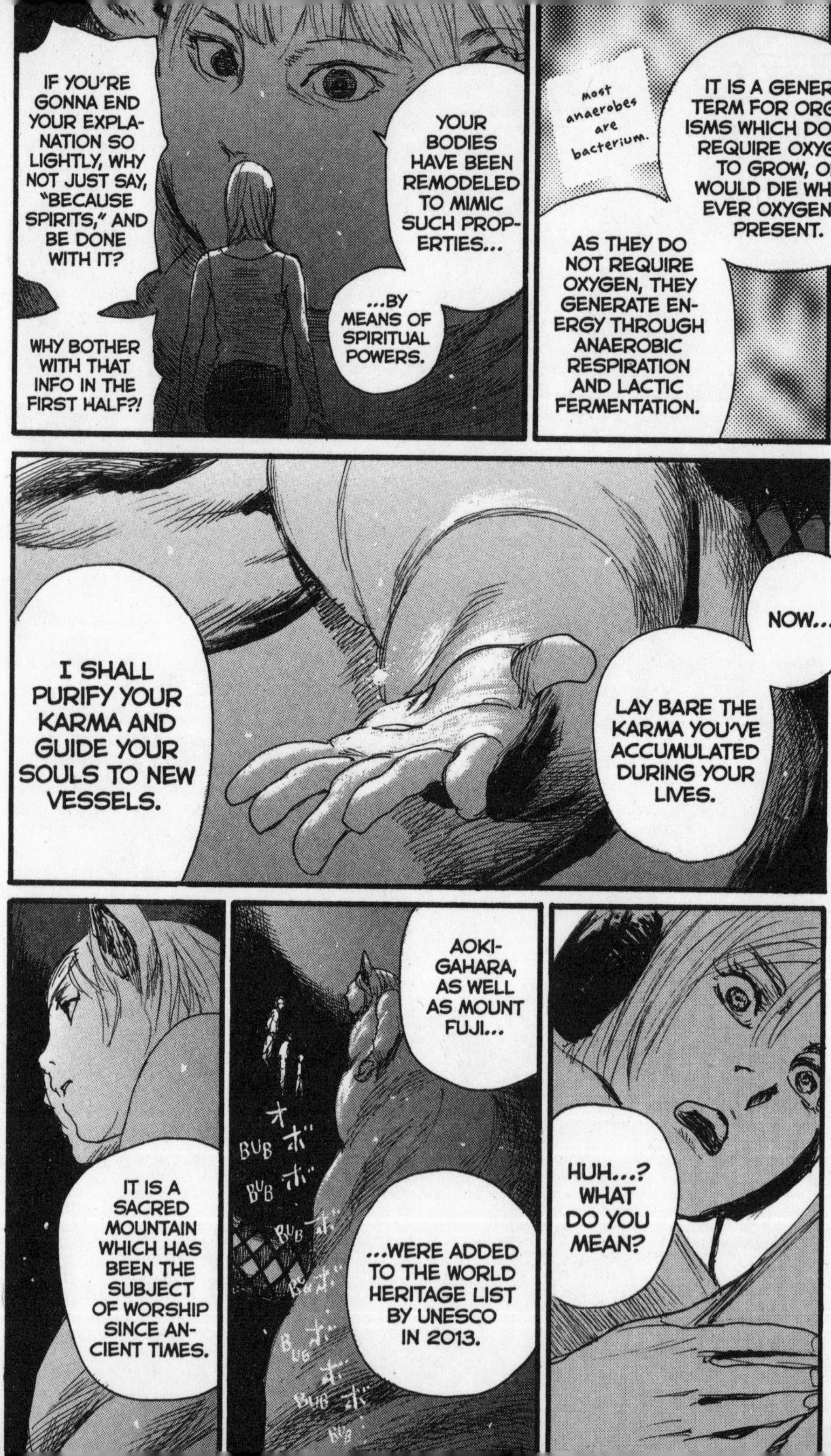
IT IS A GENERAL TERM FOR ORGANISMS WHICH DO NOT REQUIRE OXYGEN TO GROW, OR WOULD DIE WHEREVER OXYGEN IS PRESENT.
Most anaerobes are bacterium.
AS THEY DO NOT REQUIRE OXYGEN, THEY GENERATE ENERGY THROUGH ANAEROBIC RESPIRATION AND LACTIC FERMENTATION.
YOUR BODIES HAVE BEEN REMODELED TO MIMIC SUCH PROPERTIES...
...BY MEANS OF SPIRITUAL POWERS.
IF YOU'RE GONNA END YOUR EXPLANATION SO LIGHTLY, WHY NOT JUST SAY, "BECAUSE SPIRITS," AND BE DONE WITH IT?
WHY BOTHER WITH THAT INFO IN THE FIRST HALF?!
NOW...
LAY BARE THE KARMA YOU'VE ACCUMULATED DURING YOUR LIVES.
I SHALL PURIFY YOUR KARMA AND GUIDE YOUR SOULS TO NEW VESSELS.
HUH...? WHAT DO YOU MEAN?
AOKI-GAHARA, AS WELL AS MOUNT FUJI...
...WERE ADDED TO THE WORLD HERITAGE LIST BY UNESCO IN 2013.
オボ
BUB
ボ
BUB
ボ
BUB
ボ
BUB
ボ
BUB
ボ
BUB
ボ
BUB
IT IS A SACRED MOUNTAIN WHICH HAS BEEN THE SUBJECT OF WORSHIP SINCE ANCIENT TIMES.

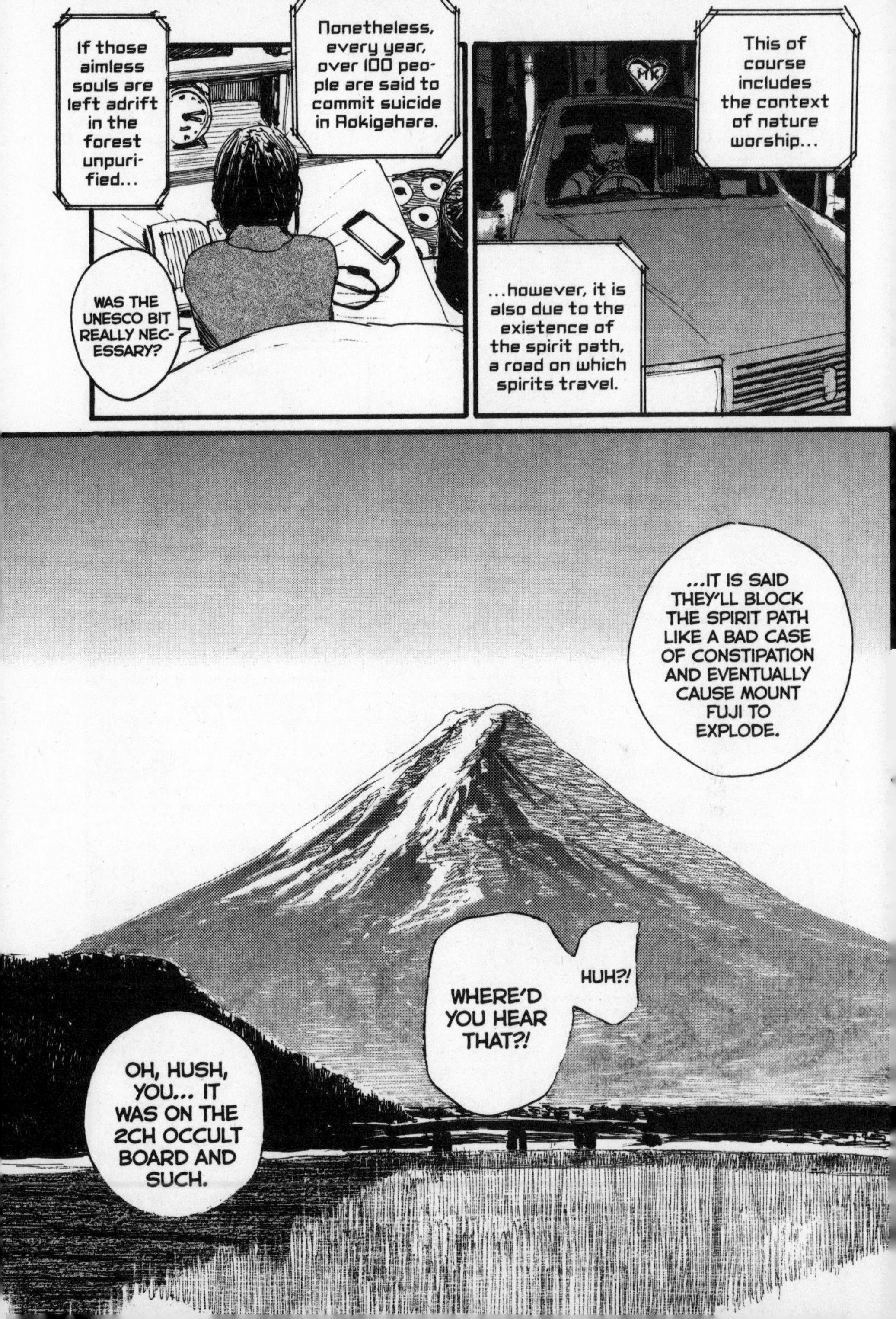
This of course includes the context of nature worship...
...however, it is also due to the existence of the spirit path, a road on which spirits travel.
Nonetheless, every year, over 100 peo-ple are said to commit suicide in Aokigahara.
If those aimless souls are left adrift in the forest unpuri-fied...
WAS THE UNESCO BIT REALLY NEC-ESSARY?
...IT IS SAID THEY'LL BLOCK THE SPIRIT PATH LIKE A BAD CASE OF CONSTIPATION AND EVENTUALLY CAUSE MOUNT FUJI TO EXPLODE.
HUH?!
WHERE'D YOU HEAR THAT?!
OH, HUSH, YOU... IT WAS ON THE 2CH OCCULT BOARD AND SUCH.

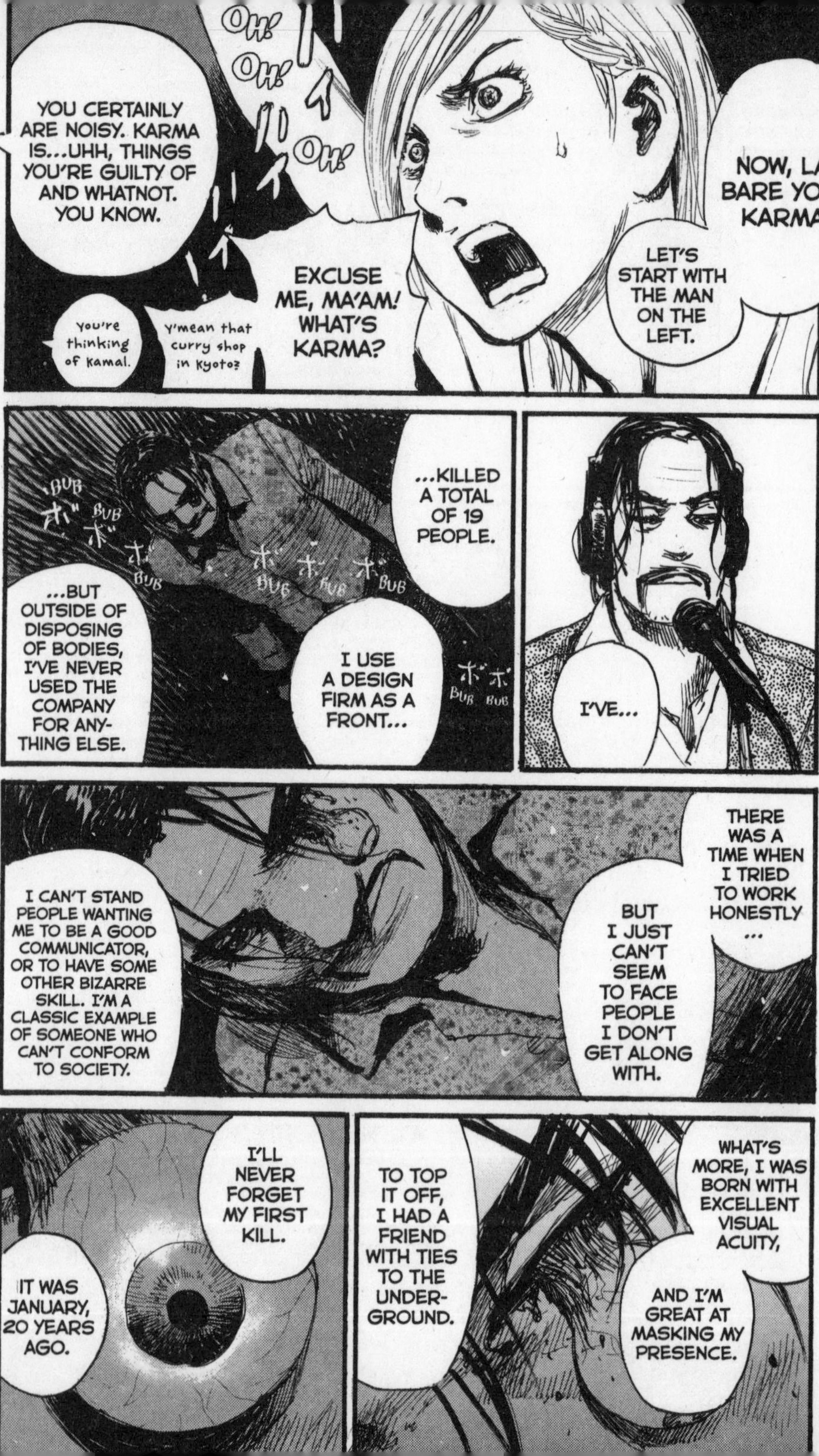
NOW, LAY BARE YOUR KARMA!
LET'S START WITH THE MAN ON THE LEFT.
OH! OH! OH!
EXCUSE ME, MA'AM! WHAT'S KARMA?
YOU CERTAINLY ARE NOISY. KARMA IS...UHH, THINGS YOU'RE GUILTY OF AND WHATNOT. YOU KNOW.
Y'mean that curry shop in Kyoto?
You're thinking of Kamal.
I'VE...
...KILLED A TOTAL OF 19 PEOPLE.
BUB BUB BUB BUB BUB BUB
I USE A DESIGN FIRM AS A FRONT...
...BUT OUTSIDE OF DISPOSING OF BODIES, I'VE NEVER USED THE COMPANY FOR ANY-THING ELSE.
BUB BUB
THERE WAS A TIME WHEN I TRIED TO WORK HONESTLY...
BUT I JUST CAN'T SEEM TO FACE PEOPLE I DON'T GET ALONG WITH.
I CAN'T STAND PEOPLE WANTING ME TO BE A GOOD COMMUNICATOR, OR TO HAVE SOME OTHER BIZARRE SKILL. I'M A CLASSIC EXAMPLE OF SOMEONE WHO CAN'T CONFORM TO SOCIETY.
WHAT'S MORE, I WAS BORN WITH EXCELLENT VISUAL ACUITY,
AND I'M GREAT AT MASKING MY PRESENCE.
TO TOP IT OFF, I HAD A FRIEND WITH TIES TO THE UNDER-GROUND.
I'LL NEVER FORGET MY FIRST KILL.
IT WAS JANUARY, 20 YEARS AGO.

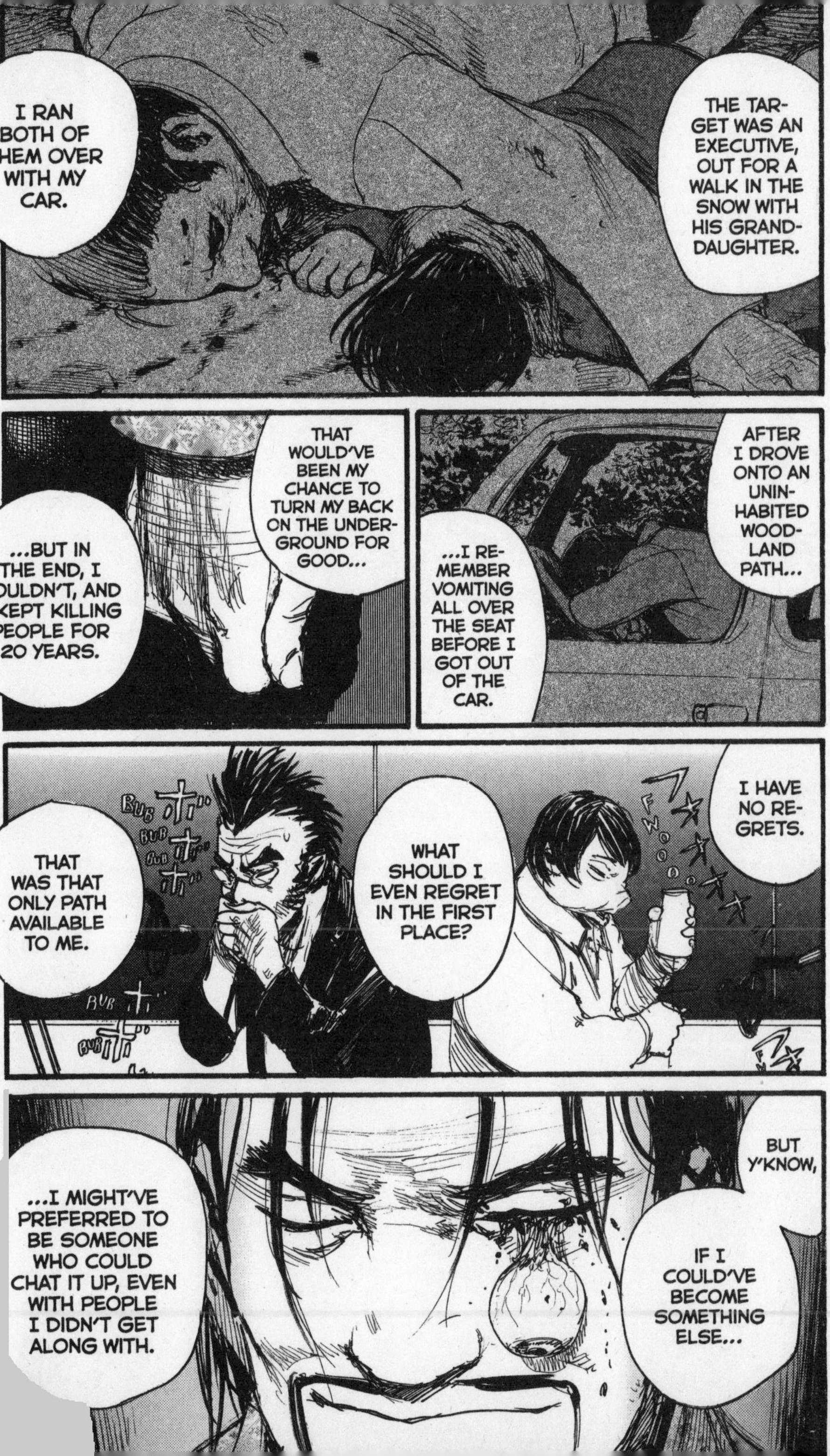
THE TARGET WAS AN EXECUTIVE, OUT FOR A WALK IN THE SNOW WITH HIS GRANDDAUGHTER.
I RAN BOTH OF THEM OVER WITH MY CAR.
AFTER I DROVE ONTO AN UNINHABITED WOODLAND PATH...
...I REMEMBER VOMITING ALL OVER THE SEAT BEFORE I GOT OUT OF THE CAR.
THAT WOULD'VE BEEN MY CHANCE TO TURN MY BACK ON THE UNDERGROUND FOR GOOD...
...BUT IN THE END, I COULDN'T, AND I KEPT KILLING PEOPLE FOR 20 YEARS.
I HAVE NO REGRETS.
FWOOO
WHAT SHOULD I EVEN REGRET IN THE FIRST PLACE?
BUB
BUB
BUB
THAT WAS THAT ONLY PATH AVAILABLE TO ME.
BUB
BUB
BUT Y'KNOW,
IF I COULD'VE BECOME SOMETHING ELSE...
...I MIGHT'VE PREFERRED TO BE SOMEONE WHO COULD CHAT IT UP, EVEN WITH PEOPLE I DIDN'T GET ALONG WITH.

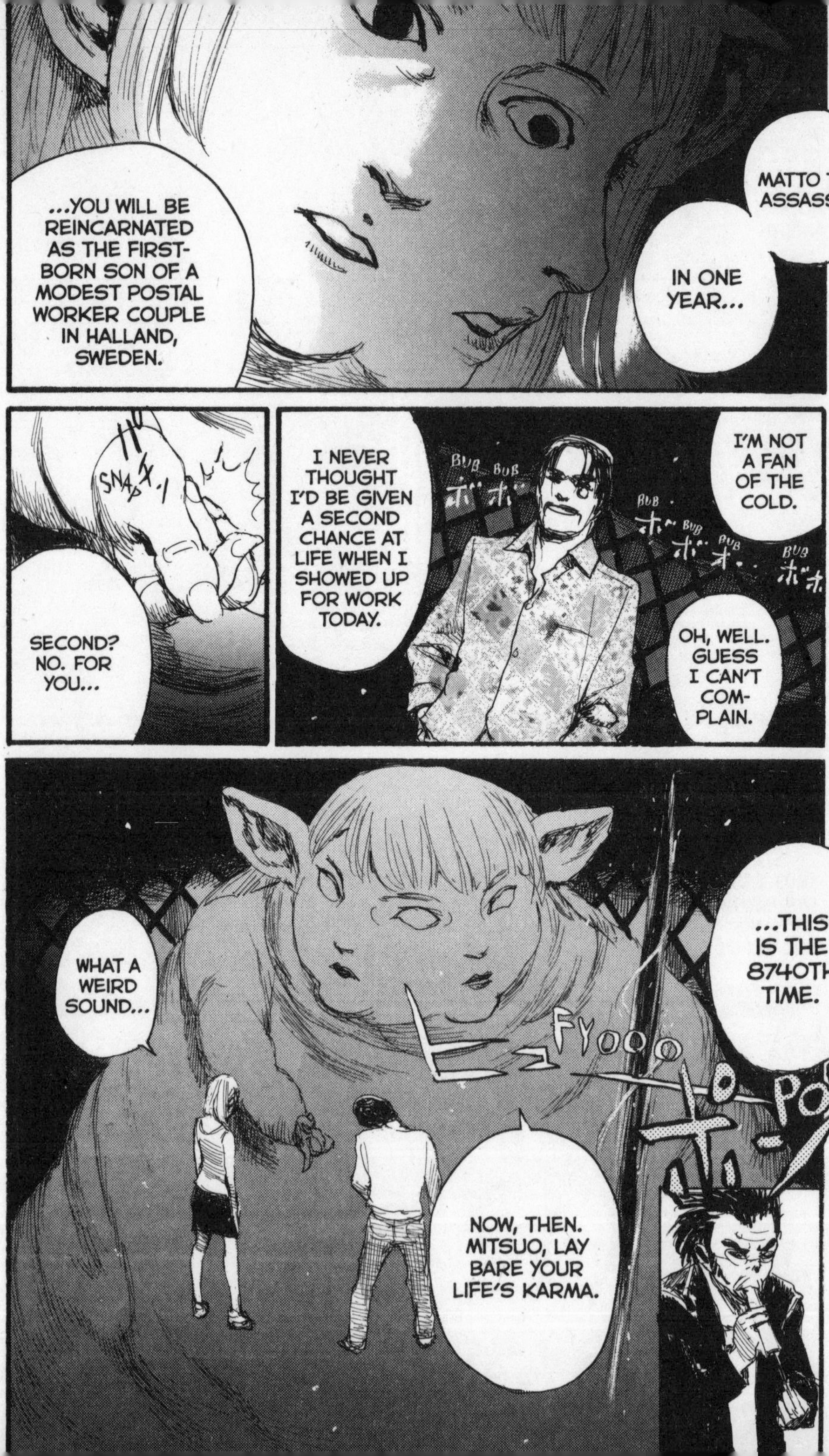
MATTO THE ASSASSIN,
IN ONE YEAR...
...YOU WILL BE REINCARNATED AS THE FIRST-BORN SON OF A MODEST POSTAL WORKER COUPLE IN HALLAND, SWEDEN.
I'M NOT A FAN OF THE COLD.
BUB BUB
BUB BUB BUB BUB
OH, WELL. GUESS I CAN'T COM-PLAIN.
I NEVER THOUGHT I'D BE GIVEN A SECOND CHANCE AT LIFE WHEN I SHOWED UP FOR WORK TODAY.
SNAP
SECOND? NO. FOR YOU...
...THIS IS THE 8740TH TIME.
FYOOO
POP
WHAT A WEIRD SOUND...
NOW, THEN. MITSUO, LAY BARE YOUR LIFE'S KARMA.

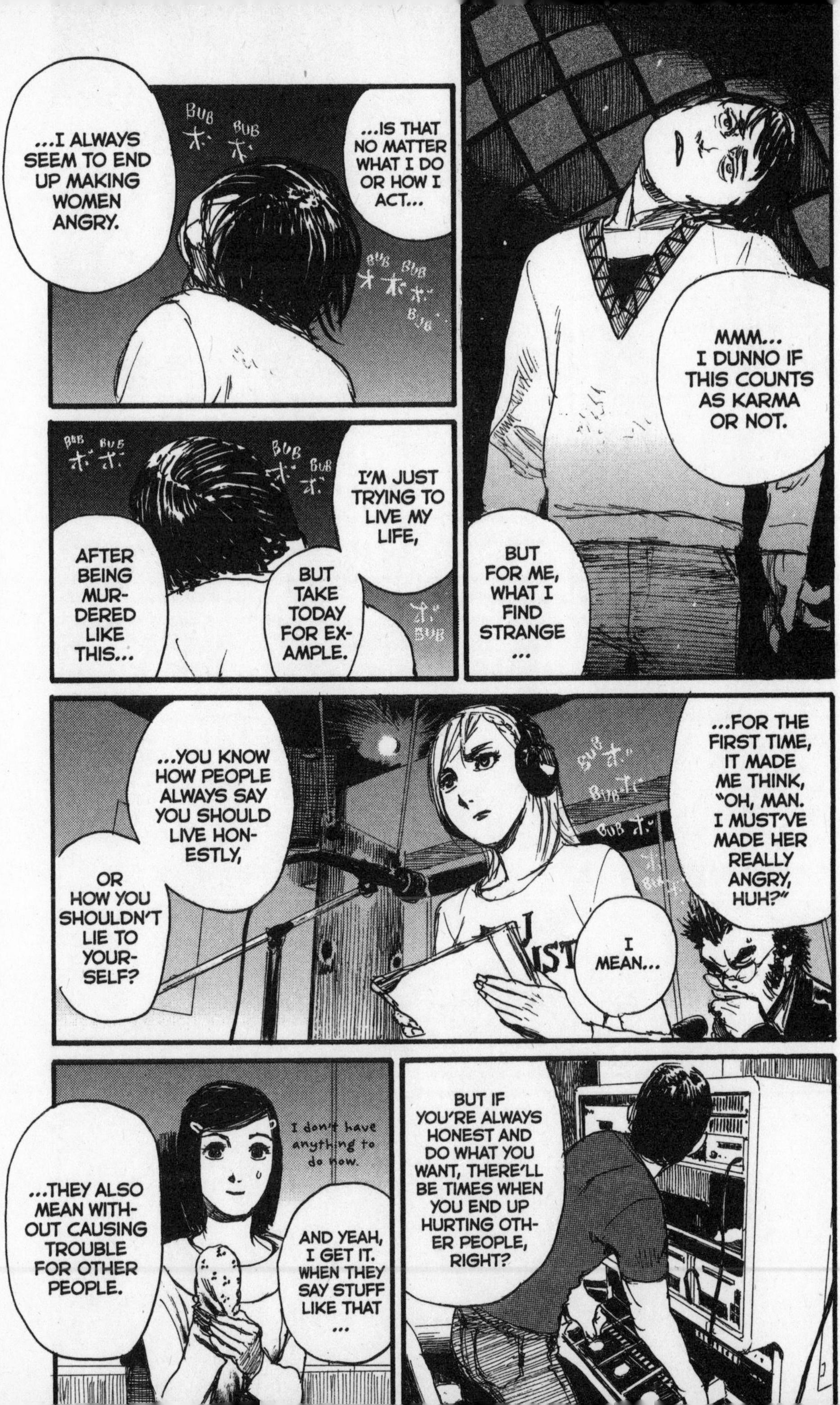
MMM... I DUNNO IF THIS COUNTS AS KARMA OR NOT.
BUT FOR ME, WHAT I FIND STRANGE...
BUB BUB
...IS THAT NO MATTER WHAT I DO OR HOW I ACT...
...I ALWAYS SEEM TO END UP MAKING WOMEN ANGRY.
BUB BUB BUB BUB
BUB BUB BUB BUB
I'M JUST TRYING TO LIVE MY LIFE,
BUB
BUT TAKE TODAY FOR EXAMPLE.
AFTER BEING MURDERED LIKE THIS...
BUB BUB BUB
...FOR THE FIRST TIME, IT MADE ME THINK, "OH, MAN. I MUST'VE MADE HER REALLY ANGRY, HUH?"
I MEAN...
...YOU KNOW HOW PEOPLE ALWAYS SAY YOU SHOULD LIVE HONESTLY,
OR HOW YOU SHOULDN'T LIE TO YOURSELF?
BUT IF YOU'RE ALWAYS HONEST AND DO WHAT YOU WANT, THERE'LL BE TIMES WHEN YOU END UP HURTING OTHER PEOPLE, RIGHT?
I don't have anything to do now.
AND YEAH, I GET IT. WHEN THEY SAY STUFF LIKE THAT...
...THEY ALSO MEAN WITHOUT CAUSING TROUBLE FOR OTHER PEOPLE.

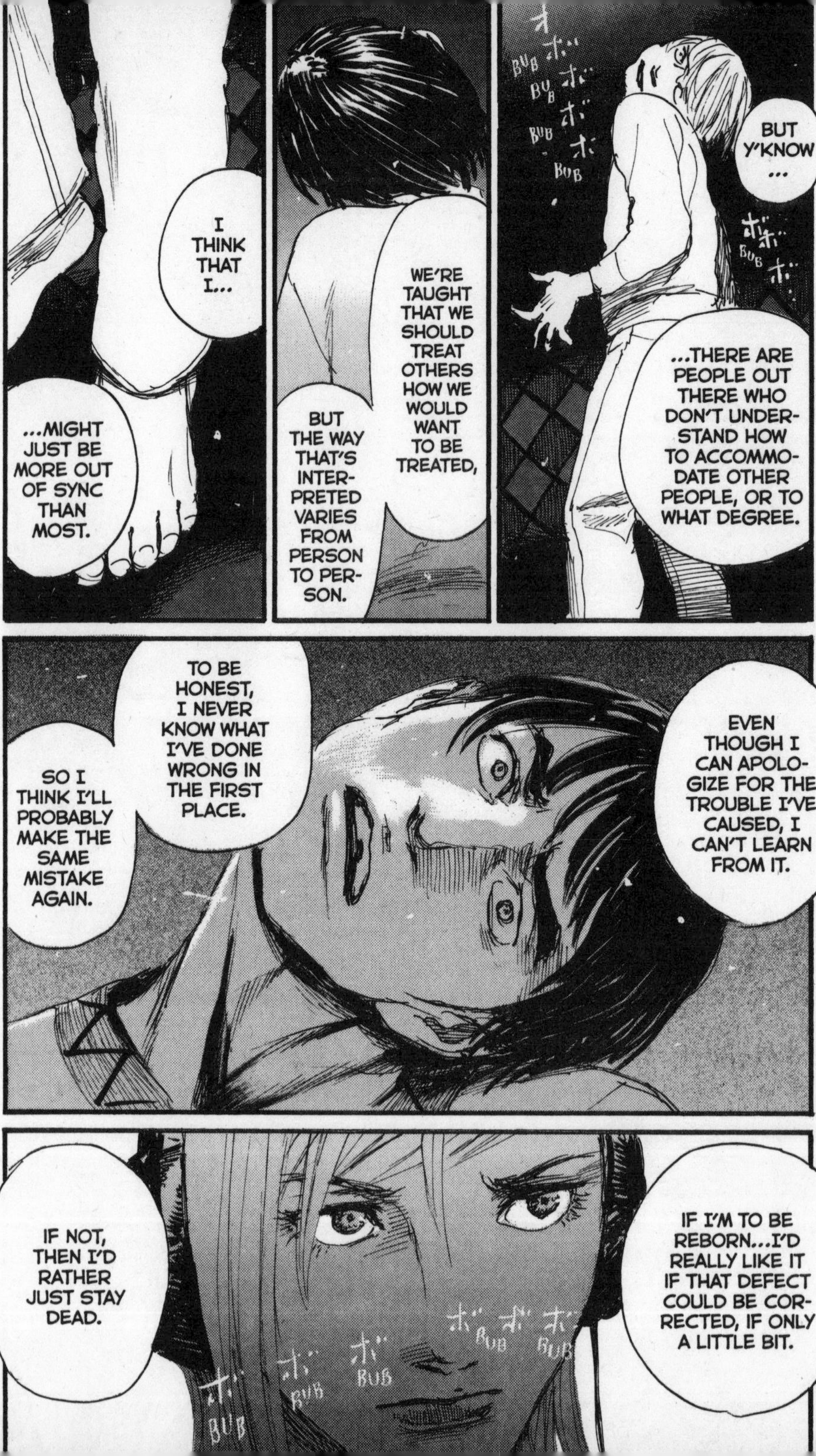
BUT Y'KNOW ...
BUB BUB BUB BUB
BUB
...THERE ARE PEOPLE OUT THERE WHO DON'T UNDER-STAND HOW TO ACCOMMO-DATE OTHER PEOPLE, OR TO WHAT DEGREE.
WE'RE TAUGHT THAT WE SHOULD TREAT OTHERS HOW WE WOULD WANT TO BE TREATED,
BUT THE WAY THAT'S INTER-PRETED VARIES FROM PERSON TO PER-SON.
I THINK THAT I...
...MIGHT JUST BE MORE OUT OF SYNC THAN MOST.
EVEN THOUGH I CAN APOLO-GIZE FOR THE TROUBLE I'VE CAUSED, I CAN'T LEARN FROM IT.
TO BE HONEST, I NEVER KNOW WHAT I'VE DONE WRONG IN THE FIRST PLACE.
SO I THINK I'LL PROBABLY MAKE THE SAME MISTAKE AGAIN.
IF I'M TO BE REBORN...I'D REALLY LIKE IT IF THAT DEFECT COULD BE COR-RECTED, IF ONLY A LITTLE BIT.
BUB BUB BUB BUB BUB
IF NOT, THEN I'D RATHER JUST STAY DEAD.

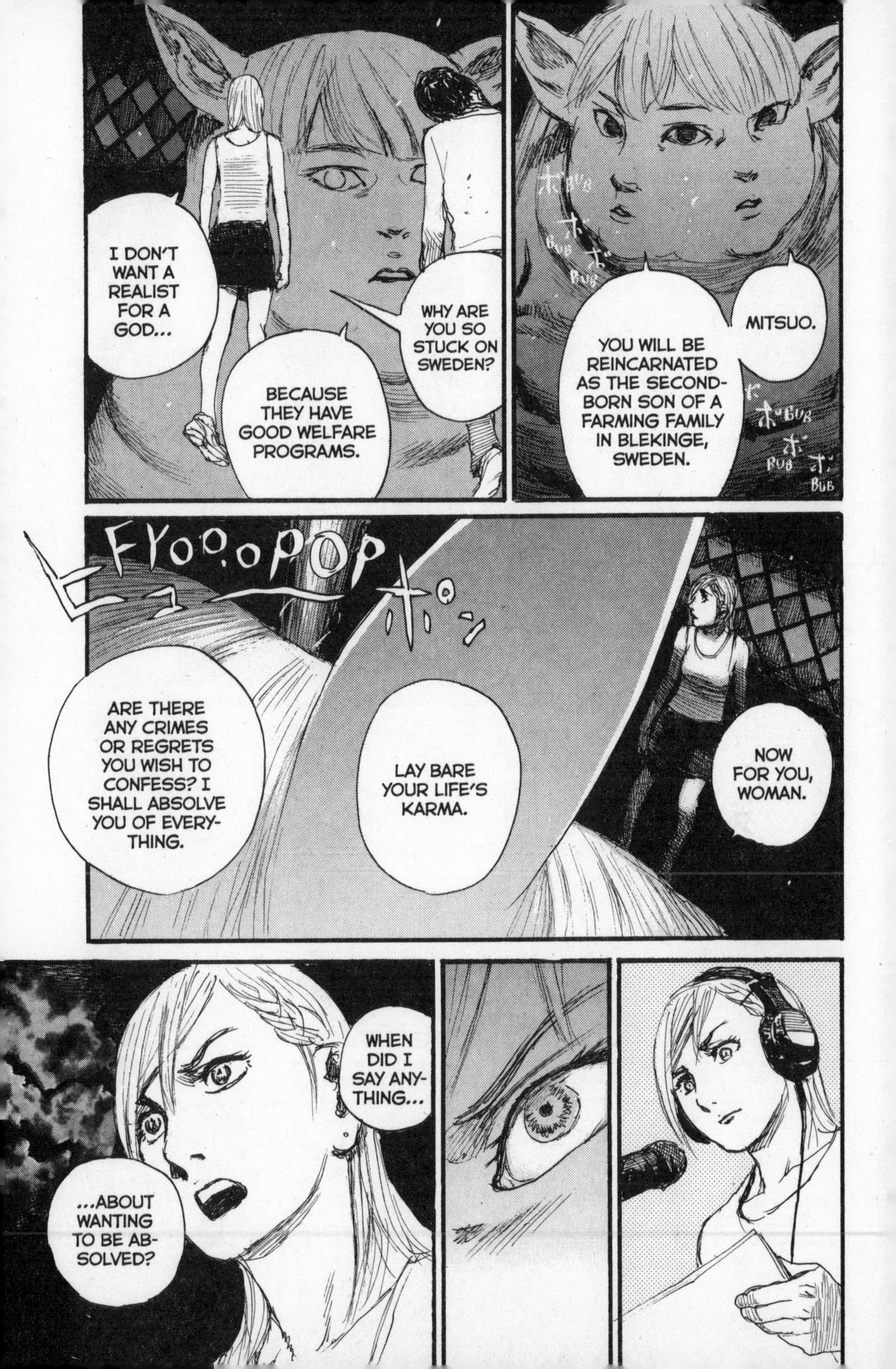
BUB BUB BUB
MITSUO.
YOU WILL BE REINCARNATED AS THE SECOND-BORN SON OF A FARMING FAMILY IN BLEKINGE, SWEDEN.
BUB BUB BUB
WHY ARE YOU SO STUCK ON SWEDEN?
BECAUSE THEY HAVE GOOD WELFARE PROGRAMS.
I DON'T WANT A REALIST FOR A GOD...
FYOOOPOP
NOW FOR YOU, WOMAN.
LAY BARE YOUR LIFE'S KARMA.
ARE THERE ANY CRIMES OR REGRETS YOU WISH TO CONFESS? I SHALL ABSOLVE YOU OF EVERYTHING.
WHEN DID I SAY ANYTHING...
...ABOUT WANTING TO BE ABSOLVED?

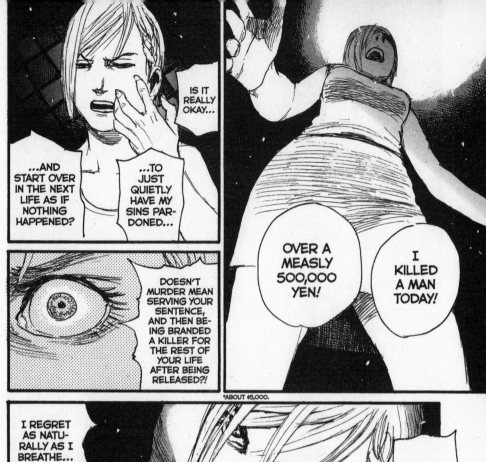

I KILLED A MAN TODAY!
OVER A MEASLY 500,000 YEN!
IS IT REALLY OKAY...
...TO JUST QUIETLY HAVE MY SINS PARDONED...
...AND START OVER IN THE NEXT LIFE AS IF NOTHING HAPPENED?
DOESN'T MURDER MEAN SERVING YOUR SENTENCE, AND THEN BEING BRANDED A KILLER FOR THE REST OF YOUR LIFE AFTER BEING RELEASED?!
YOU WANT REGRETS?
TRY EVERY MINUTE OF EVERY HOUR OF EVERY DAY.
I REGRET AS NATURALLY AS I BREATHE...
HOW I DATED A MAN WHO CAN'T TELL RIGHT FROM WRONG!
HOW I LENT HIM MONEY!
HOW I BITCHED ABOUT ALL OF IT TO A HOT OLDER DUDE I JUST MET AT A BAR!
Now for you, wom
Are there any crim
wish to confess? I s
of everything.
Minare: *Adlib from here on, b
yell your name (real) at th
then fade out.
SE – Lightning
SE – Distant
*ABOUT $5,000.

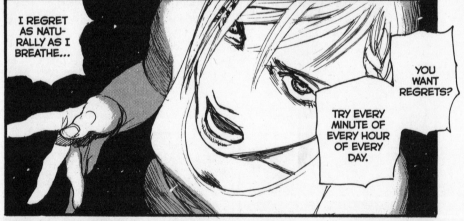

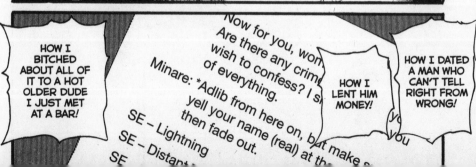

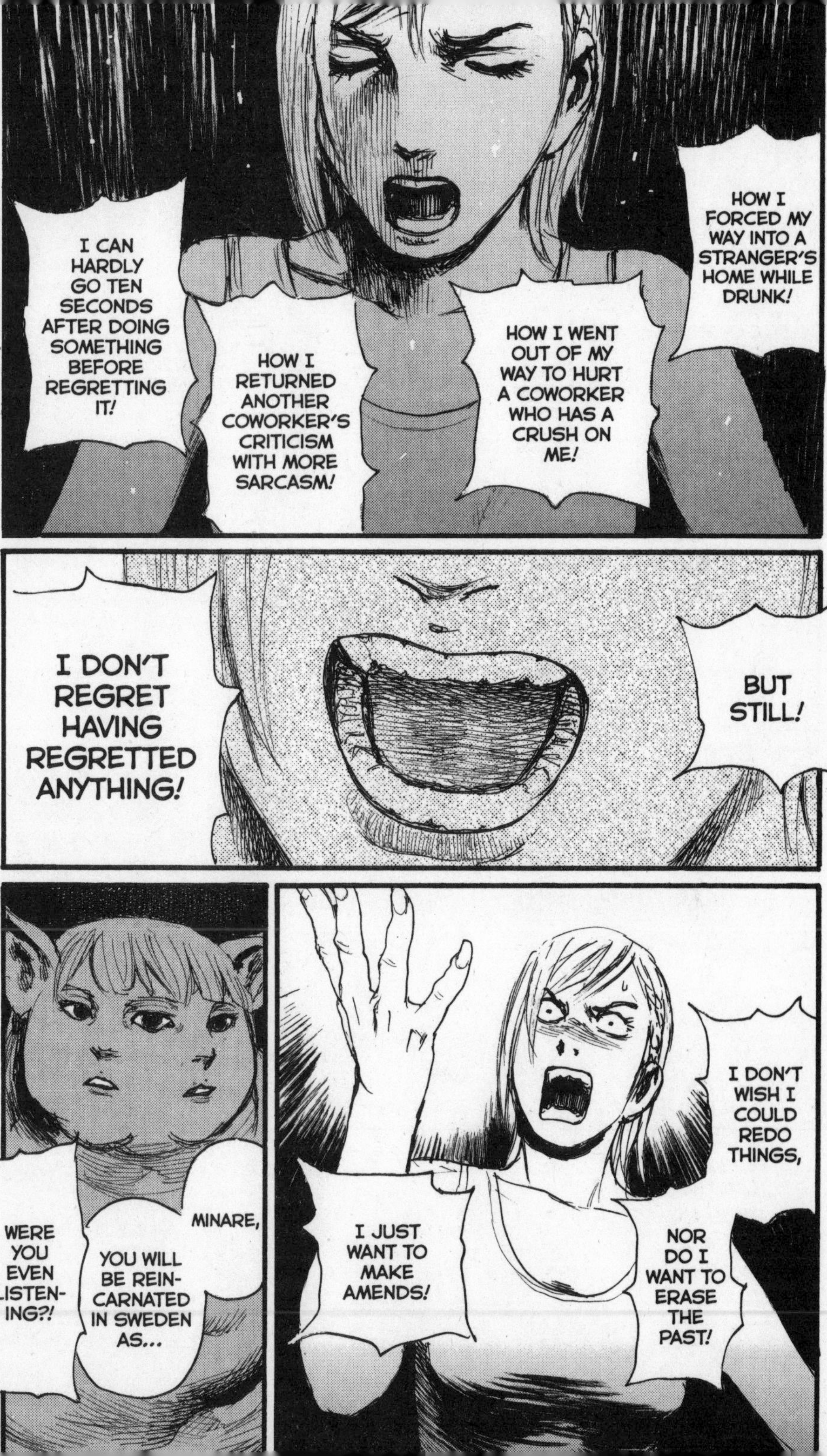
HOW I FORCED MY WAY INTO A STRANGER'S HOME WHILE DRUNK!
HOW I WENT OUT OF MY WAY TO HURT A COWORKER WHO HAS A CRUSH ON ME!
HOW I RETURNED ANOTHER COWORKER'S CRITICISM WITH MORE SARCASM!
I CAN HARDLY GO TEN SECONDS AFTER DOING SOMETHING BEFORE REGRETTING IT!
BUT STILL!
I DON'T REGRET HAVING REGRETTED ANYTHING!
I DON'T WISH I COULD REDO THINGS,
NOR DO I WANT TO ERASE THE PAST!
I JUST WANT TO MAKE AMENDS!
MINARE,
YOU WILL BE REIN-CARNATED IN SWEDEN AS...
WERE YOU EVEN LISTEN-ING?!

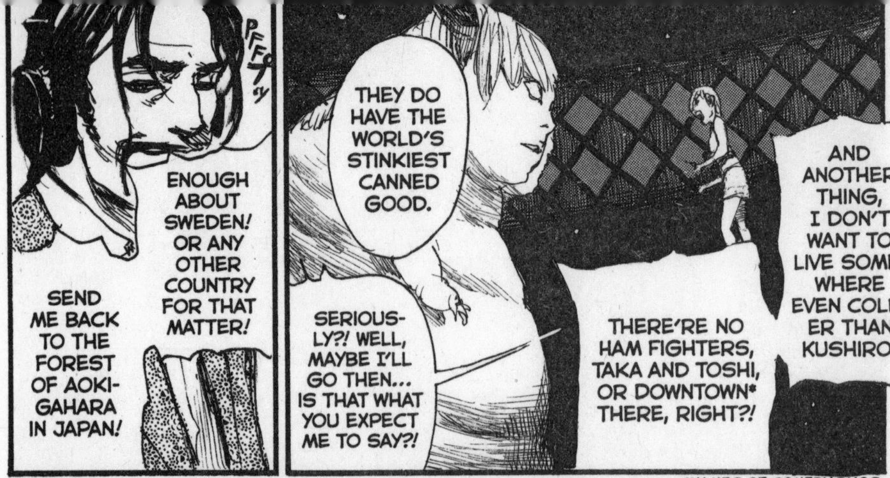
THEY DO HAVE THE WORLD'S STINKIEST CANNED GOOD.
SERIOUS-LY?! WELL, MAYBE I'LL GO THEN... IS THAT WHAT YOU EXPECT ME TO SAY?!
THERE'RE NO HAM FIGHTERS, TAKA AND TOSHI, OR DOWNTOWN* THERE, RIGHT?!
AND ANOTHER THING, I DON'T WANT TO LIVE SOME-WHERE EVEN COLD-ER THAN KUSHIRO!
PFFFT
ENOUGH ABOUT SWEDEN! OR ANY OTHER COUNTRY FOR THAT MATTER!
SEND ME BACK TO THE FOREST OF AOKI-GAHARA IN JAPAN!

*NAMES OF COMEDY DUOS.

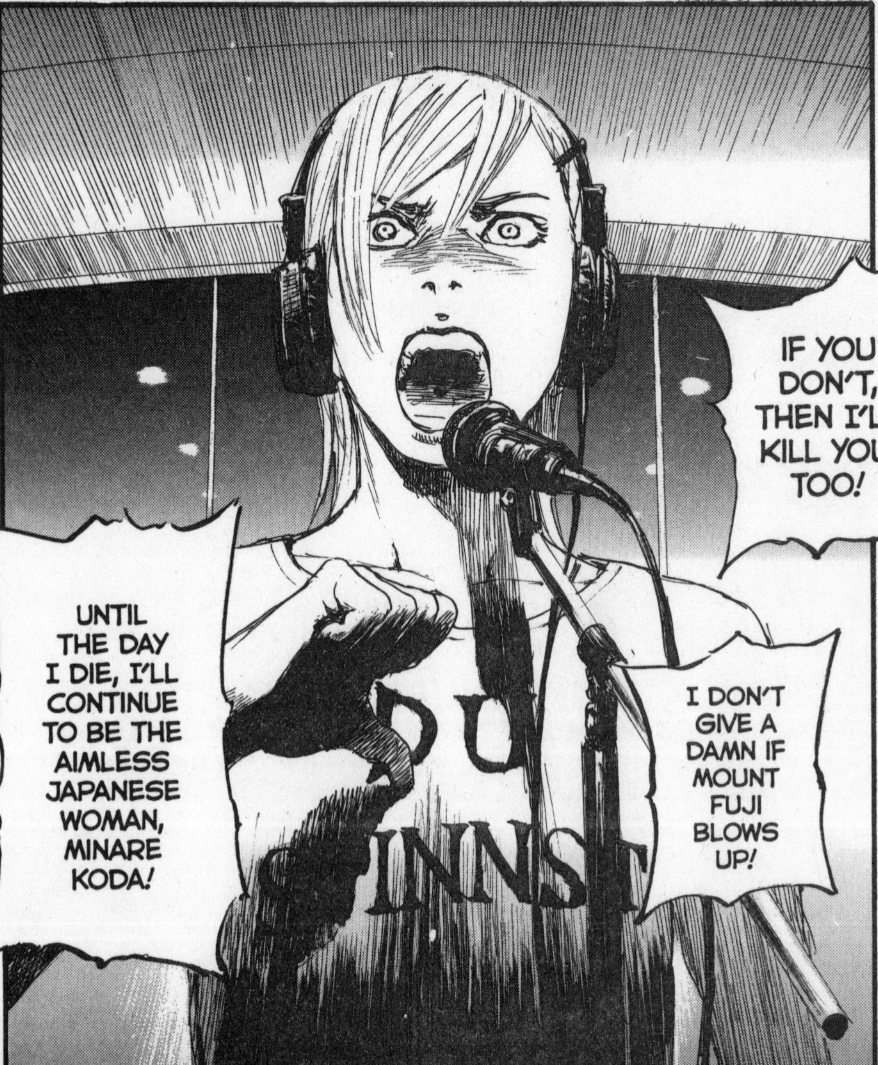
IF YOU DON'T, THEN I'LL KILL YOU, TOO!
I DON'T GIVE A DAMN IF MOUNT FUJI BLOWS UP!
UNTIL THE DAY I DIE, I'LL CONTINUE TO BE THE AIMLESS JAPANESE WOMAN, MINARE KODA!

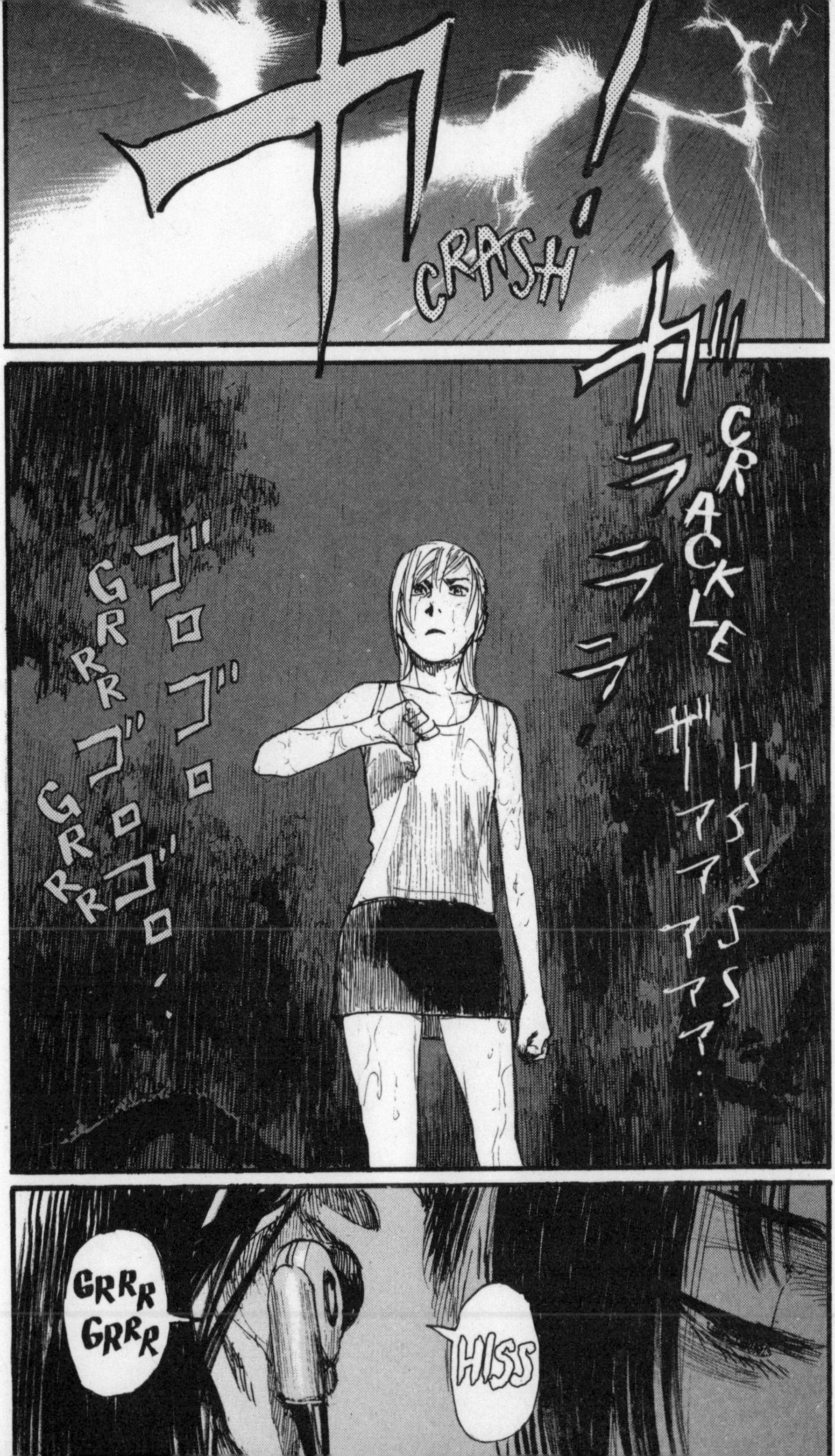

カッ!
CRASH
ガラララ…
CRACKLE
ザァアアアア…
HISSSS
ゴロゴロゴロゴロ…
GRRR GRRR
HISS
GRRR GRRR

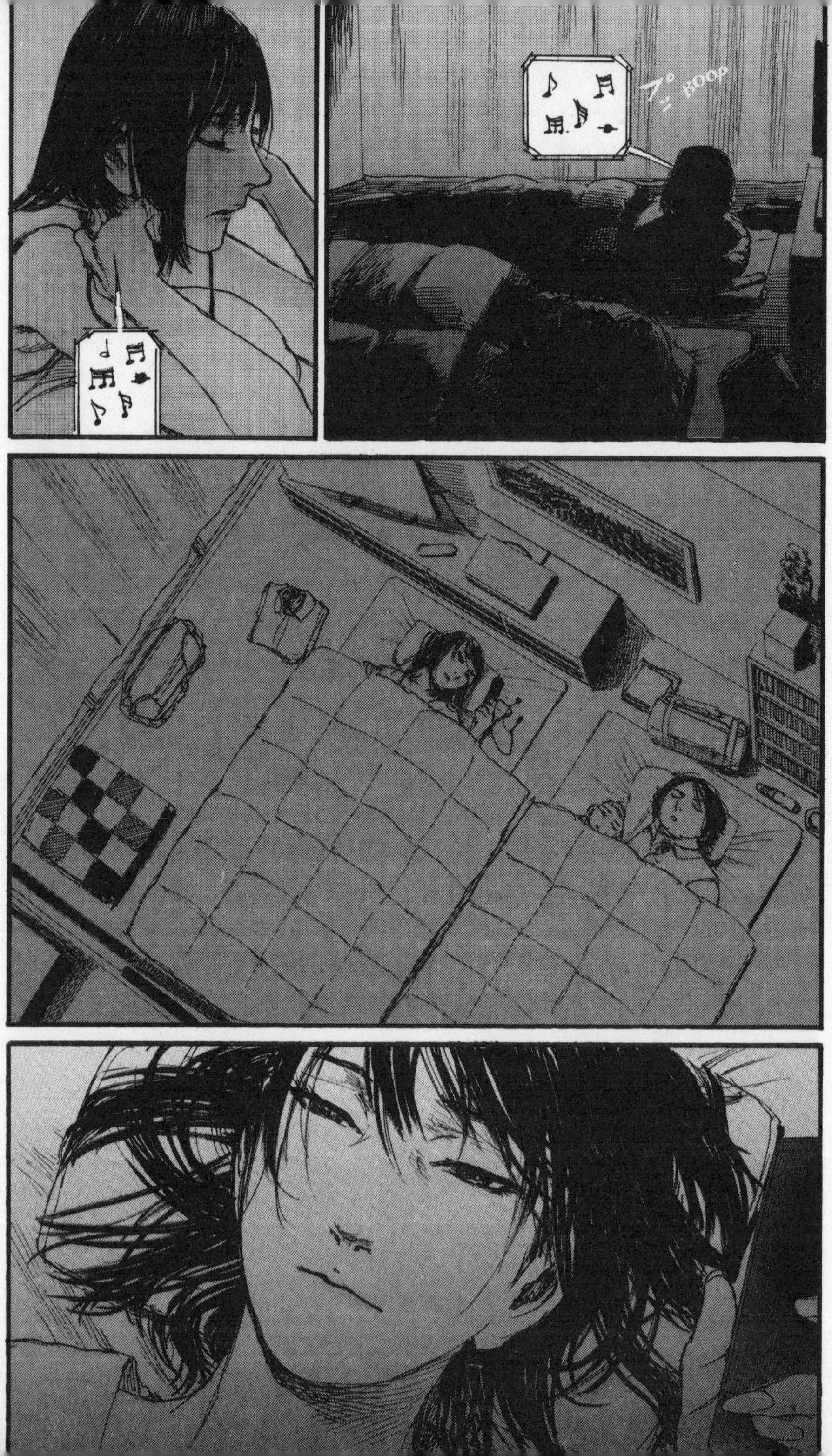

プッ
KOOP

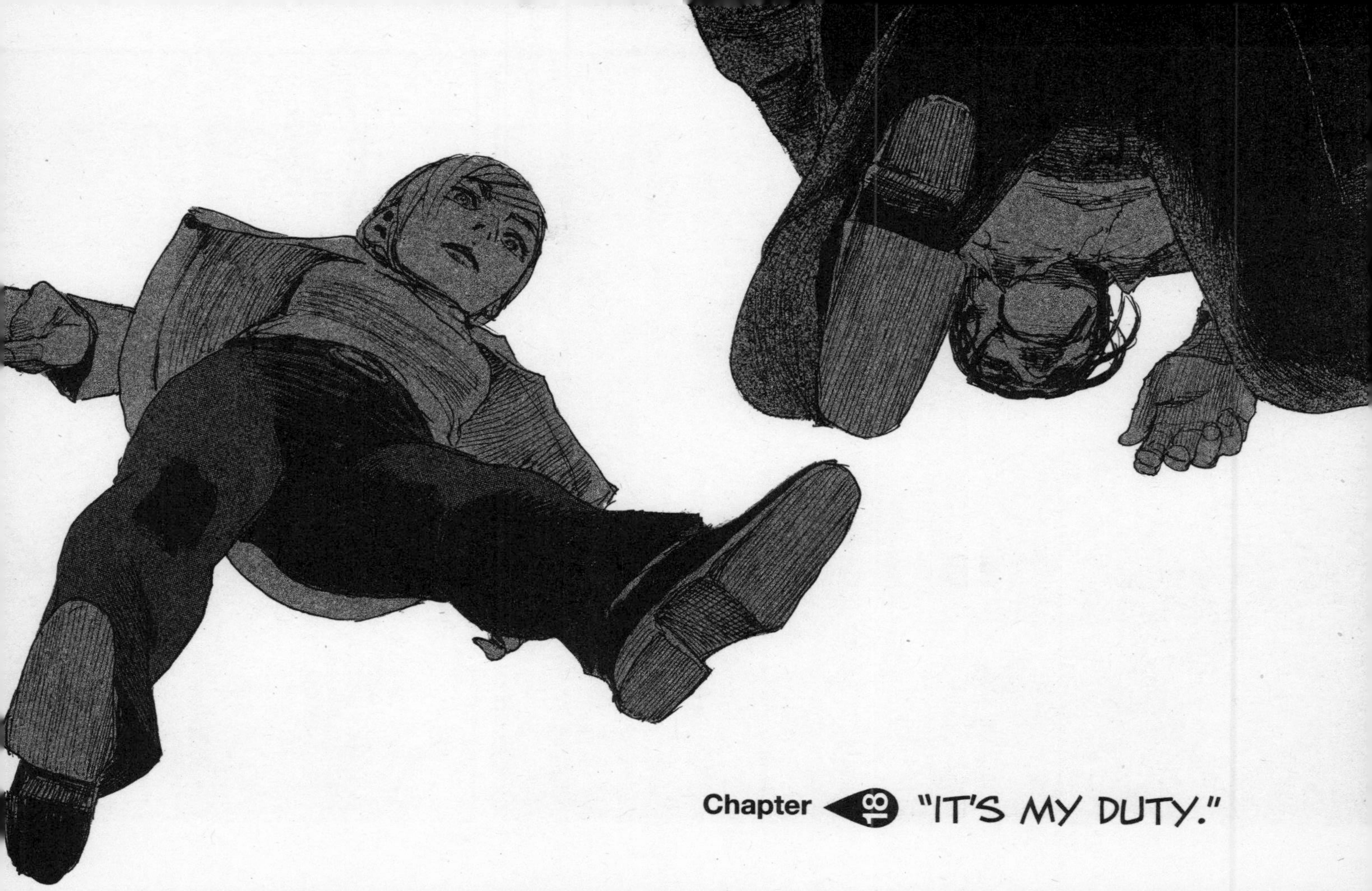

Chapter 18 "IT'S MY DUTY."

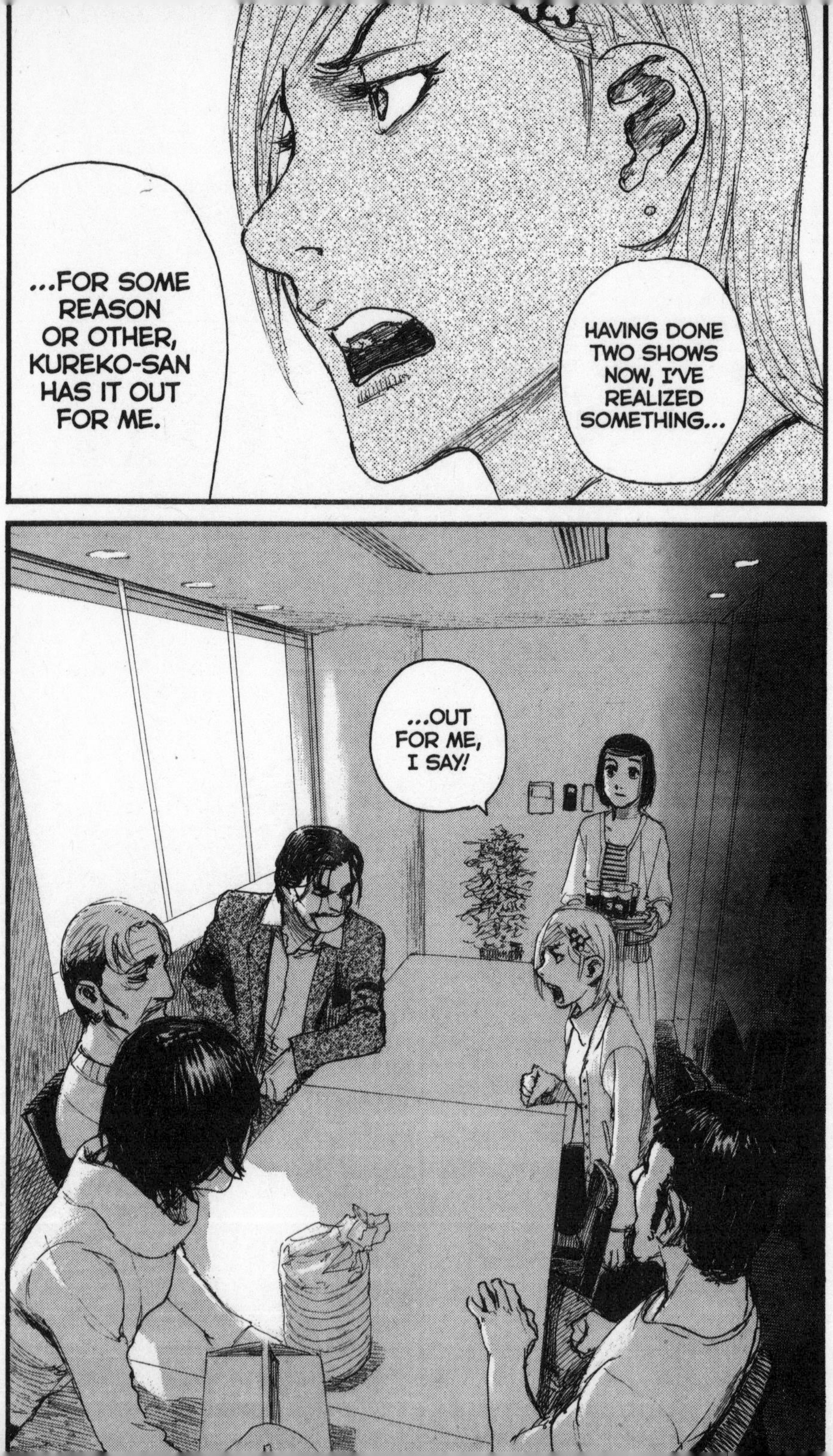
HAVING DONE TWO SHOWS NOW, I'VE REALIZED SOMETHING...
...FOR SOME REASON OR OTHER, KUREKO-SAN HAS IT OUT FOR ME.
...OUT FOR ME, I SAY!

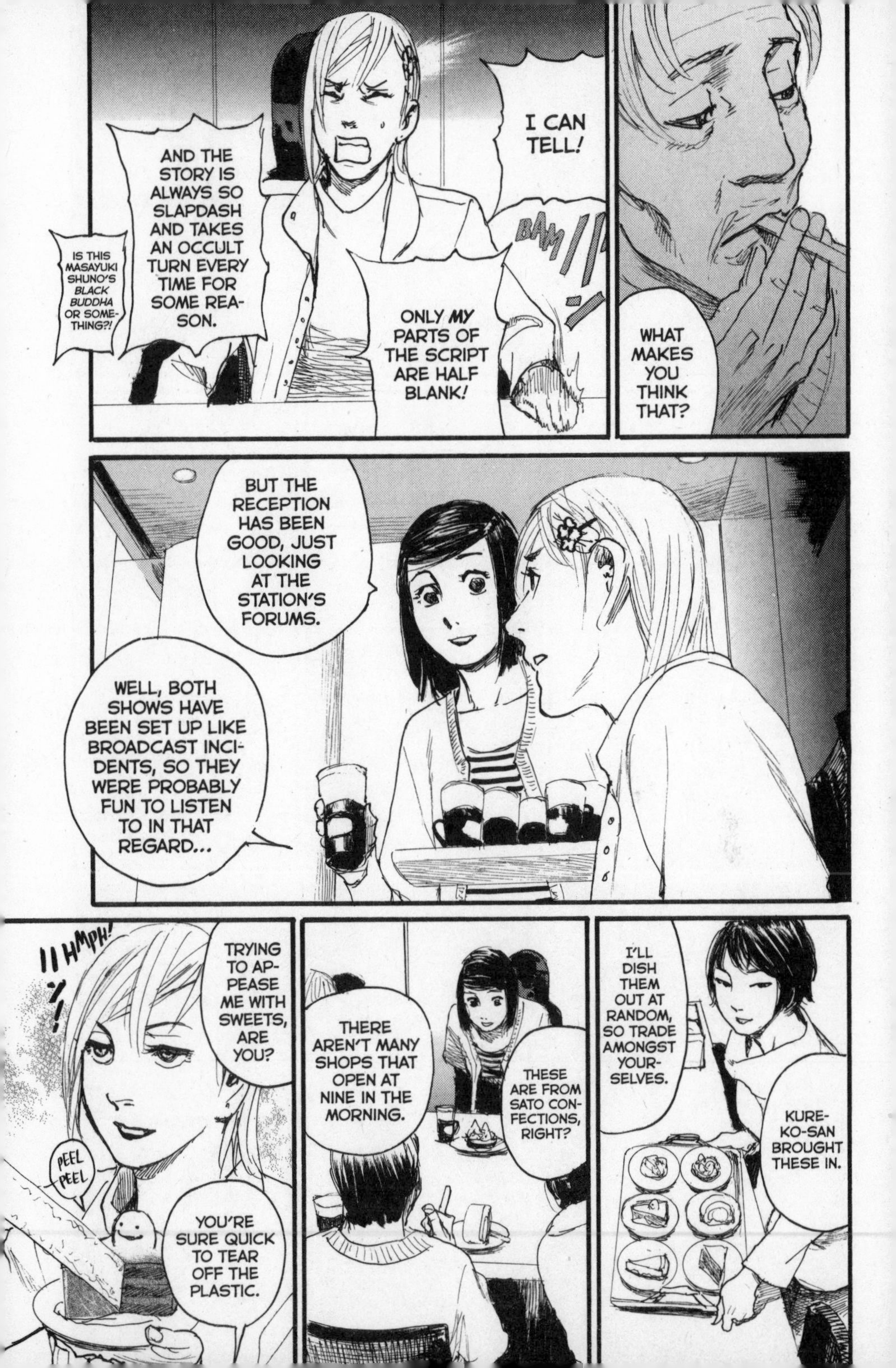
WHAT MAKES YOU THINK THAT?
I CAN TELL!
BAM
ONLY *MY* PARTS OF THE SCRIPT ARE HALF BLANK!
AND THE STORY IS ALWAYS SO SLAPDASH AND TAKES AN OCCULT TURN EVERY TIME FOR SOME REA-SON.
IS THIS MASAYUKI SHUNO'S *BLACK BUDDHA* OR SOME-THING?!
BUT THE RECEPTION HAS BEEN GOOD, JUST LOOKING AT THE STATION'S FORUMS.
WELL, BOTH SHOWS HAVE BEEN SET UP LIKE BROADCAST INCI-DENTS, SO THEY WERE PROBABLY FUN TO LISTEN TO IN THAT REGARD...
I'LL DISH THEM OUT AT RANDOM, SO TRADE AMONGST YOUR-SELVES.
KURE-KO-SAN BROUGHT THESE IN.
THESE ARE FROM SATO CON-FECTIONS, RIGHT?
THERE AREN'T MANY SHOPS THAT OPEN AT NINE IN THE MORNING.
TRYING TO AP-PEASE ME WITH SWEETS, ARE YOU?
HMPH!
PEEL PEEL
YOU'RE SURE QUICK TO TEAR OFF THE PLASTIC.

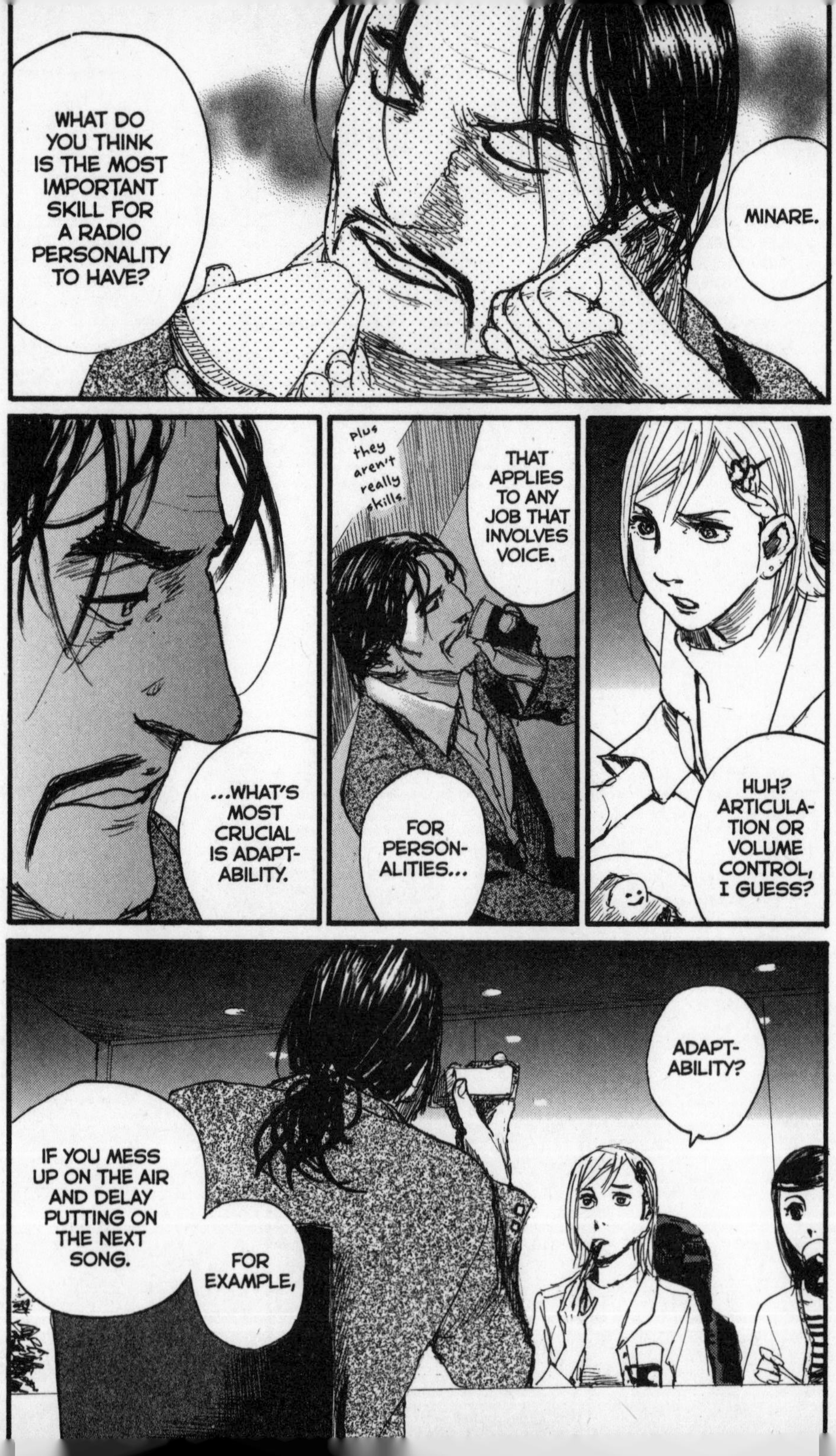
MINARE.
WHAT DO YOU THINK IS THE MOST IMPORTANT SKILL FOR A RADIO PERSONALITY TO HAVE?
HUH? ARTICULATION OR VOLUME CONTROL, I GUESS?
THAT APPLIES TO ANY JOB THAT INVOLVES VOICE.
plus they aren't really skills.
FOR PERSONALITIES...
...WHAT'S MOST CRUCIAL IS ADAPTABILITY.
ADAPTABILITY?
FOR EXAMPLE,
IF YOU MESS UP ON THE AIR AND DELAY PUTTING ON THE NEXT SONG.

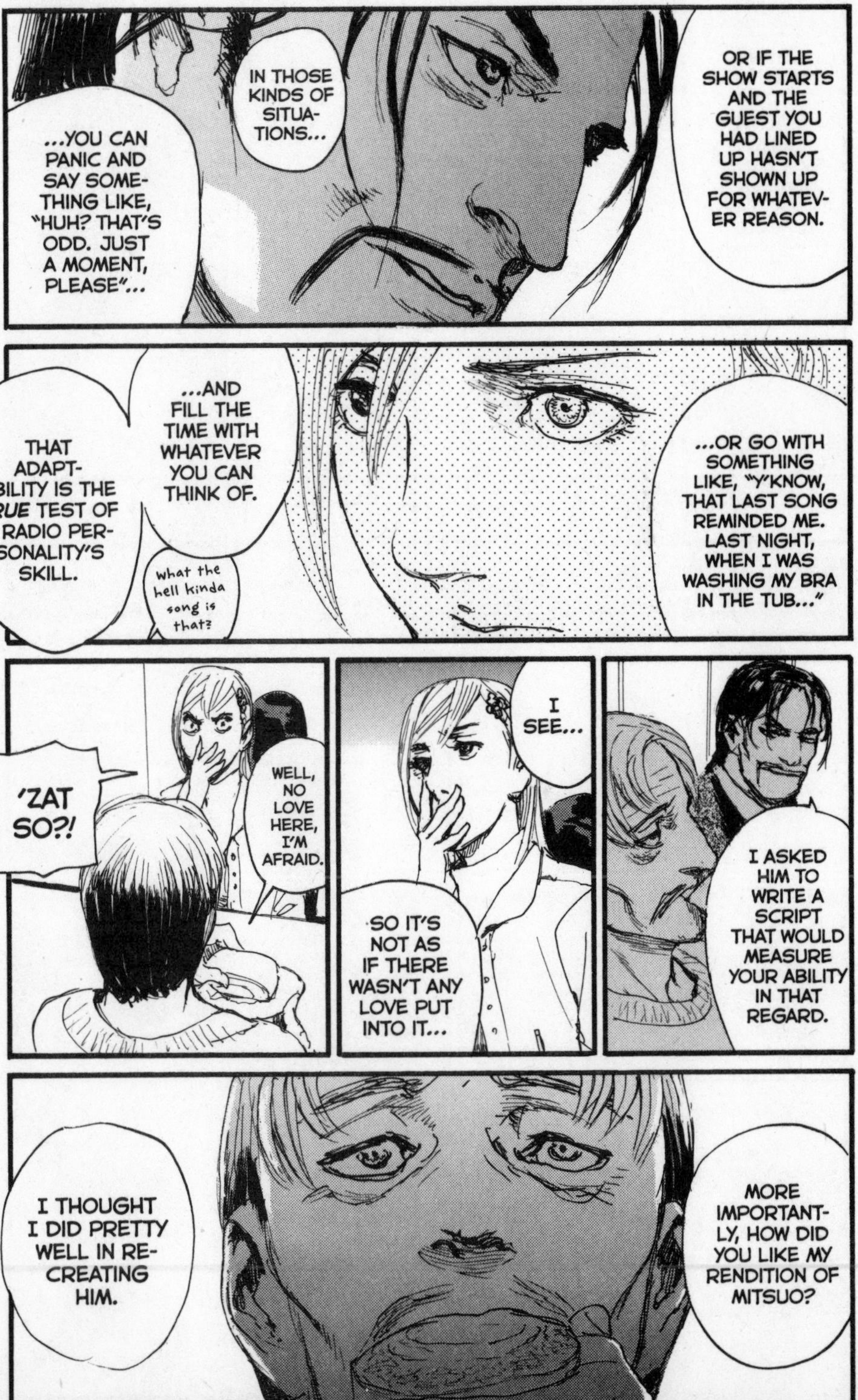
OR IF THE SHOW STARTS AND THE GUEST YOU HAD LINED UP HASN'T SHOWN UP FOR WHATEVER REASON.
IN THOSE KINDS OF SITUATIONS...
...YOU CAN PANIC AND SAY SOMETHING LIKE, "HUH? THAT'S ODD. JUST A MOMENT, PLEASE"...
...OR GO WITH SOMETHING LIKE, "Y'KNOW, THAT LAST SONG REMINDED ME. LAST NIGHT, WHEN I WAS WASHING MY BRA IN THE TUB..."
...AND FILL THE TIME WITH WHATEVER YOU CAN THINK OF.
THAT ADAPTABILITY IS THE *TRUE* TEST OF A RADIO PERSONALITY'S SKILL.
what the hell kinda song is that?
I ASKED HIM TO WRITE A SCRIPT THAT WOULD MEASURE YOUR ABILITY IN THAT REGARD.
I SEE...
SO IT'S NOT AS IF THERE WASN'T ANY LOVE PUT INTO IT...
WELL, NO LOVE HERE, I'M AFRAID.
'ZAT SO?!
MORE IMPORTANTLY, HOW DID YOU LIKE MY RENDITION OF MITSUO?
I THOUGHT I DID PRETTY WELL IN RECREATING HIM.

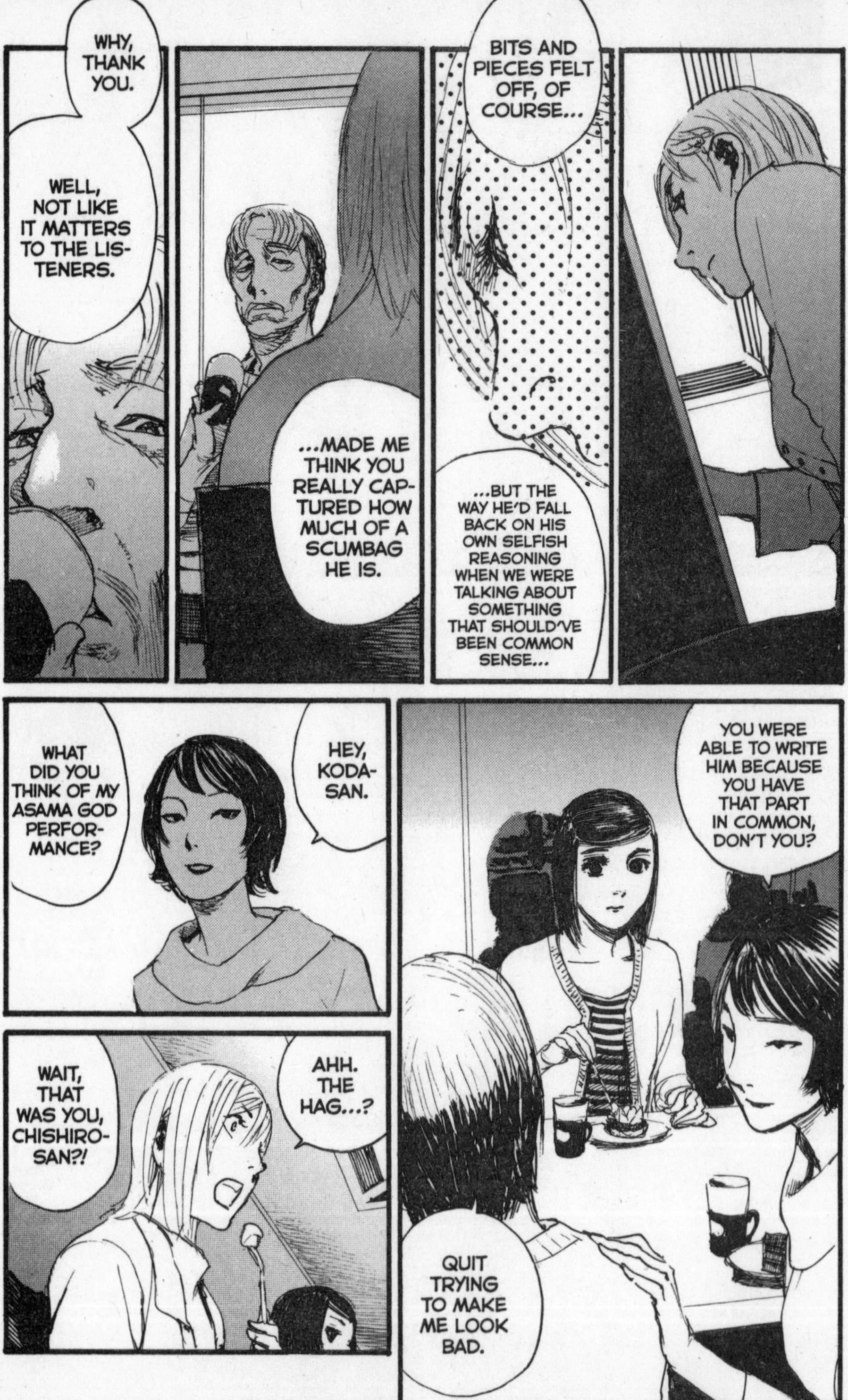
BITS AND PIECES FELT OFF, OF COURSE...
...BUT THE WAY HE'D FALL BACK ON HIS OWN SELFISH REASONING WHEN WE WERE TALKING ABOUT SOMETHING THAT SHOULD'VE BEEN COMMON SENSE...
...MADE ME THINK YOU REALLY CAPTURED HOW MUCH OF A SCUMBAG HE IS.
WHY, THANK YOU.
WELL, NOT LIKE IT MATTERS TO THE LISTENERS.
YOU WERE ABLE TO WRITE HIM BECAUSE YOU HAVE THAT PART IN COMMON, DON'T YOU?
QUIT TRYING TO MAKE ME LOOK BAD.
HEY, KODA-SAN.
WHAT DID YOU THINK OF MY ASAMA GOD PERFORMANCE?
AHH. THE HAG...?
WAIT, THAT WAS YOU, CHISHIRO-SAN?!

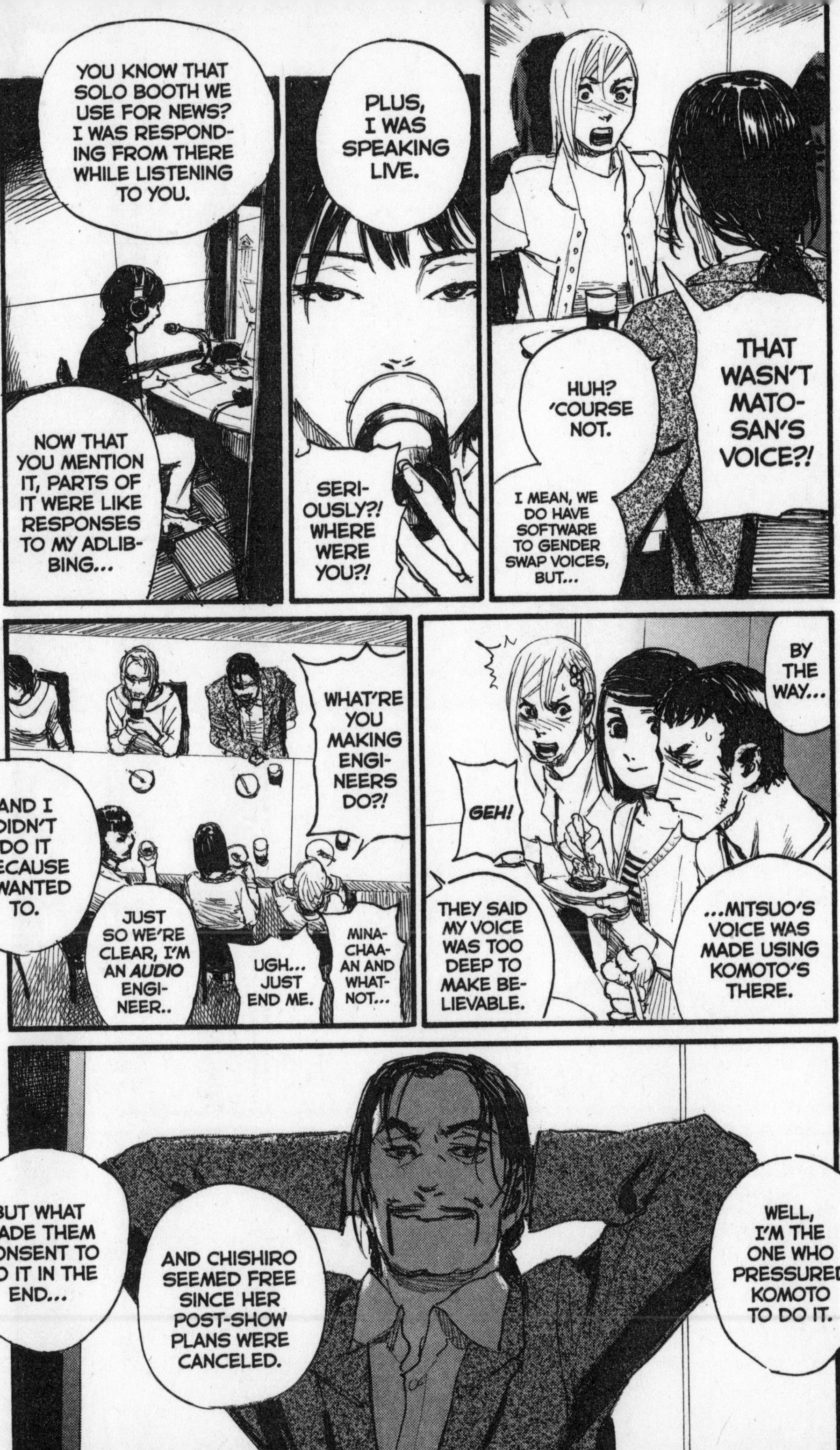
THAT WASN'T MATO-SAN'S VOICE?!
HUH? 'COURSE NOT.
I MEAN, WE DO HAVE SOFTWARE TO GENDER SWAP VOICES, BUT...
PLUS, I WAS SPEAKING LIVE.
SERI-OUSLY?! WHERE WERE YOU?!
YOU KNOW THAT SOLO BOOTH WE USE FOR NEWS? I WAS RESPOND-ING FROM THERE WHILE LISTENING TO YOU.
NOW THAT YOU MENTION IT, PARTS OF IT WERE LIKE RESPONSES TO MY ADLIB-BING...
BY THE WAY...
...MITSUO'S VOICE WAS MADE USING KOMOTO'S THERE.
GEH!
THEY SAID MY VOICE WAS TOO DEEP TO MAKE BE-LIEVABLE.
WHAT'RE YOU MAKING ENGI-NEERS DO?!
AND I DIDN'T DO IT BECAUSE I WANTED TO.
MINA-CHAA-AN AND WHAT-NOT...
UGH... JUST END ME.
JUST SO WE'RE CLEAR, I'M AN *AUDIO* ENGI-NEER..
WELL, I'M THE ONE WHO PRESSURED KOMOTO TO DO IT.
AND CHISHIRO SEEMED FREE SINCE HER POST-SHOW PLANS WERE CANCELED.
BUT WHAT MADE THEM CONSENT TO DO IT IN THE END...

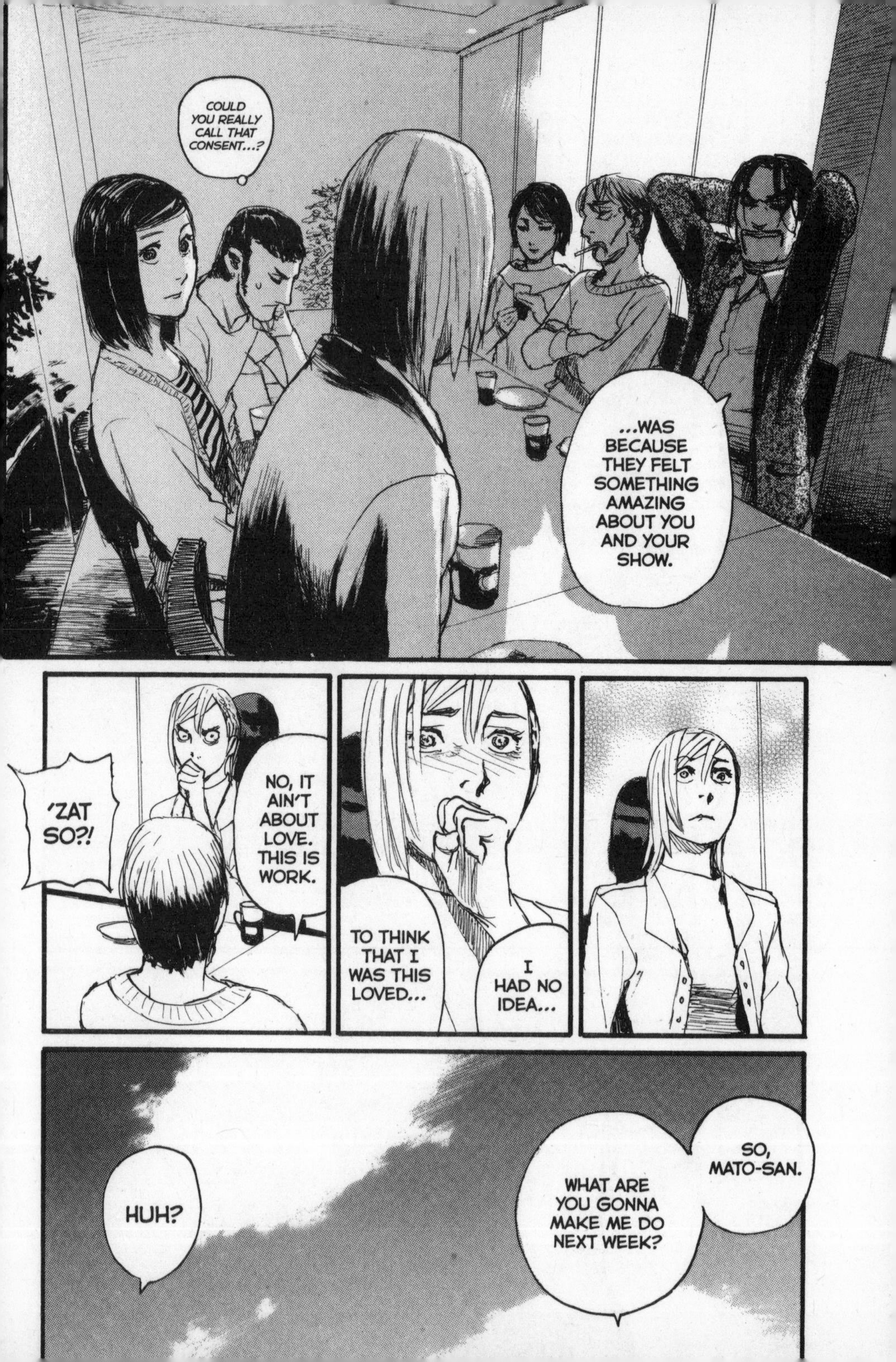
...WAS BECAUSE THEY FELT SOMETHING AMAZING ABOUT YOU AND YOUR SHOW.
COULD YOU REALLY CALL THAT CONSENT...?
I HAD NO IDEA...
TO THINK THAT I WAS THIS LOVED...
NO, IT AIN'T ABOUT LOVE. THIS IS WORK.
'ZAT SO?!
SO, MATO-SAN.
WHAT ARE YOU GONNA MAKE ME DO NEXT WEEK?
HUH?

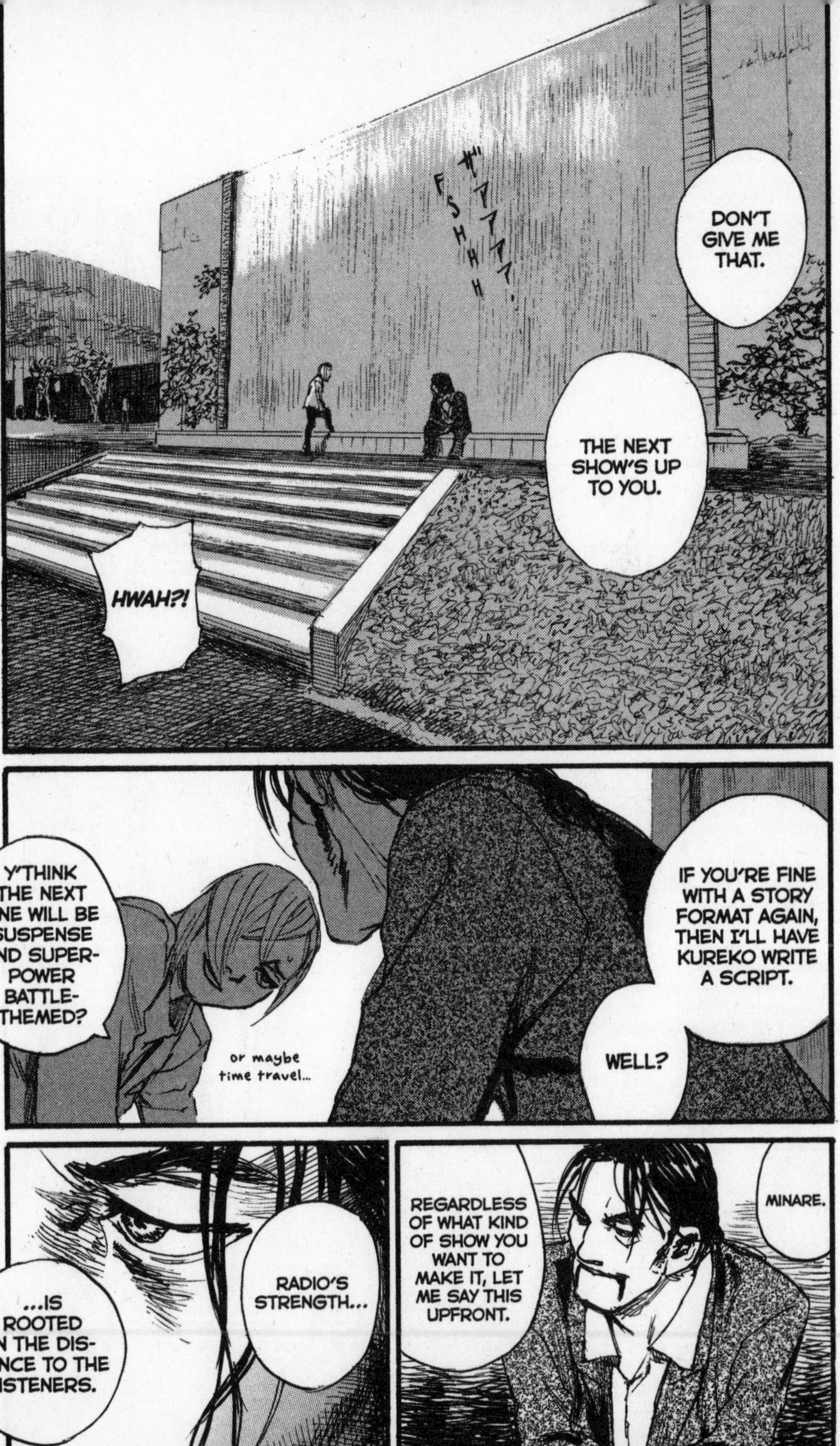
DON'T GIVE ME THAT.
FSHHH
THE NEXT SHOW'S UP TO YOU.
HWAH?!
IF YOU'RE FINE WITH A STORY FORMAT AGAIN, THEN I'LL HAVE KUREKO WRITE A SCRIPT.
WELL?
Y'THINK THE NEXT ONE WILL BE SUSPENSE AND SUPER-POWER BATTLE-THEMED?
or maybe time travel...
MINARE.
REGARDLESS OF WHAT KIND OF SHOW YOU WANT TO MAKE IT, LET ME SAY THIS UPFRONT.
RADIO'S STRENGTH...
...IS ROOTED IN THE DISTANCE TO THE LISTENERS.

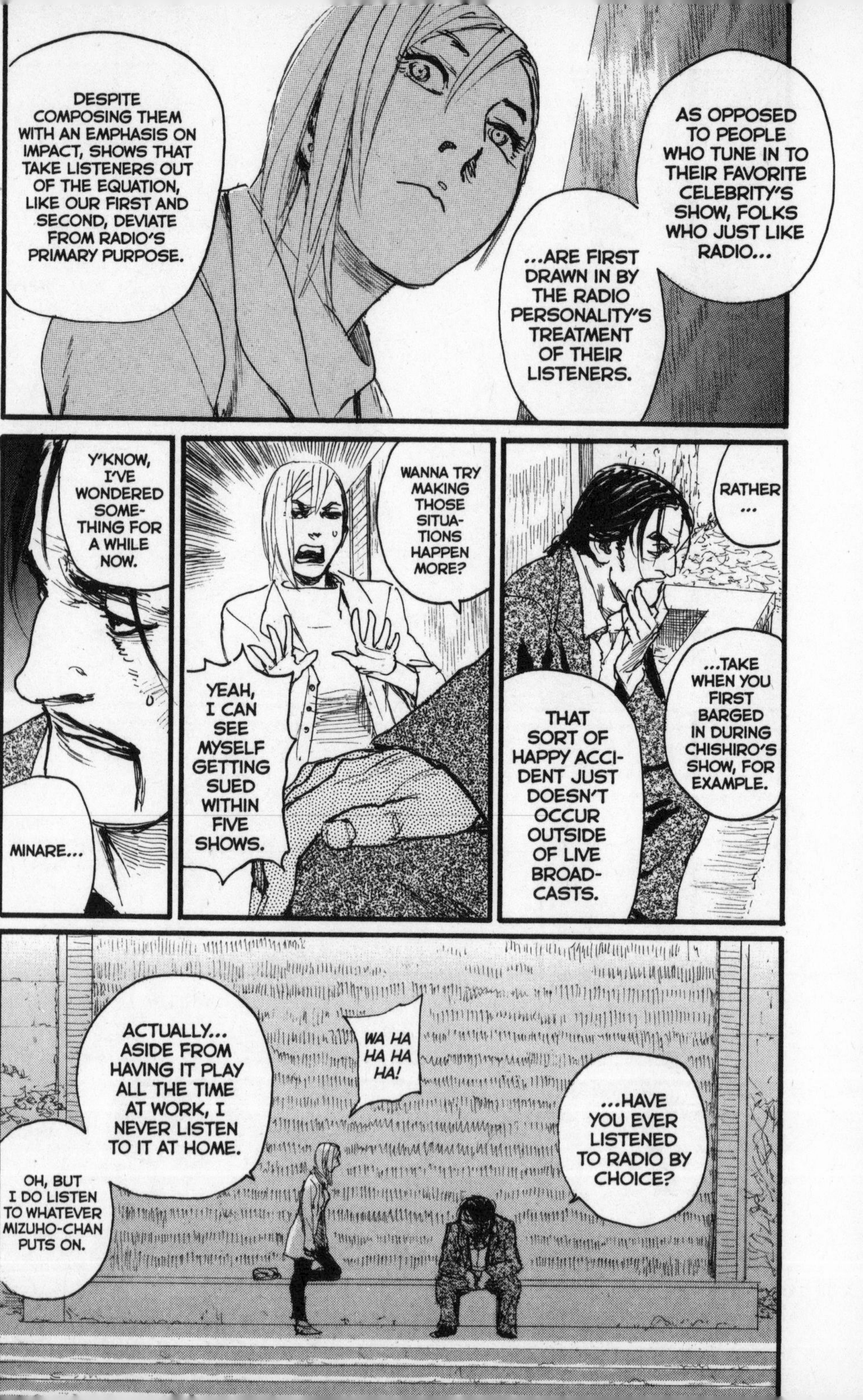
AS OPPOSED TO PEOPLE WHO TUNE IN TO THEIR FAVORITE CELEBRITY'S SHOW, FOLKS WHO JUST LIKE RADIO...
...ARE FIRST DRAWN IN BY THE RADIO PERSONALITY'S TREATMENT OF THEIR LISTENERS.
DESPITE COMPOSING THEM WITH AN EMPHASIS ON IMPACT, SHOWS THAT TAKE LISTENERS OUT OF THE EQUATION, LIKE OUR FIRST AND SECOND, DEVIATE FROM RADIO'S PRIMARY PURPOSE.
RATHER...
...TAKE WHEN YOU FIRST BARGED IN DURING CHISHIRO'S SHOW, FOR EXAMPLE.
THAT SORT OF HAPPY ACCI-DENT JUST DOESN'T OCCUR OUTSIDE OF LIVE BROAD-CASTS.
WANNA TRY MAKING THOSE SITUA-TIONS HAPPEN MORE?
YEAH, I CAN SEE MYSELF GETTING SUED WITHIN FIVE SHOWS.
Y'KNOW, I'VE WONDERED SOME-THING FOR A WHILE NOW.
MINARE...
...HAVE YOU EVER LISTENED TO RADIO BY CHOICE?
WA HA HA HA HA!
ACTUALLY... ASIDE FROM HAVING IT PLAY ALL THE TIME AT WORK, I NEVER LISTEN TO IT AT HOME.
OH, BUT I DO LISTEN TO WHATEVER MIZUHO-CHAN PUTS ON.

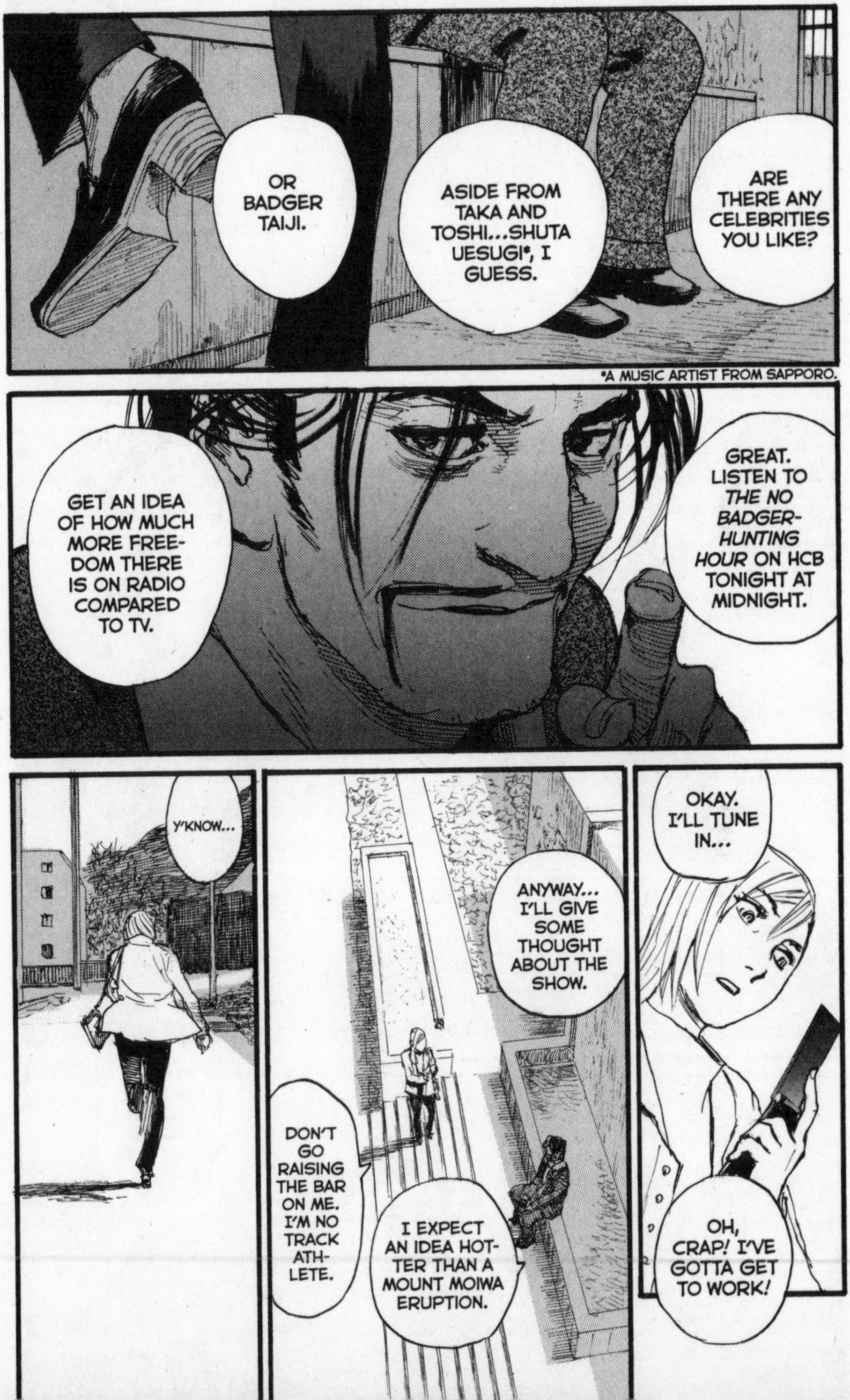
ARE THERE ANY CELEBRITIES YOU LIKE?
ASIDE FROM TAKA AND TOSHI...SHUTA UESUGI*, I GUESS.
OR BADGER TAIJI.
GREAT. LISTEN TO *THE NO BADGER-HUNTING HOUR* ON HCB TONIGHT AT MIDNIGHT.
GET AN IDEA OF HOW MUCH MORE FREE-DOM THERE IS ON RADIO COMPARED TO TV.
OKAY. I'LL TUNE IN...
OH, CRAP! I'VE GOTTA GET TO WORK!
ANYWAY... I'LL GIVE SOME THOUGHT ABOUT THE SHOW.
I EXPECT AN IDEA HOT-TER THAN A MOUNT MOIWA ERUPTION.
DON'T GO RAISING THE BAR ON ME. I'M NO TRACK ATH-LETE.
Y'KNOW...

*A MUSIC ARTIST FROM SAPPORO.

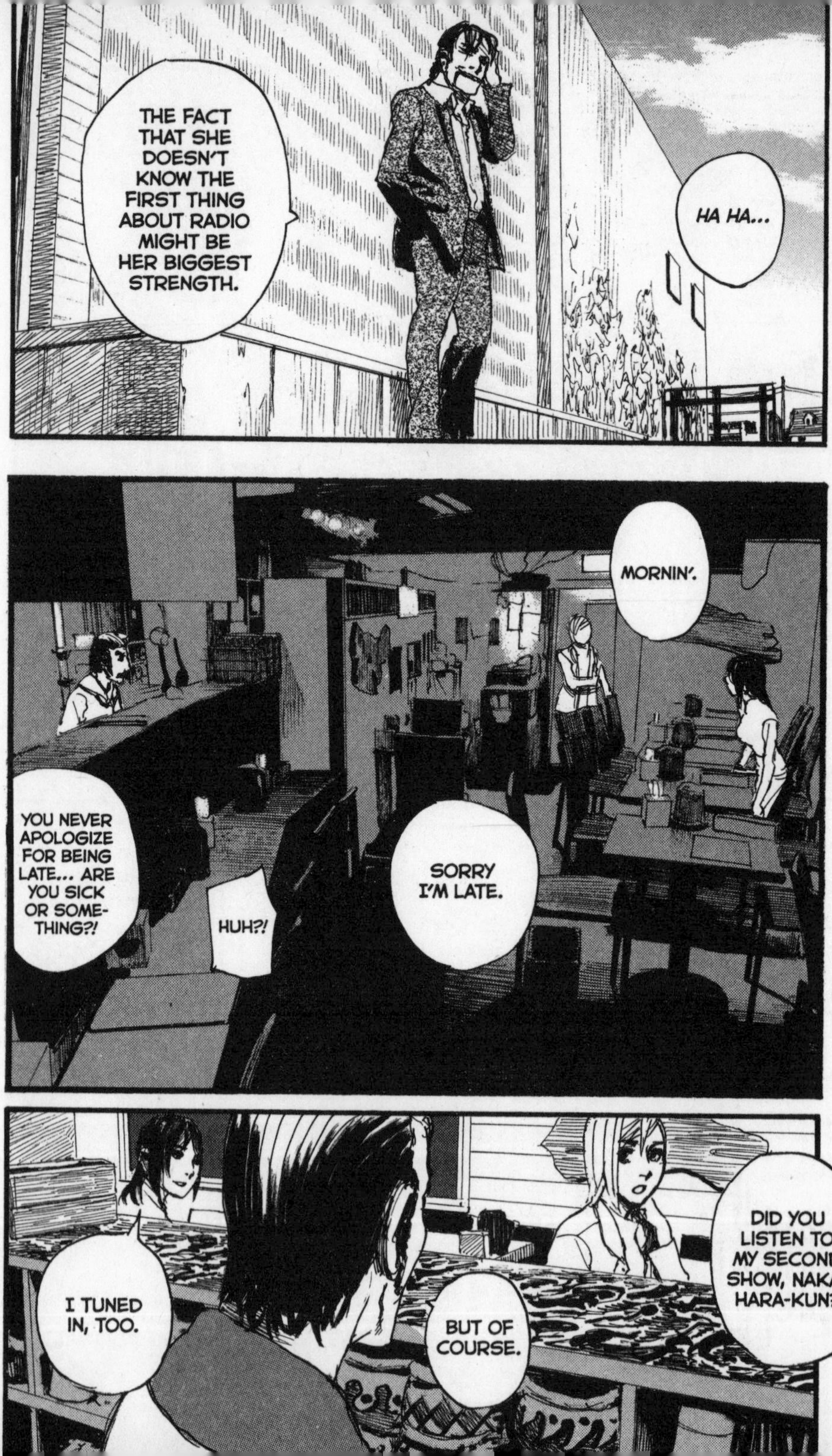
HA HA...
THE FACT THAT SHE DOESN'T KNOW THE FIRST THING ABOUT RADIO MIGHT BE HER BIGGEST STRENGTH.
MORNIN'.
SORRY I'M LATE.
HUH?!
YOU NEVER APOLOGIZE FOR BEING LATE... ARE YOU SICK OR SOMETHING?!
DID YOU LISTEN TO MY SECOND SHOW, NAKAHARA-KUN?
BUT OF COURSE.
I TUNED IN, TOO.

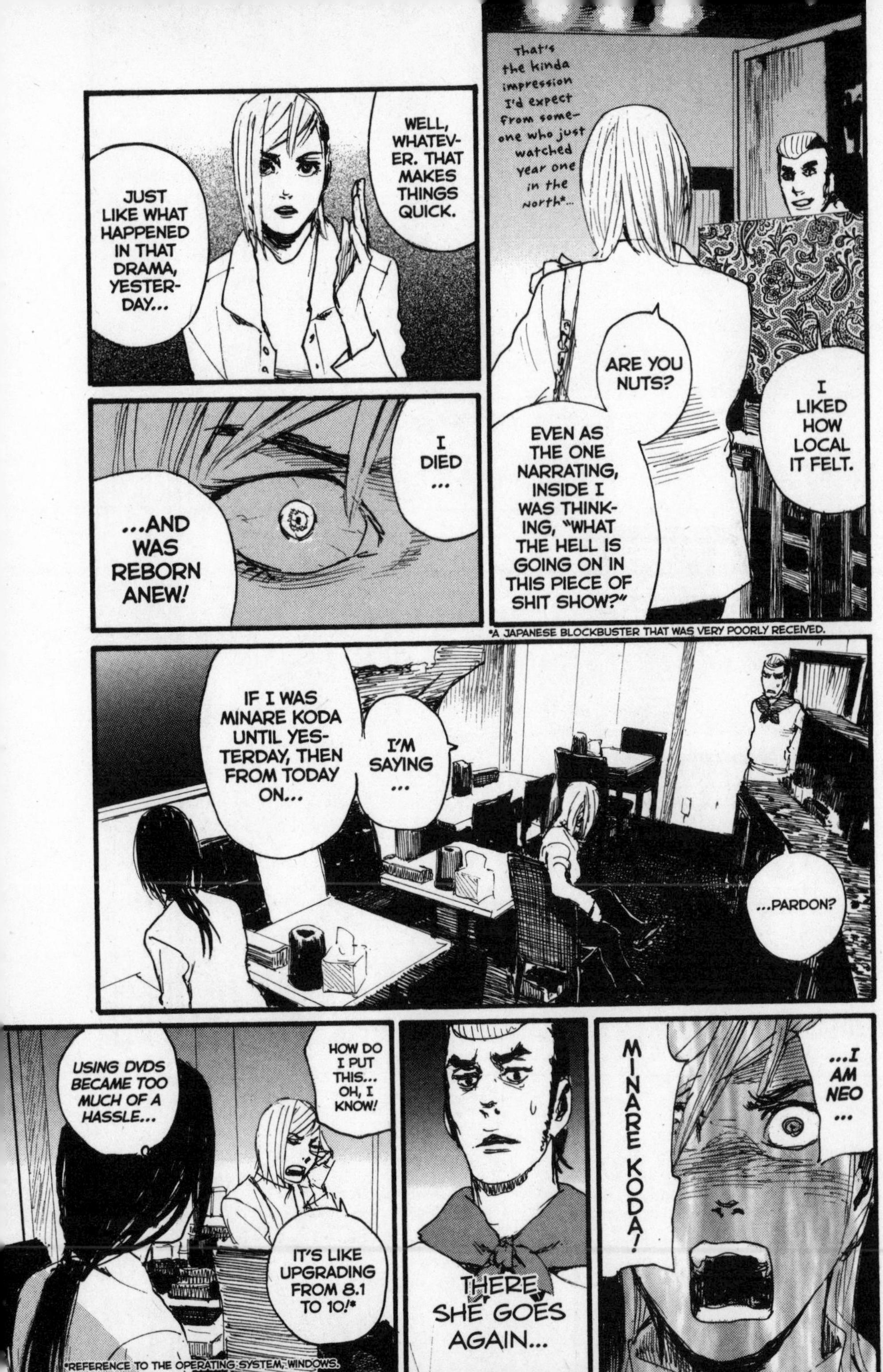
That's the kinda impression I'd expect from some-one who just watched year one in the north*...
I LIKED HOW LOCAL IT FELT.
ARE YOU NUTS?
EVEN AS THE ONE NARRATING, INSIDE I WAS THINK-ING, "WHAT THE HELL IS GOING ON IN THIS PIECE OF SHIT SHOW?"
*A JAPANESE BLOCKBUSTER THAT WAS VERY POORLY RECEIVED.
WELL, WHATEV-ER. THAT MAKES THINGS QUICK.
JUST LIKE WHAT HAPPENED IN THAT DRAMA, YESTER-DAY...
I DIED...
...AND WAS REBORN ANEW!
I'M SAYING...
IF I WAS MINARE KODA UNTIL YES-TERDAY, THEN FROM TODAY ON...
...PARDON?
...I AM NEO...
MINARE KODA!
THERE SHE GOES AGAIN...
HOW DO I PUT THIS... OH, I KNOW!
USING DVDS BECAME TOO MUCH OF A HASSLE...
IT'S LIKE UPGRADING FROM 8.1 TO 10!*
*REFERENCE TO THE OPERATING SYSTEM, WINDOWS.

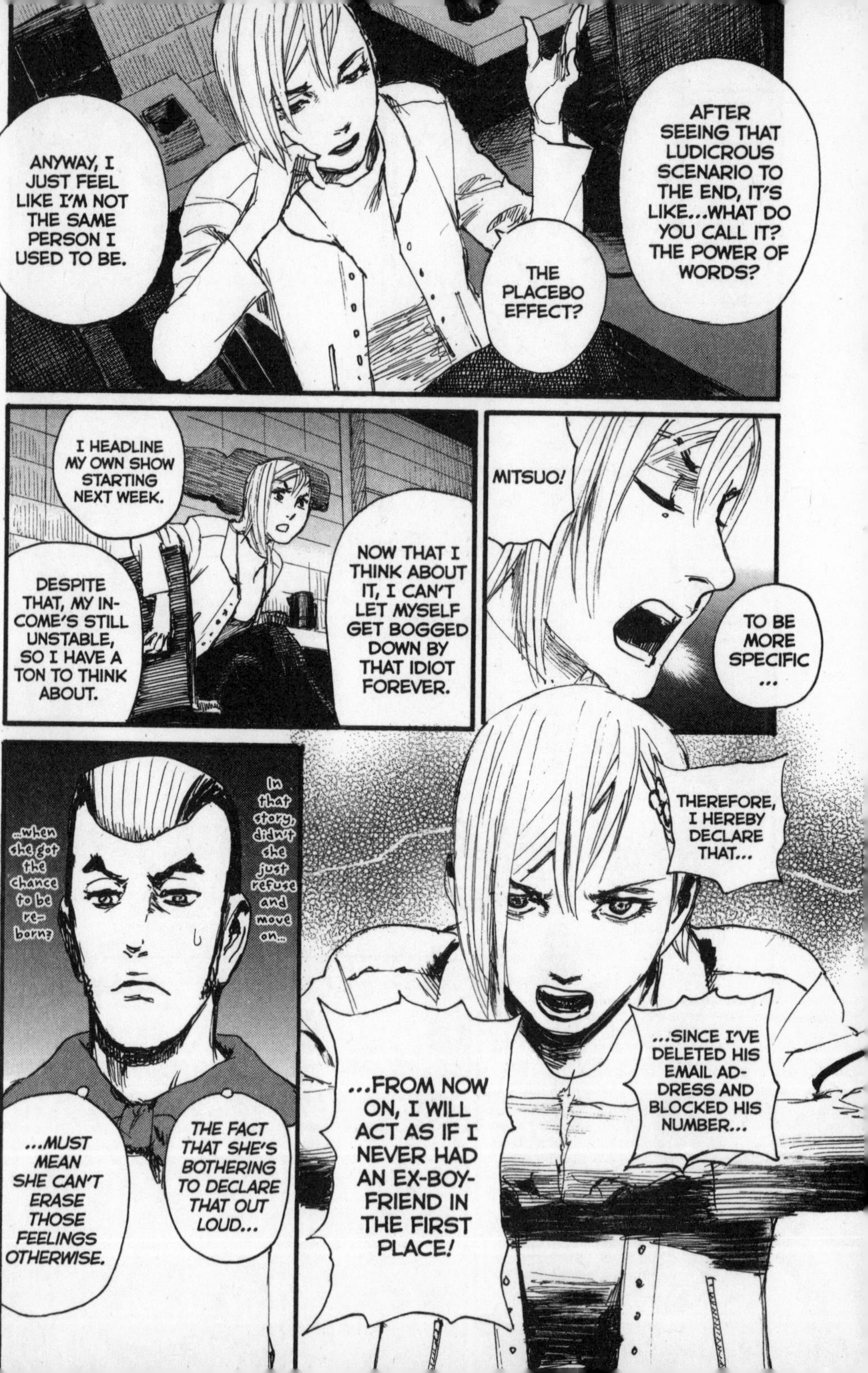
AFTER SEEING THAT LUDICROUS SCENARIO TO THE END, IT'S LIKE...WHAT DO YOU CALL IT? THE POWER OF WORDS?
THE PLACEBO EFFECT?
ANYWAY, I JUST FEEL LIKE I'M NOT THE SAME PERSON I USED TO BE.
MITSUO!
TO BE MORE SPECIFIC...
I HEADLINE MY OWN SHOW STARTING NEXT WEEK.
DESPITE THAT, MY INCOME'S STILL UNSTABLE, SO I HAVE A TON TO THINK ABOUT.
NOW THAT I THINK ABOUT IT, I CAN'T LET MYSELF GET BOGGED DOWN BY THAT IDIOT FOREVER.
THEREFORE, I HEREBY DECLARE THAT...
...SINCE I'VE DELETED HIS EMAIL ADDRESS AND BLOCKED HIS NUMBER...
...FROM NOW ON, I WILL ACT AS IF I NEVER HAD AN EX-BOYFRIEND IN THE FIRST PLACE!
In that story, didn't she just refuse and move on...
...when she got the chance to be reborn?
THE FACT THAT SHE'S BOTHERING TO DECLARE THAT OUT LOUD...
...MUST MEAN SHE CAN'T ERASE THOSE FEELINGS OTHERWISE.

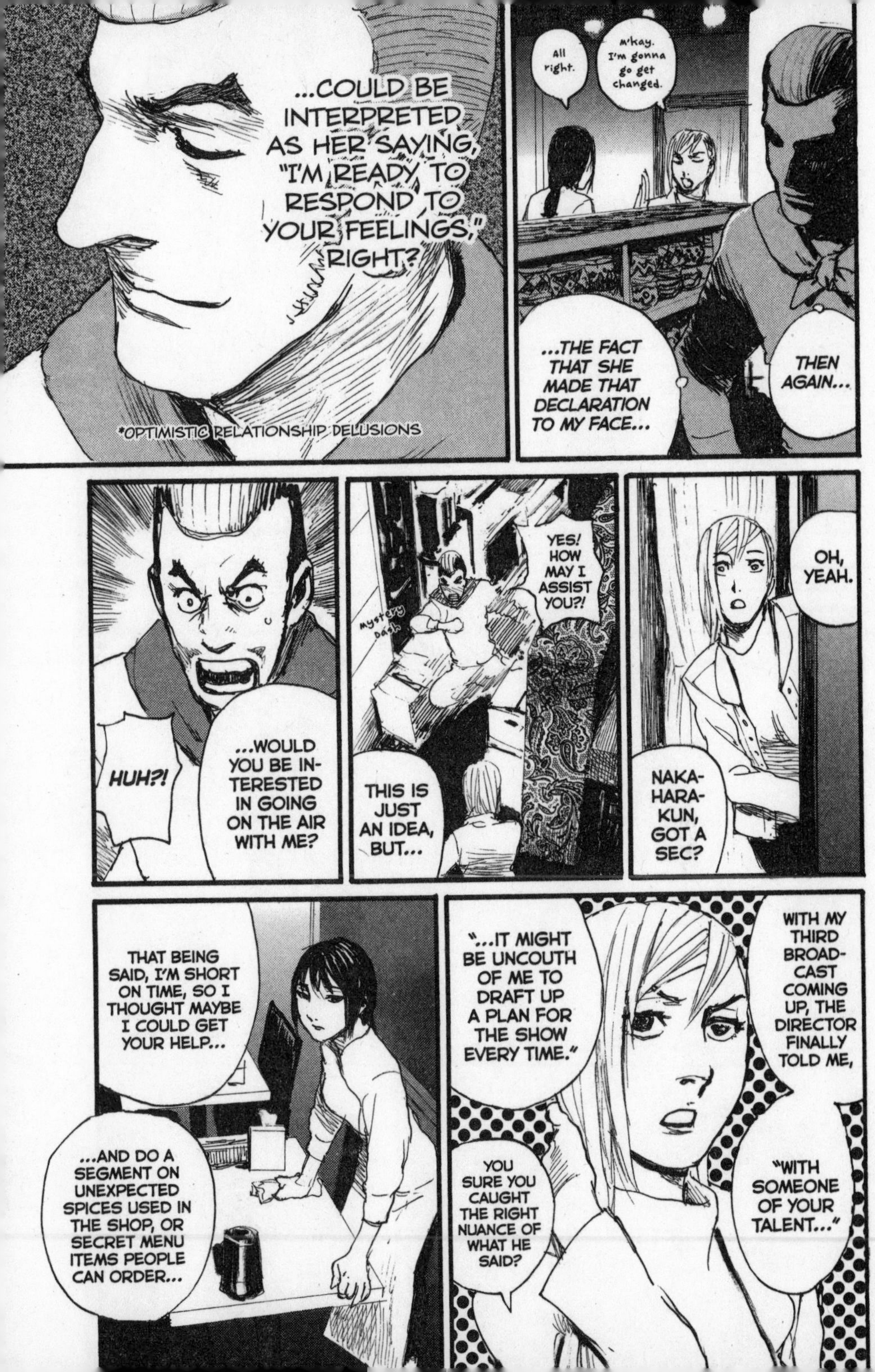
M'kay. I'm gonna go get changed.
All right.
THEN AGAIN...
...THE FACT THAT SHE MADE THAT DECLARATION TO MY FACE...
...COULD BE INTERPRETED AS HER SAYING, "I'M READY TO RESPOND TO YOUR FEELINGS," RIGHT?
*OPTIMISTIC RELATIONSHIP DELUSIONS
OH, YEAH.
NAKA-HARA-KUN, GOT A SEC?
YES! HOW MAY I ASSIST YOU?!
Mystery Dash
THIS IS JUST AN IDEA, BUT...
...WOULD YOU BE INTERESTED IN GOING ON THE AIR WITH ME?
HUH?!
WITH MY THIRD BROADCAST COMING UP, THE DIRECTOR FINALLY TOLD ME,
"...IT MIGHT BE UNCOUTH OF ME TO DRAFT UP A PLAN FOR THE SHOW EVERY TIME."
"WITH SOMEONE OF YOUR TALENT..."
YOU SURE YOU CAUGHT THE RIGHT NUANCE OF WHAT HE SAID?
THAT BEING SAID, I'M SHORT ON TIME, SO I THOUGHT MAYBE I COULD GET YOUR HELP...
...AND DO A SEGMENT ON UNEXPECTED SPICES USED IN THE SHOP, OR SECRET MENU ITEMS PEOPLE CAN ORDER...

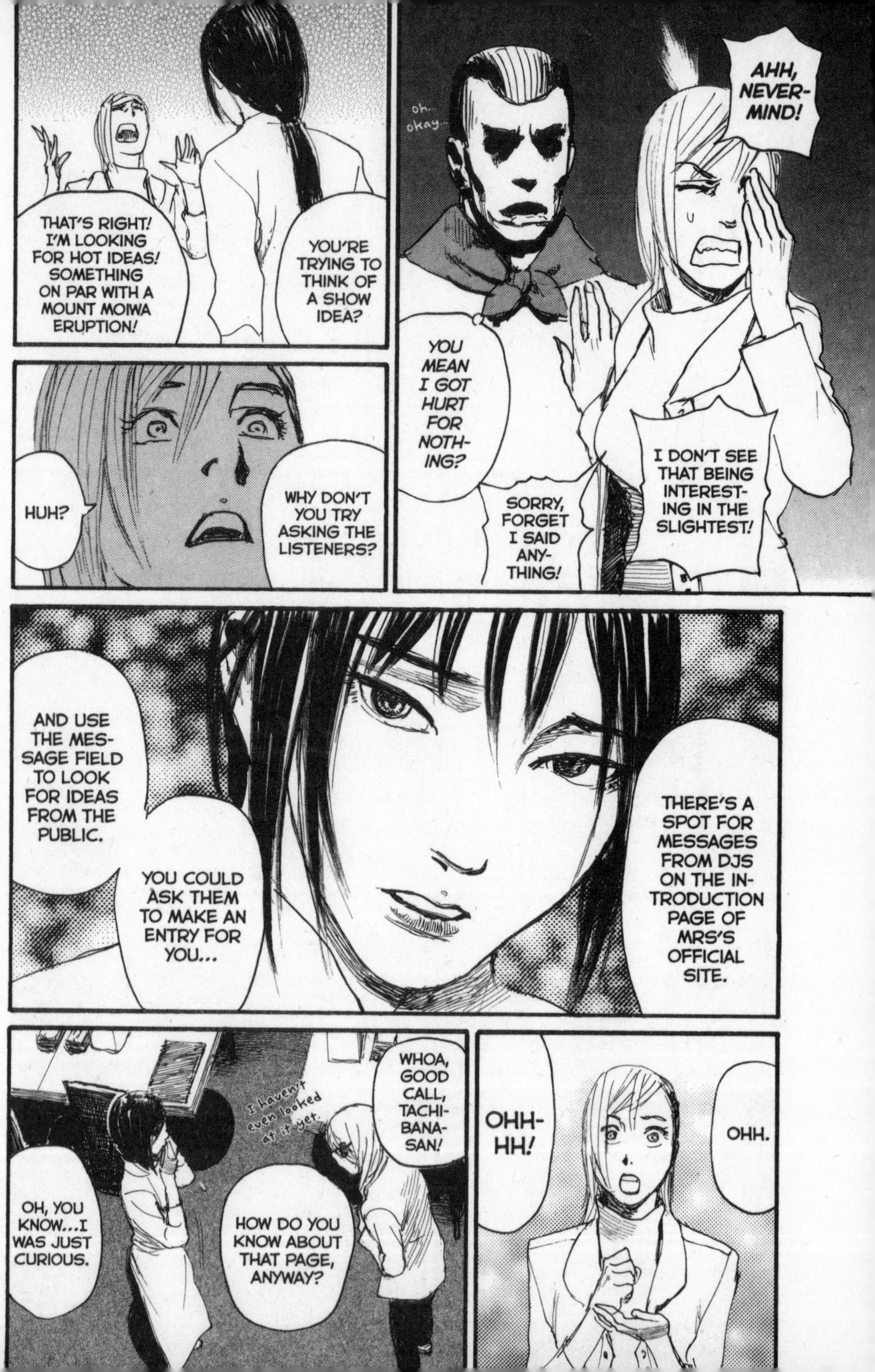
AHH, NEVER-MIND!
oh... okay...
I DON'T SEE THAT BEING INTEREST-ING IN THE SLIGHTEST!
SORRY, FORGET I SAID ANY-THING!
YOU MEAN I GOT HURT FOR NOTH-ING?
YOU'RE TRYING TO THINK OF A SHOW IDEA?
THAT'S RIGHT! I'M LOOKING FOR HOT IDEAS! SOMETHING ON PAR WITH A MOUNT MOIWA ERUPTION!
WHY DON'T YOU TRY ASKING THE LISTENERS?
HUH?
THERE'S A SPOT FOR MESSAGES FROM DJS ON THE IN-TRODUCTION PAGE OF MRS'S OFFICIAL SITE.
AND USE THE MES-SAGE FIELD TO LOOK FOR IDEAS FROM THE PUBLIC.
YOU COULD ASK THEM TO MAKE AN ENTRY FOR YOU...
OHH.
OHH-HH!
WHOA, GOOD CALL, TACHI-BANA-SAN!
I haven't even looked at it yet.
HOW DO YOU KNOW ABOUT THAT PAGE, ANYWAY?
OH, YOU KNOW...I WAS JUST CURIOUS.

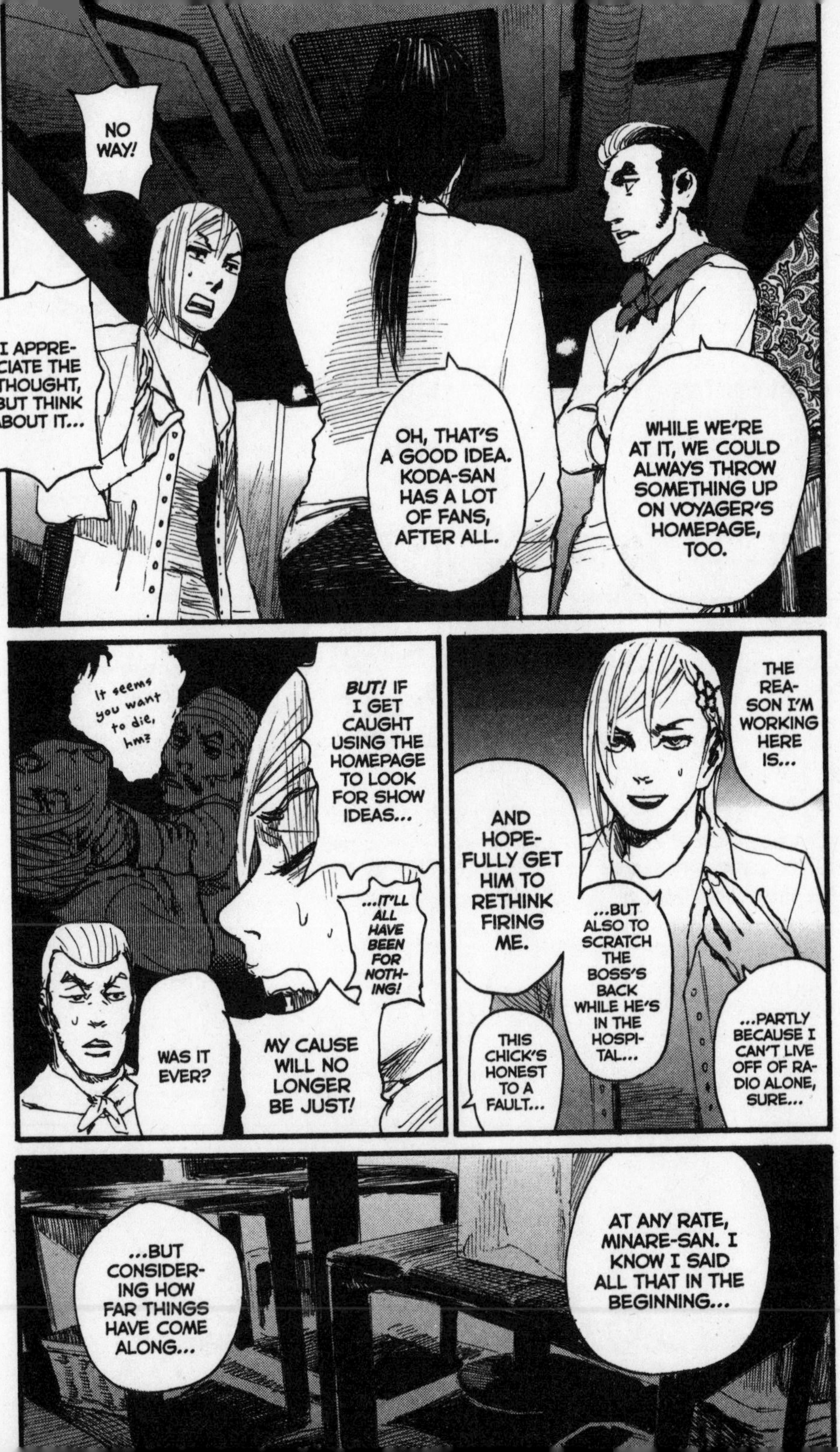
WHILE WE'RE AT IT, WE COULD ALWAYS THROW SOMETHING UP ON VOYAGER'S HOMEPAGE, TOO.
OH, THAT'S A GOOD IDEA. KODA-SAN HAS A LOT OF FANS, AFTER ALL.
NO WAY!
I APPRECIATE THE THOUGHT, BUT THINK ABOUT IT...
THE REASON I'M WORKING HERE IS...
...PARTLY BECAUSE I CAN'T LIVE OFF OF RADIO ALONE, SURE...
...BUT ALSO TO SCRATCH THE BOSS'S BACK WHILE HE'S IN THE HOSPITAL...
AND HOPEFULLY GET HIM TO RETHINK FIRING ME.
THIS CHICK'S HONEST TO A FAULT...
BUT! IF I GET CAUGHT USING THE HOMEPAGE TO LOOK FOR SHOW IDEAS...
...IT'LL ALL HAVE BEEN FOR NOTHING!
MY CAUSE WILL NO LONGER BE JUST!
It seems you want to die, hm?
WAS IT EVER?
AT ANY RATE, MINARE-SAN. I KNOW I SAID ALL THAT IN THE BEGINNING...
...BUT CONSIDERING HOW FAR THINGS HAVE COME ALONG...

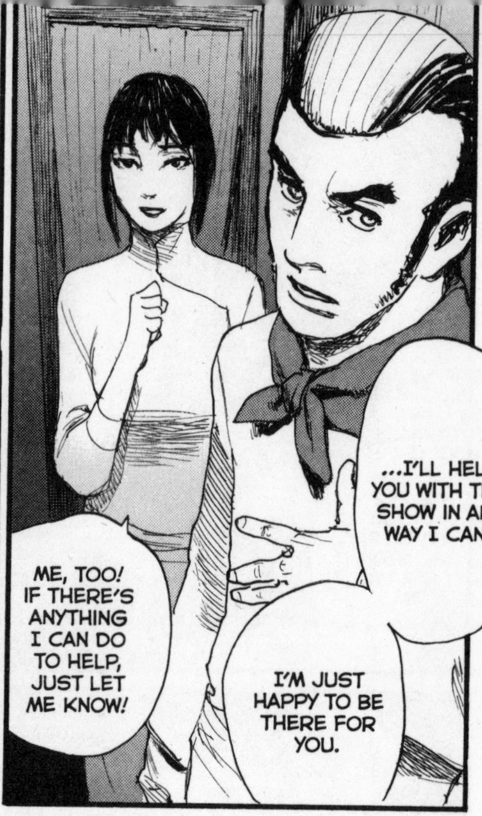
...I'LL HELP YOU WITH THE SHOW IN ANY WAY I CAN.
I'M JUST HAPPY TO BE THERE FOR YOU.
ME, TOO! IF THERE'S ANYTHING I CAN DO TO HELP, JUST LET ME KNOW!

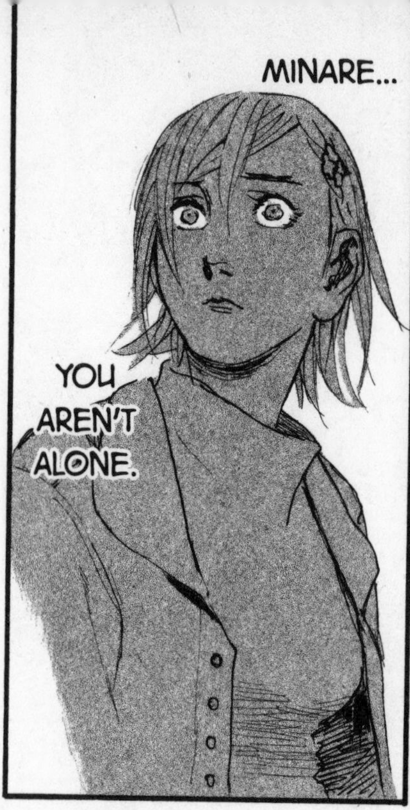
MINARE...
YOU AREN'T ALONE.

RADIO HOSTS ARE DIFFERENT FROM COMEDIANS. THERE IS NO NEED FOR YOU TO MAKE PEOPLE LAUGH ON YOUR EFFORTS ALONE.

THE EXPERIENCES OF YOUR FRIENDS, THE WORKS OF ARTISTS, THE WORDS OF THE LISTENERS...

ALL YOU NEED TO BE IS A COORDINATOR WHO CAN SKILLFULLY ARRANGE SUCH PIECES INTO A MOSAIC MEANT TO PLEASE YOUR AUDIENCE.

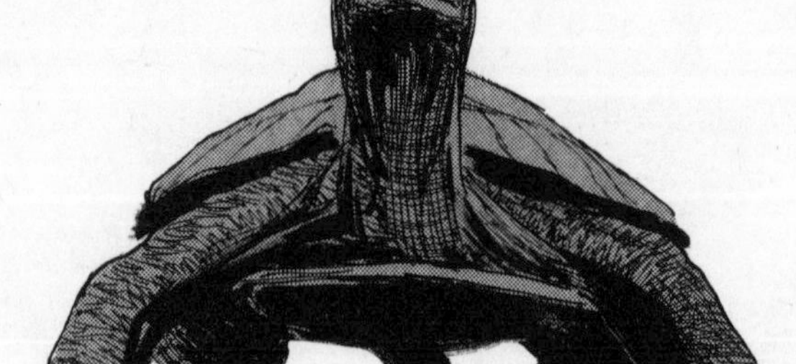

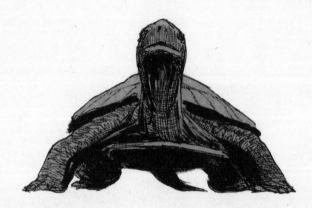

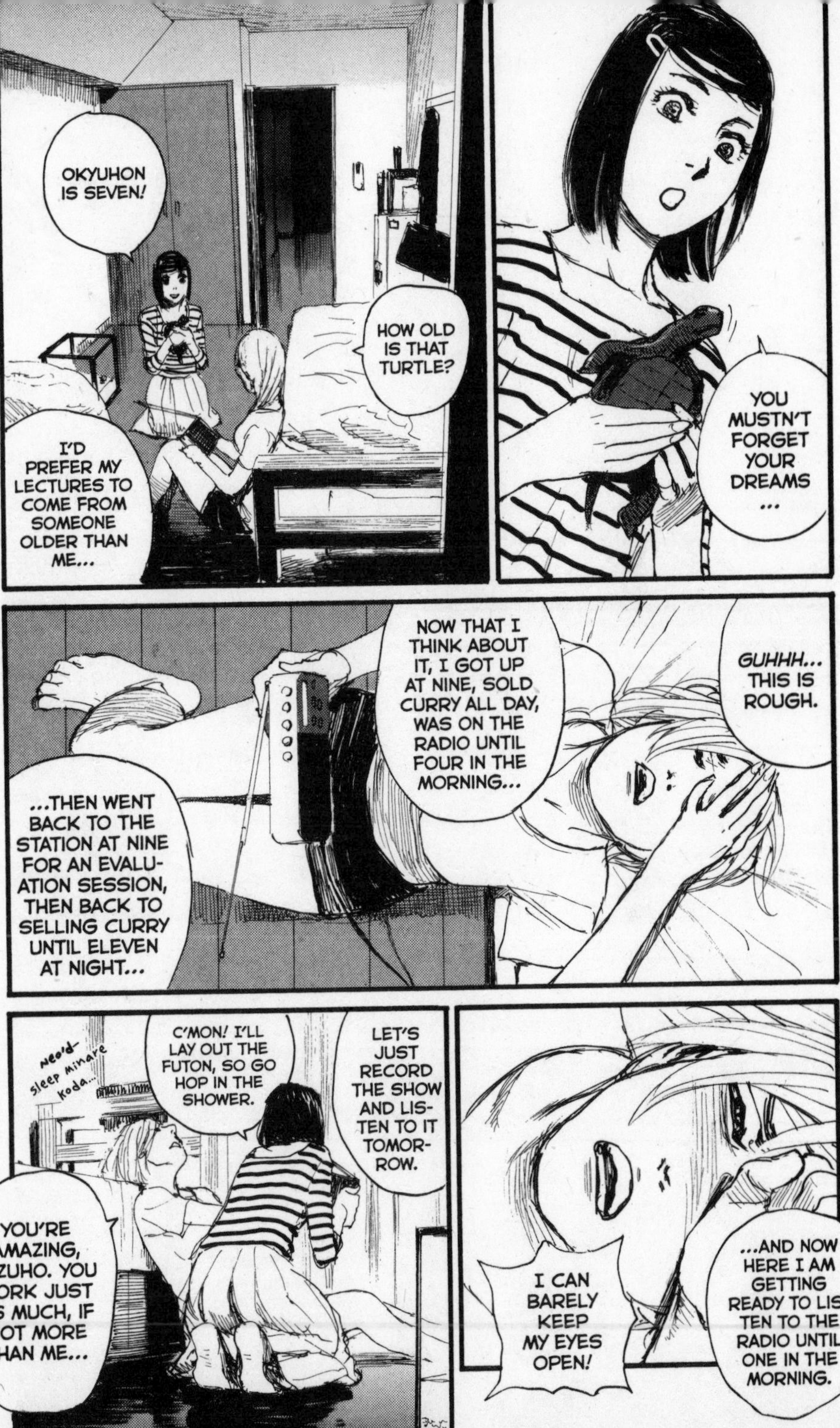
YOU MUSTN'T FORGET YOUR DREAMS ...
HOW OLD IS THAT TURTLE?
OKYUHON IS SEVEN!
I'D PREFER MY LECTURES TO COME FROM SOMEONE OLDER THAN ME...
GUHHH... THIS IS ROUGH.
NOW THAT I THINK ABOUT IT, I GOT UP AT NINE, SOLD CURRY ALL DAY, WAS ON THE RADIO UNTIL FOUR IN THE MORNING...
...THEN WENT BACK TO THE STATION AT NINE FOR AN EVALU-ATION SESSION, THEN BACK TO SELLING CURRY UNTIL ELEVEN AT NIGHT...
...AND NOW HERE I AM GETTING READY TO LIS-TEN TO THE RADIO UNTIL ONE IN THE MORNING.
I CAN BARELY KEEP MY EYES OPEN!
LET'S JUST RECORD THE SHOW AND LIS-TEN TO IT TOMOR-ROW.
C'MON! I'LL LAY OUT THE FUTON, SO GO HOP IN THE SHOWER.
YOU'RE AMAZING, MIZUHO. YOU WORK JUST AS MUCH, IF NOT MORE THAN ME...

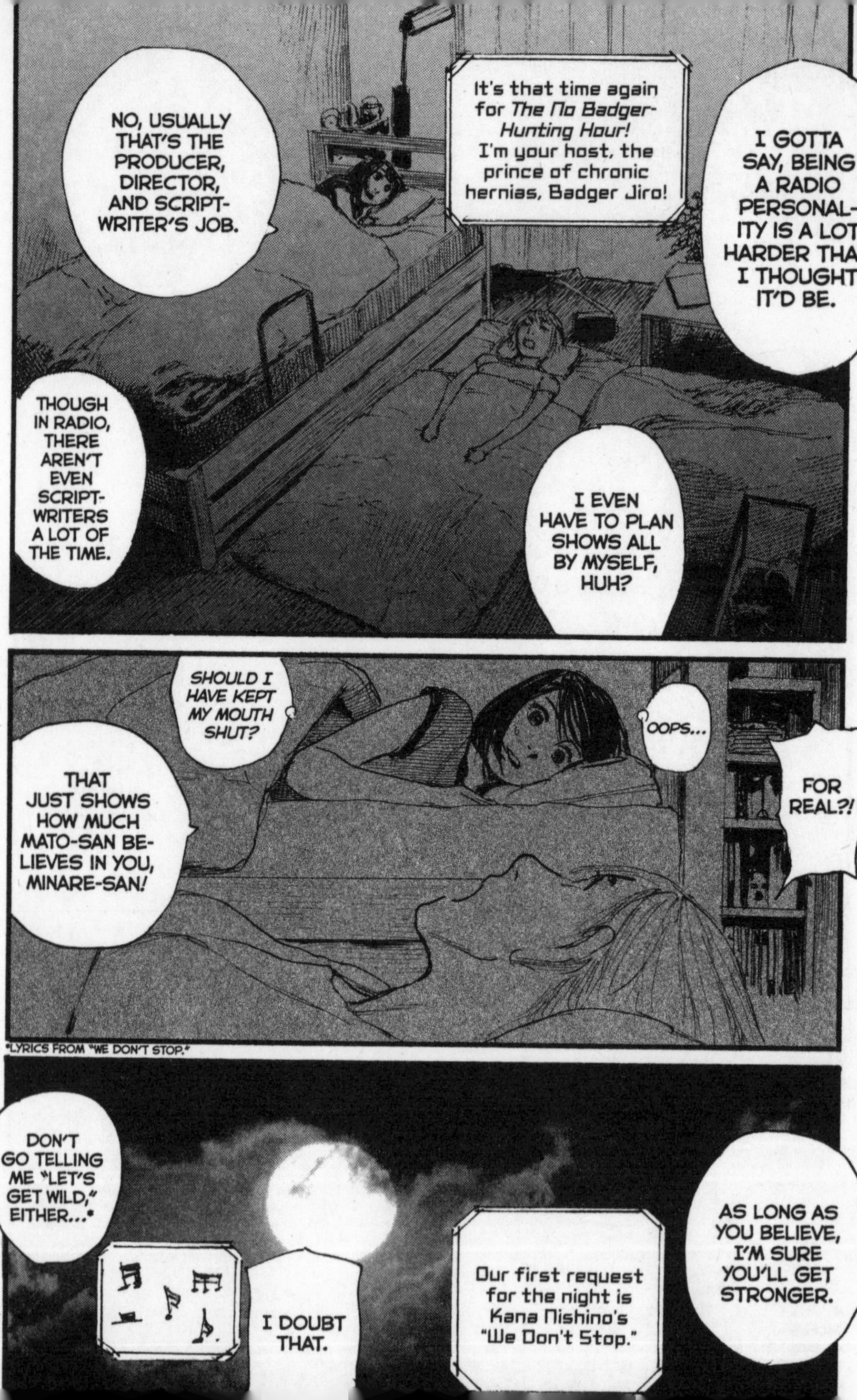
I GOTTA SAY, BEING A RADIO PERSONALITY IS A LOT HARDER THAN I THOUGHT IT'D BE.
It's that time again for *The No Badger-Hunting Hour!* I'm your host, the prince of chronic hernias, Badger Jiro!
NO, USUALLY THAT'S THE PRODUCER, DIRECTOR, AND SCRIPT-WRITER'S JOB.
I EVEN HAVE TO PLAN SHOWS ALL BY MYSELF, HUH?
THOUGH IN RADIO, THERE AREN'T EVEN SCRIPT-WRITERS A LOT OF THE TIME.
FOR REAL?!
OOPS...
SHOULD I HAVE KEPT MY MOUTH SHUT?
THAT JUST SHOWS HOW MUCH MATO-SAN BELIEVES IN YOU, MINARE-SAN!
*LYRICS FROM "WE DON'T STOP."
AS LONG AS YOU BELIEVE, I'M SURE YOU'LL GET STRONGER.
Our first request for the night is Kana Nishino's "We Don't Stop."
I DOUBT THAT.
DON'T GO TELLING ME "LET'S GET WILD," EITHER...*

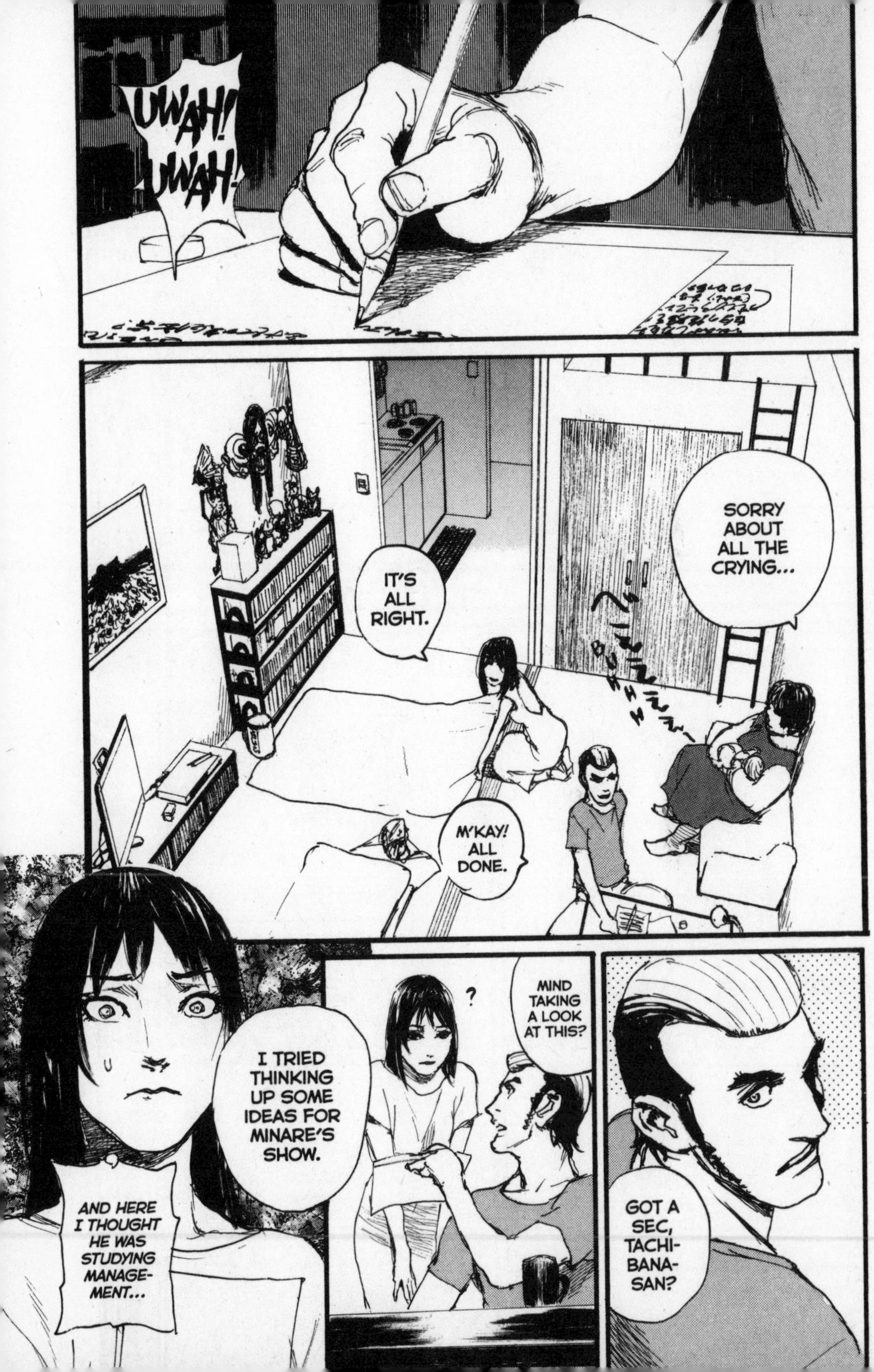
UWAH! A UWAH!
SORRY ABOUT ALL THE CRYING...
IT'S ALL RIGHT.
M'KAY! ALL DONE.
GOT A SEC, TACHI-BANA-SAN?
MIND TAKING A LOOK AT THIS?
?
I TRIED THINKING UP SOME IDEAS FOR MINARE'S SHOW.
AND HERE I THOUGHT HE WAS STUDYING MANAGE-MENT...

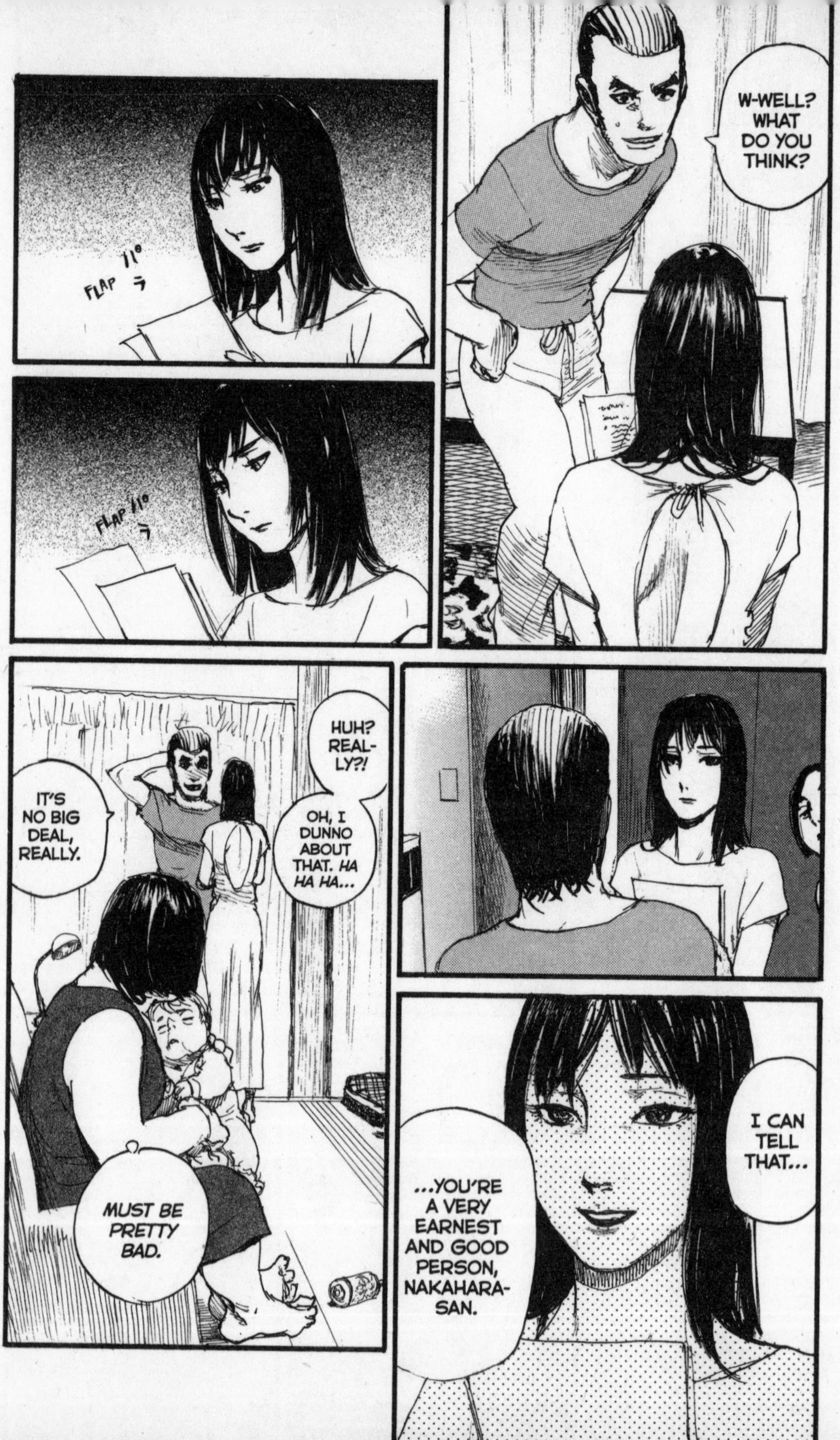

W-WELL? WHAT DO YOU THINK?
FLAP パラ
FLAP パラ
I CAN TELL THAT...
...YOU'RE A VERY EARNEST AND GOOD PERSON, NAKAHARA-SAN.
HUH? REALLY?!
OH, I DUNNO ABOUT THAT. *HA HA HA...*
IT'S NO BIG DEAL, REALLY.
MUST BE PRETTY BAD.

Chapter 19 "I WANT TO WARM YOU UP."

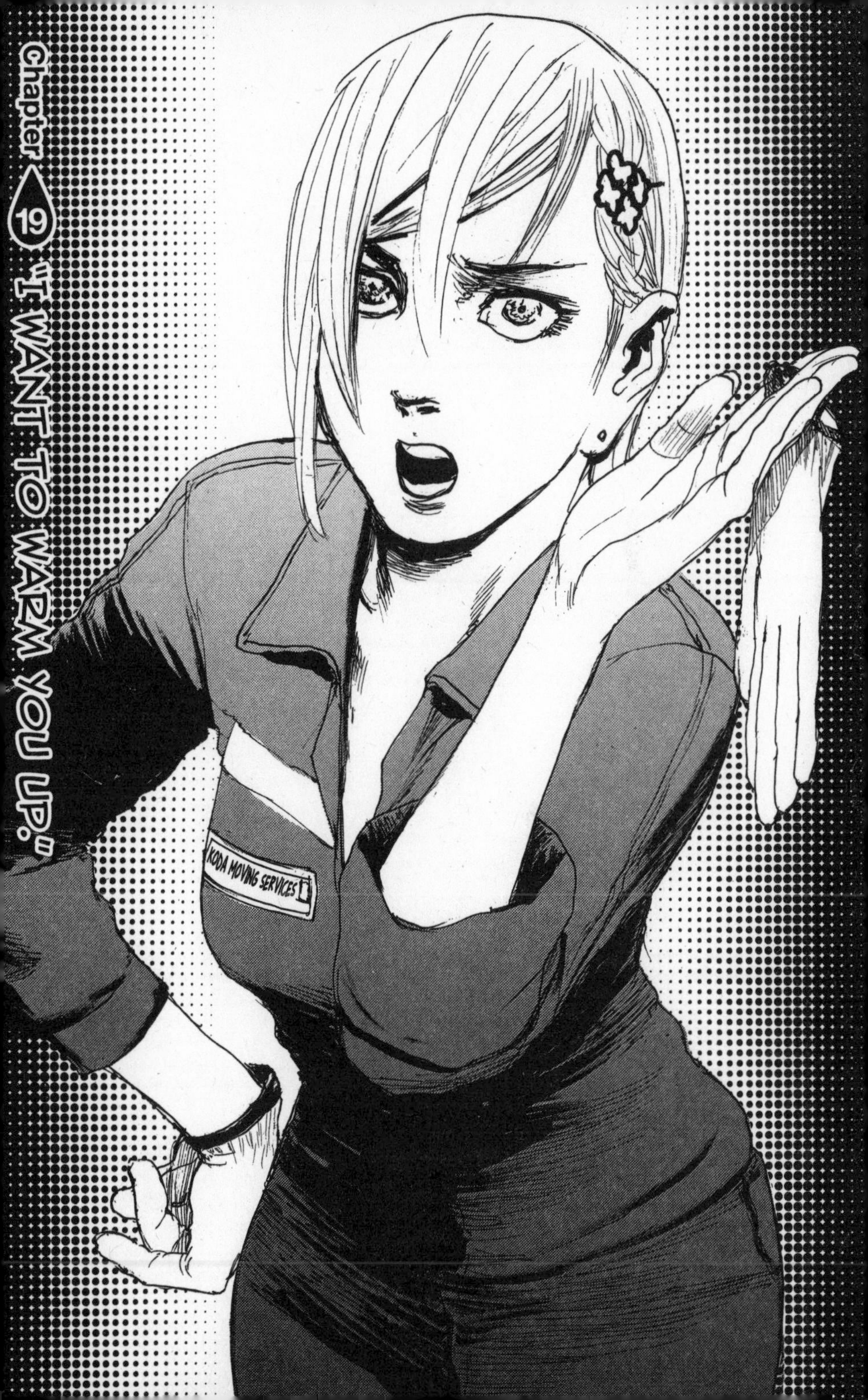
KODA MOVING SERVICES

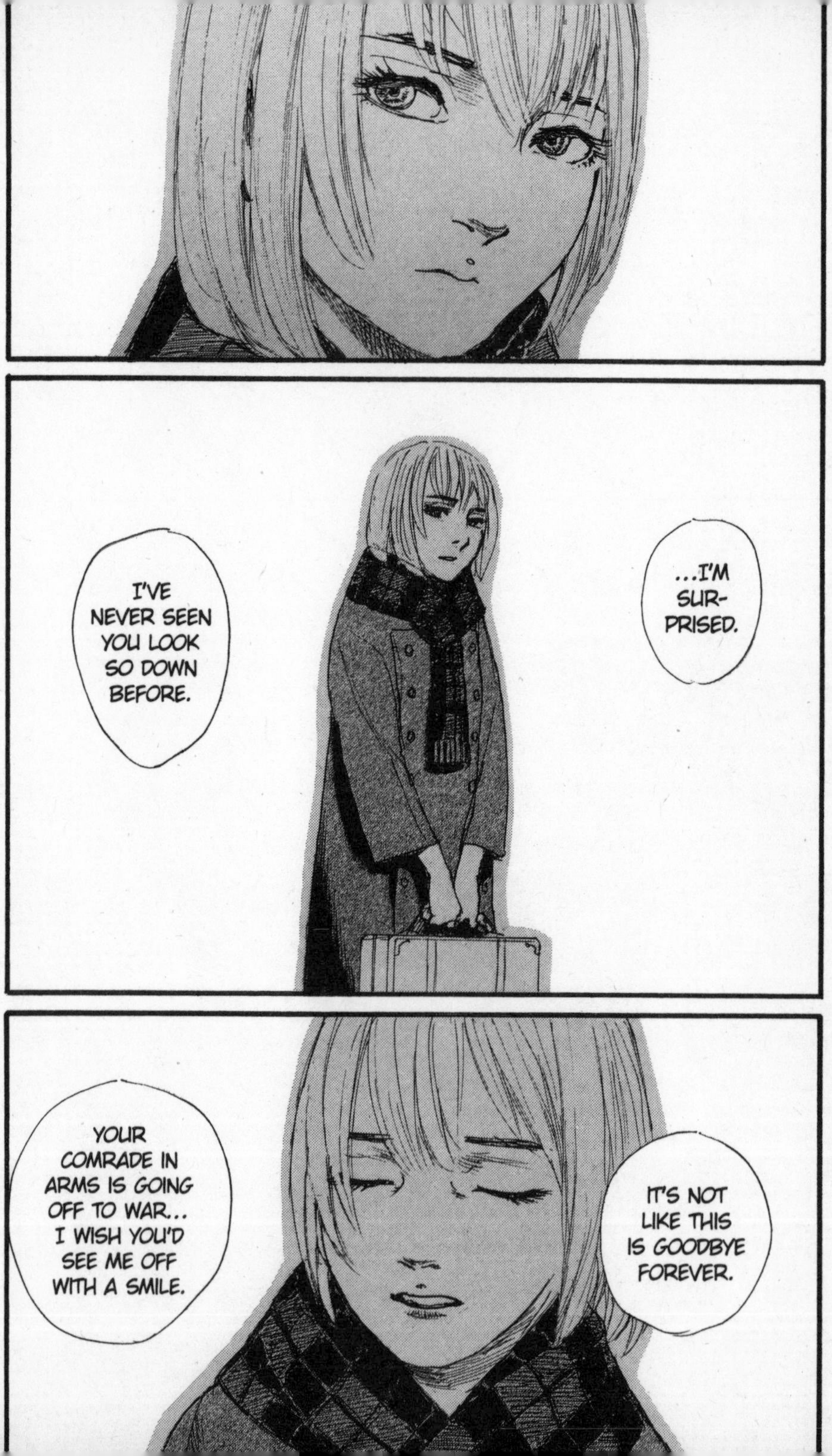
...I'M SUR-PRISED.
I'VE NEVER SEEN YOU LOOK SO DOWN BEFORE.
IT'S NOT LIKE THIS IS GOODBYE FOREVER.
YOUR COMRADE IN ARMS IS GOING OFF TO WAR... I WISH YOU'D SEE ME OFF WITH A SMILE.

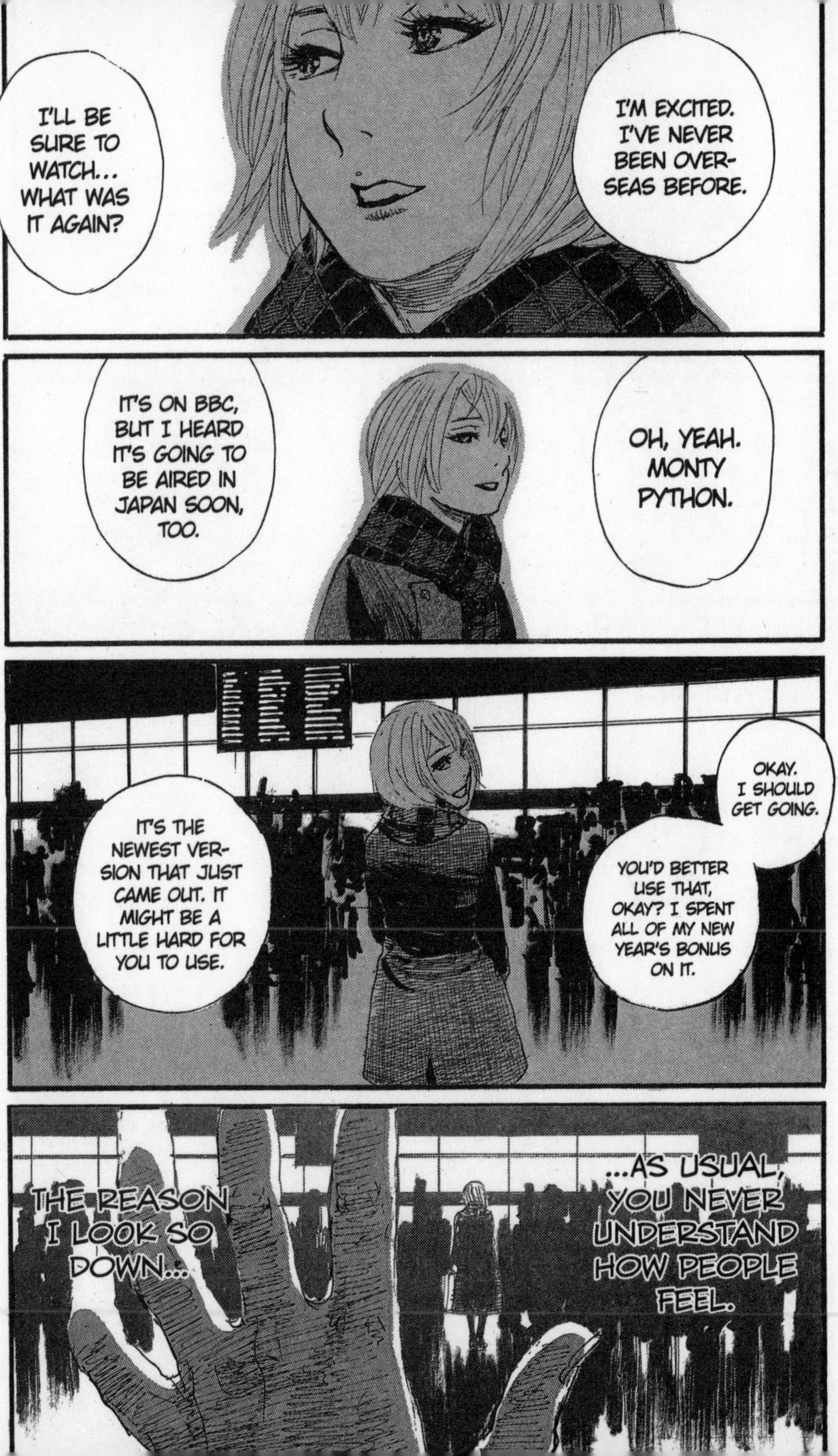
I'M EXCITED. I'VE NEVER BEEN OVERSEAS BEFORE.
I'LL BE SURE TO WATCH... WHAT WAS IT AGAIN?
OH, YEAH. MONTY PYTHON.
IT'S ON BBC, BUT I HEARD IT'S GOING TO BE AIRED IN JAPAN SOON, TOO.
OKAY. I SHOULD GET GOING.
YOU'D BETTER USE THAT, OKAY? I SPENT ALL OF MY NEW YEAR'S BONUS ON IT.
IT'S THE NEWEST VERSION THAT JUST CAME OUT. IT MIGHT BE A LITTLE HARD FOR YOU TO USE.
...AS USUAL, YOU NEVER UNDERSTAND HOW PEOPLE FEEL.
THE REASON I LOOK SO DOWN...

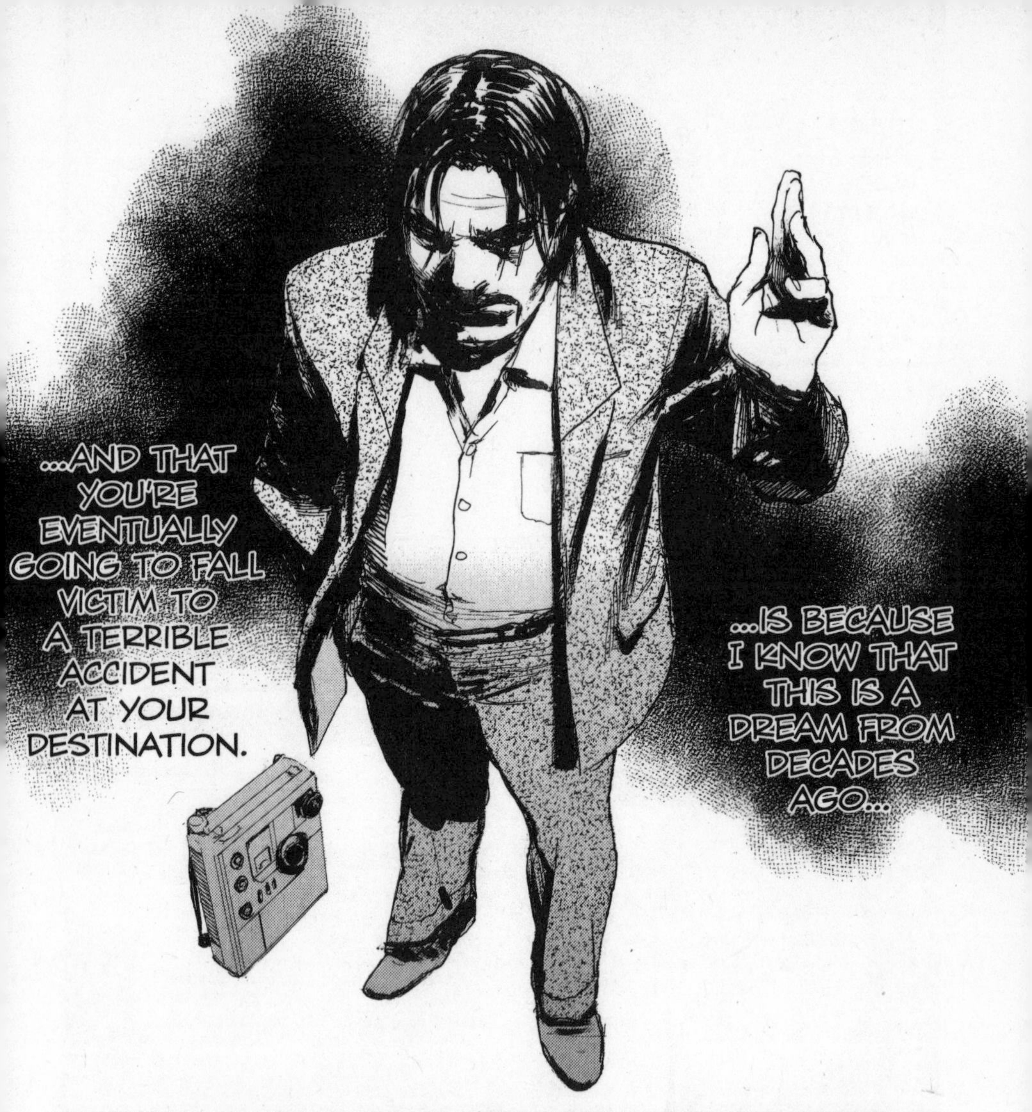
...AND THAT YOU'RE EVENTUALLY GOING TO FALL VICTIM TO A TERRIBLE ACCIDENT AT YOUR DESTINATION.
...IS BECAUSE I KNOW THAT THIS IS A DREAM FROM DECADES AGO...

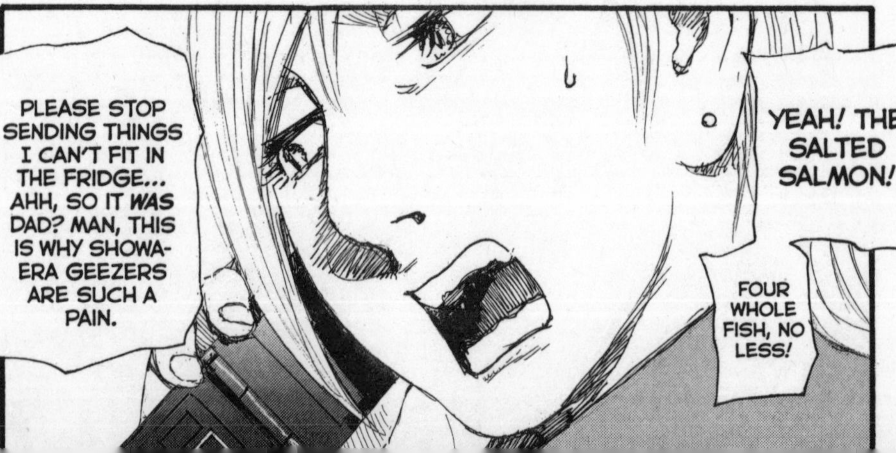
YEAH! THE SALTED SALMON!
FOUR WHOLE FISH, NO LESS!
PLEASE STOP SENDING THINGS I CAN'T FIT IN THE FRIDGE... AHH, SO IT *WAS* DAD? MAN, THIS IS WHY SHOWA-ERA GEEZERS ARE SUCH A PAIN.

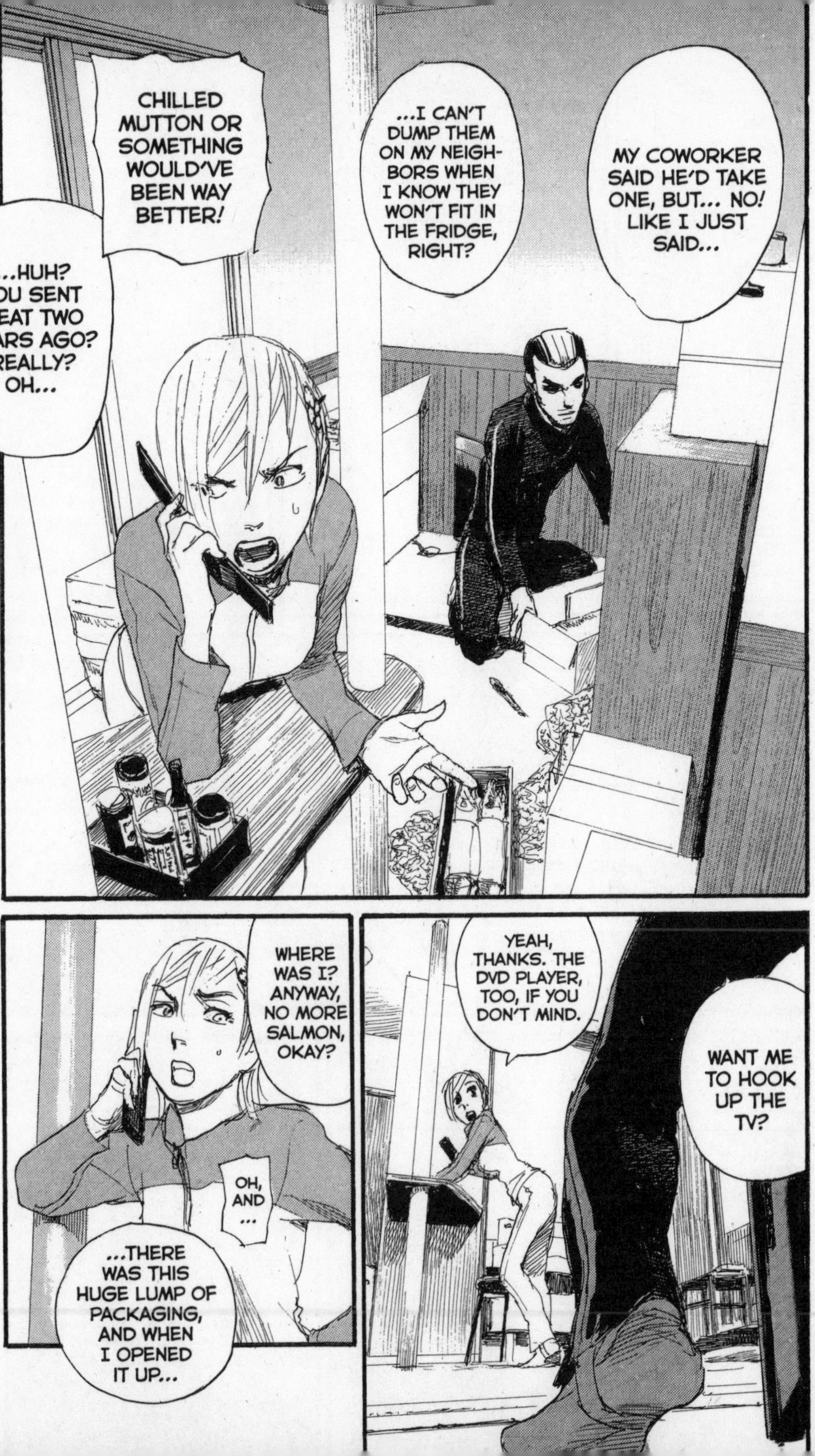
MY COWORKER SAID HE'D TAKE ONE, BUT... NO! LIKE I JUST SAID...
...I CAN'T DUMP THEM ON MY NEIGH-BORS WHEN I KNOW THEY WON'T FIT IN THE FRIDGE, RIGHT?
CHILLED MUTTON OR SOMETHING WOULD'VE BEEN WAY BETTER!
...HUH? YOU SENT MEAT TWO YEARS AGO? REALLY? OH...
WANT ME TO HOOK UP THE TV?
YEAH, THANKS. THE DVD PLAYER, TOO, IF YOU DON'T MIND.
WHERE WAS I? ANYWAY, NO MORE SALMON, OKAY?
OH, AND ...
...THERE WAS THIS HUGE LUMP OF PACKAGING, AND WHEN I OPENED IT UP...

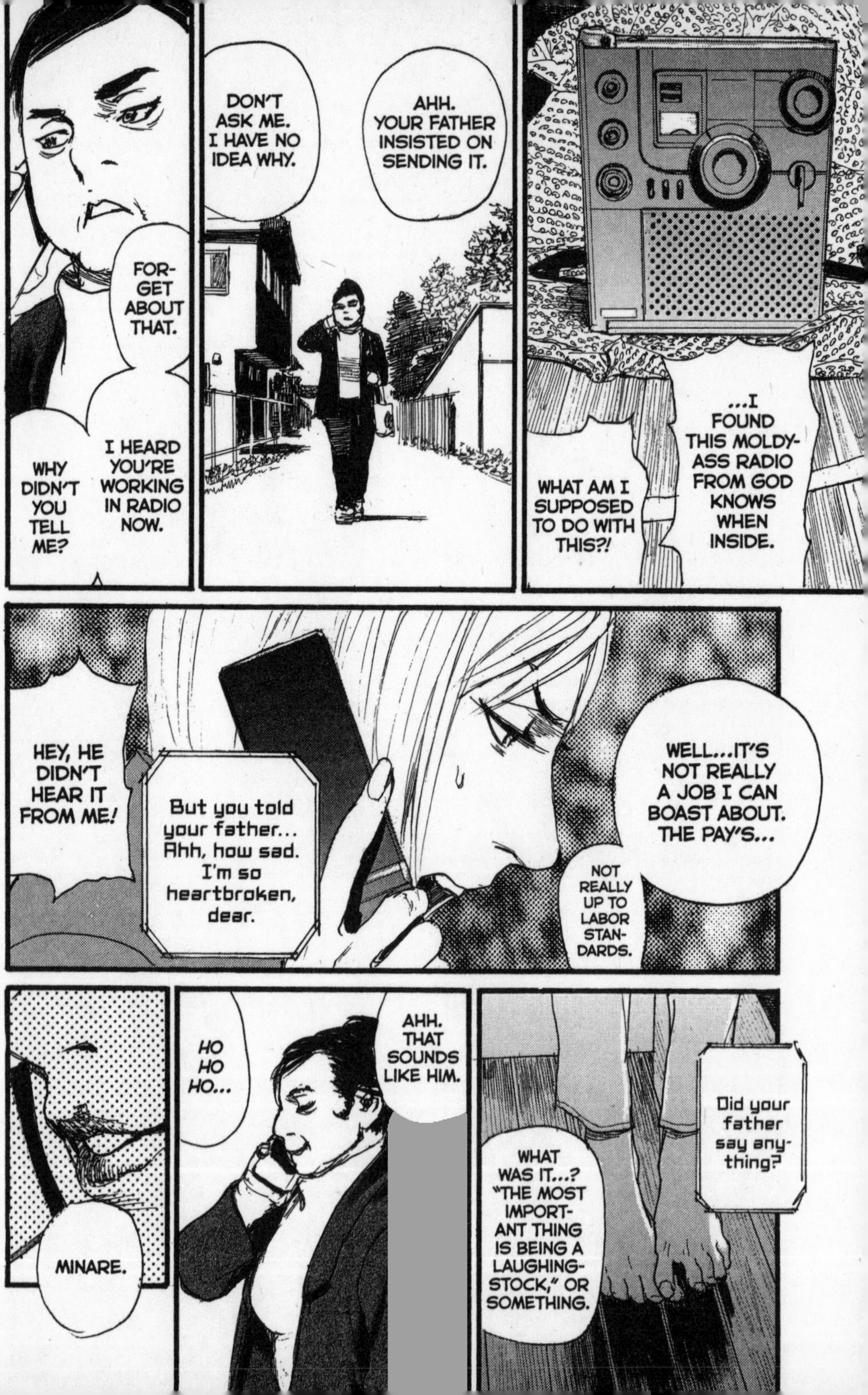
...I FOUND THIS MOLDY-ASS RADIO FROM GOD KNOWS WHEN INSIDE.
WHAT AM I SUPPOSED TO DO WITH THIS?!
AHH. YOUR FATHER INSISTED ON SENDING IT.
DON'T ASK ME. I HAVE NO IDEA WHY.
FORGET ABOUT THAT.
I HEARD YOU'RE WORKING IN RADIO NOW.
WHY DIDN'T YOU TELL ME?
WELL...IT'S NOT REALLY A JOB I CAN BOAST ABOUT. THE PAY'S...
NOT REALLY UP TO LABOR STANDARDS.
But you told your father... Ahh, how sad. I'm so heartbroken, dear.
HEY, HE DIDN'T HEAR IT FROM ME!
Did your father say anything?
WHAT WAS IT...? "THE MOST IMPORTANT THING IS BEING A LAUGHINGSTOCK," OR SOMETHING.
AHH. THAT SOUNDS LIKE HIM.
HO HO HO...
MINARE.

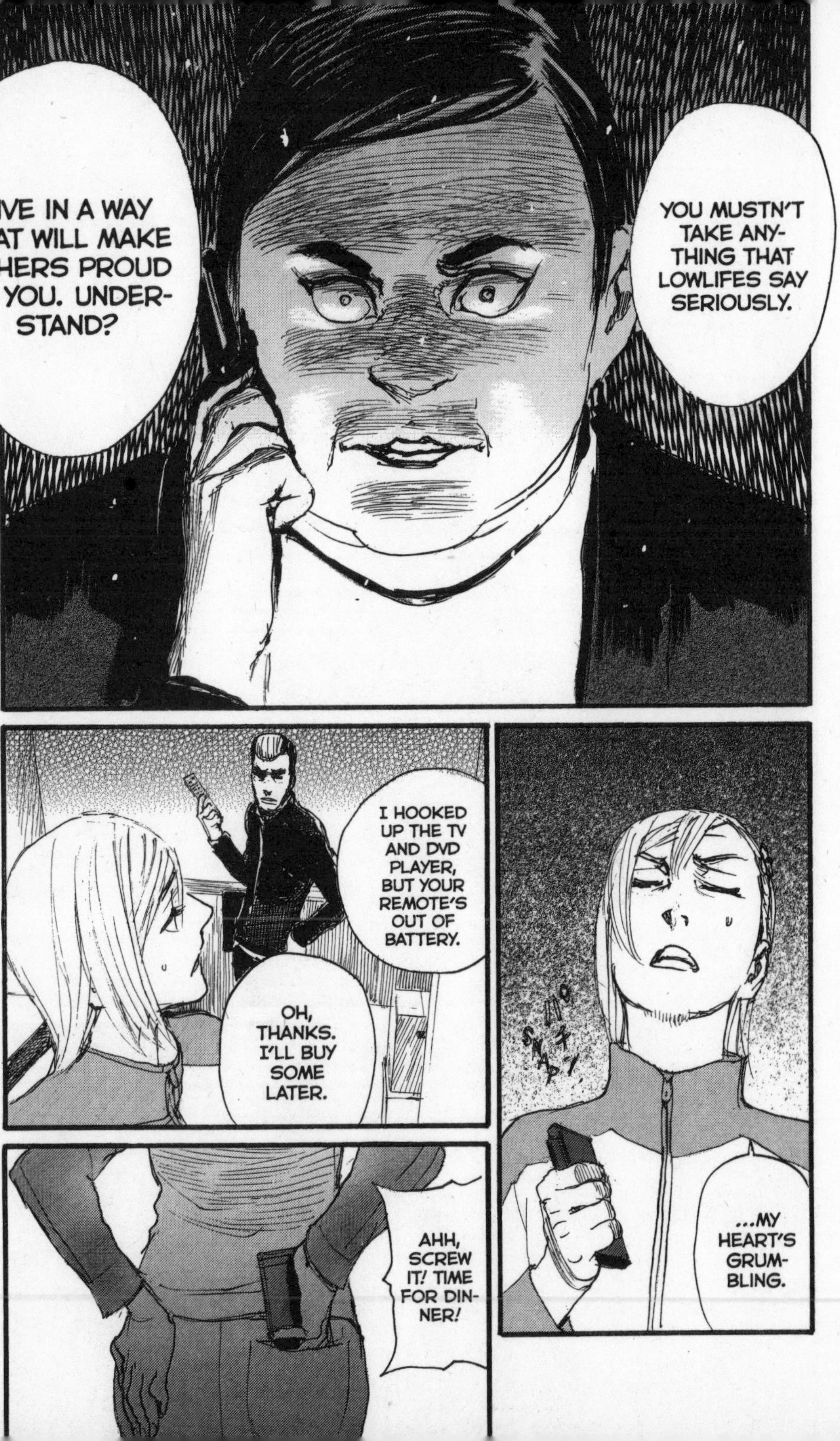
YOU MUSTN'T TAKE ANY-THING THAT LOWLIFES SAY SERIOUSLY.
LIVE IN A WAY THAT WILL MAKE OTHERS PROUD OF YOU. UNDER-STAND?
SNAP
...MY HEART'S GRUM-BLING.
I HOOKED UP THE TV AND DVD PLAYER, BUT YOUR REMOTE'S OUT OF BATTERY.
OH, THANKS. I'LL BUY SOME LATER.
AHH, SCREW IT! TIME FOR DIN-NER!

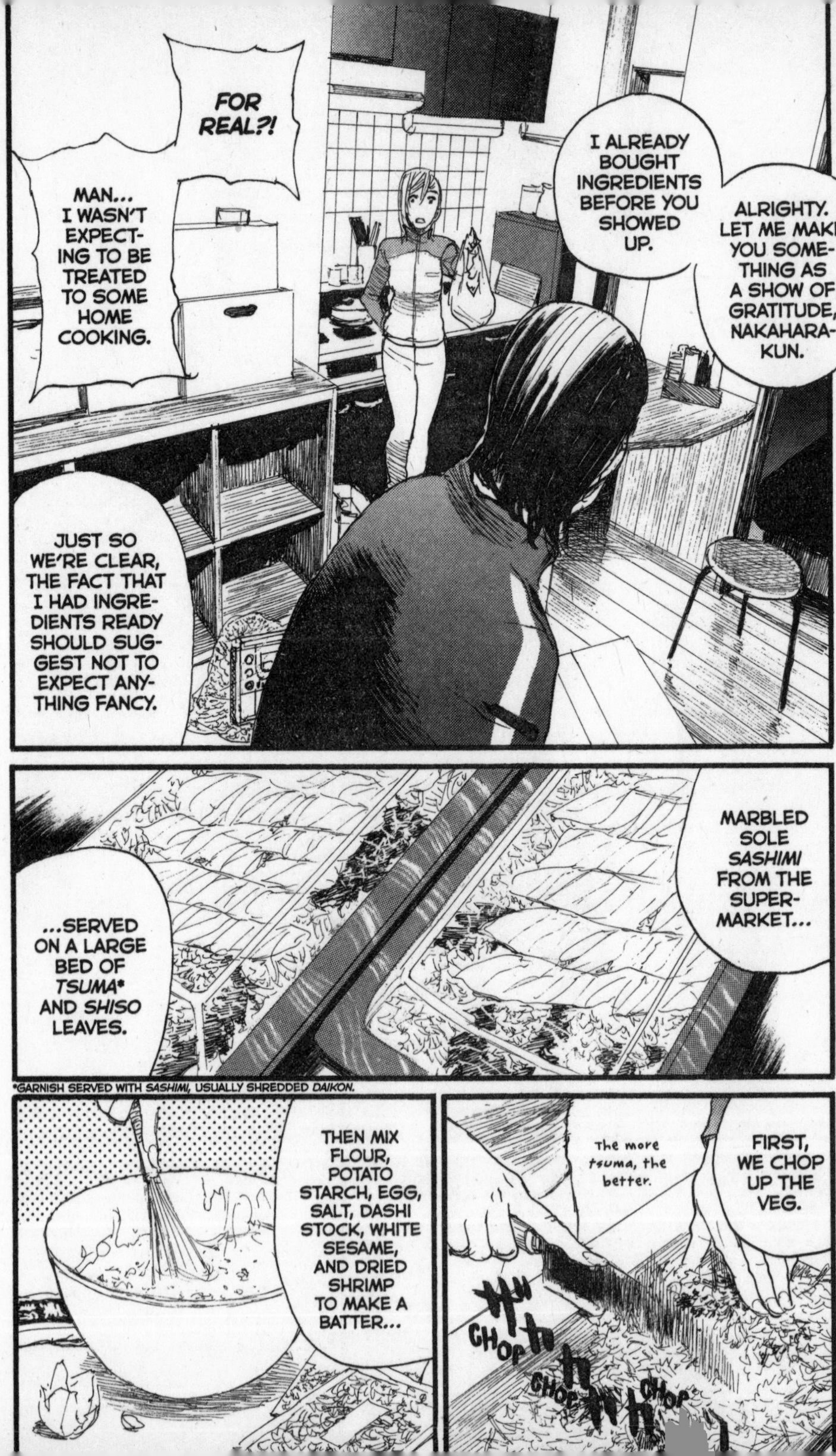
ALRIGHTY. LET ME MAKE YOU SOMETHING AS A SHOW OF GRATITUDE, NAKAHARA-KUN.
I ALREADY BOUGHT INGREDIENTS BEFORE YOU SHOWED UP.
FOR REAL?!
MAN... I WASN'T EXPECTING TO BE TREATED TO SOME HOME COOKING.
JUST SO WE'RE CLEAR, THE FACT THAT I HAD INGREDIENTS READY SHOULD SUGGEST NOT TO EXPECT ANYTHING FANCY.
MARBLED SOLE *SASHIMI* FROM THE SUPERMARKET...
...SERVED ON A LARGE BED OF *TSUMA** AND *SHISO* LEAVES.
FIRST, WE CHOP UP THE VEG.
The more *tsuma*, the better.
CHOP
CHOP
CHOP
THEN MIX FLOUR, POTATO STARCH, EGG, SALT, DASHI STOCK, WHITE SESAME, AND DRIED SHRIMP TO MAKE A BATTER...

*GARNISH SERVED WITH *SASHIMI*, USUALLY SHREDDED *DAIKON*.

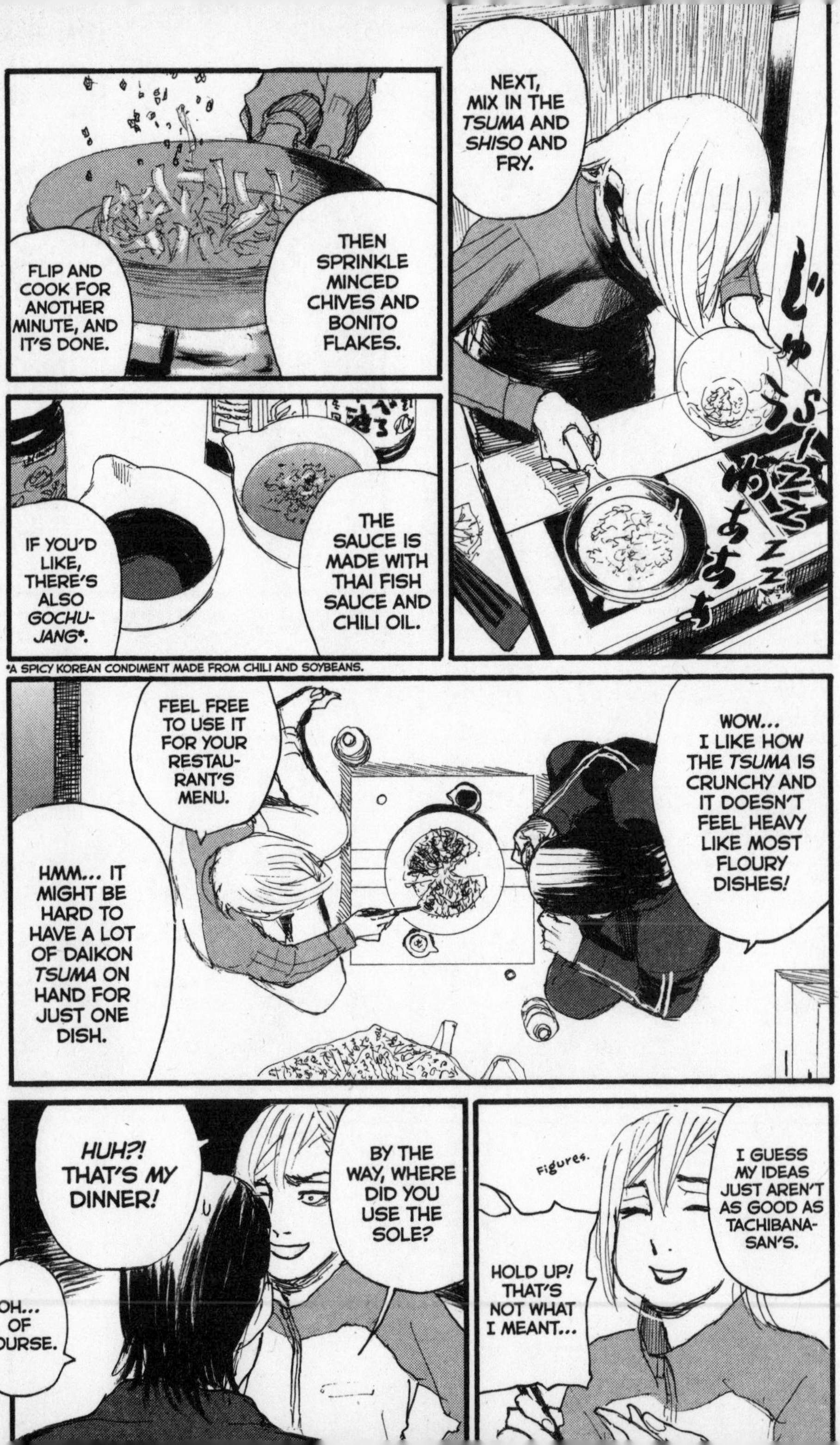
NEXT, MIX IN THE *TSUMA* AND *SHISO* AND FRY.
THEN SPRINKLE MINCED CHIVES AND BONITO FLAKES.
FLIP AND COOK FOR ANOTHER MINUTE, AND IT'S DONE.
THE SAUCE IS MADE WITH THAI FISH SAUCE AND CHILI OIL.
IF YOU'D LIKE, THERE'S ALSO *GOCHUJANG**.
*A SPICY KOREAN CONDIMENT MADE FROM CHILI AND SOYBEANS.
WOW... I LIKE HOW THE *TSUMA* IS CRUNCHY AND IT DOESN'T FEEL HEAVY LIKE MOST FLOURY DISHES!
FEEL FREE TO USE IT FOR YOUR RESTAU-RANT'S MENU.
HMM... IT MIGHT BE HARD TO HAVE A LOT OF DAIKON *TSUMA* ON HAND FOR JUST ONE DISH.
I GUESS MY IDEAS JUST AREN'T AS GOOD AS TACHIBANA-SAN'S.
Figures.
HOLD UP! THAT'S NOT WHAT I MEANT...
BY THE WAY, WHERE DID YOU USE THE SOLE?
HUH?! THAT'S *MY* DINNER!
OH... OF COURSE.

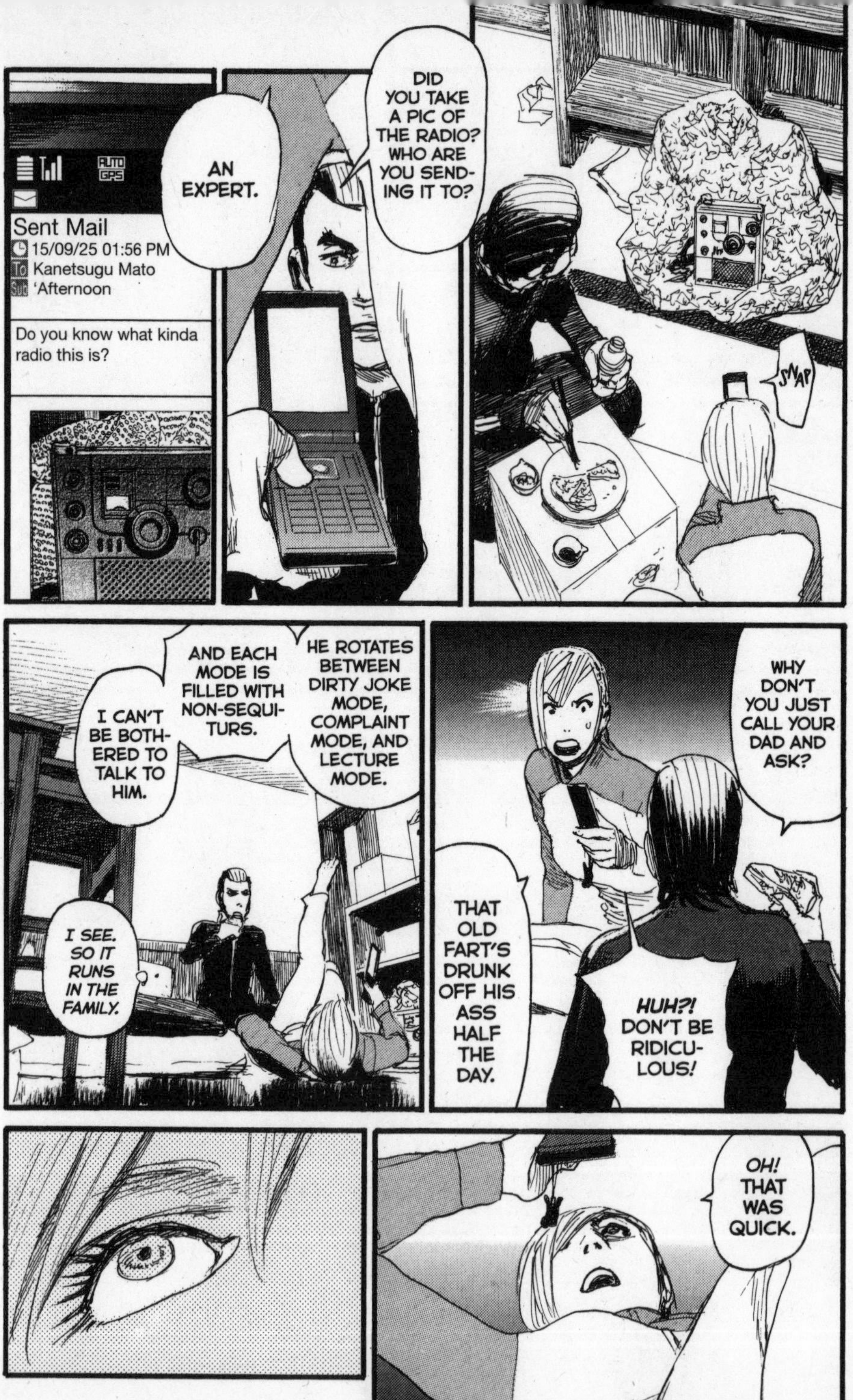
SNAP
DID YOU TAKE A PIC OF THE RADIO? WHO ARE YOU SENDING IT TO?
AN EXPERT.
AUTO GPS
Sent Mail
15/09/25 01:56 PM
Kanetsugu Mato
'Afternoon
Do you know what kinda radio this is?
WHY DON'T YOU JUST CALL YOUR DAD AND ASK?
HUH?! DON'T BE RIDICULOUS!
THAT OLD FART'S DRUNK OFF HIS ASS HALF THE DAY.
HE ROTATES BETWEEN DIRTY JOKE MODE, COMPLAINT MODE, AND LECTURE MODE.
AND EACH MODE IS FILLED WITH NON-SEQUITURS.
I CAN'T BE BOTHERED TO TALK TO HIM.
I SEE. SO IT RUNS IN THE FAMILY.
OH! THAT WAS QUICK.

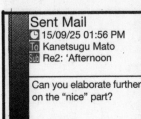

01:56
nbox
15/09/25 01:56 PM
Kanetsugu Mato
Re: 'Afternoon
MAKE A NOTE.
That's a Skysensor 5900.
It's one of Sony's best models.
Your old man has a nice radio.
Sent Mail
15/09/25 01:56 PM
To Kanetsugu Mato
Sub Re2: 'Afternoon
Can you elaborate further on the "nice" part?
ピロリ〜ン..
BRING DING
Sub Re3: 'Afternoon
MAKE A NOTE.
Later. We're about to go on the air.
Give me a call sometime after 10.
MAN, DON'T LEAVE ME HANGING.
NAH, THE OPPOSITE. I'M NOT EVEN THE LEAST BIT INTERESTED IN IT.
YOU REALLY LIKE THAT RADIO, HUH?
I WANT TO LEAVE IT OUT ON THE NEXT NON-COMBUSTIBLE TRASH DAY...
...BUT WOULDN'T IT BE SICK IF IT TURNS OUT I CAN SELL IT FOR LIKE A MILLION YEN OR SOMETHING?
SHE'S HEARTLESS...

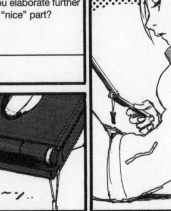

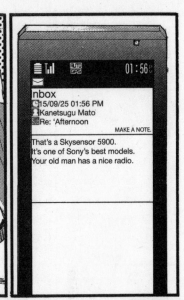

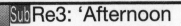

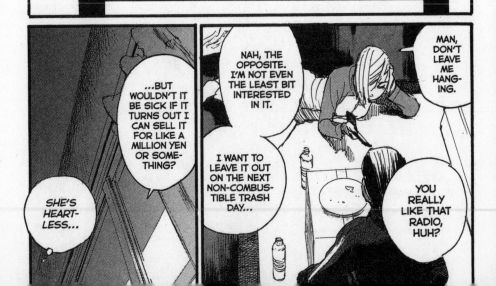

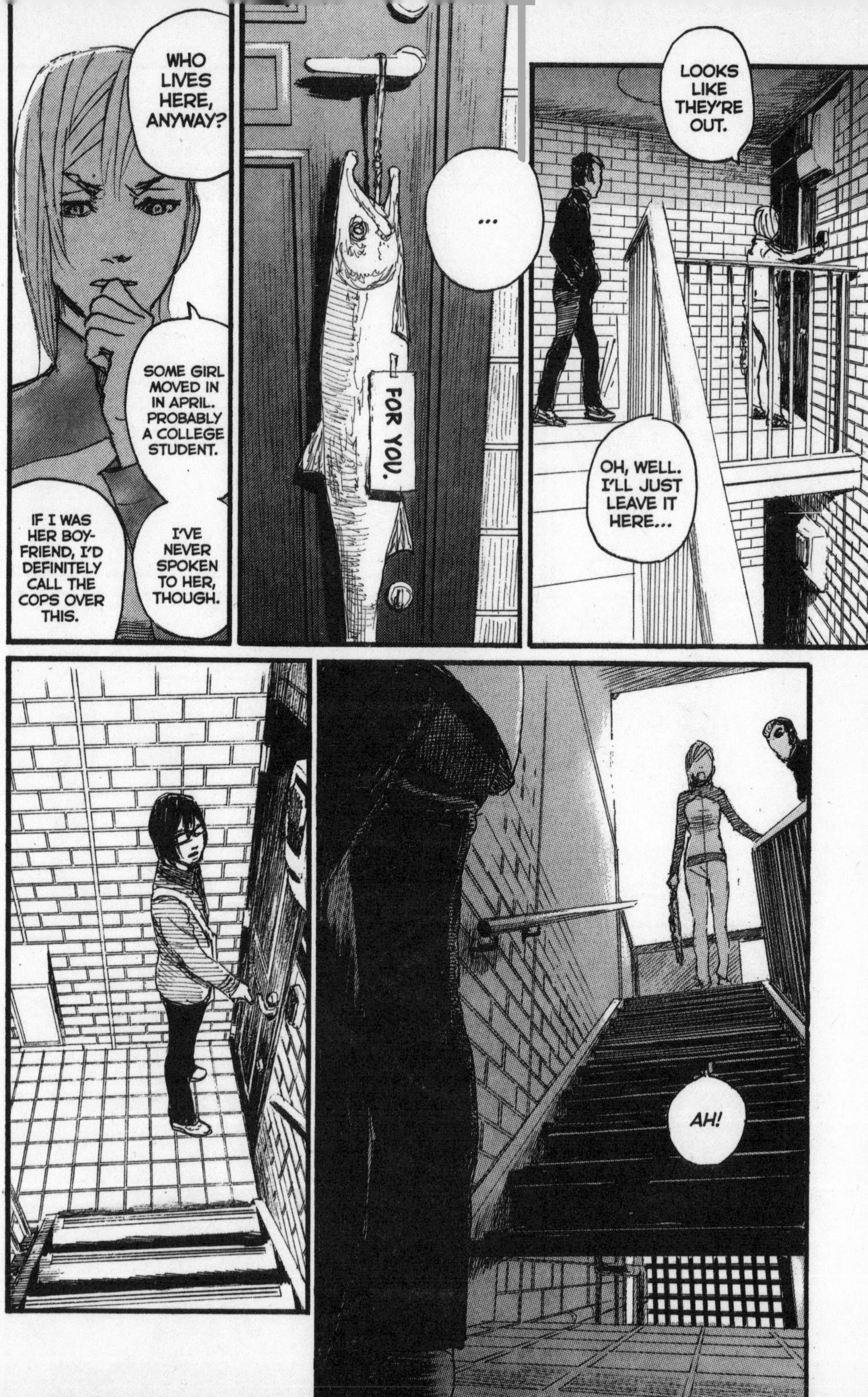
LOOKS LIKE THEY'RE OUT.
OH, WELL. I'LL JUST LEAVE IT HERE...
...
FOR YOU.
WHO LIVES HERE, ANYWAY?
SOME GIRL MOVED IN IN APRIL. PROBABLY A COLLEGE STUDENT.
I'VE NEVER SPOKEN TO HER, THOUGH.
IF I WAS HER BOY-FRIEND, I'D DEFINITELY CALL THE COPS OVER THIS.
AH!

SORRY AGAIN FOR THE OTHER DAY...

OH, UHH...

SEN-PAI!

PLEASE TAKE THIS AND DON'T SAY ANYTHING!

CAN I HELP YOU?

OH! WAIT JUST A SEC, PLEASE.

OW OW... IT'S TANGLED AROUND MY FINGERS.

The police?

...AHH.

YOU'RE THE WOMAN I CALLED THE POLICE ON...

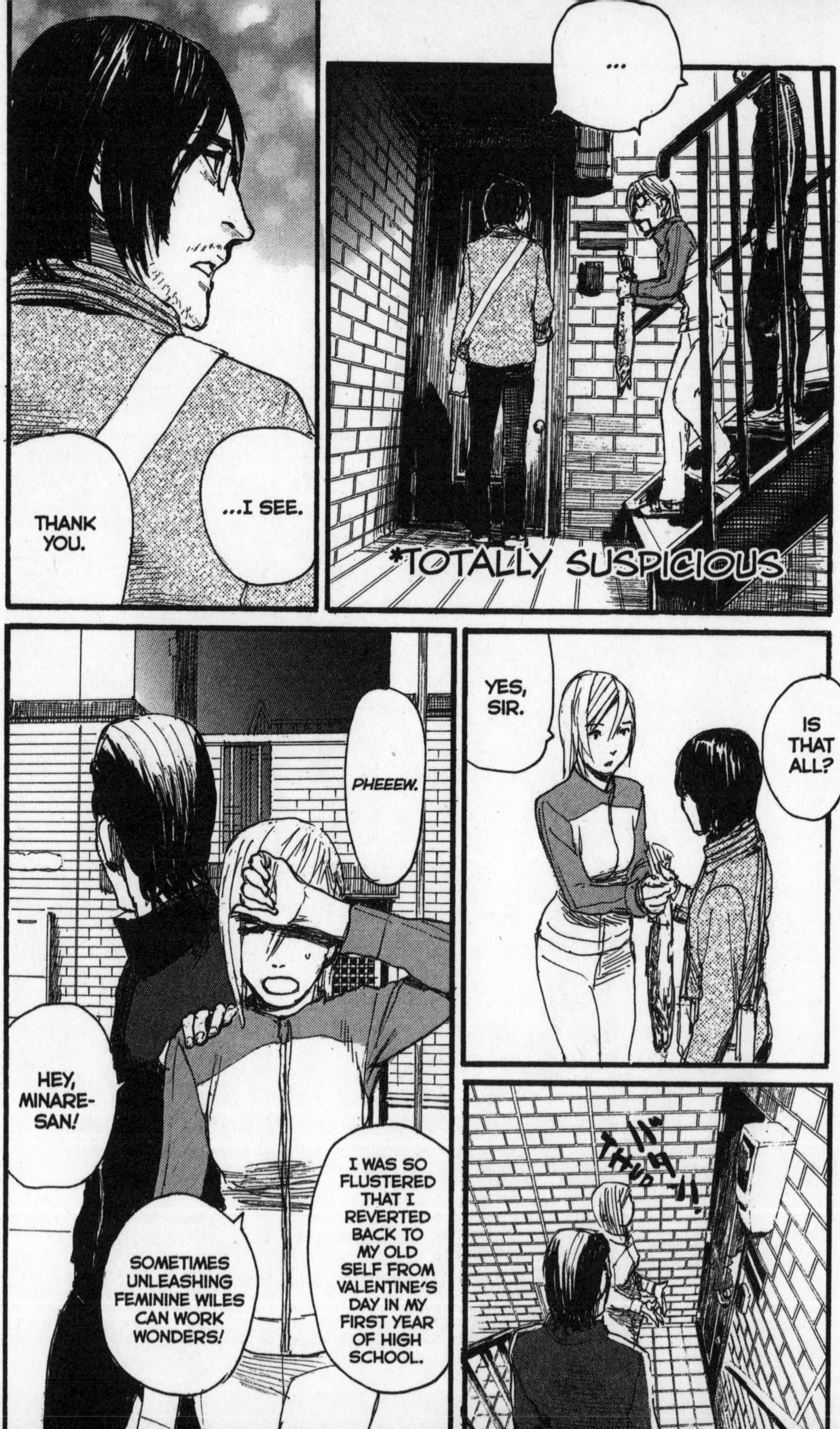
...
*TOTALLY SUSPICIOUS
...I SEE.
THANK YOU.
IS THAT ALL?
YES, SIR.
バタン!!
THUD
PHEEEW.
I WAS SO FLUSTERED THAT I REVERTED BACK TO MY OLD SELF FROM VALENTINE'S DAY IN MY FIRST YEAR OF HIGH SCHOOL.
HEY, MINARE-SAN!
SOMETIMES UNLEASHING FEMININE WILES CAN WORK WONDERS!

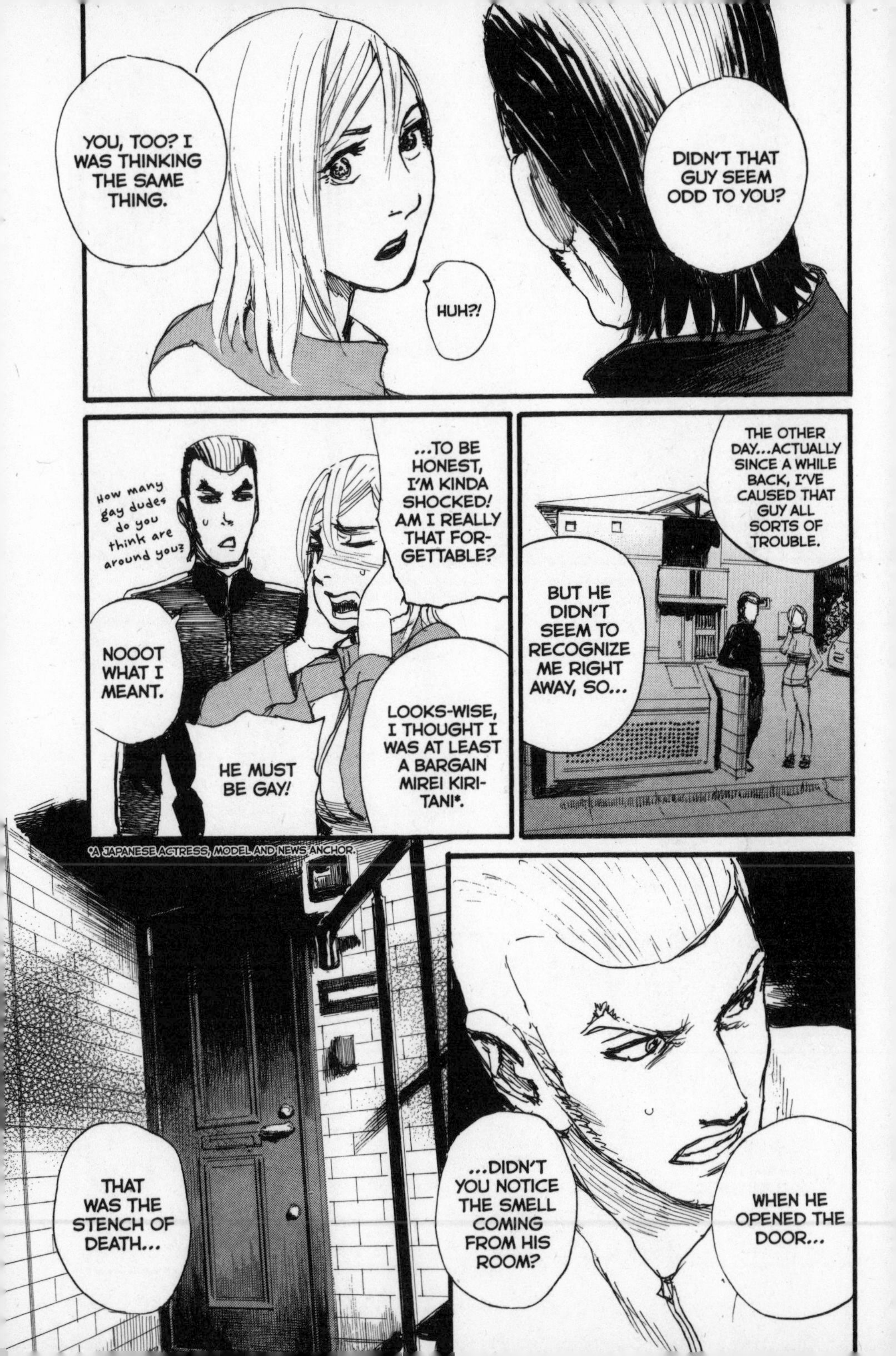
DIDN'T THAT GUY SEEM ODD TO YOU?
HUH?!
YOU, TOO? I WAS THINKING THE SAME THING.
THE OTHER DAY...ACTUALLY SINCE A WHILE BACK, I'VE CAUSED THAT GUY ALL SORTS OF TROUBLE.
BUT HE DIDN'T SEEM TO RECOGNIZE ME RIGHT AWAY, SO...
...TO BE HONEST, I'M KINDA SHOCKED! AM I REALLY THAT FORGETTABLE?
LOOKS-WISE, I THOUGHT I WAS AT LEAST A BARGAIN MIREI KIRITANI*.
HE MUST BE GAY!
NOOOT WHAT I MEANT.
How many gay dudes do you think are around you?
WHEN HE OPENED THE DOOR...
...DIDN'T YOU NOTICE THE SMELL COMING FROM HIS ROOM?
THAT WAS THE STENCH OF DEATH...

*A JAPANESE ACTRESS, MODEL AND NEWS ANCHOR.

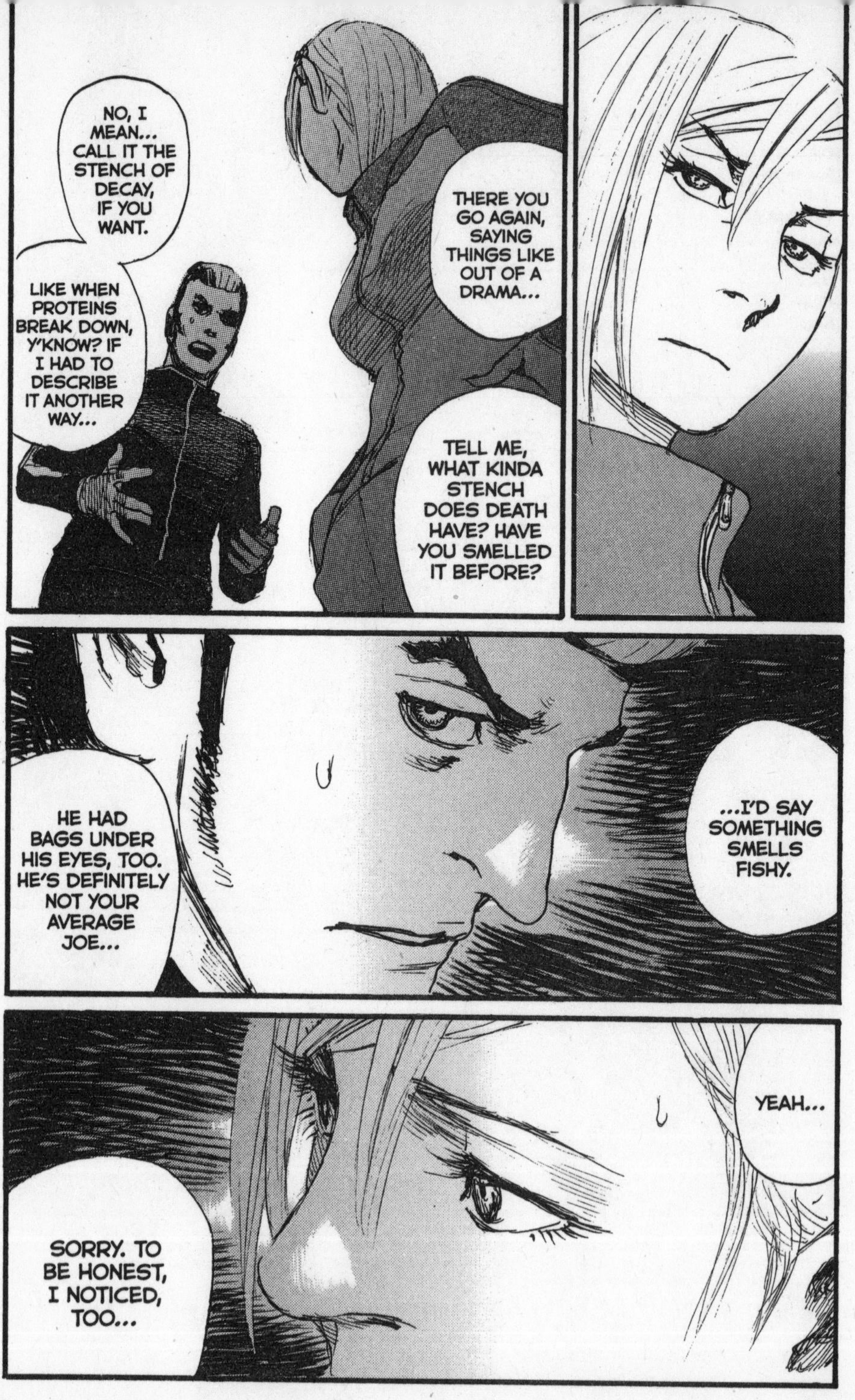
THERE YOU GO AGAIN, SAYING THINGS LIKE OUT OF A DRAMA...
TELL ME, WHAT KINDA STENCH DOES DEATH HAVE? HAVE YOU SMELLED IT BEFORE?
NO, I MEAN... CALL IT THE STENCH OF DECAY, IF YOU WANT.
LIKE WHEN PROTEINS BREAK DOWN, Y'KNOW? IF I HAD TO DESCRIBE IT ANOTHER WAY...
...I'D SAY SOMETHING SMELLS FISHY.
HE HAD BAGS UNDER HIS EYES, TOO. HE'S DEFINITELY NOT YOUR AVERAGE JOE...
YEAH...
SORRY. TO BE HONEST, I NOTICED, TOO...

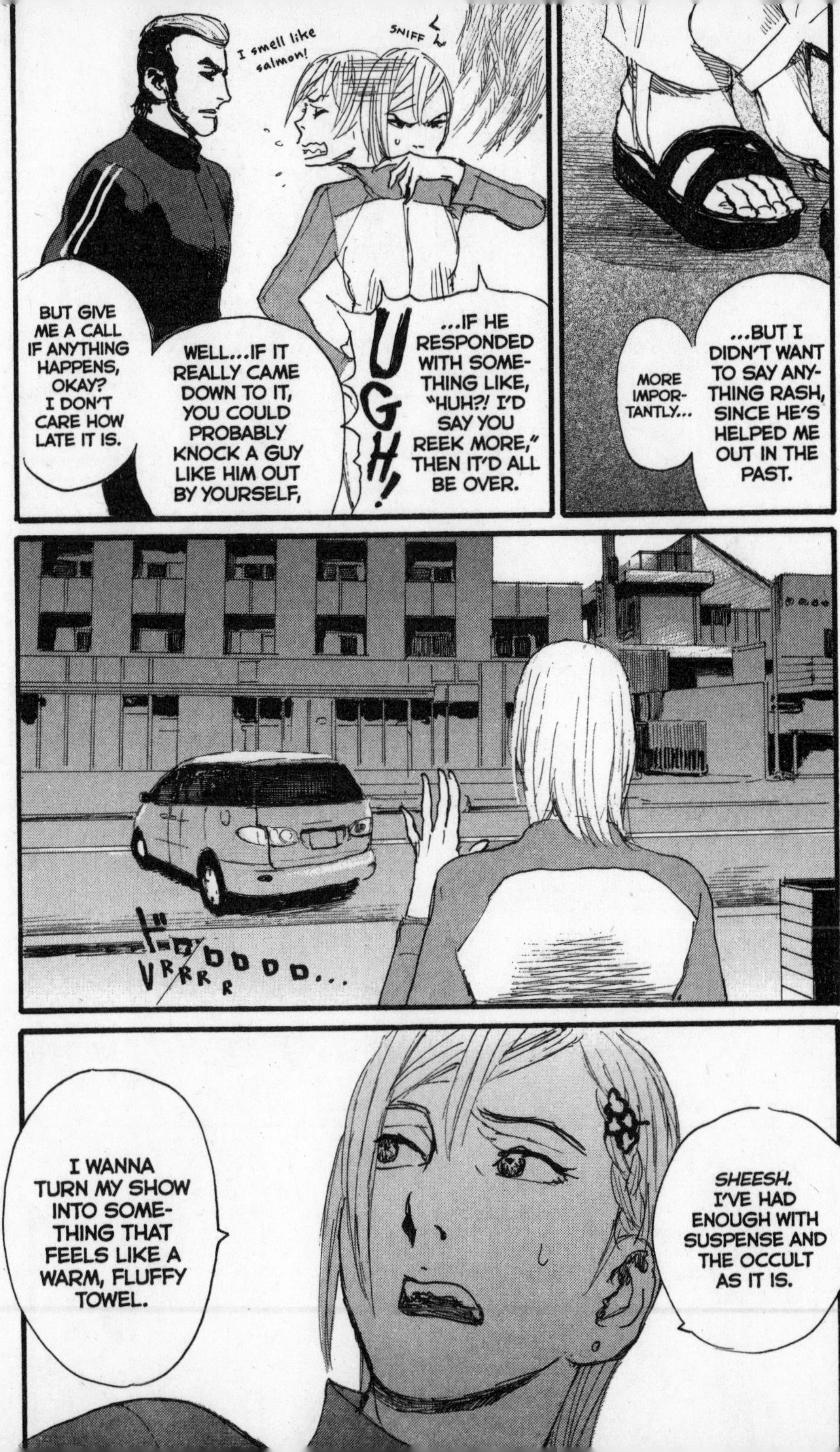
...BUT I DIDN'T WANT TO SAY ANYTHING RASH, SINCE HE'S HELPED ME OUT IN THE PAST.
MORE IMPORTANTLY...
SNIFF
I smell like salmon!
...IF HE RESPONDED WITH SOMETHING LIKE, "HUH?! I'D SAY YOU REEK MORE," THEN IT'D ALL BE OVER.
UGH!
WELL...IF IT REALLY CAME DOWN TO IT, YOU COULD PROBABLY KNOCK A GUY LIKE HIM OUT BY YOURSELF,
BUT GIVE ME A CALL IF ANYTHING HAPPENS, OKAY? I DON'T CARE HOW LATE IT IS.
VRRRR
SHEESH. I'VE HAD ENOUGH WITH SUSPENSE AND THE OCCULT AS IT IS.
I WANNA TURN MY SHOW INTO SOMETHING THAT FEELS LIKE A WARM, FLUFFY TOWEL.

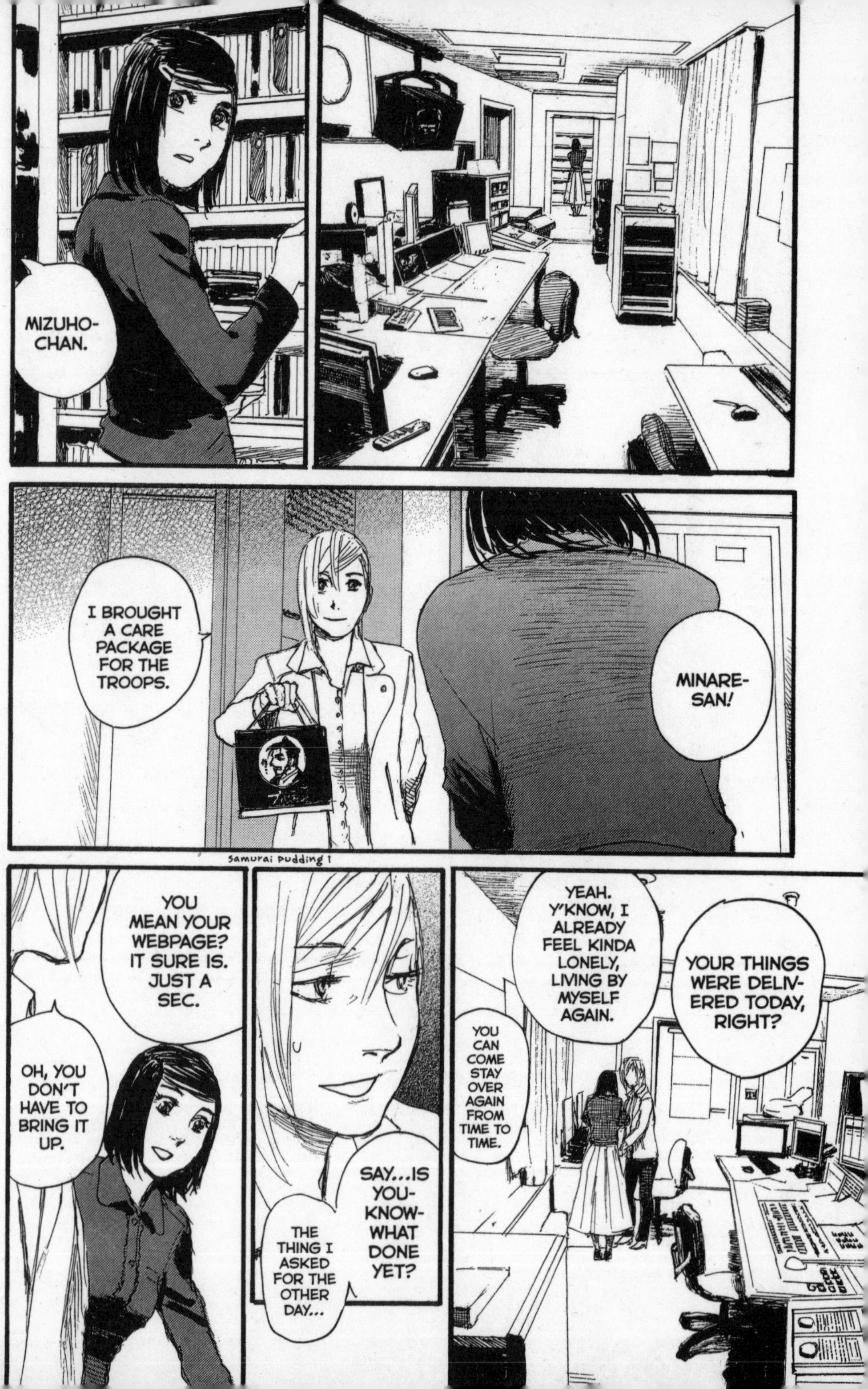
MIZUHO-CHAN.
MINARE-SAN!
I BROUGHT A CARE PACKAGE FOR THE TROOPS.
Samurai pudding!
YOUR THINGS WERE DELIVERED TODAY, RIGHT?
YEAH. Y'KNOW, I ALREADY FEEL KINDA LONELY, LIVING BY MYSELF AGAIN.
YOU CAN COME STAY OVER AGAIN FROM TIME TO TIME.
SAY...IS YOU-KNOW-WHAT DONE YET?
THE THING I ASKED FOR THE OTHER DAY...
YOU MEAN YOUR WEBPAGE? IT SURE IS. JUST A SEC.
OH, YOU DON'T HAVE TO BRING IT UP.

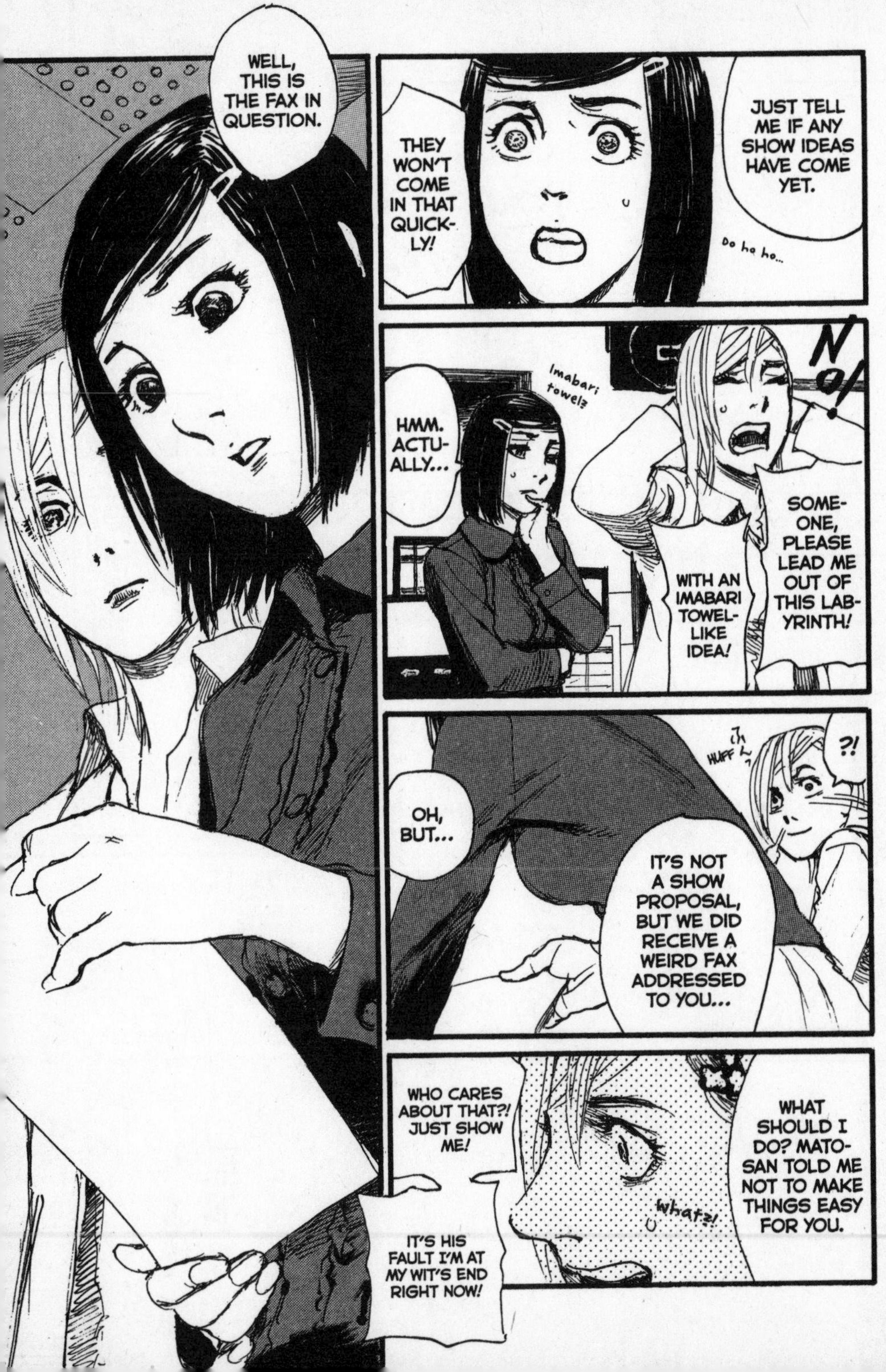
JUST TELL ME IF ANY SHOW IDEAS HAVE COME YET.
Do ho ho...
THEY WON'T COME IN THAT QUICK-LY!
NO!
SOME-ONE, PLEASE LEAD ME OUT OF THIS LAB-YRINTH!
WITH AN IMABARI TOWEL-LIKE IDEA!
Imabari towel?
HMM. ACTU-ALLY...
?!
HUFF
IT'S NOT A SHOW PROPOSAL, BUT WE DID RECEIVE A WEIRD FAX ADDRESSED TO YOU...
OH, BUT...
WHAT SHOULD I DO? MATO-SAN TOLD ME NOT TO MAKE THINGS EASY FOR YOU.
What?!
WHO CARES ABOUT THAT?! JUST SHOW ME!
IT'S HIS FAULT I'M AT MY WIT'S END RIGHT NOW!
WELL, THIS IS THE FAX IN QUESTION.

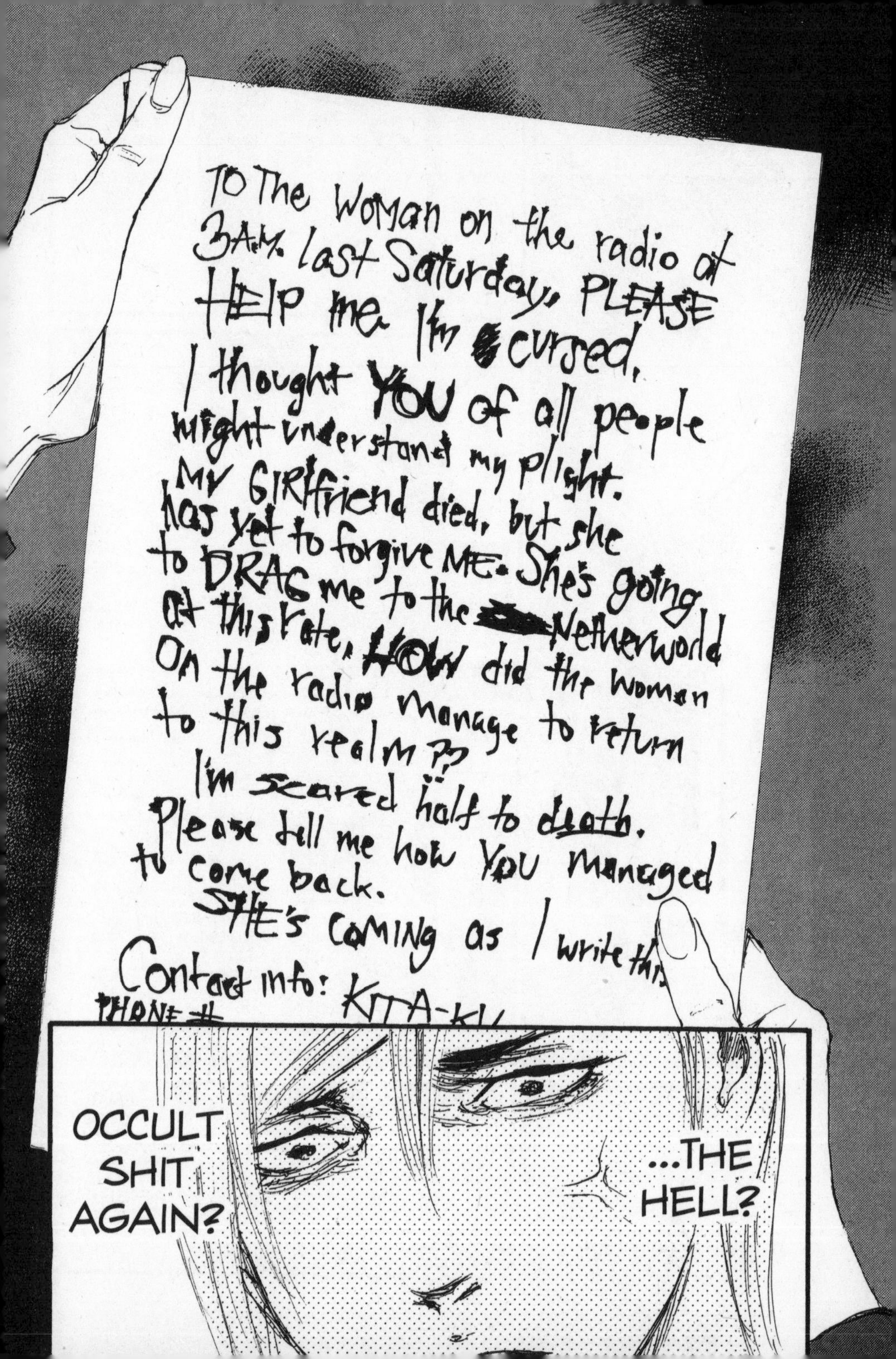
TO The WOMAN on the radio at
3A.M. last Saturday. PLEASE
HELP me. I'm cursed.
I thought YOU of all people
might understand my plight.
MY GIRlfriend died, but she
has yet to forgive ME. She's going
to DRAG me to the Netherworld
at this rate. HOW did the woman
On the radio manage to return
to this realm??
I'm scared half to death.
Please tell me how YOU managed
to come back.
SHE's COMING as I write this
Contact info: KITA-KU
PHONE #
...THE HELL?
OCCULT SHIT AGAIN?

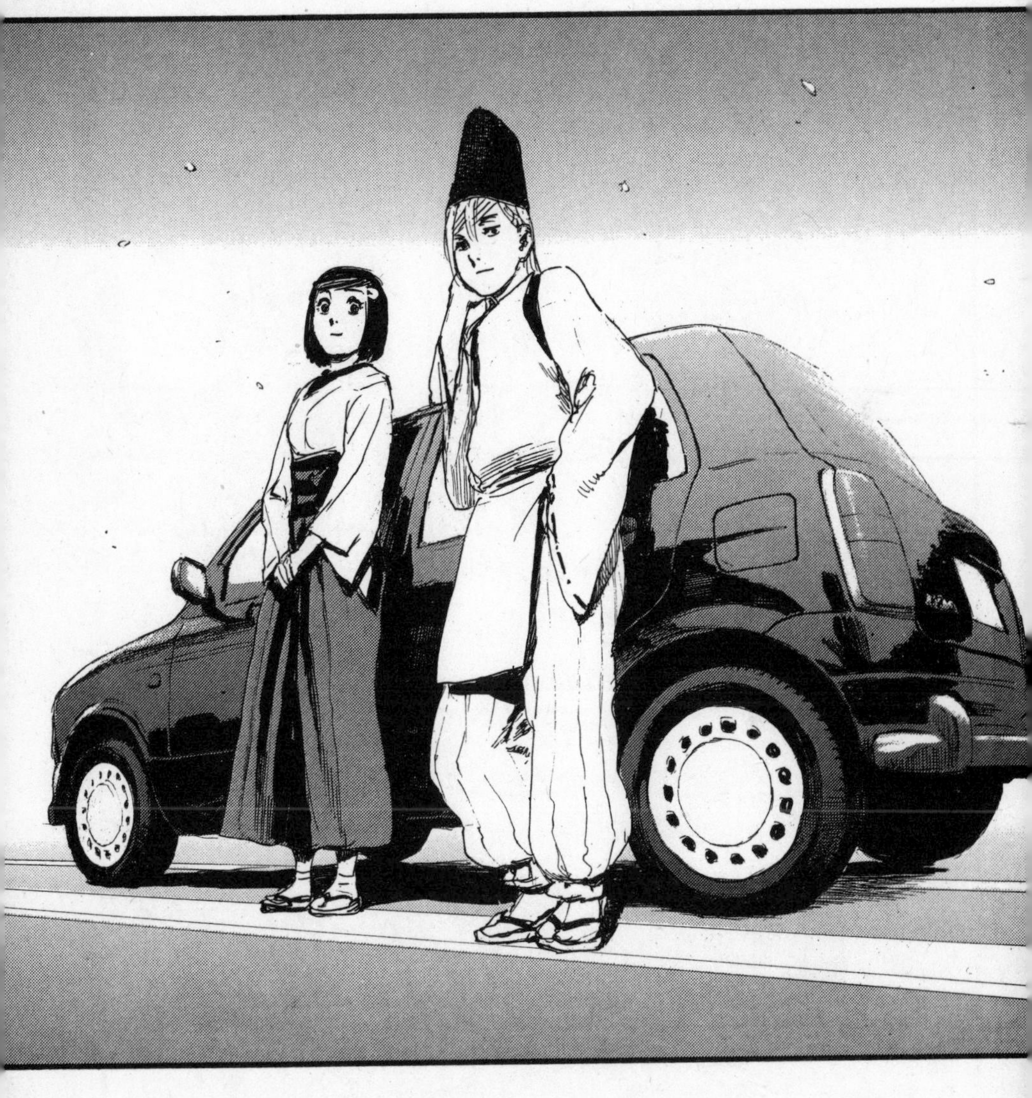

Chapter 20 "THEY DON'T EXIST."

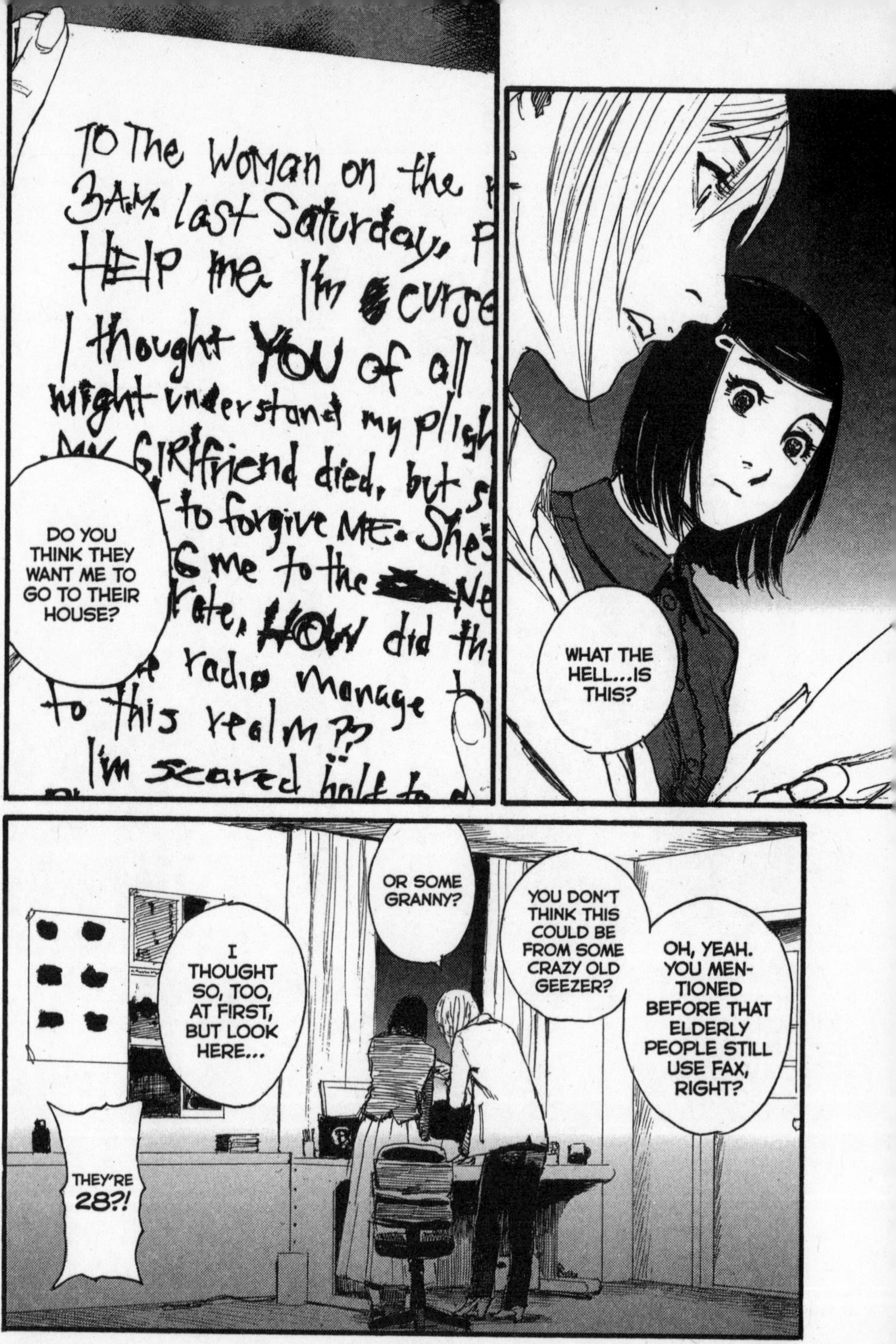
WHAT THE HELL...IS THIS?
TO The WOMAN on the
3A.M. last Saturday,
HELP me. I'm CURSE
I thought YOU of all
might understand my pligh
MY GIRLfriend died, but s
to forgive ME. She's
me to the Ne
rate, HOW did th
radio manage t
to this realm??
I'm scared
DO YOU THINK THEY WANT ME TO GO TO THEIR HOUSE?
OH, YEAH. YOU MENTIONED BEFORE THAT ELDERLY PEOPLE STILL USE FAX, RIGHT?
YOU DON'T THINK THIS COULD BE FROM SOME CRAZY OLD GEEZER?
OR SOME GRANNY?
I THOUGHT SO, TOO, AT FIRST, BUT LOOK HERE...
THEY'RE 28?!

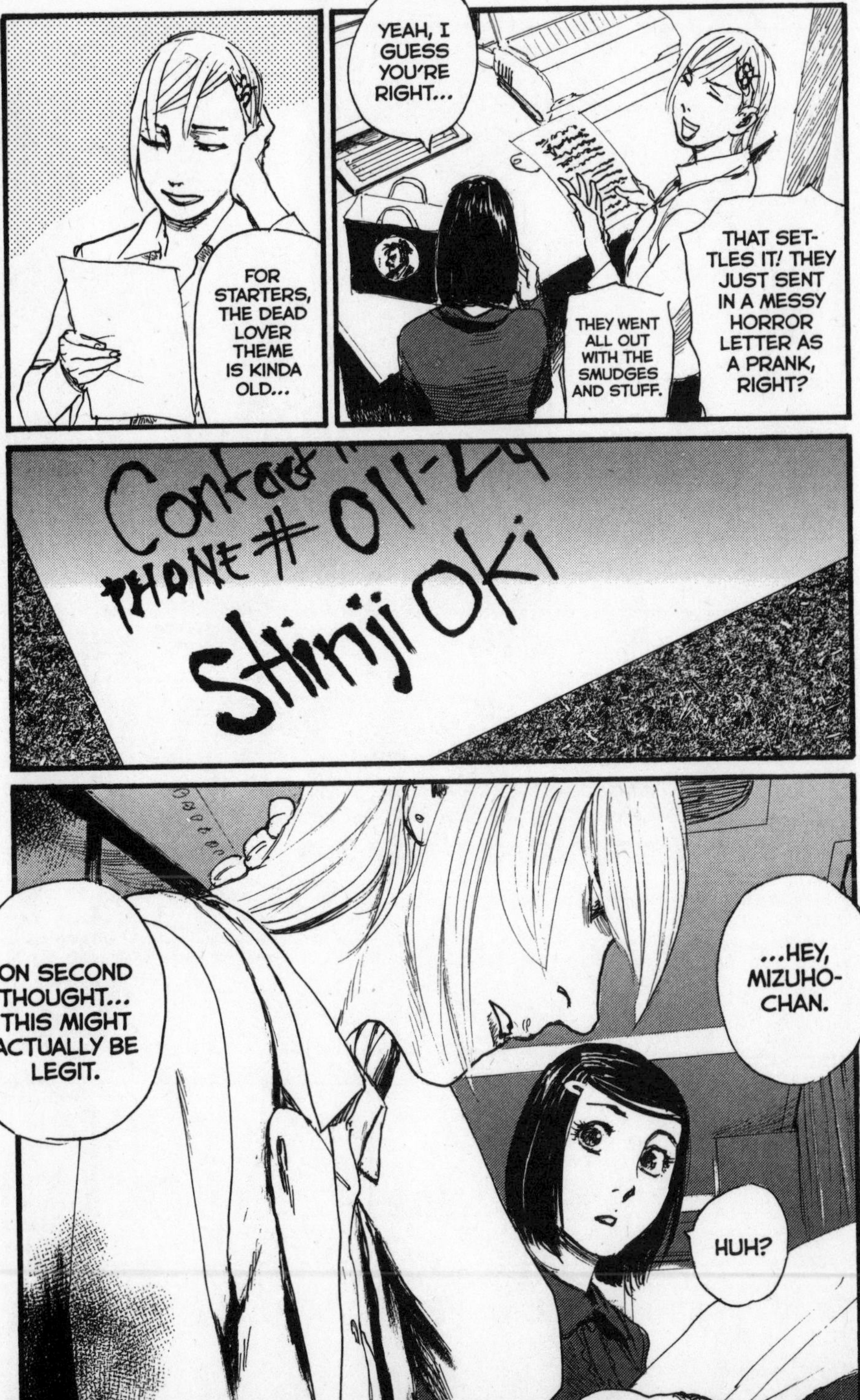
THAT SET-TLES IT! THEY JUST SENT IN A MESSY HORROR LETTER AS A PRANK, RIGHT?
THEY WENT ALL OUT WITH THE SMUDGES AND STUFF.
YEAH, I GUESS YOU'RE RIGHT...
FOR STARTERS, THE DEAD LOVER THEME IS KINDA OLD...
Contact
PHONE # 011-24
Shinji OKI
...HEY, MIZUHO-CHAN.
HUH?
ON SECOND THOUGHT... THIS MIGHT ACTUALLY BE LEGIT.

IF WE DON'T THINK THINGS THROUGH AND JUST KEEP TAKING SHOTS IN THE DARK, THEN WE'RE BOUND TO DRAW IN SOME CRAZIES! LOOK!

THIS IS WHAT I'M TALKING ABOUT, MATO-SAN!

WHAT'S UP?

HM? I DIDN'T KNOW YOU DROPPED BY.

The woman on the radio at last Saturday, PLEASE help me. I'm cursed. I thought YOU of all people might understand my plight. My girlfriend died, but she has yet to forgive me. She's got to DRAG me to the slightest on this rate, HOW did this woman to this realm?? On the radio manage to I'm scared half to death. Please tell me how You me me back. I'll be coming as I write.

OH, MAN, THIS IS WILD. HA HA HA!

...HMM.

I JUST KNEW YOU'D HELP ME OUT!

AH! YES, SIR! ♡

ABOUT THE MATE- RIAL FOR THE THIRD SHOW...

MI- NARE.

IF THAT KINDA REACTION FLEW, THEN WE WOULDN'T NEED POLICE...

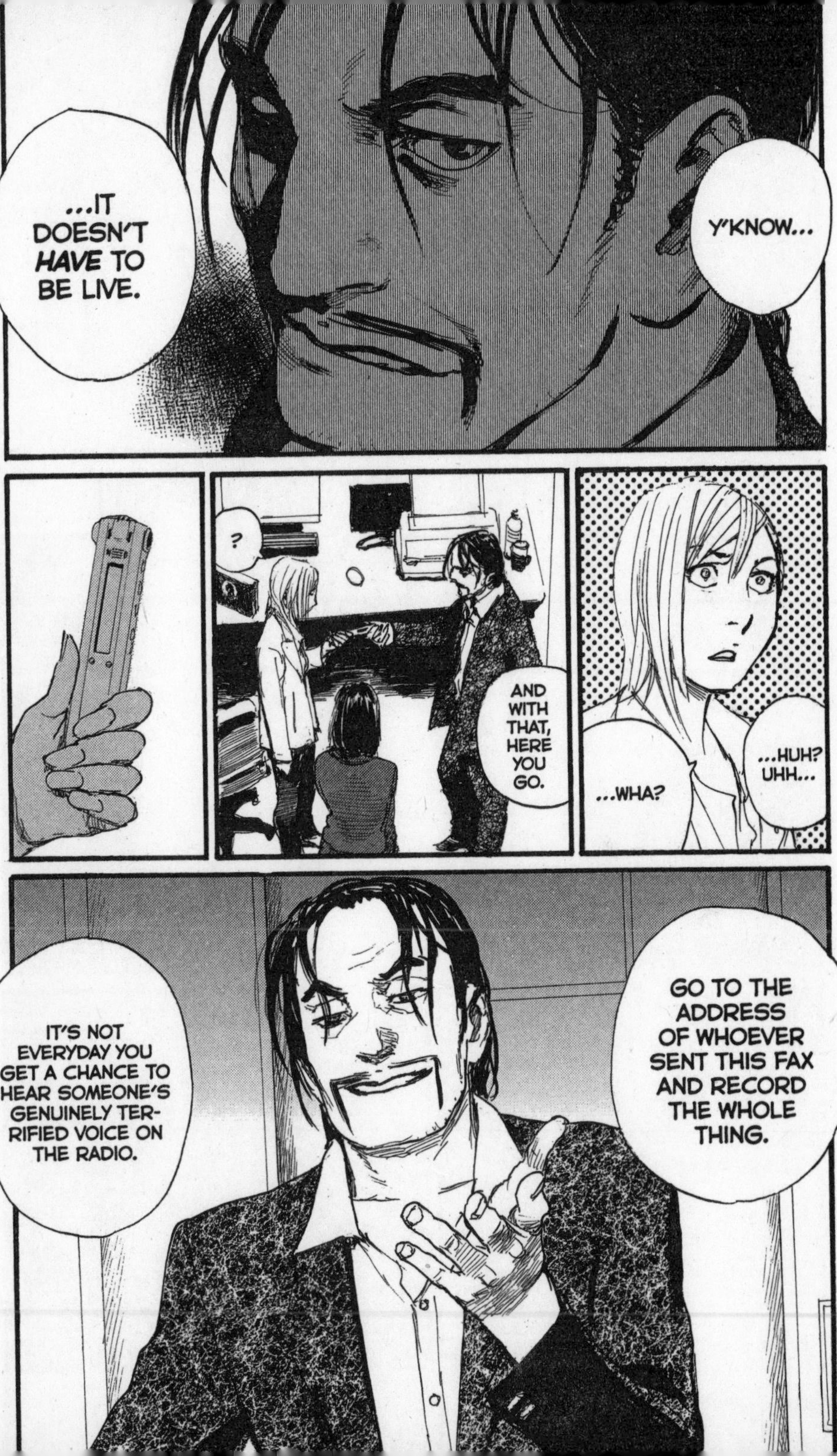
Y'KNOW...
...IT DOESN'T *HAVE* TO BE LIVE.
...HUH? UHH...
...WHA?
?
AND WITH THAT, HERE YOU GO.
GO TO THE ADDRESS OF WHOEVER SENT THIS FAX AND RECORD THE WHOLE THING.
IT'S NOT EVERYDAY YOU GET A CHANCE TO HEAR SOMEONE'S GENUINELY TERRIFIED VOICE ON THE RADIO.

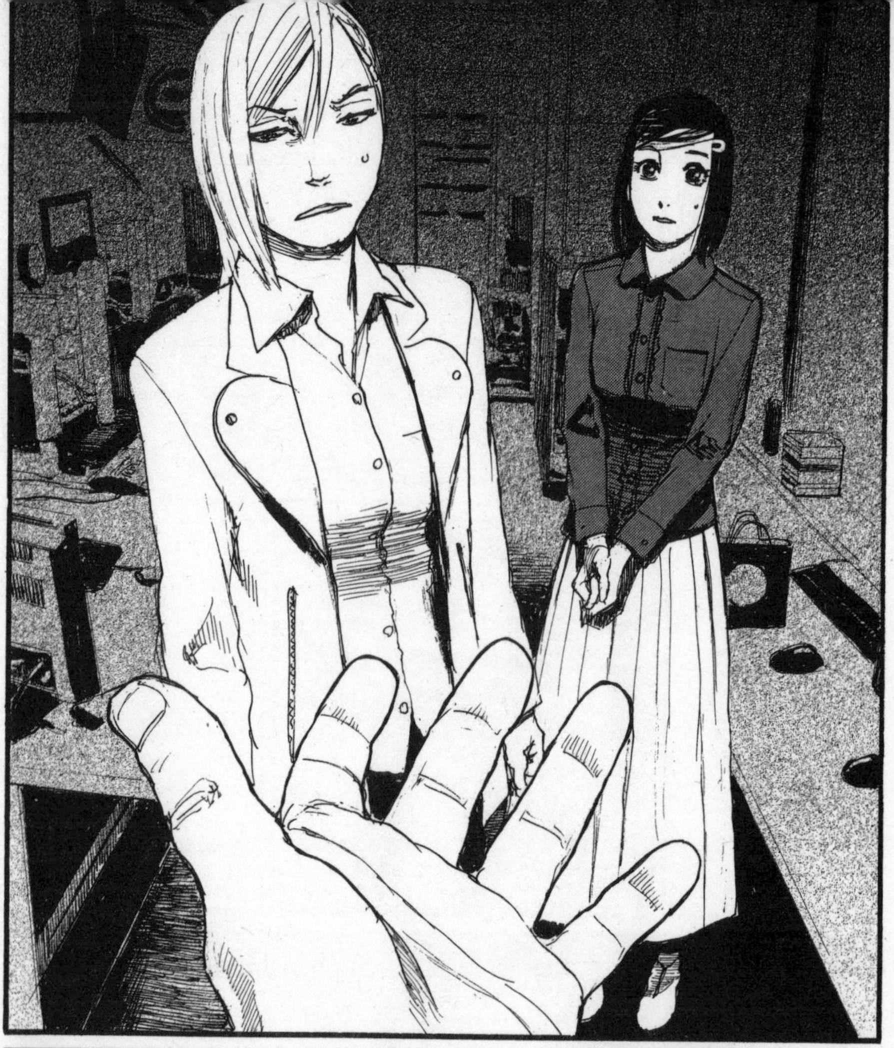

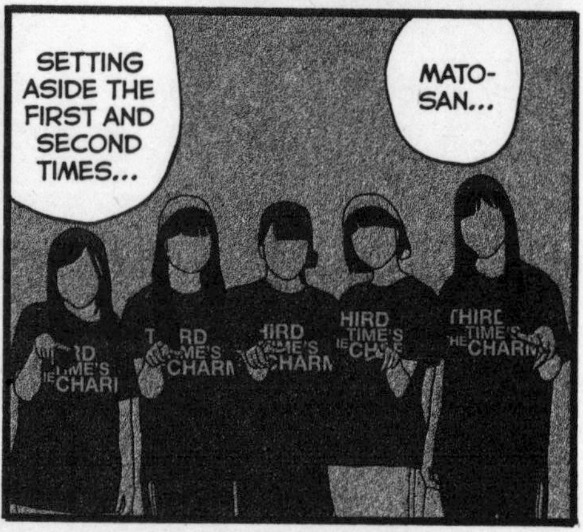
MATO-SAN...
SETTING ASIDE THE FIRST AND SECOND TIMES...

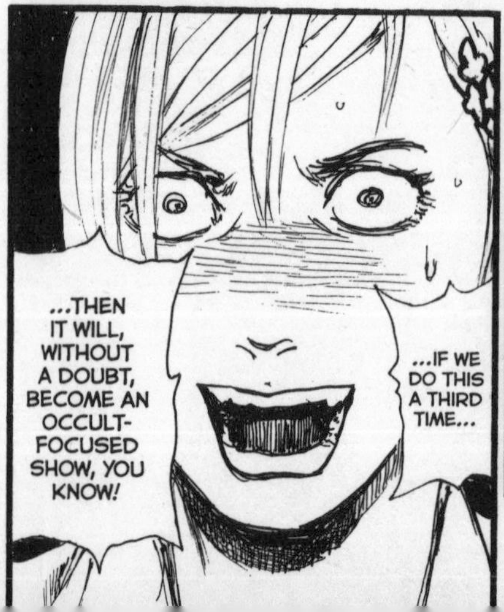
...IF WE DO THIS A THIRD TIME...
...THEN IT WILL, WITHOUT A DOUBT, BECOME AN OCCULT-FOCUSED SHOW, YOU KNOW!

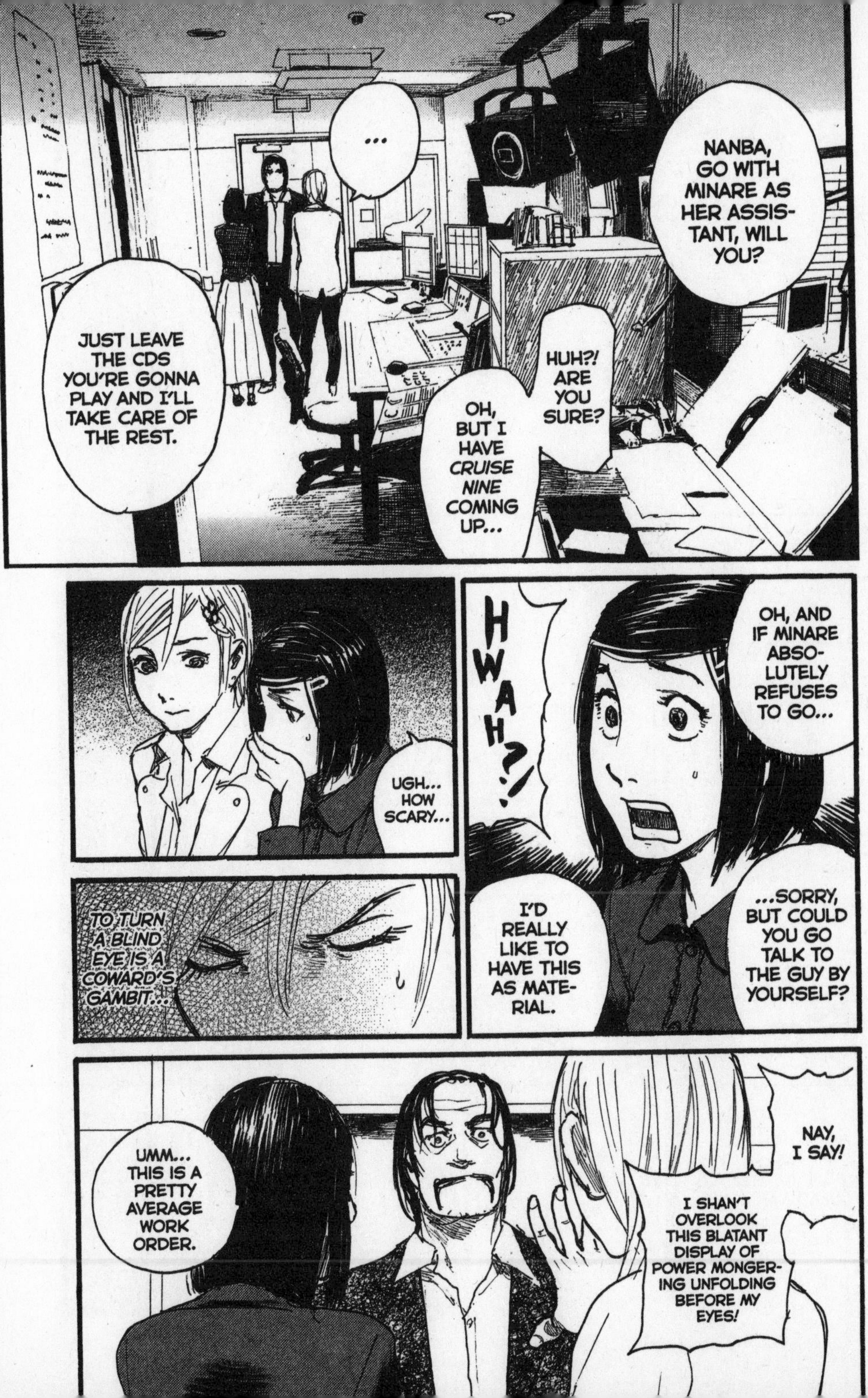
NANBA, GO WITH MINARE AS HER ASSISTANT, WILL YOU?
...
HUH?! ARE YOU SURE?
OH, BUT I HAVE *CRUISE NINE* COMING UP...
JUST LEAVE THE CDS YOU'RE GONNA PLAY AND I'LL TAKE CARE OF THE REST.
OH, AND IF MINARE ABSOLUTELY REFUSES TO GO...
HWAH?!
...SORRY, BUT COULD YOU GO TALK TO THE GUY BY YOURSELF?
I'D REALLY LIKE TO HAVE THIS AS MATERIAL.
UGH... HOW SCARY...
TO TURN A BLIND EYE IS A COWARD'S GAMBIT...
NAY, I SAY!
I SHAN'T OVERLOOK THIS BLATANT DISPLAY OF POWER MONGERING UNFOLDING BEFORE MY EYES!
UMM... THIS IS A PRETTY AVERAGE WORK ORDER.

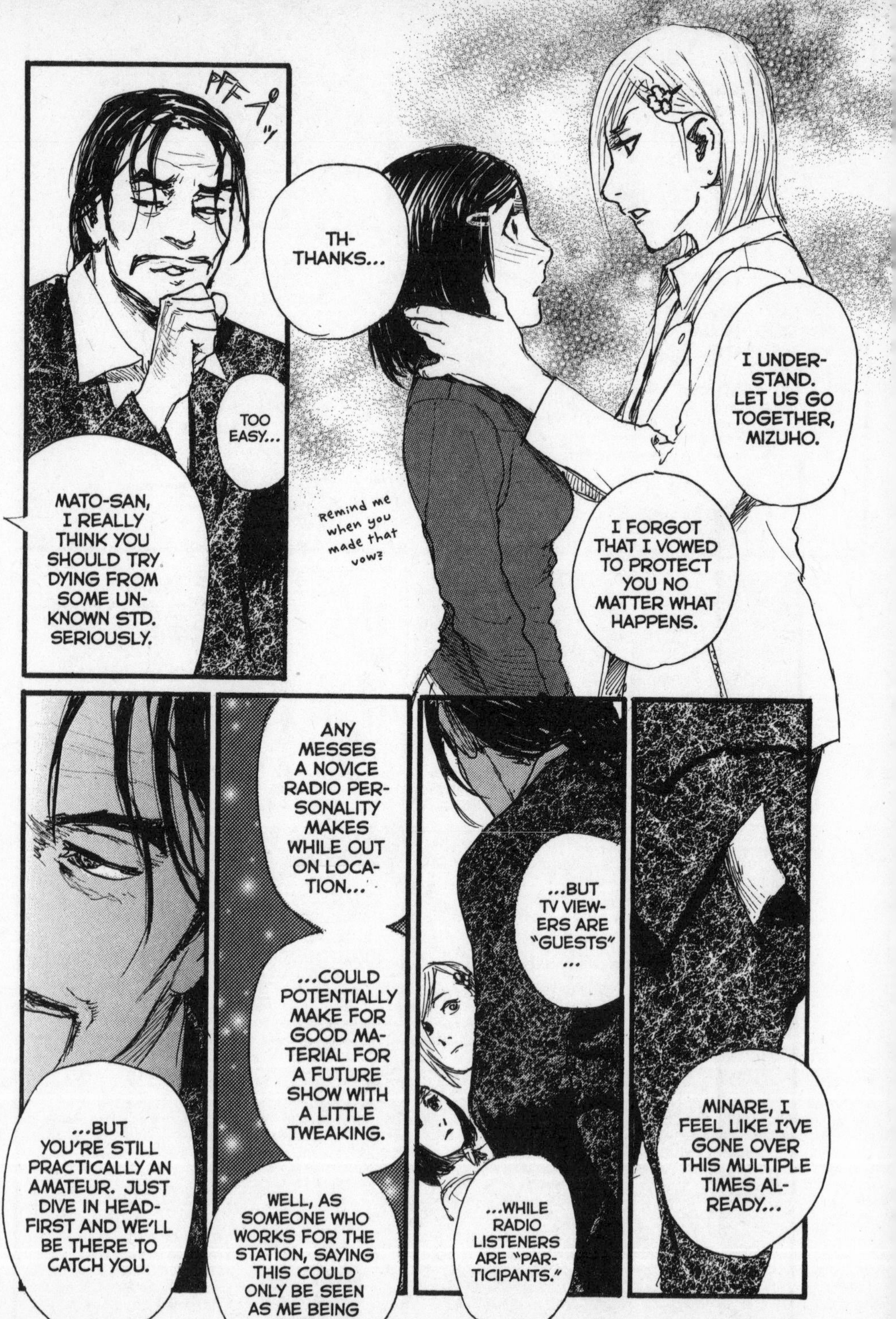
TH-THANKS...
I UNDERSTAND. LET US GO TOGETHER, MIZUHO.
I FORGOT THAT I VOWED TO PROTECT YOU NO MATTER WHAT HAPPENS.
Remind me when you made that vow?
PFF
TOO EASY...
MATO-SAN, I REALLY THINK YOU SHOULD TRY DYING FROM SOME UNKNOWN STD. SERIOUSLY.
MINARE, I FEEL LIKE I'VE GONE OVER THIS MULTIPLE TIMES ALREADY...
...BUT TV VIEWERS ARE "GUESTS"...
...WHILE RADIO LISTENERS ARE "PARTICIPANTS."
ANY MESSES A NOVICE RADIO PERSONALITY MAKES WHILE OUT ON LOCATION...
...COULD POTENTIALLY MAKE FOR GOOD MATERIAL FOR A FUTURE SHOW WITH A LITTLE TWEAKING.
WELL, AS SOMEONE WHO WORKS FOR THE STATION, SAYING THIS COULD ONLY BE SEEN AS ME BEING SOFT...
...BUT YOU'RE STILL PRACTICALLY AN AMATEUR. JUST DIVE IN HEADFIRST AND WE'LL BE THERE TO CATCH YOU.

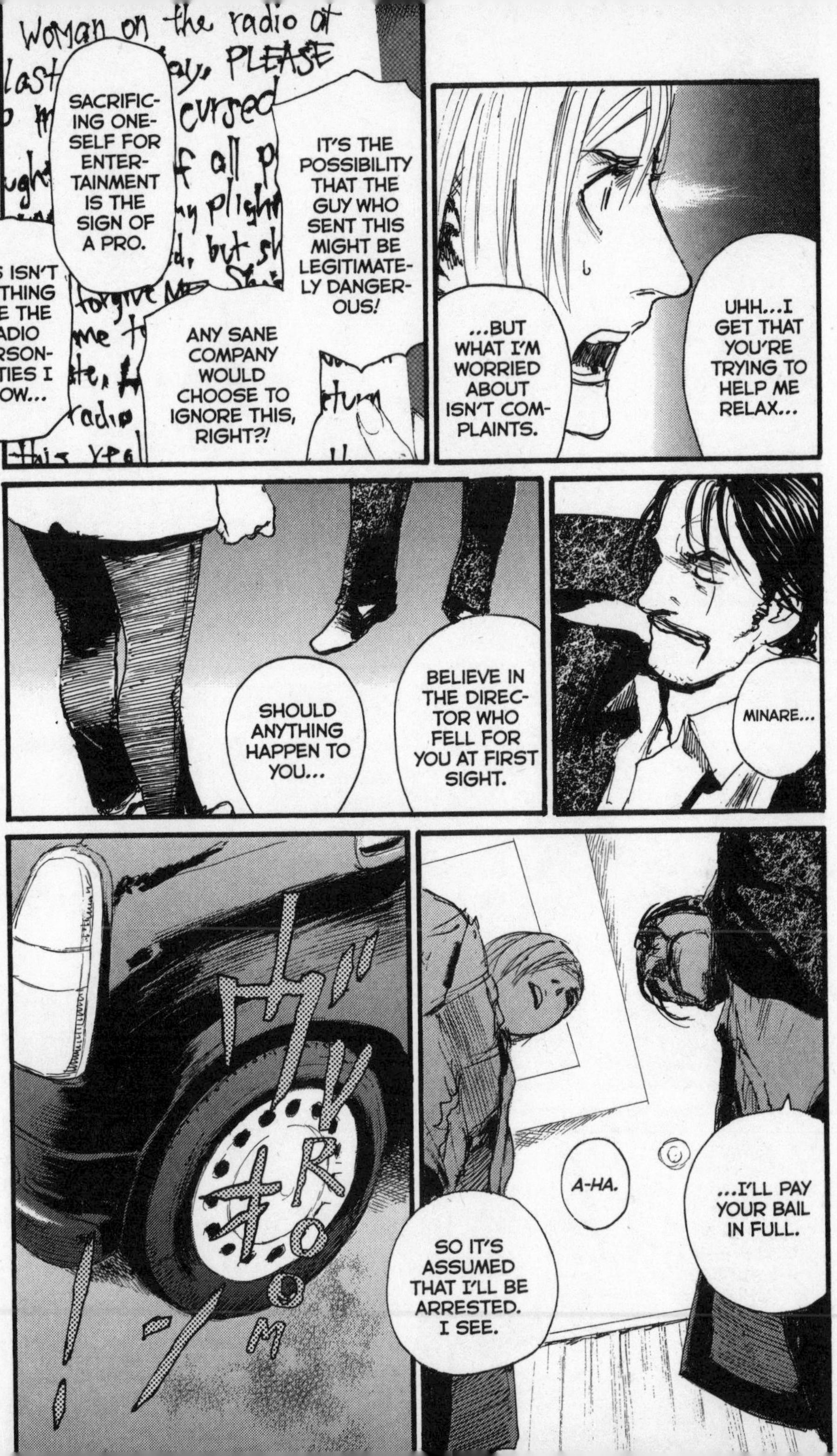
UHH...I GET THAT YOU'RE TRYING TO HELP ME RELAX...
...BUT WHAT I'M WORRIED ABOUT ISN'T COMPLAINTS.
Woman on the radio at
PLEASE
cursed
IT'S THE POSSIBILITY THAT THE GUY WHO SENT THIS MIGHT BE LEGITIMATELY DANGEROUS!
ANY SANE COMPANY WOULD CHOOSE TO IGNORE THIS, RIGHT?!
SACRIFICING ONESELF FOR ENTERTAINMENT IS THE SIGN OF A PRO.
THIS ISN'T ANYTHING LIKE THE RADIO PERSONALITIES I KNOW...
MINARE...
BELIEVE IN THE DIRECTOR WHO FELL FOR YOU AT FIRST SIGHT.
SHOULD ANYTHING HAPPEN TO YOU...
...I'LL PAY YOUR BAIL IN FULL.
A-HA.
SO IT'S ASSUMED THAT I'LL BE ARRESTED. I SEE.

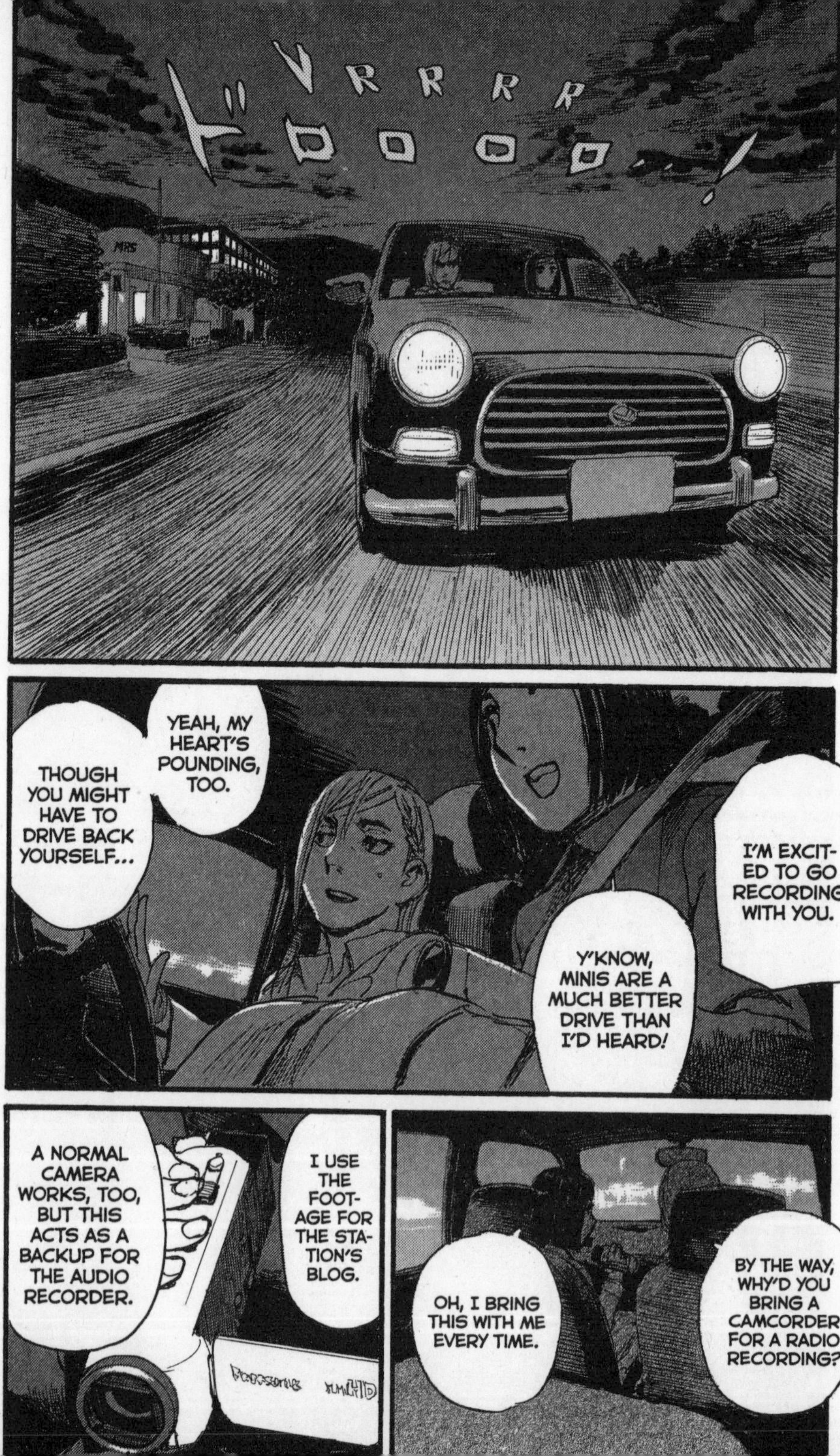
ドVRRRRDOOOO...!
I'M EXCITED TO GO RECORDING WITH YOU.
Y'KNOW, MINIS ARE A MUCH BETTER DRIVE THAN I'D HEARD!
YEAH, MY HEART'S POUNDING, TOO.
THOUGH YOU MIGHT HAVE TO DRIVE BACK YOURSELF...
BY THE WAY, WHY'D YOU BRING A CAMCORDER FOR A RADIO RECORDING?
OH, I BRING THIS WITH ME EVERY TIME.
I USE THE FOOTAGE FOR THE STATION'S BLOG.
A NORMAL CAMERA WORKS, TOO, BUT THIS ACTS AS A BACKUP FOR THE AUDIO RECORDER.

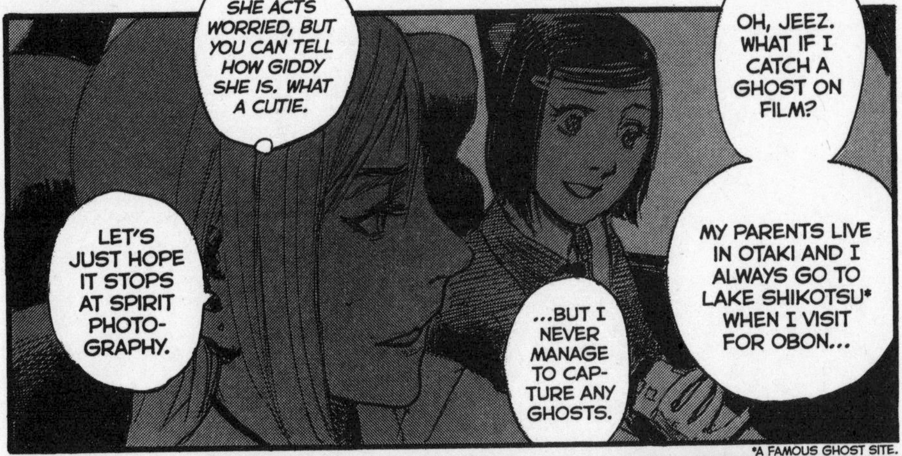
OH, JEEZ. WHAT IF I CATCH A GHOST ON FILM?
MY PARENTS LIVE IN OTAKI AND I ALWAYS GO TO LAKE SHIKOTSU* WHEN I VISIT FOR OBON...
...BUT I NEVER MANAGE TO CAPTURE ANY GHOSTS.
SHE ACTS WORRIED, BUT YOU CAN TELL HOW GIDDY SHE IS. WHAT A CUTIE.
LET'S JUST HOPE IT STOPS AT SPIRIT PHOTOGRAPHY.
*A FAMOUS GHOST SITE.

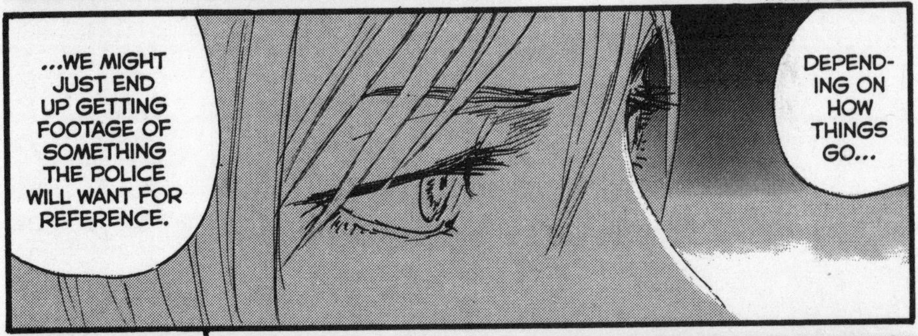
DEPENDING ON HOW THINGS GO...
...WE MIGHT JUST END UP GETTING FOOTAGE OF SOMETHING THE POLICE WILL WANT FOR REFERENCE.

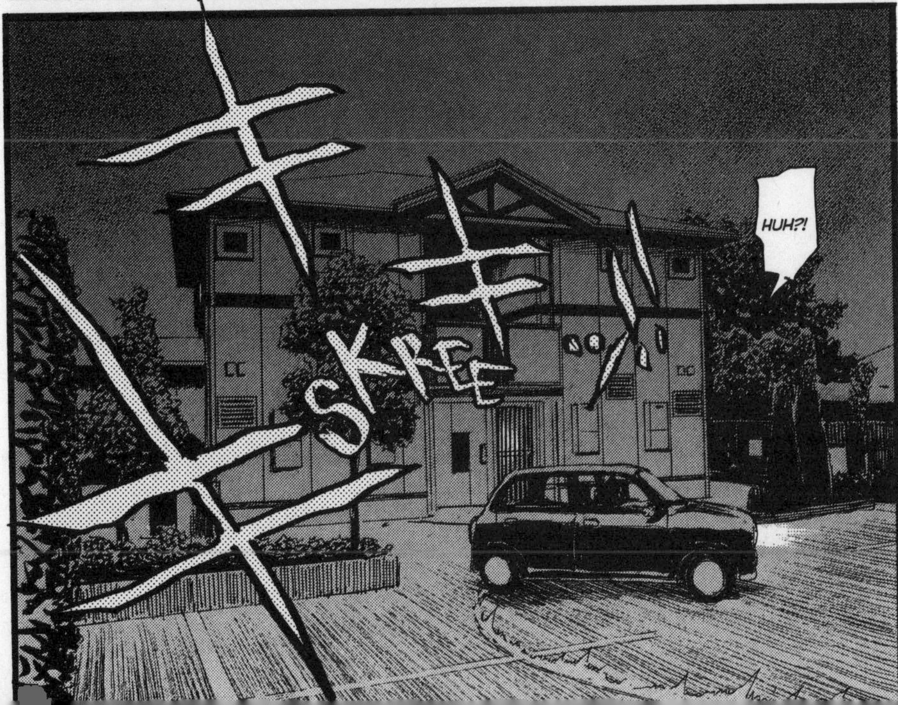
HUH?!
SKREE

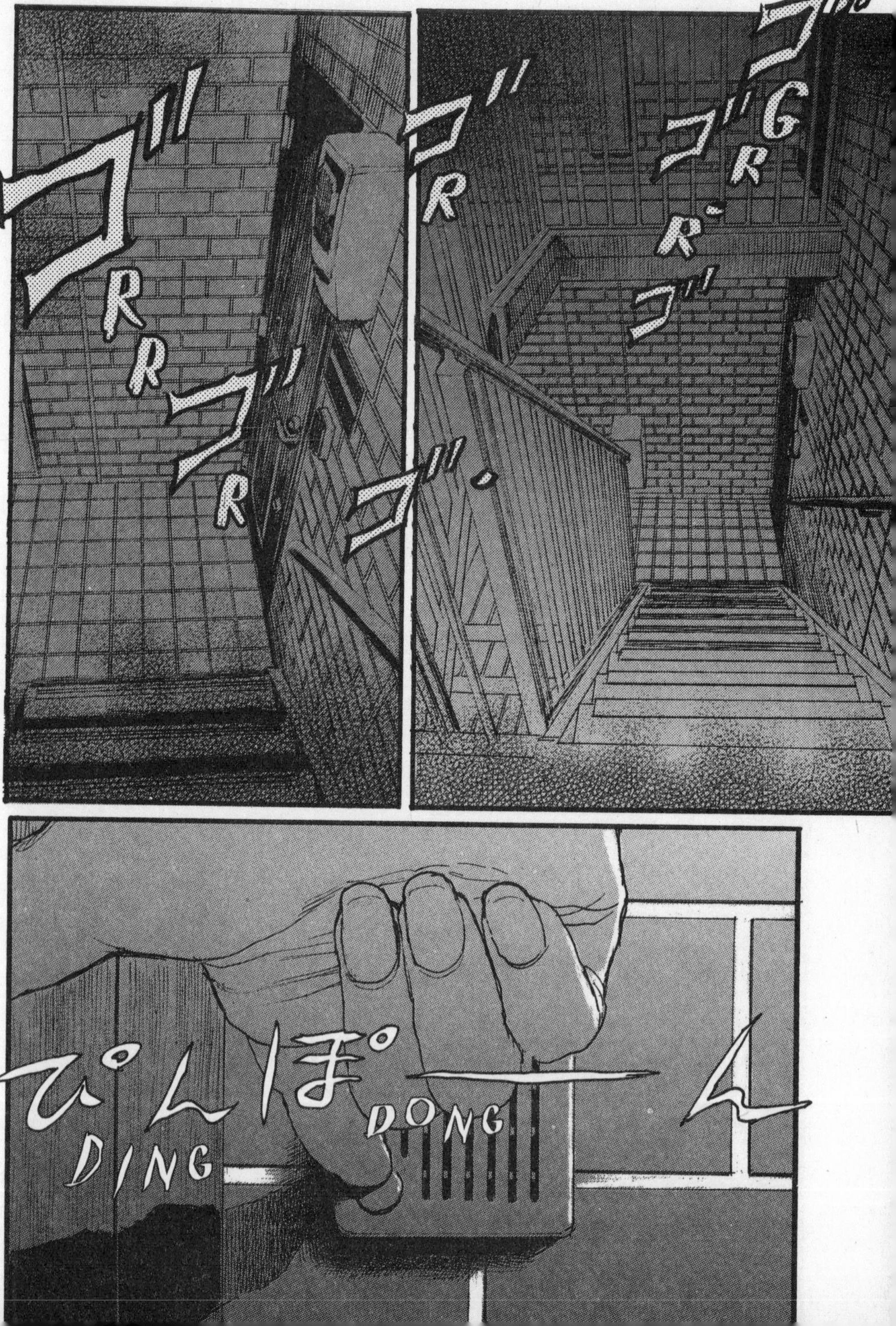
ゴ
GR
ゴ
R
ゴ
R
ゴ
ゴ
R
ゴ
RR
ゴ
R
ゴ
ぴんぽ——ん
DING
DONG

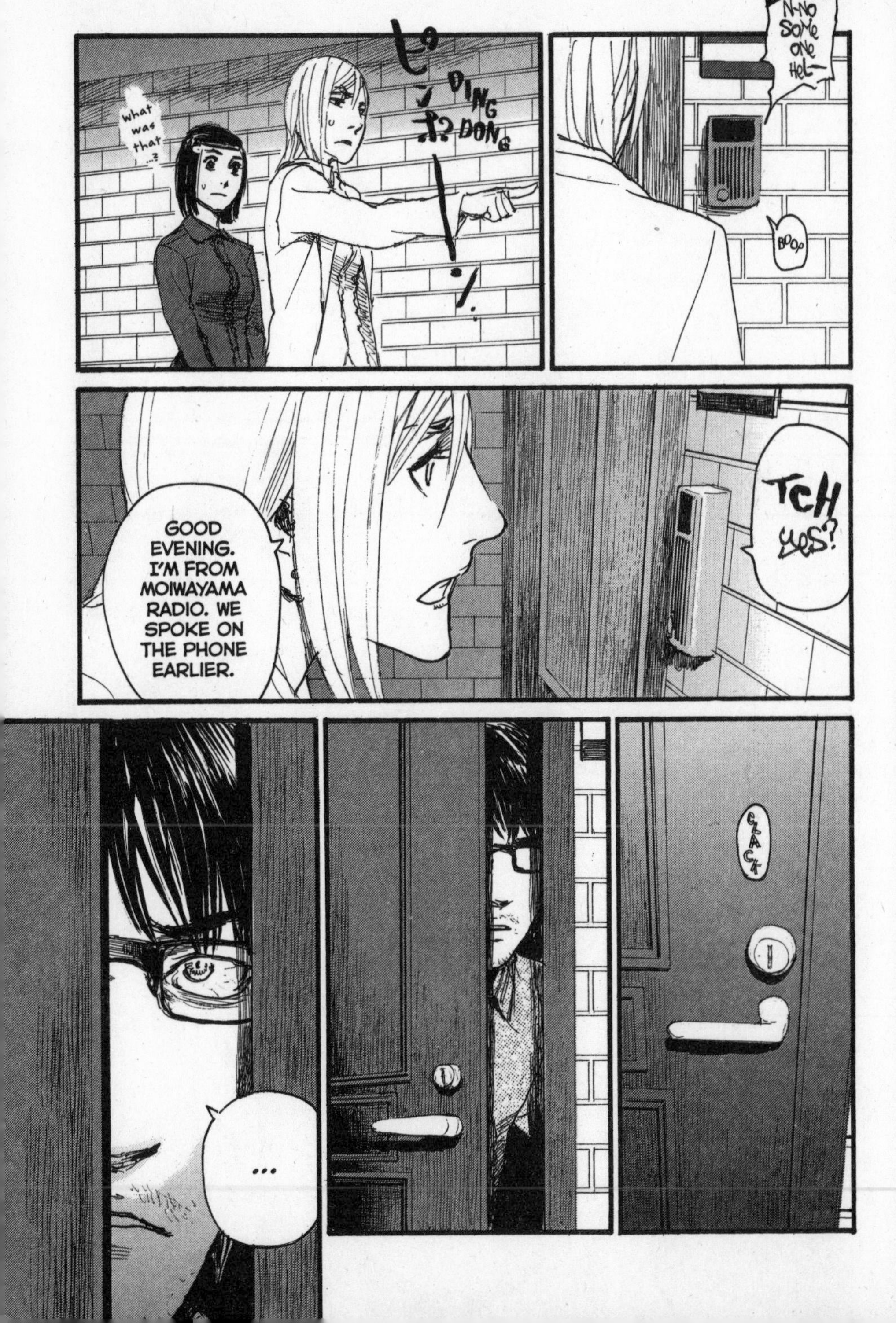
ZTCH
N-NO SOME ONE HEL—
BOOP
DING DONG
what was that ...?
TCH yes?
GOOD EVENING. I'M FROM MOIWAYAMA RADIO. WE SPOKE ON THE PHONE EARLIER.
CLACK
...

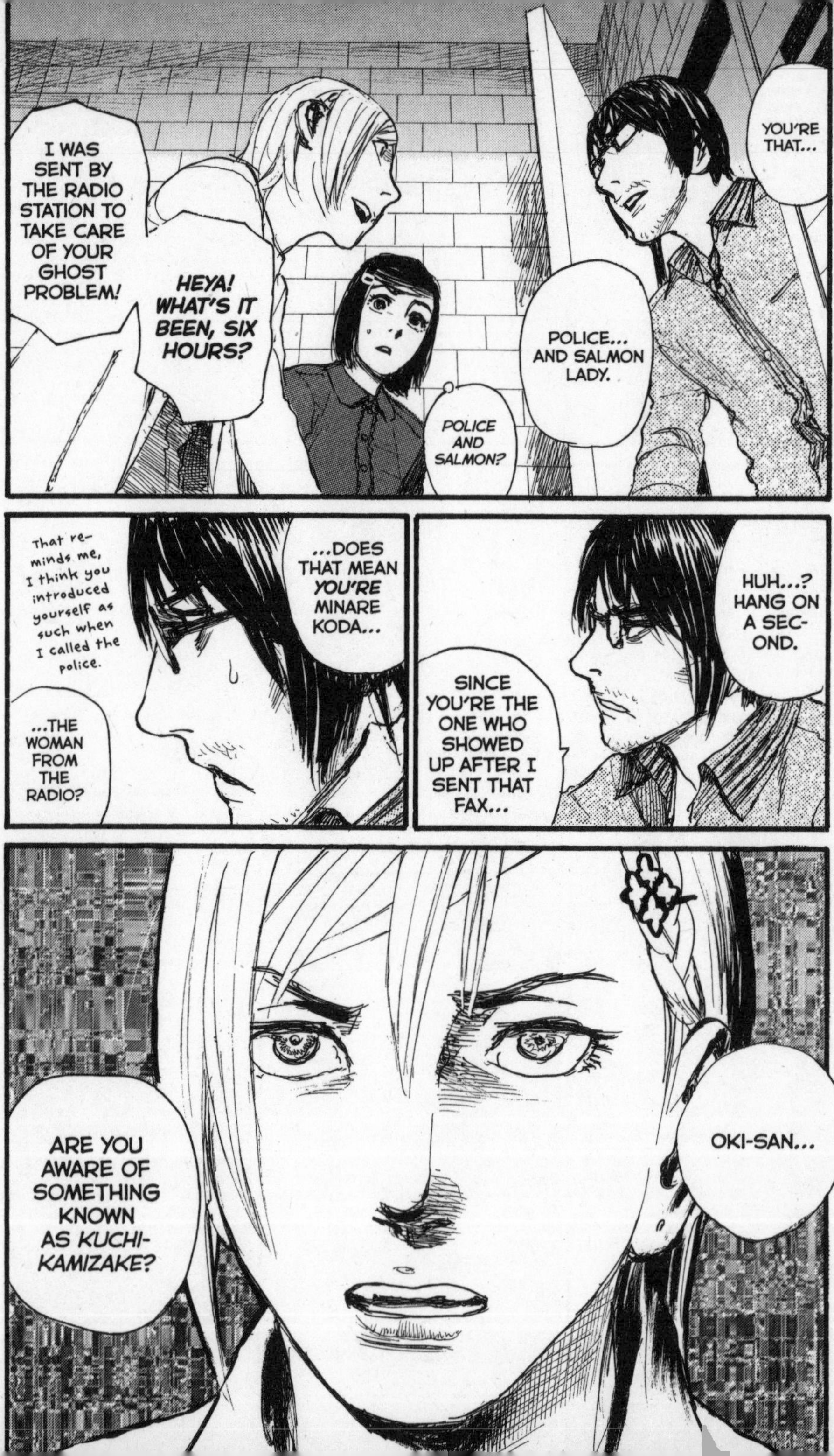

YOU'RE THAT...
POLICE... AND SALMON LADY.
POLICE AND SALMON?
HEYA! WHAT'S IT BEEN, SIX HOURS?
I WAS SENT BY THE RADIO STATION TO TAKE CARE OF YOUR GHOST PROBLEM!
HUH...? HANG ON A SEC- OND.
SINCE YOU'RE THE ONE WHO SHOWED UP AFTER I SENT THAT FAX...
...DOES THAT MEAN YOU'RE MINARE KODA...
That re- minds me, I think you introduced yourself as such when I called the police.
...THE WOMAN FROM THE RADIO?
OKI-SAN...
ARE YOU AWARE OF SOMETHING KNOWN AS KUCHI- KAMIZAKE?

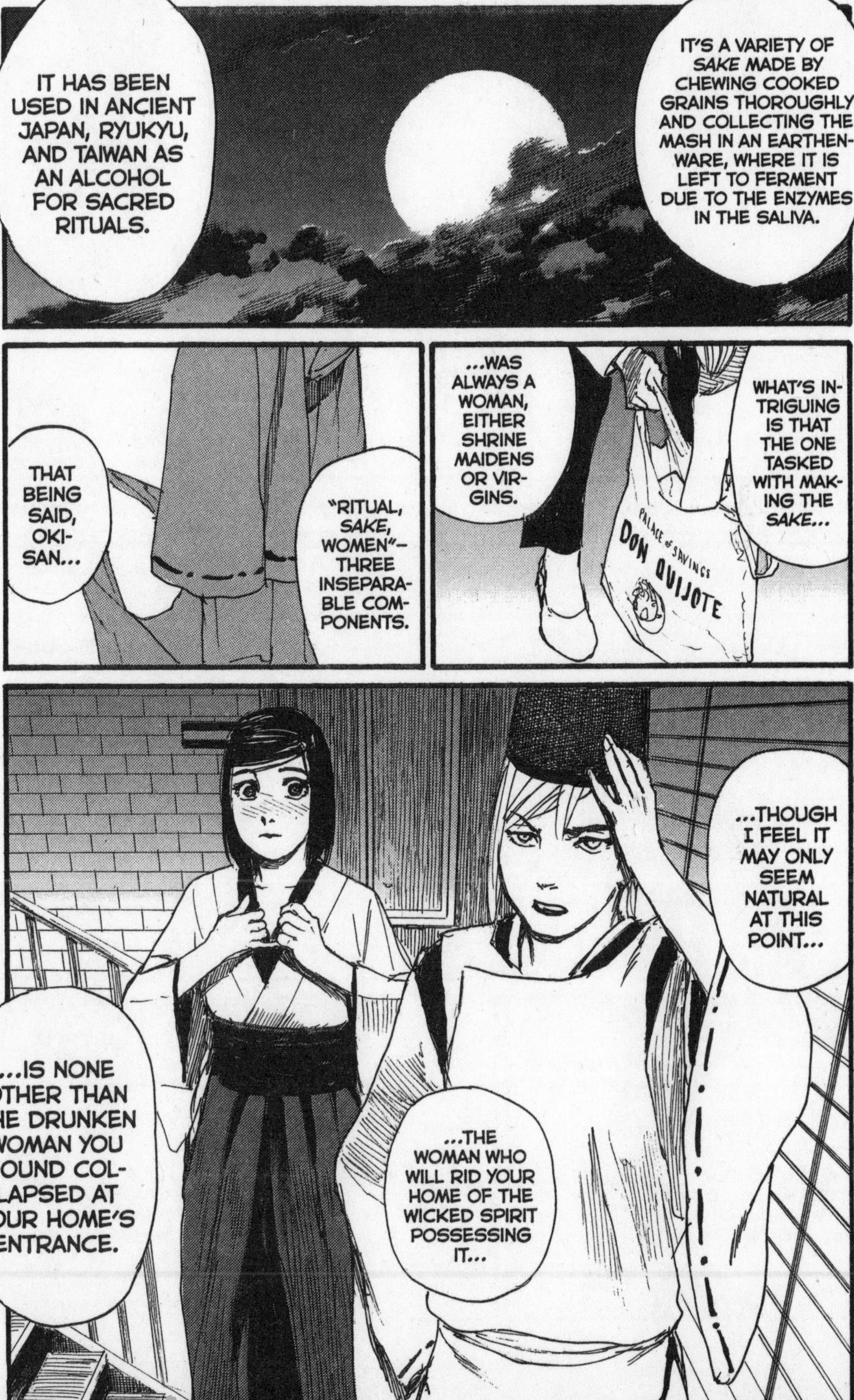

IT'S A VARIETY OF SAKE MADE BY CHEWING COOKED GRAINS THOROUGHLY AND COLLECTING THE MASH IN AN EARTHENWARE, WHERE IT IS LEFT TO FERMENT DUE TO THE ENZYMES IN THE SALIVA.
IT HAS BEEN USED IN ANCIENT JAPAN, RYUKYU, AND TAIWAN AS AN ALCOHOL FOR SACRED RITUALS.
WHAT'S INTRIGUING IS THAT THE ONE TASKED WITH MAKING THE SAKE...
...WAS ALWAYS A WOMAN, EITHER SHRINE MAIDENS OR VIRGINS.
PALACE of SAVINGS
DON QUIJOTE
"RITUAL, SAKE, WOMEN"—THREE INSEPARABLE COMPONENTS.
THAT BEING SAID, OKI-SAN...
...THOUGH I FEEL IT MAY ONLY SEEM NATURAL AT THIS POINT...
...THE WOMAN WHO WILL RID YOUR HOME OF THE WICKED SPIRIT POSSESSING IT...
...IS NONE OTHER THAN THE DRUNKEN WOMAN YOU FOUND COLLAPSED AT YOUR HOME'S ENTRANCE.

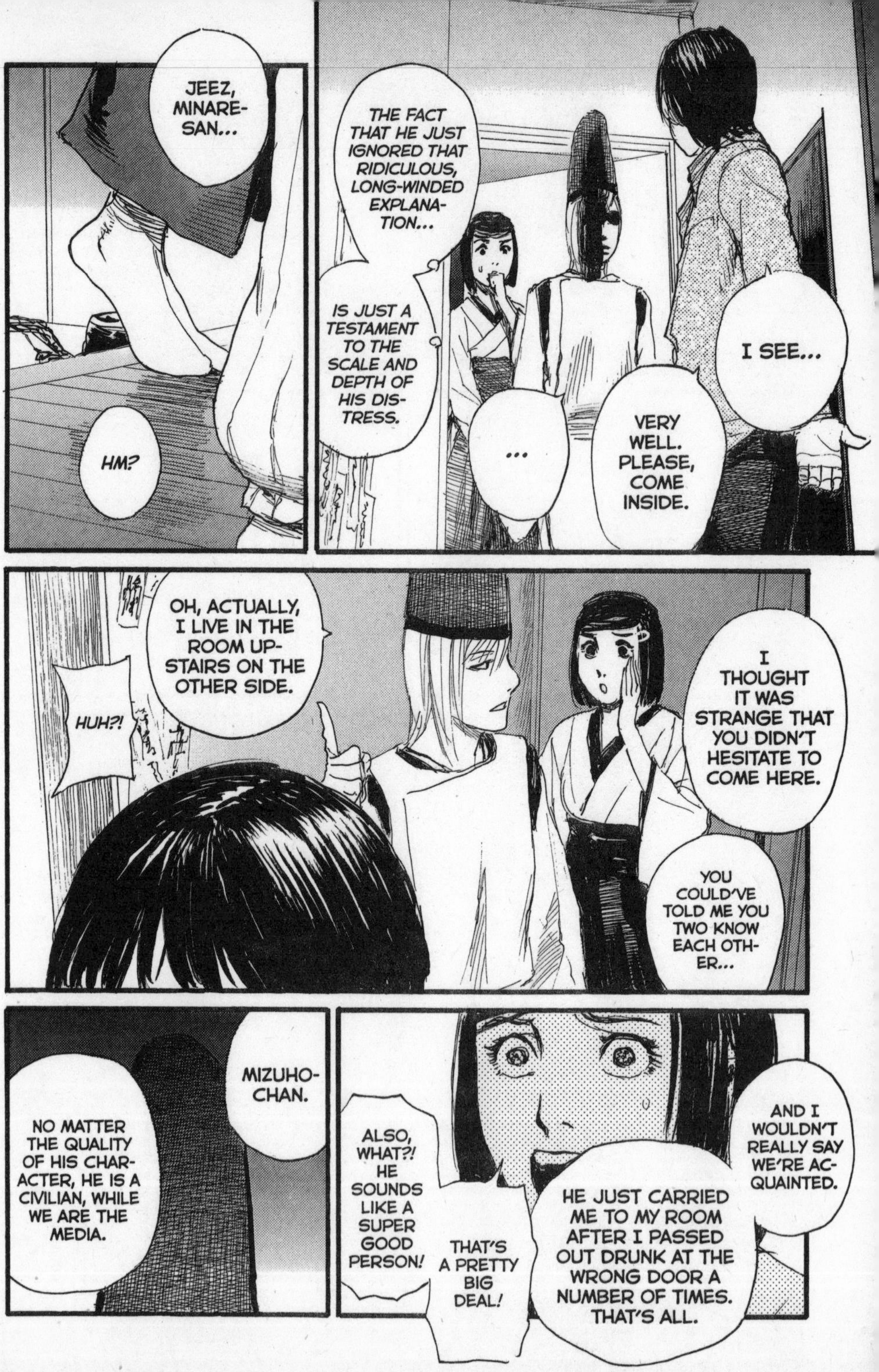
I SEE...
VERY WELL. PLEASE, COME INSIDE.
...
THE FACT THAT HE JUST IGNORED THAT RIDICULOUS, LONG-WINDED EXPLANATION...
IS JUST A TESTAMENT TO THE SCALE AND DEPTH OF HIS DISTRESS.
JEEZ, MINARE-SAN...
HM?
I THOUGHT IT WAS STRANGE THAT YOU DIDN'T HESITATE TO COME HERE.
YOU COULD'VE TOLD ME YOU TWO KNOW EACH OTHER...
OH, ACTUALLY, I LIVE IN THE ROOM UPSTAIRS ON THE OTHER SIDE.
HUH?!
AND I WOULDN'T REALLY SAY WE'RE ACQUAINTED.
HE JUST CARRIED ME TO MY ROOM AFTER I PASSED OUT DRUNK AT THE WRONG DOOR A NUMBER OF TIMES. THAT'S ALL.
ALSO, WHAT?! HE SOUNDS LIKE A SUPER GOOD PERSON!
THAT'S A PRETTY BIG DEAL!
MIZUHO-CHAN.
NO MATTER THE QUALITY OF HIS CHARACTER, HE IS A CIVILIAN, WHILE WE ARE THE MEDIA.

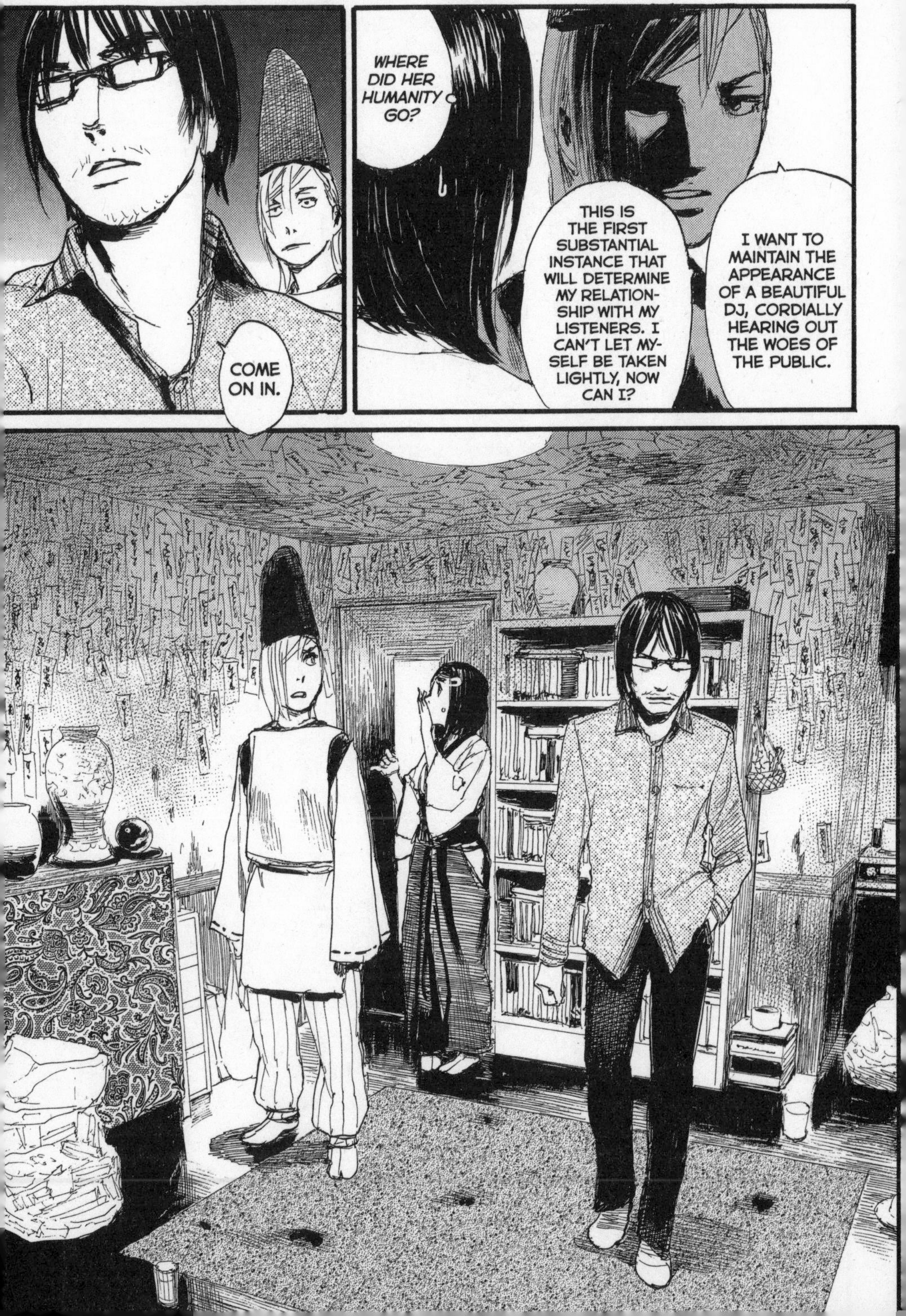
I WANT TO MAINTAIN THE APPEARANCE OF A BEAUTIFUL DJ, CORDIALLY HEARING OUT THE WOES OF THE PUBLIC.
THIS IS THE FIRST SUBSTANTIAL INSTANCE THAT WILL DETERMINE MY RELATIONSHIP WITH MY LISTENERS. I CAN'T LET MYSELF BE TAKEN LIGHTLY, NOW CAN I?
WHERE DID HER HUMANITY GO?
COME ON IN.

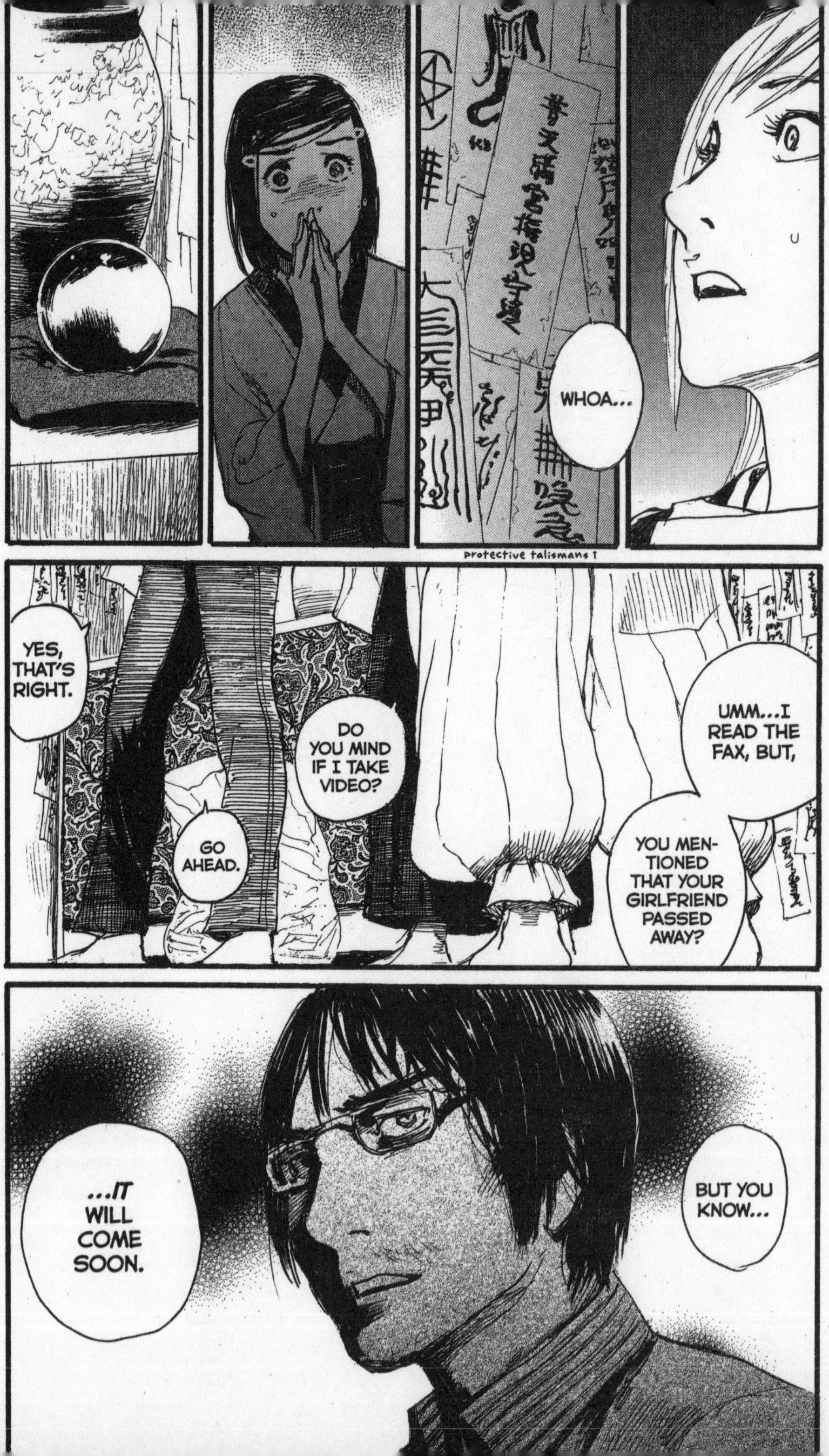
WHOA...
protective talismans!
UMM...I READ THE FAX, BUT,
YOU MEN-TIONED THAT YOUR GIRLFRIEND PASSED AWAY?
YES, THAT'S RIGHT.
DO YOU MIND IF I TAKE VIDEO?
GO AHEAD.
BUT YOU KNOW...
...IT WILL COME SOON.

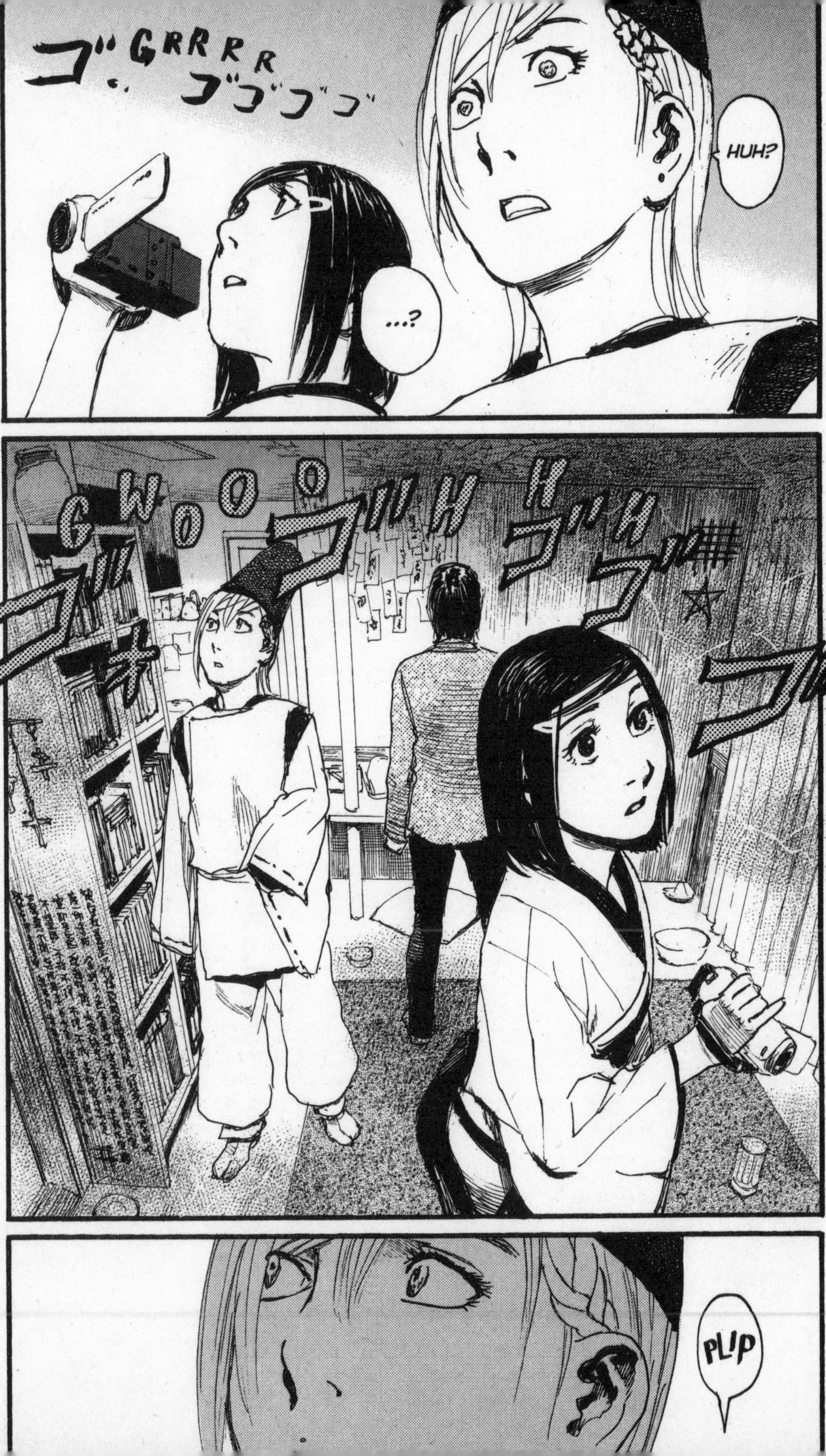
HUH?
GRRRR
...?
GWOOOHHH
PLIP

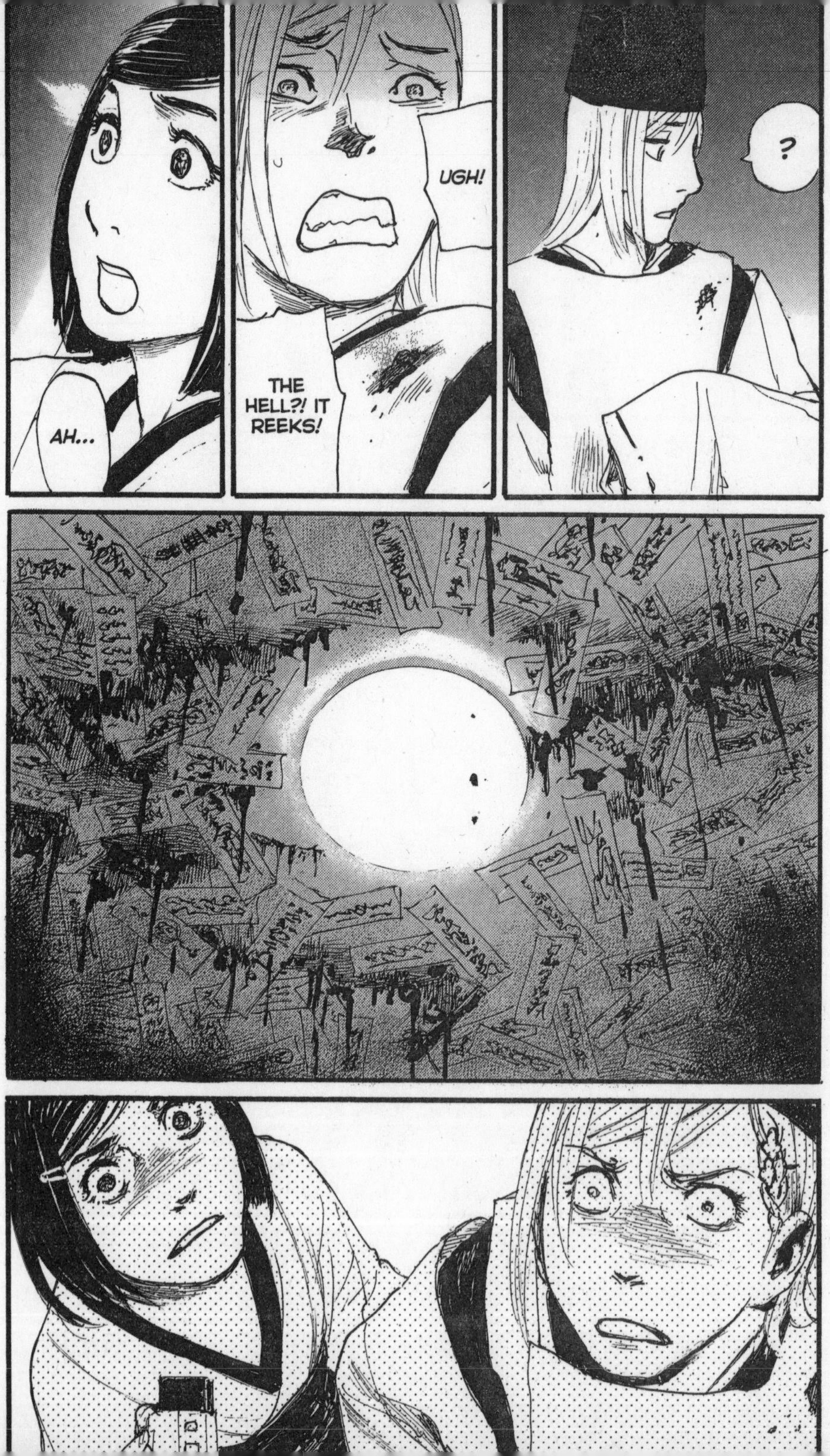
?
UGH!
THE HELL?! IT REEKS!
AH...

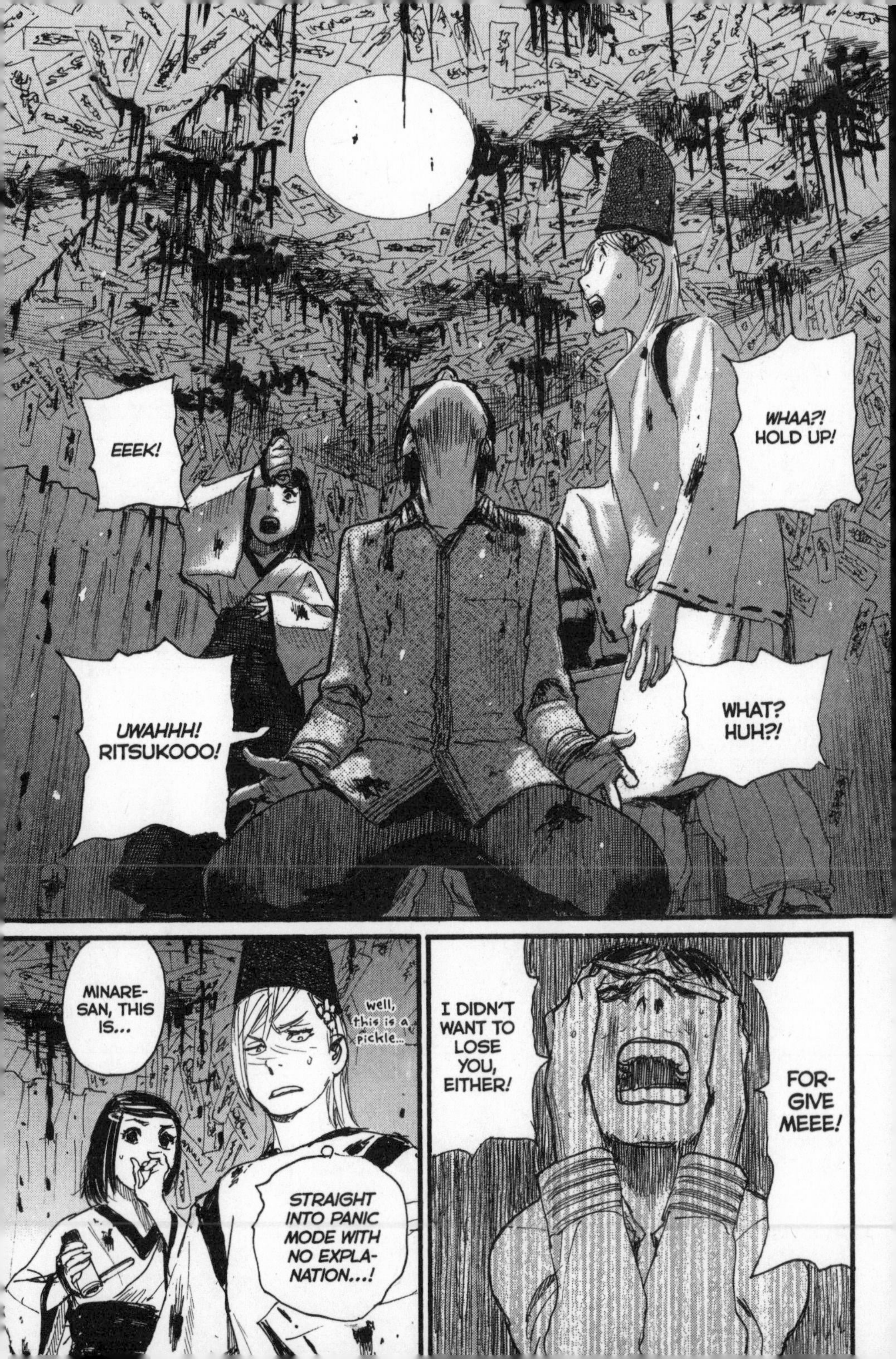
WHAA?! HOLD UP!
EEEK!
WHAT? HUH?!
UWAHHH! RITSUKOOO!
I DIDN'T WANT TO LOSE YOU, EITHER!
FOR-GIVE MEEE!
MINARE-SAN, THIS IS...
well, this is a pickle...
STRAIGHT INTO PANIC MODE WITH NO EXPLA-NATION...!

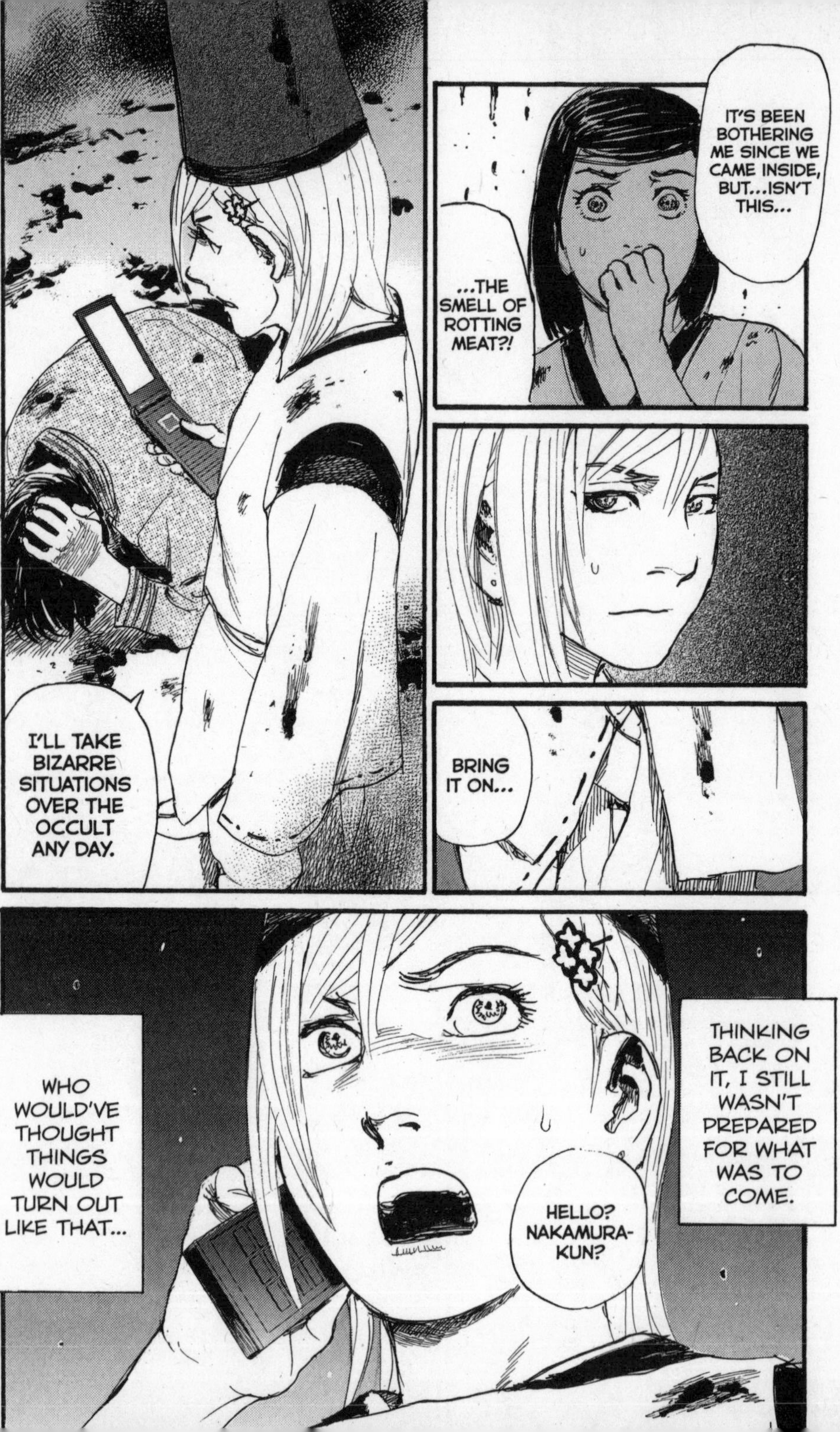
IT'S BEEN BOTHERING ME SINCE WE CAME INSIDE, BUT...ISN'T THIS...
...THE SMELL OF ROTTING MEAT?!
BRING IT ON...
I'LL TAKE BIZARRE SITUATIONS OVER THE OCCULT ANY DAY.
THINKING BACK ON IT, I STILL WASN'T PREPARED FOR WHAT WAS TO COME.
HELLO? NAKAMURA-KUN?
WHO WOULD'VE THOUGHT THINGS WOULD TURN OUT LIKE THAT...

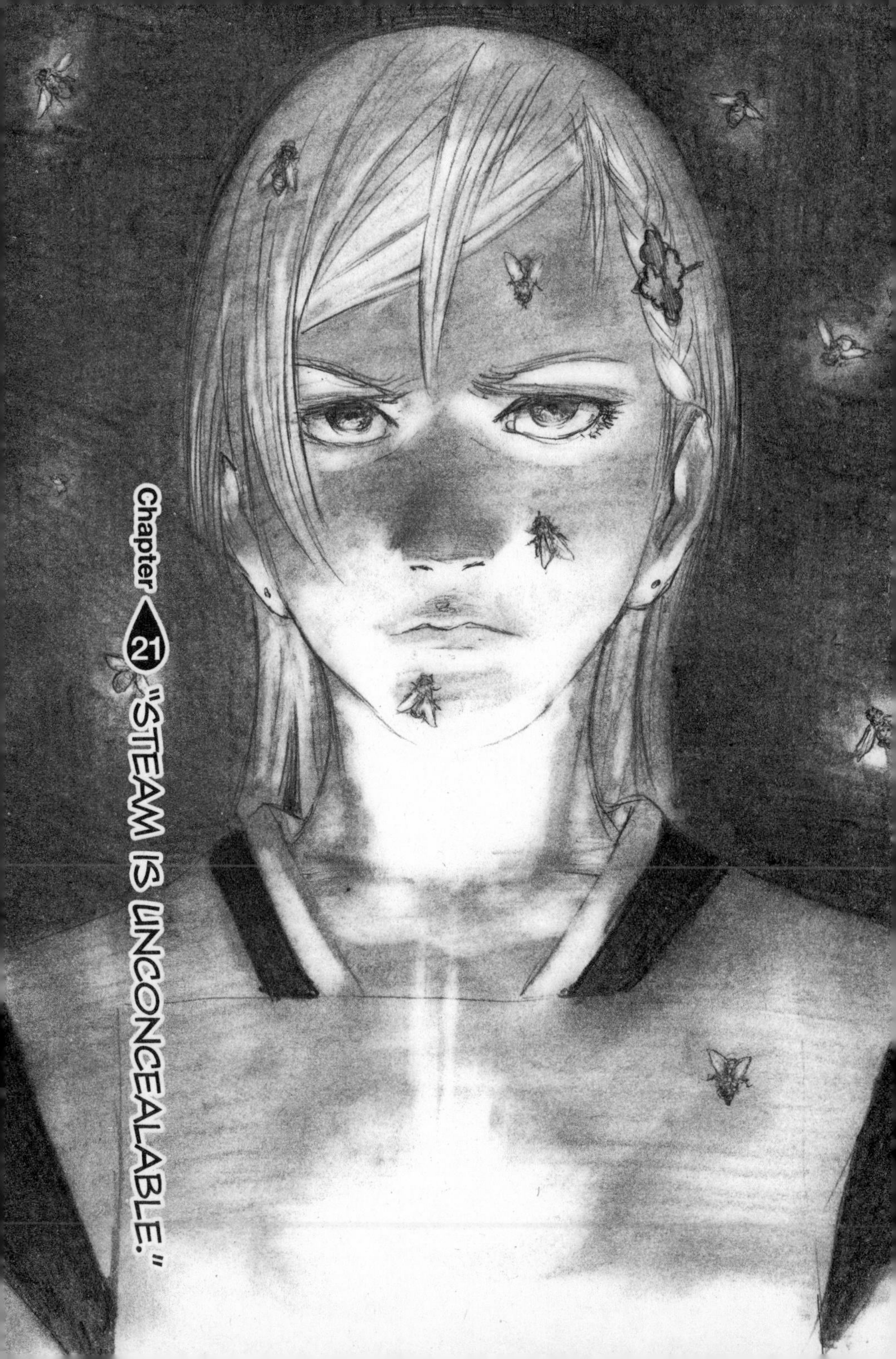
Chapter 21
"STEAM IS UNCONCEALABLE."

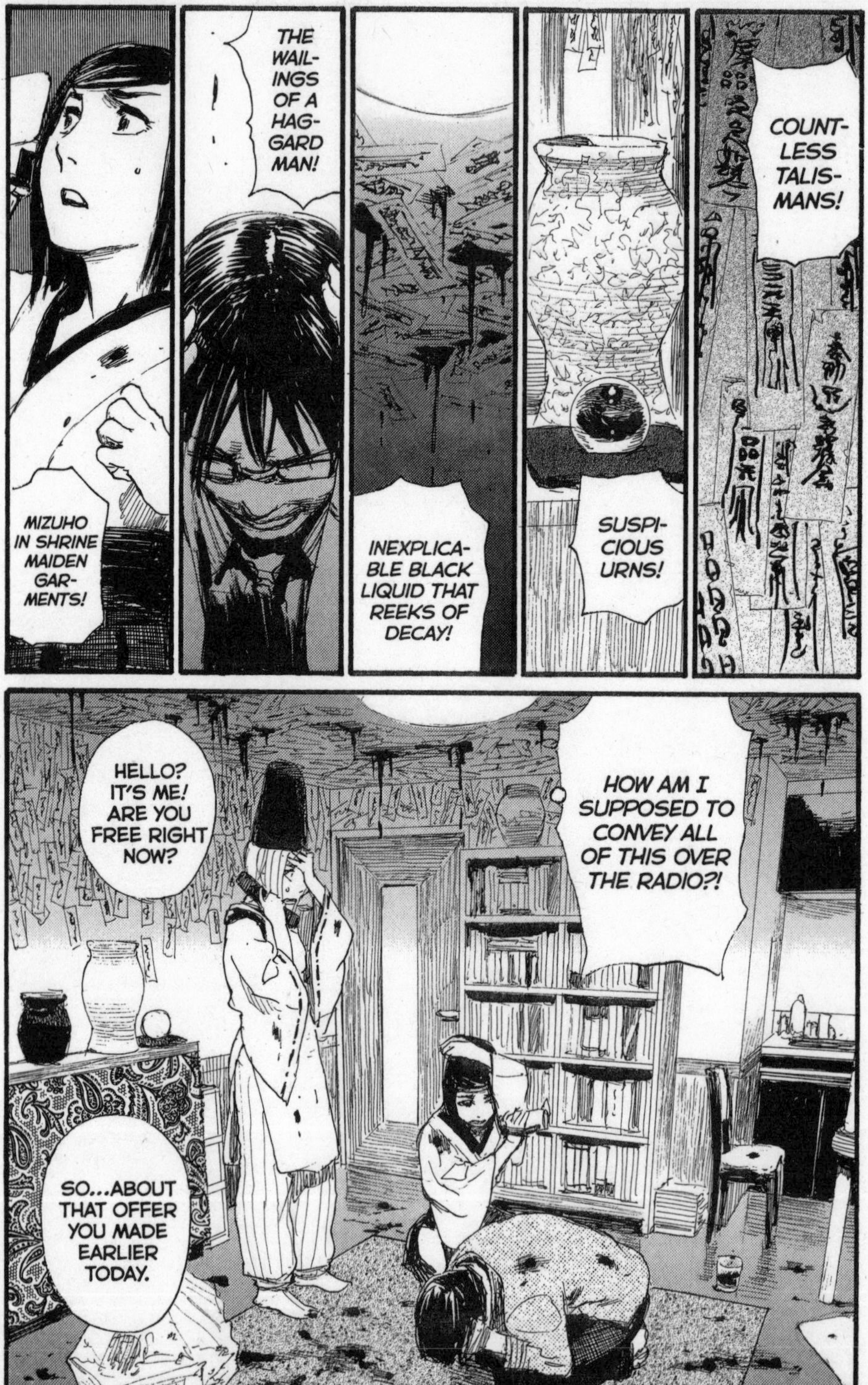
COUNTLESS TALISMANS!
SUSPICIOUS URNS!
INEXPLICABLE BLACK LIQUID THAT REEKS OF DECAY!
THE WAILINGS OF A HAGGARD MAN!
MIZUHO IN SHRINE MAIDEN GARMENTS!
HOW AM I SUPPOSED TO CONVEY ALL OF THIS OVER THE RADIO?!
HELLO? IT'S ME! ARE YOU FREE RIGHT NOW?
SO...ABOUT THAT OFFER YOU MADE EARLIER TODAY.

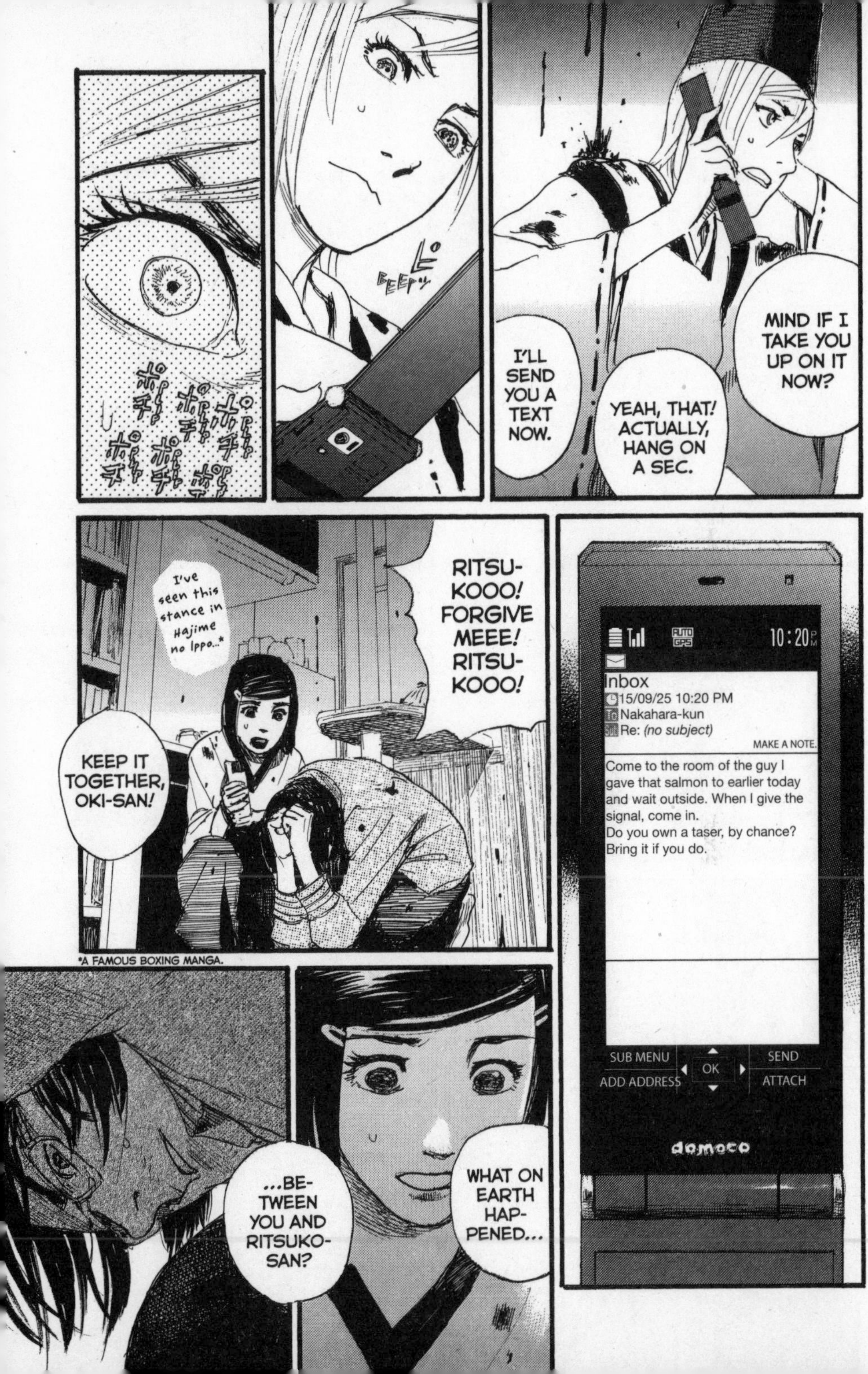
MIND IF I TAKE YOU UP ON IT NOW?
YEAH, THAT! ACTUALLY, HANG ON A SEC.
I'LL SEND YOU A TEXT NOW.
BEEP
10:20 PM
Inbox
15/09/25 10:20 PM
Nakahara-kun
Re: (no subject)
MAKE A NOTE.
Come to the room of the guy I gave that salmon to earlier today and wait outside. When I give the signal, come in.
Do you own a taser, by chance?
Bring it if you do.
SUB MENU
ADD ADDRESS
OK
SEND
ATTACH
domoco
RITSU-KOOO! FORGIVE MEEE! RITSU-KOOO!
I've seen this stance in Hajime no Ippo...*
KEEP IT TOGETHER, OKI-SAN!
WHAT ON EARTH HAPPENED...
...BETWEEN YOU AND RITSUKO-SAN?
*A FAMOUS BOXING MANGA.

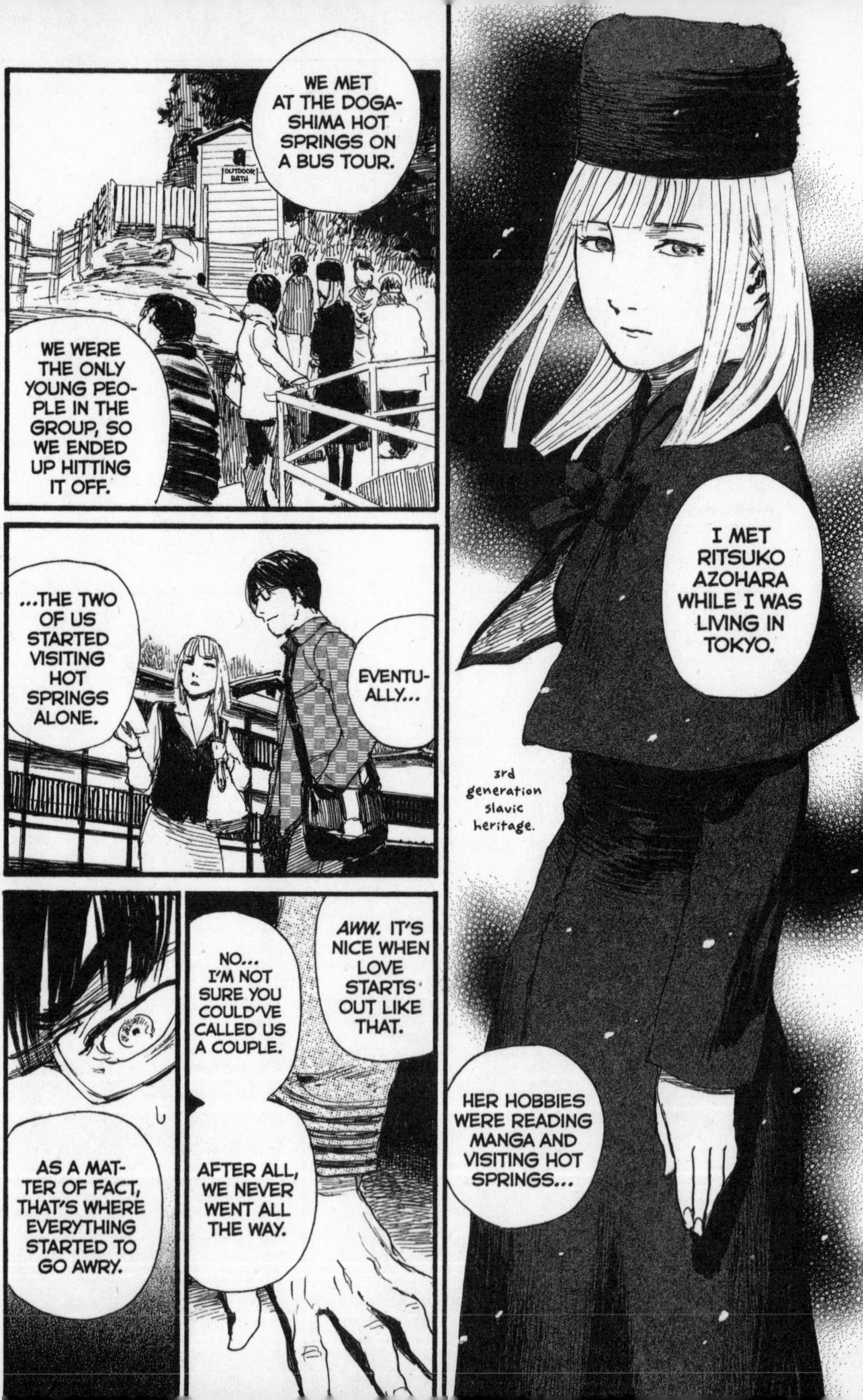
I MET RITSUKO AZOHARA WHILE I WAS LIVING IN TOKYO.
3rd generation slavic heritage.
HER HOBBIES WERE READING MANGA AND VISITING HOT SPRINGS...
WE MET AT THE DOGA-SHIMA HOT SPRINGS ON A BUS TOUR.
OUTDOOR BATH
WE WERE THE ONLY YOUNG PEOPLE IN THE GROUP, SO WE ENDED UP HITTING IT OFF.
EVENTUALLY...
...THE TWO OF US STARTED VISITING HOT SPRINGS ALONE.
AWW. IT'S NICE WHEN LOVE STARTS OUT LIKE THAT.
NO... I'M NOT SURE YOU COULD'VE CALLED US A COUPLE.
AFTER ALL, WE NEVER WENT ALL THE WAY.
AS A MATTER OF FACT, THAT'S WHERE EVERYTHING STARTED TO GO AWRY.

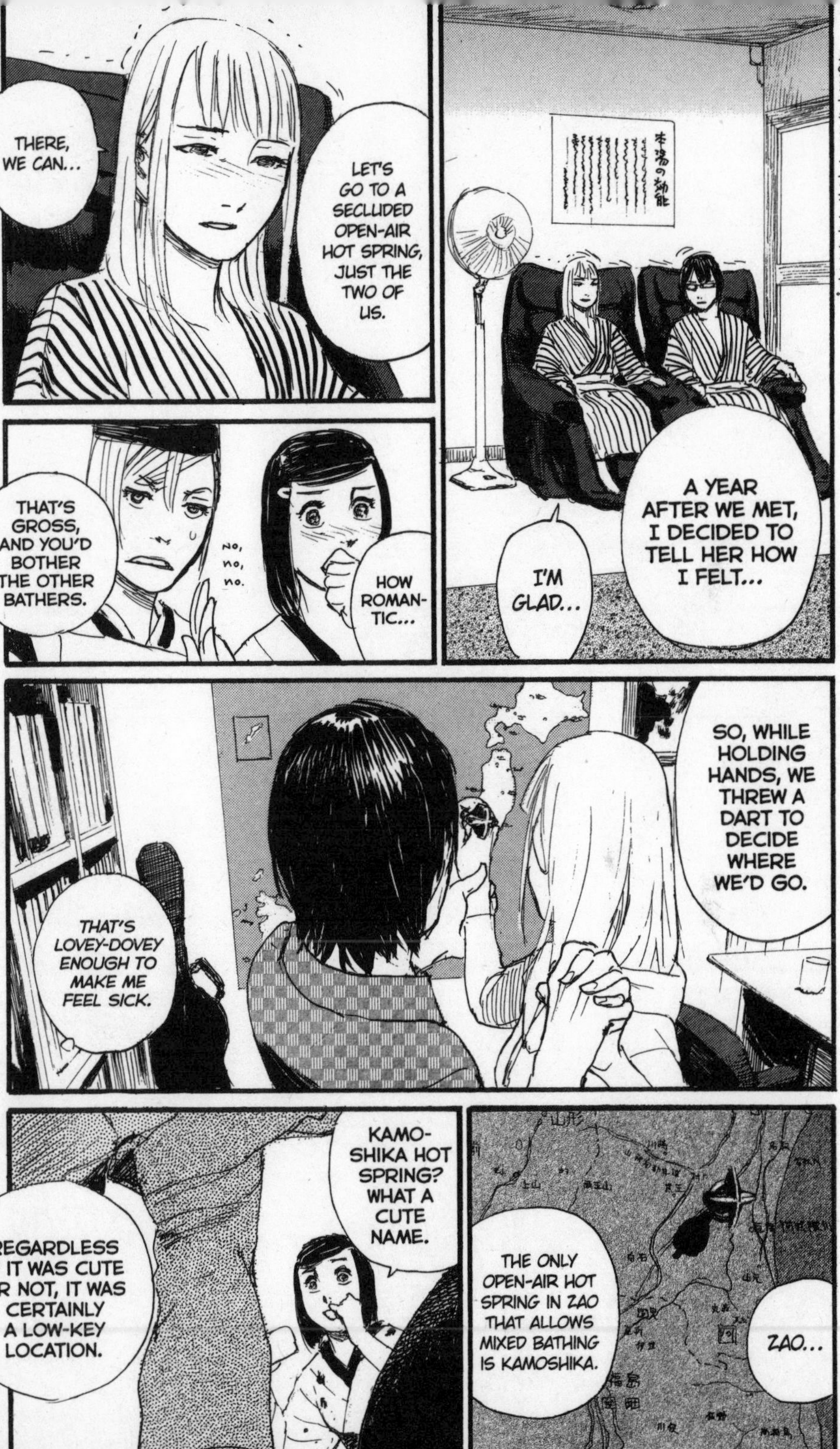
A YEAR AFTER WE MET, I DECIDED TO TELL HER HOW I FELT...
I'M GLAD...
LET'S GO TO A SECLUDED OPEN-AIR HOT SPRING, JUST THE TWO OF US.
THERE, WE CAN...
HOW ROMANTIC...
no, no, no.
THAT'S GROSS, AND YOU'D BOTHER THE OTHER BATHERS.
SO, WHILE HOLDING HANDS, WE THREW A DART TO DECIDE WHERE WE'D GO.
THAT'S LOVEY-DOVEY ENOUGH TO MAKE ME FEEL SICK.
ZAO...
THE ONLY OPEN-AIR HOT SPRING IN ZAO THAT ALLOWS MIXED BATHING IS KAMOSHIKA.
山形
福島
KAMOSHIKA HOT SPRING? WHAT A CUTE NAME.
REGARDLESS IF IT WAS CUTE OR NOT, IT WAS CERTAINLY A LOW-KEY LOCATION.

↑ The sign lists the hot spring's benefits

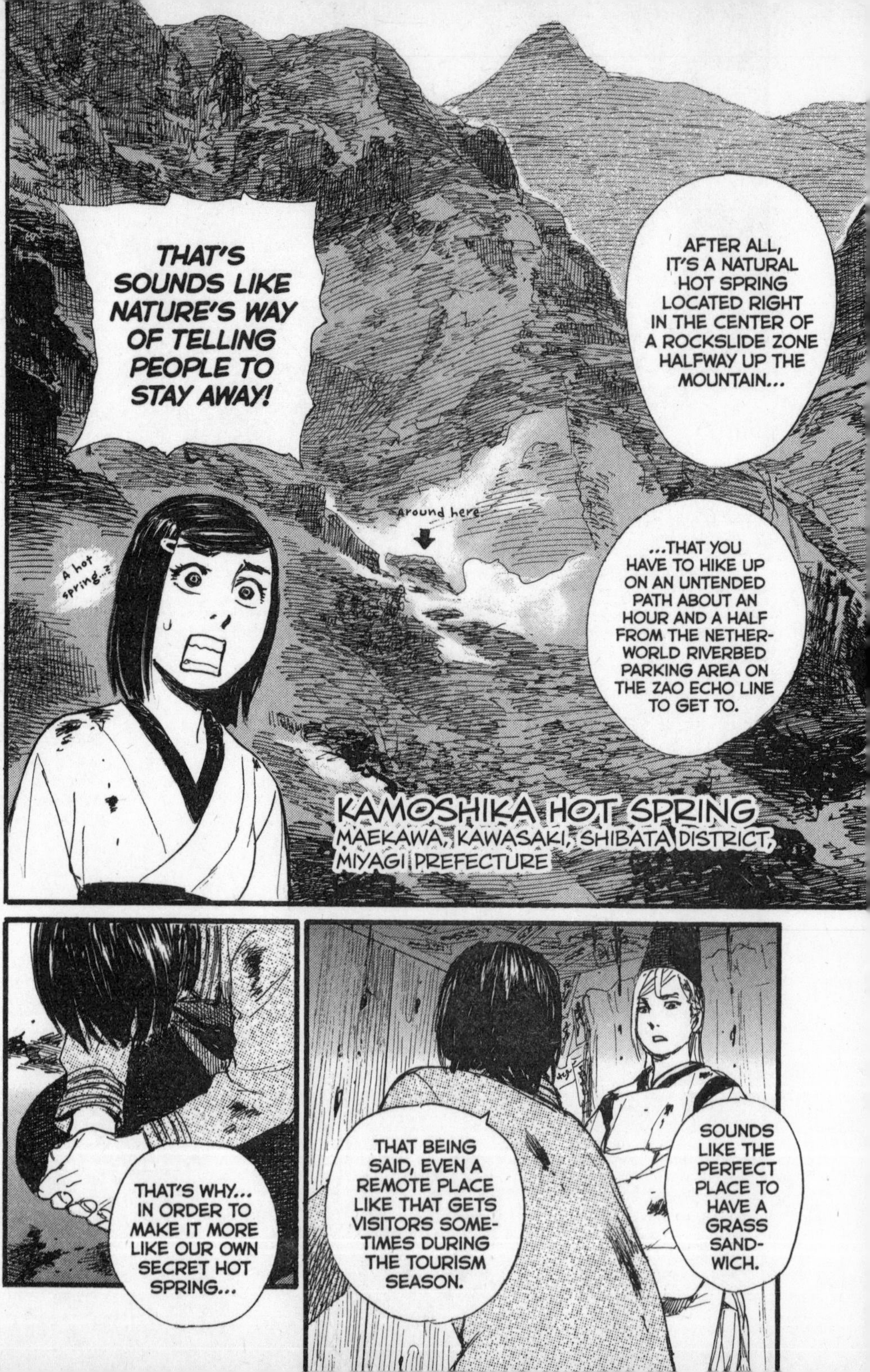
AFTER ALL, IT'S A NATURAL HOT SPRING LOCATED RIGHT IN THE CENTER OF A ROCKSLIDE ZONE HALFWAY UP THE MOUNTAIN...
...THAT YOU HAVE TO HIKE UP ON AN UNTENDED PATH ABOUT AN HOUR AND A HALF FROM THE NETHER-WORLD RIVERBED PARKING AREA ON THE ZAO ECHO LINE TO GET TO.
Around here
THAT'S SOUNDS LIKE NATURE'S WAY OF TELLING PEOPLE TO STAY AWAY!
A hot spring..?
KAMOSHIKA HOT SPRING
MAEKAWA, KAWASAKI, SHIBATA DISTRICT, MIYAGI PREFECTURE
SOUNDS LIKE THE PERFECT PLACE TO HAVE A GRASS SAND-WICH.
THAT BEING SAID, EVEN A REMOTE PLACE LIKE THAT GETS VISITORS SOME-TIMES DURING THE TOURISM SEASON.
THAT'S WHY... IN ORDER TO MAKE IT MORE LIKE OUR OWN SECRET HOT SPRING...

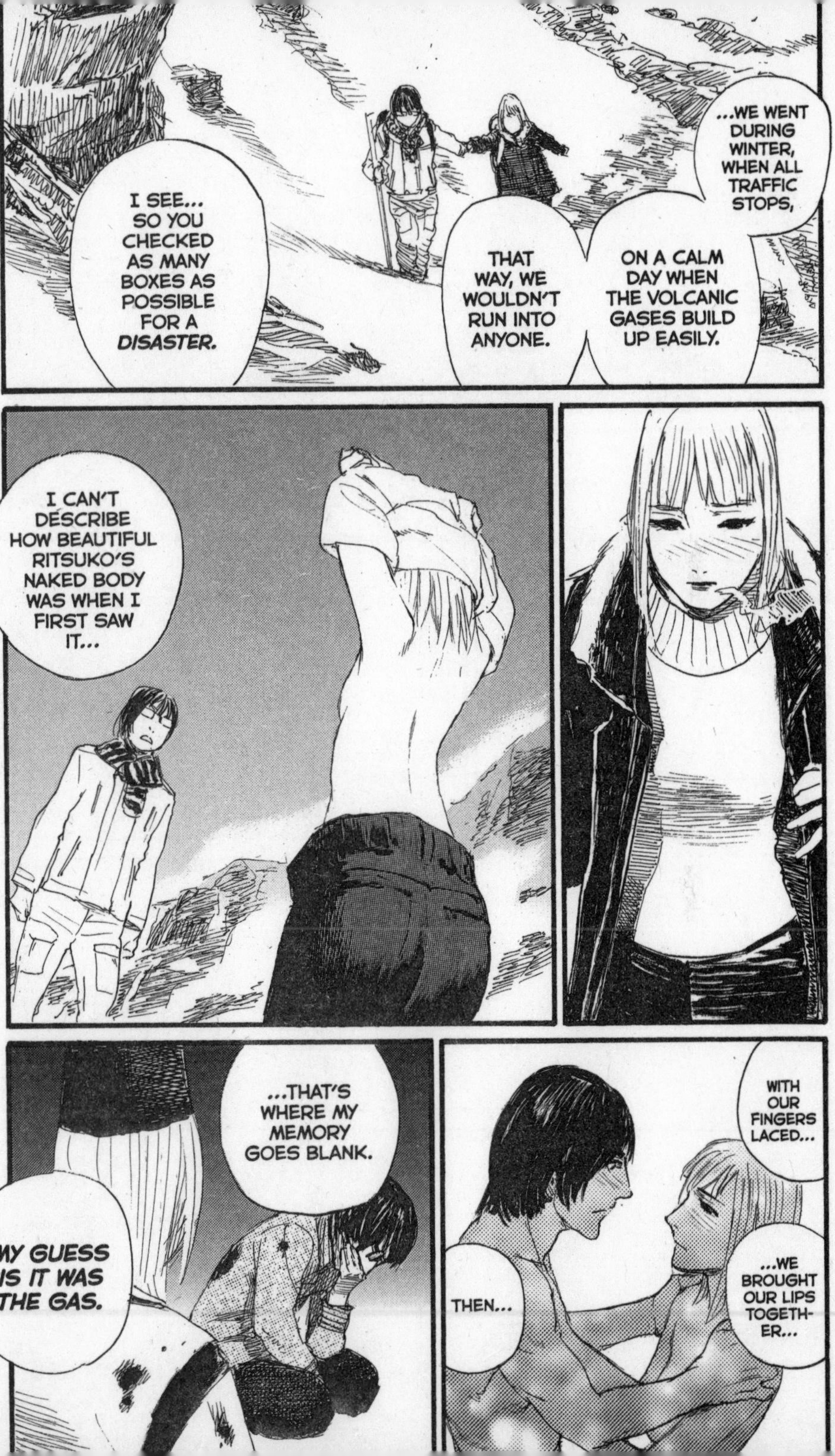
...WE WENT DURING WINTER, WHEN ALL TRAFFIC STOPS,
ON A CALM DAY WHEN THE VOLCANIC GASES BUILD UP EASILY.
THAT WAY, WE WOULDN'T RUN INTO ANYONE.
I SEE... SO YOU CHECKED AS MANY BOXES AS POSSIBLE FOR A *DISASTER.*
I CAN'T DESCRIBE HOW BEAUTIFUL RITSUKO'S NAKED BODY WAS WHEN I FIRST SAW IT...
WITH OUR FINGERS LACED...
...WE BROUGHT OUR LIPS TOGETHER...
THEN...
...THAT'S WHERE MY MEMORY GOES BLANK.
MY GUESS IS IT WAS THE GAS.

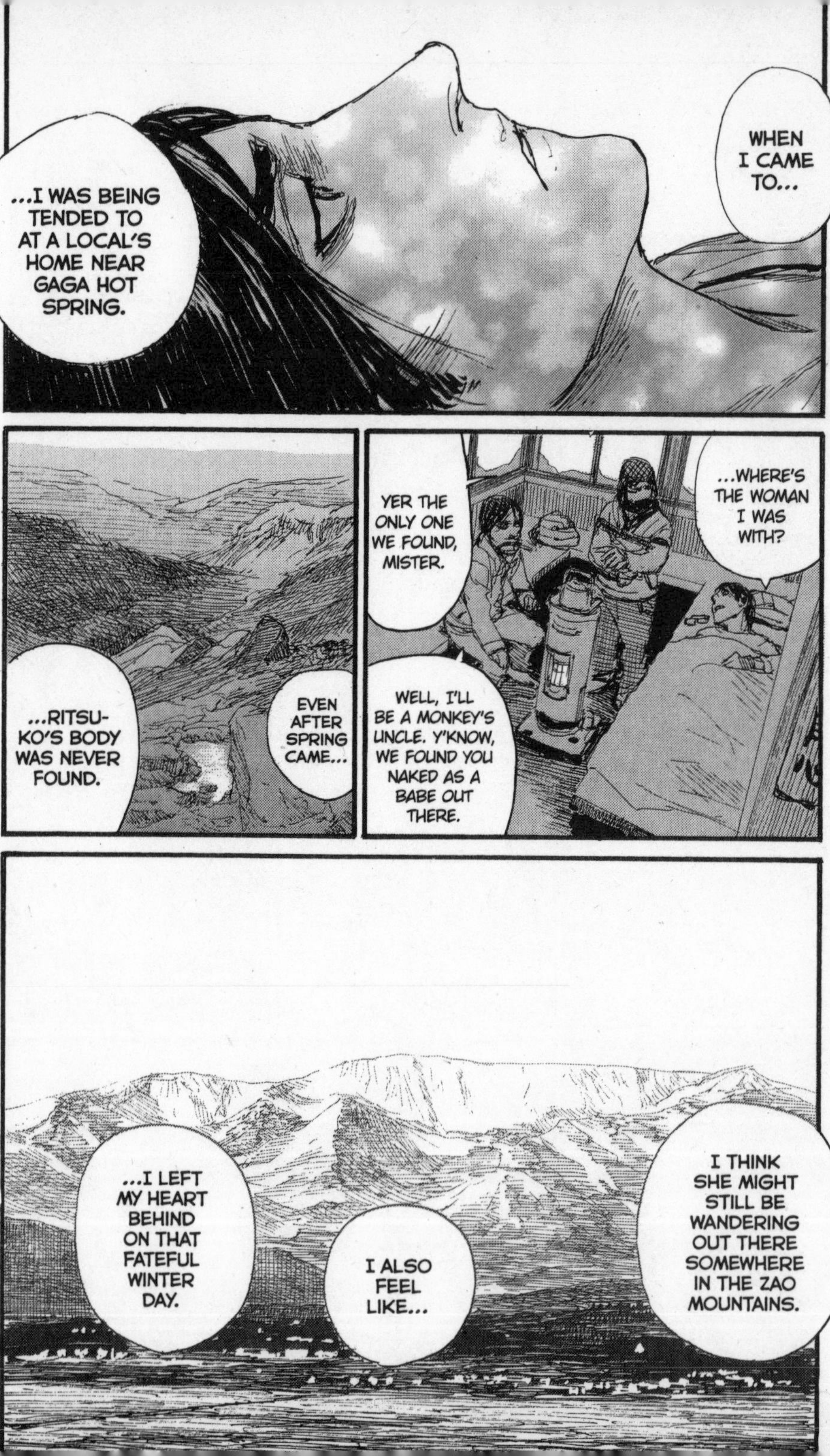
WHEN I CAME TO...
...I WAS BEING TENDED TO AT A LOCAL'S HOME NEAR GAGA HOT SPRING.
...WHERE'S THE WOMAN I WAS WITH?
YER THE ONLY ONE WE FOUND, MISTER.
WELL, I'LL BE A MONKEY'S UNCLE. Y'KNOW, WE FOUND YOU NAKED AS A BABE OUT THERE.
EVEN AFTER SPRING CAME...
...RITSU-KO'S BODY WAS NEVER FOUND.
I THINK SHE MIGHT STILL BE WANDERING OUT THERE SOMEWHERE IN THE ZAO MOUNTAINS.
I ALSO FEEL LIKE...
...I LEFT MY HEART BEHIND ON THAT FATEFUL WINTER DAY.

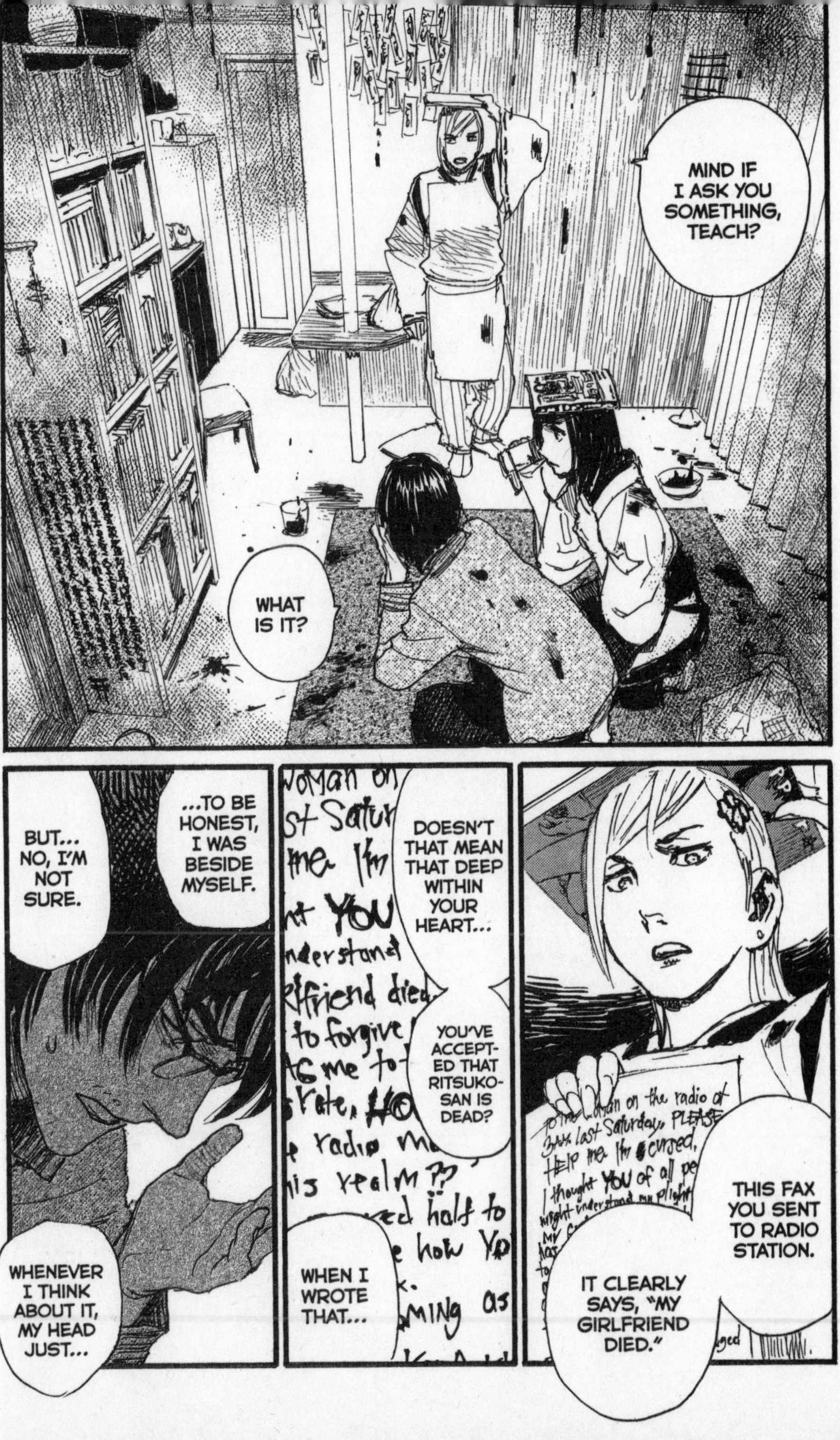
MIND IF I ASK YOU SOMETHING, TEACH?
WHAT IS IT?
THIS FAX YOU SENT TO RADIO STATION.
IT CLEARLY SAYS, "MY GIRLFRIEND DIED."
DOESN'T THAT MEAN THAT DEEP WITHIN YOUR HEART...
YOU'VE ACCEPTED THAT RITSUKO-SAN IS DEAD?
WHEN I WROTE THAT...
...TO BE HONEST, I WAS BESIDE MYSELF.
BUT... NO, I'M NOT SURE.
WHENEVER I THINK ABOUT IT, MY HEAD JUST...

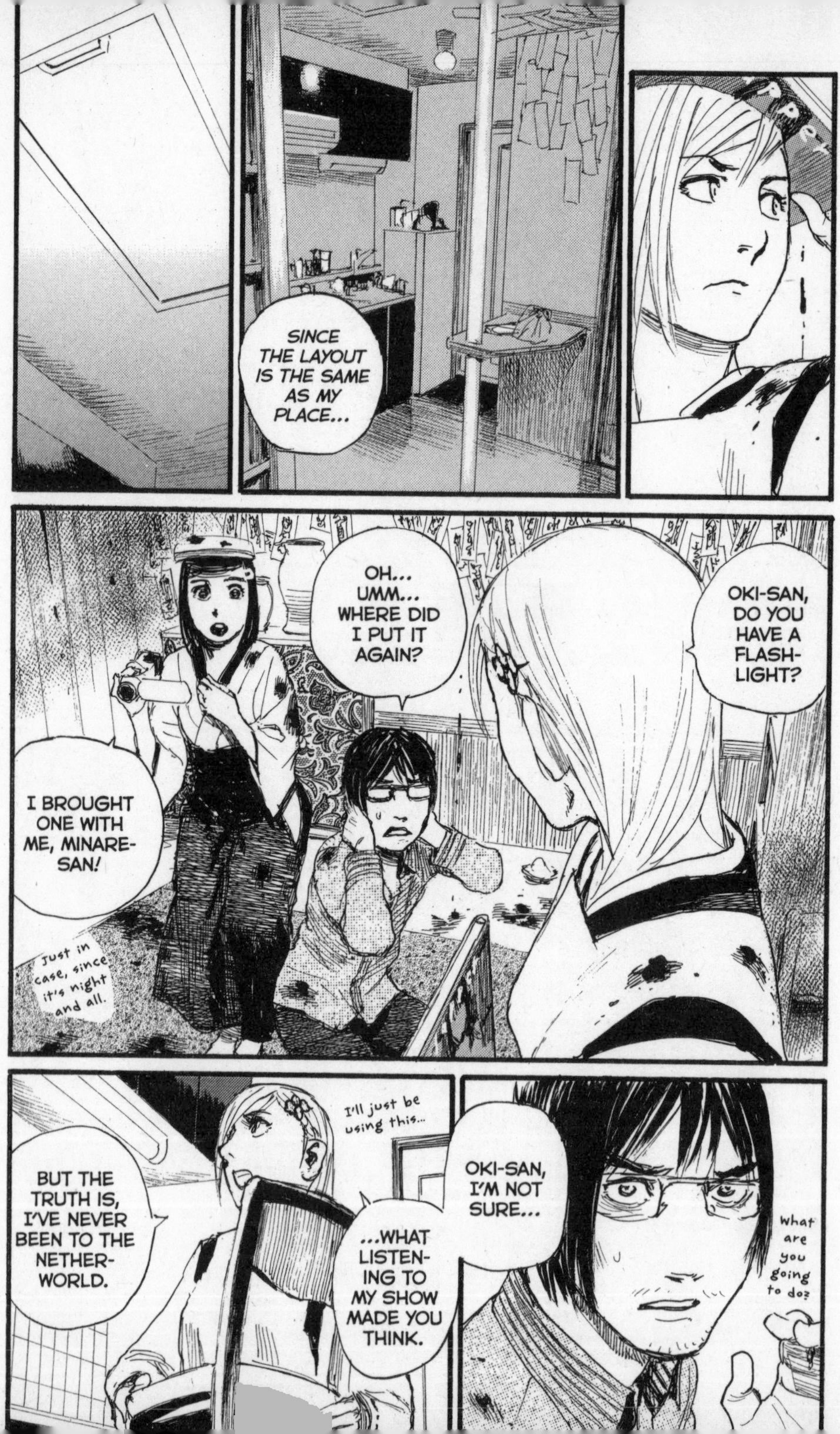
SINCE THE LAYOUT IS THE SAME AS MY PLACE...
OKI-SAN, DO YOU HAVE A FLASH-LIGHT?
OH... UMM... WHERE DID I PUT IT AGAIN?
I BROUGHT ONE WITH ME, MINARE-SAN!
Just in case, since it's night and all.
OKI-SAN, I'M NOT SURE...
What are you going to do?
I'll just be using this...
...WHAT LISTEN-ING TO MY SHOW MADE YOU THINK.
BUT THE TRUTH IS, I'VE NEVER BEEN TO THE NETHER-WORLD.

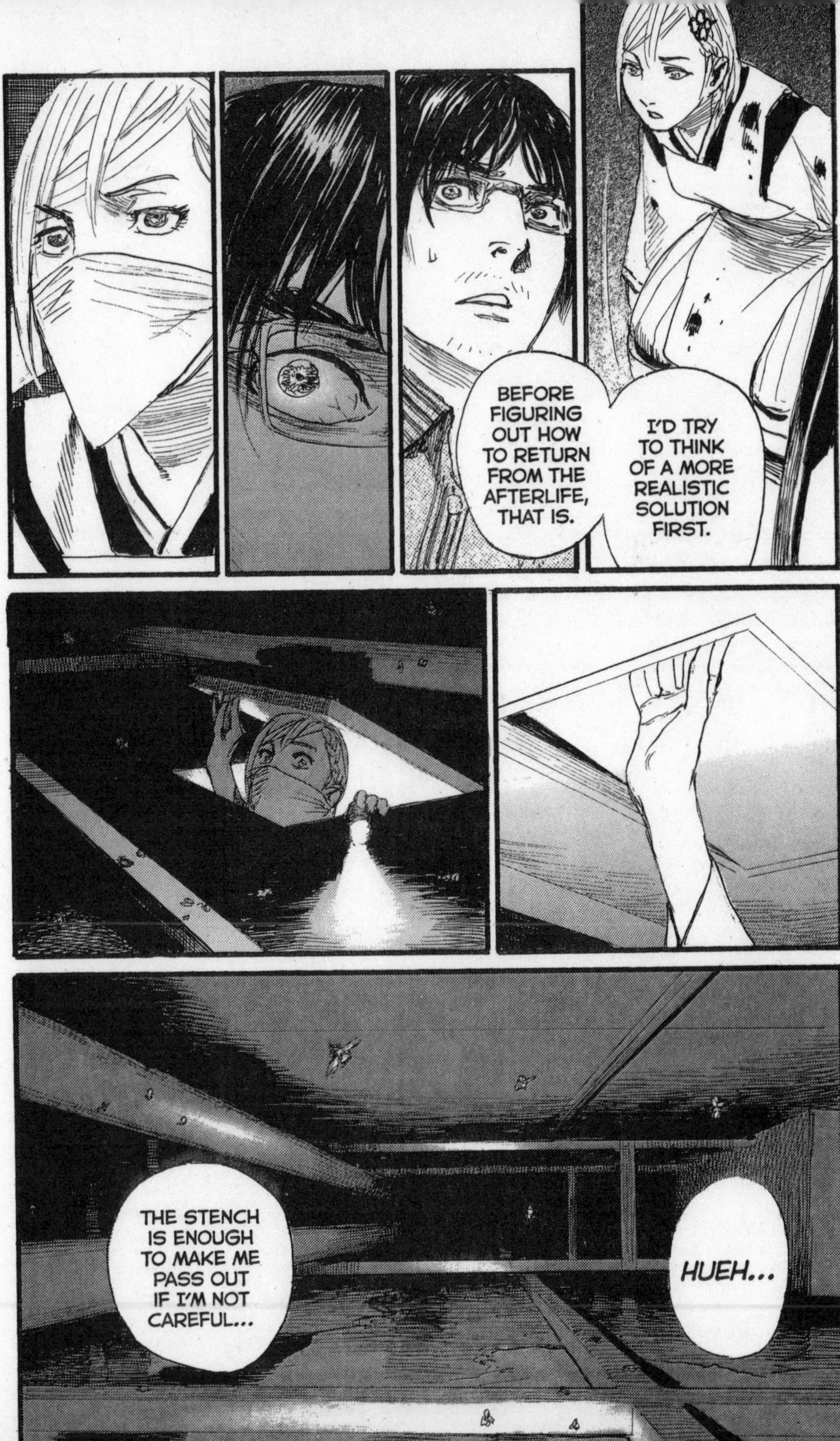
I'D TRY TO THINK OF A MORE REALISTIC SOLUTION FIRST.
BEFORE FIGURING OUT HOW TO RETURN FROM THE AFTERLIFE, THAT IS.
HUEH...
THE STENCH IS ENOUGH TO MAKE ME PASS OUT IF I'M NOT CAREFUL...

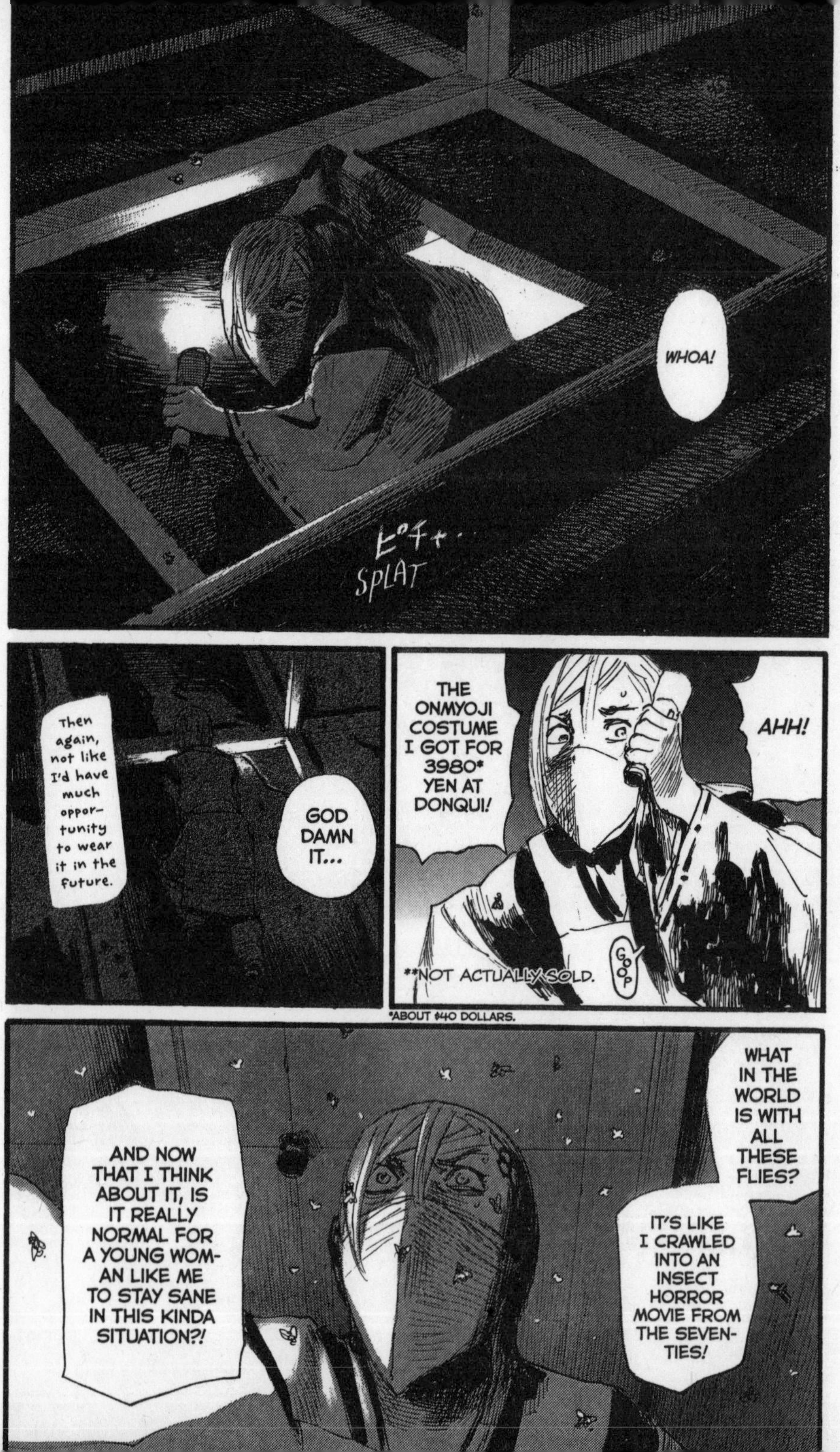
WHOA!
ピチャ…
SPLAT
AHH!
THE ONMYOJI COSTUME I GOT FOR 3980* YEN AT DONQUI!
GOOP
**NOT ACTUALLY SOLD.
GOD DAMN IT...
Then again, not like I'd have much opportunity to wear it in the future.
*ABOUT $40 DOLLARS.
WHAT IN THE WORLD IS WITH ALL THESE FLIES?
IT'S LIKE I CRAWLED INTO AN INSECT HORROR MOVIE FROM THE SEVENTIES!
AND NOW THAT I THINK ABOUT IT, IS IT REALLY NORMAL FOR A YOUNG WOMAN LIKE ME TO STAY SANE IN THIS KINDA SITUATION?!

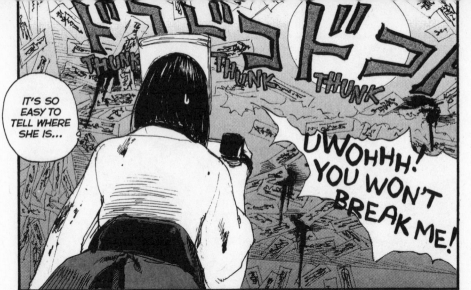

THUNK
THUNK
THUNK
UWOHHH! YOU WON'T BREAK ME!
IT'S SO EASY TO TELL WHERE SHE IS...
WHRR
WHRRRRR
...
THIS SOUND...
WHRR
I HEARD IT BEFORE THE ROTTING JUICES STARTED DRIP-PING.
MEAN-ING...
!
SHHH

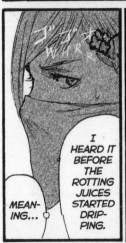

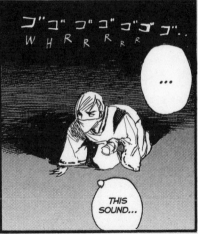

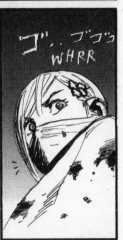

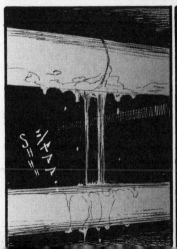

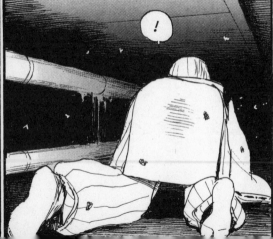

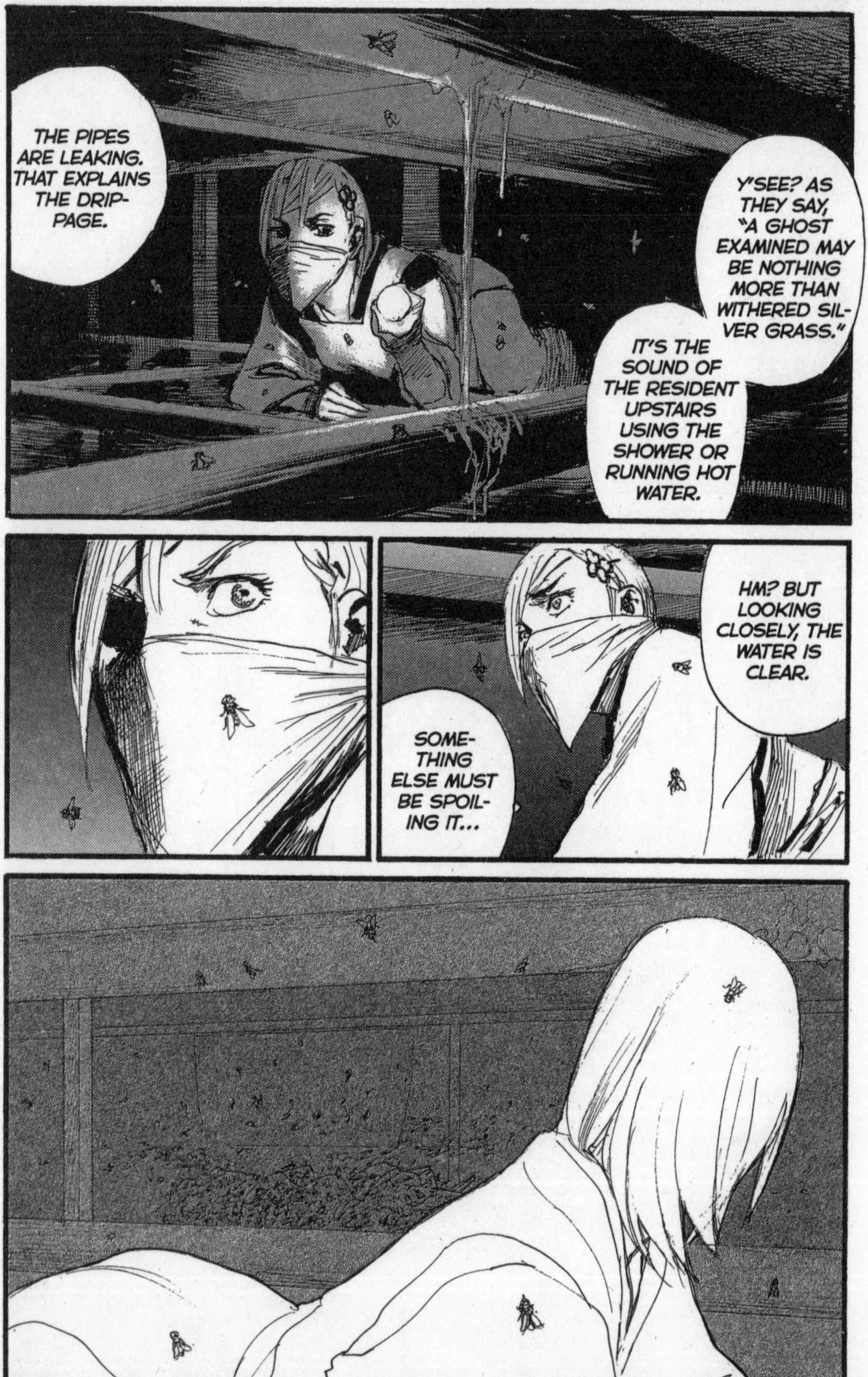
THE PIPES ARE LEAKING. THAT EXPLAINS THE DRIP-PAGE.
IT'S THE SOUND OF THE RESIDENT UPSTAIRS USING THE SHOWER OR RUNNING HOT WATER.
Y'SEE? AS THEY SAY, "A GHOST EXAMINED MAY BE NOTHING MORE THAN WITHERED SIL-VER GRASS."
HM? BUT LOOKING CLOSELY, THE WATER IS CLEAR.
SOME-THING ELSE MUST BE SPOIL-ING IT...

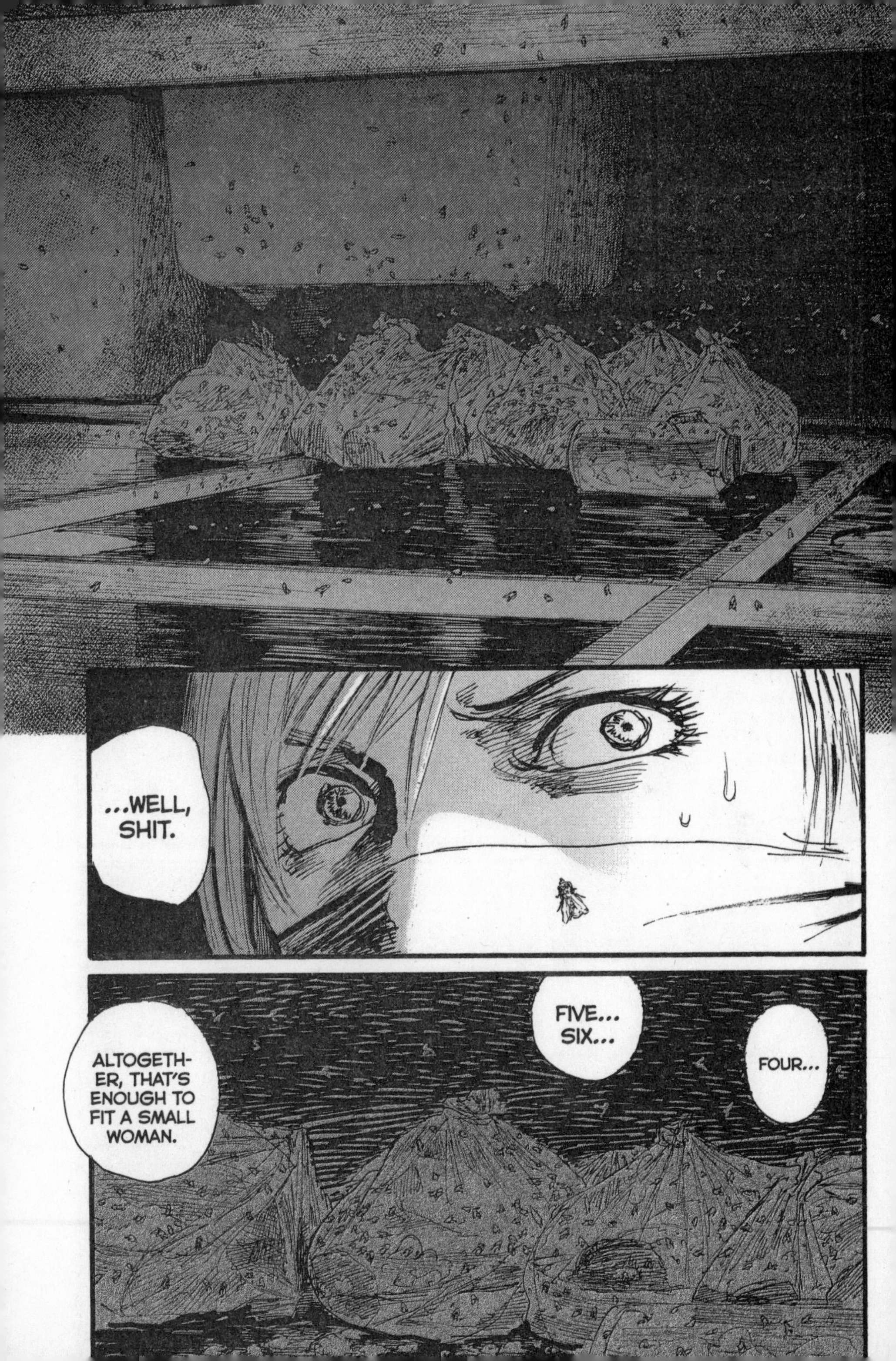
...WELL, SHIT.
FOUR...
FIVE... SIX...
ALTOGETH-ER, THAT'S ENOUGH TO FIT A SMALL WOMAN.

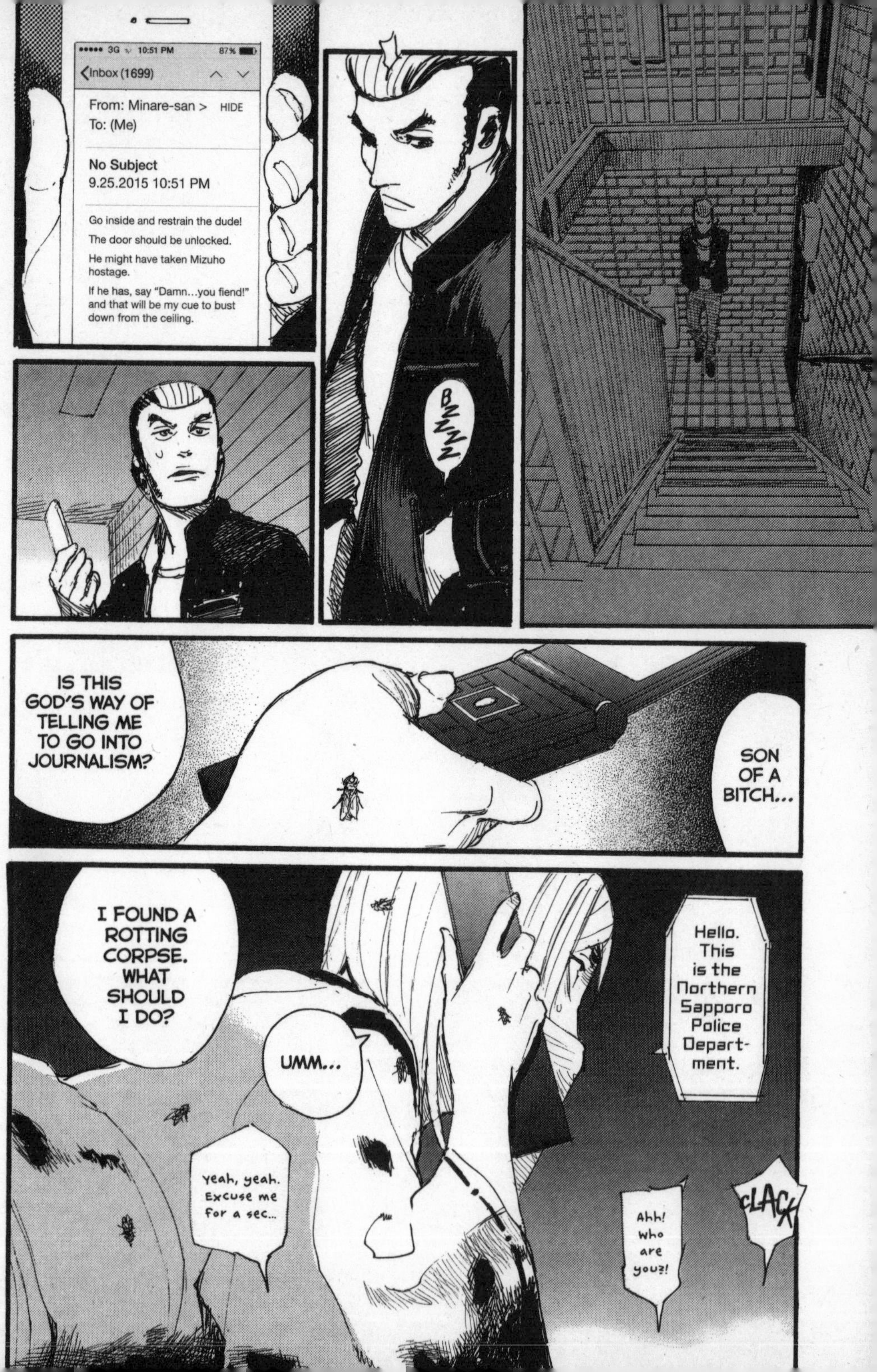
BZZZ
3G 10:51 PM 87%
Inbox (1699)
From: Minare-san > HIDE
To: (Me)
No Subject
9.25.2015 10:51 PM
Go inside and restrain the dude!
The door should be unlocked.
He might have taken Mizuho hostage.
If he has, say "Damn…you fiend!" and that will be my cue to bust down from the ceiling.
SON OF A BITCH...
IS THIS GOD'S WAY OF TELLING ME TO GO INTO JOURNALISM?
Hello. This is the Northern Sapporo Police Depart-ment.
I FOUND A ROTTING CORPSE. WHAT SHOULD I DO?
UMM...
CLACK
Ahh! Who are you?!
Yeah, yeah. Excuse me for a sec...

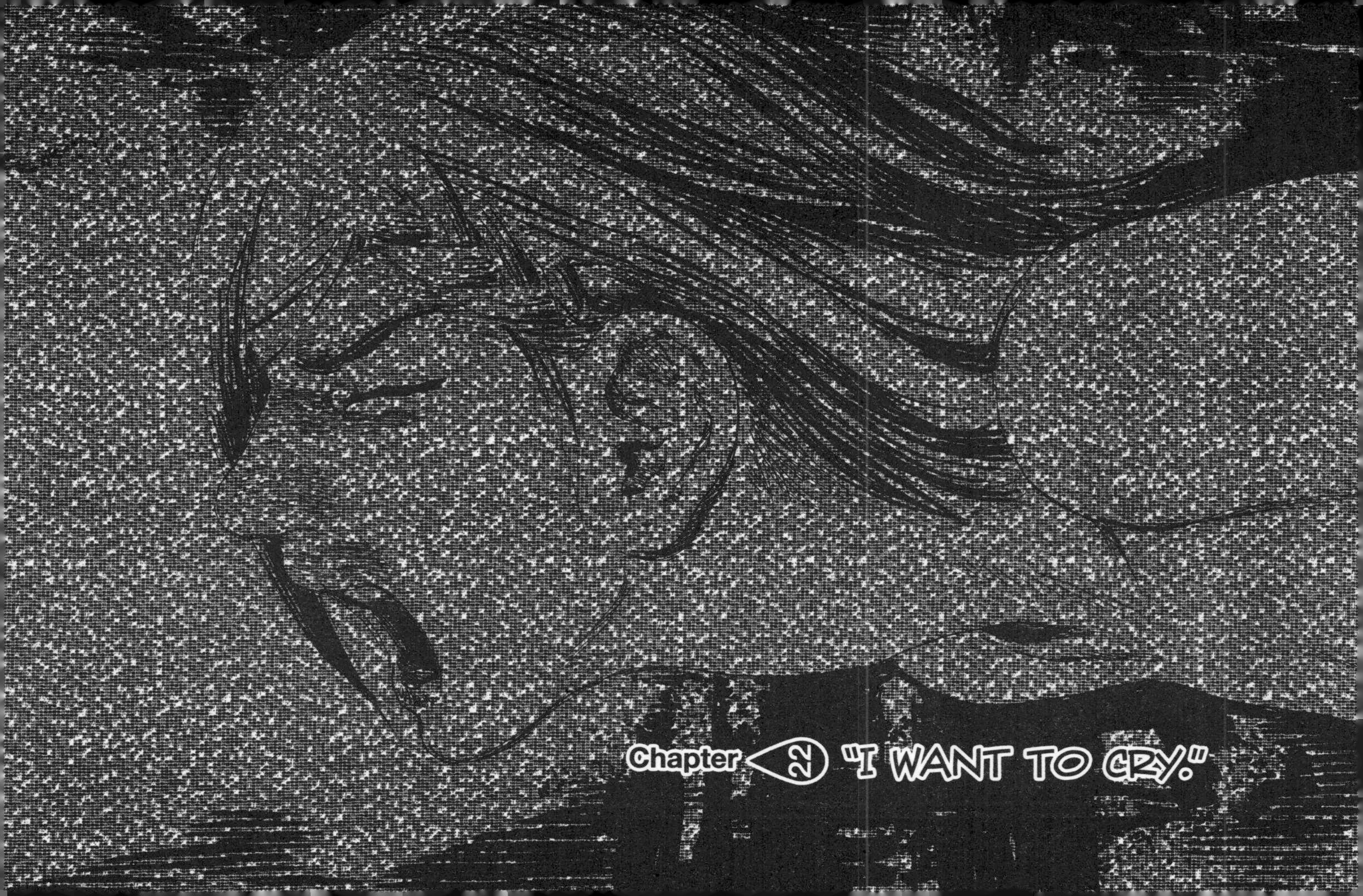
Chapter 22 "I WANT TO CRY."

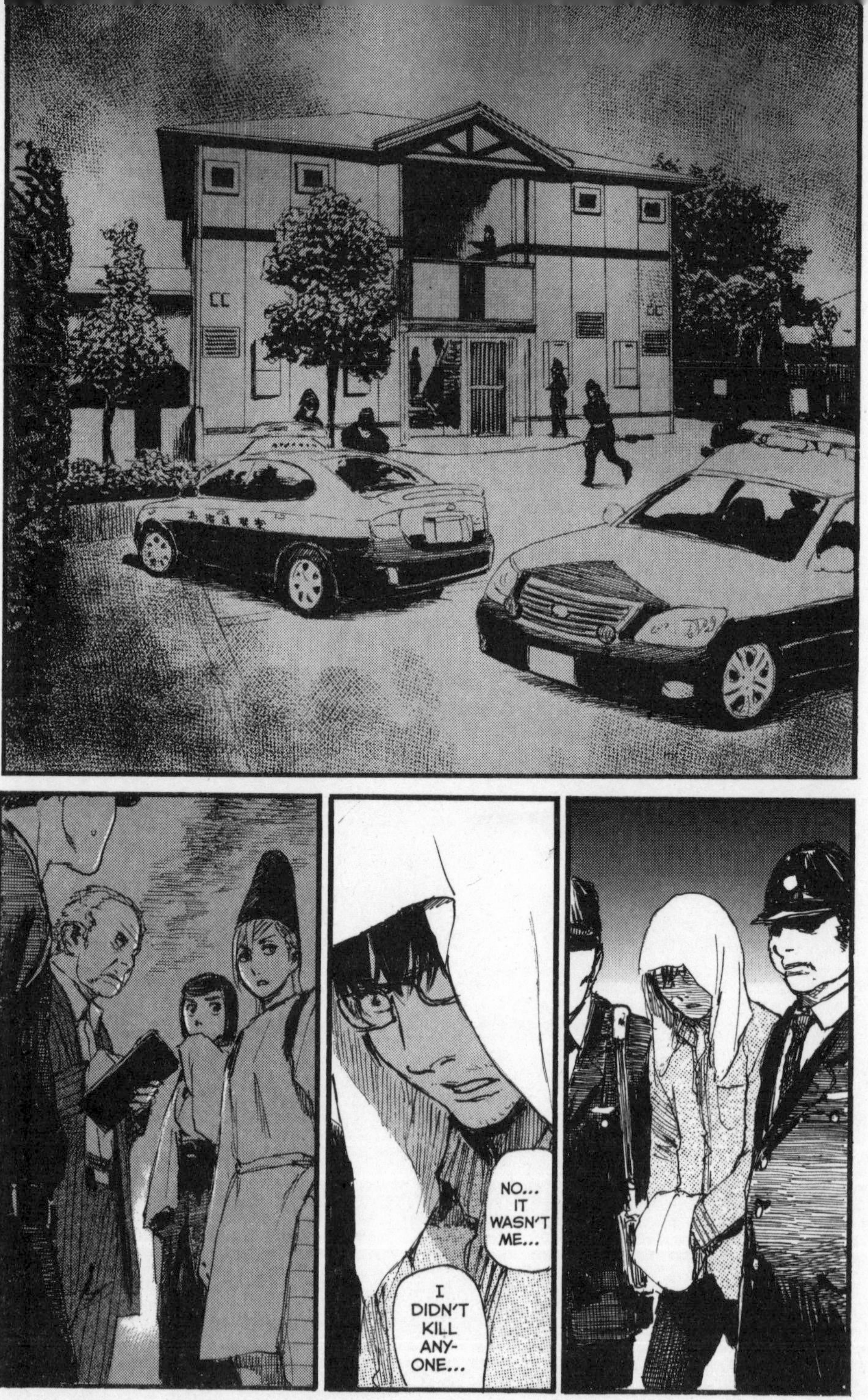
NO... IT WASN'T ME...
I DIDN'T KILL ANY-ONE...

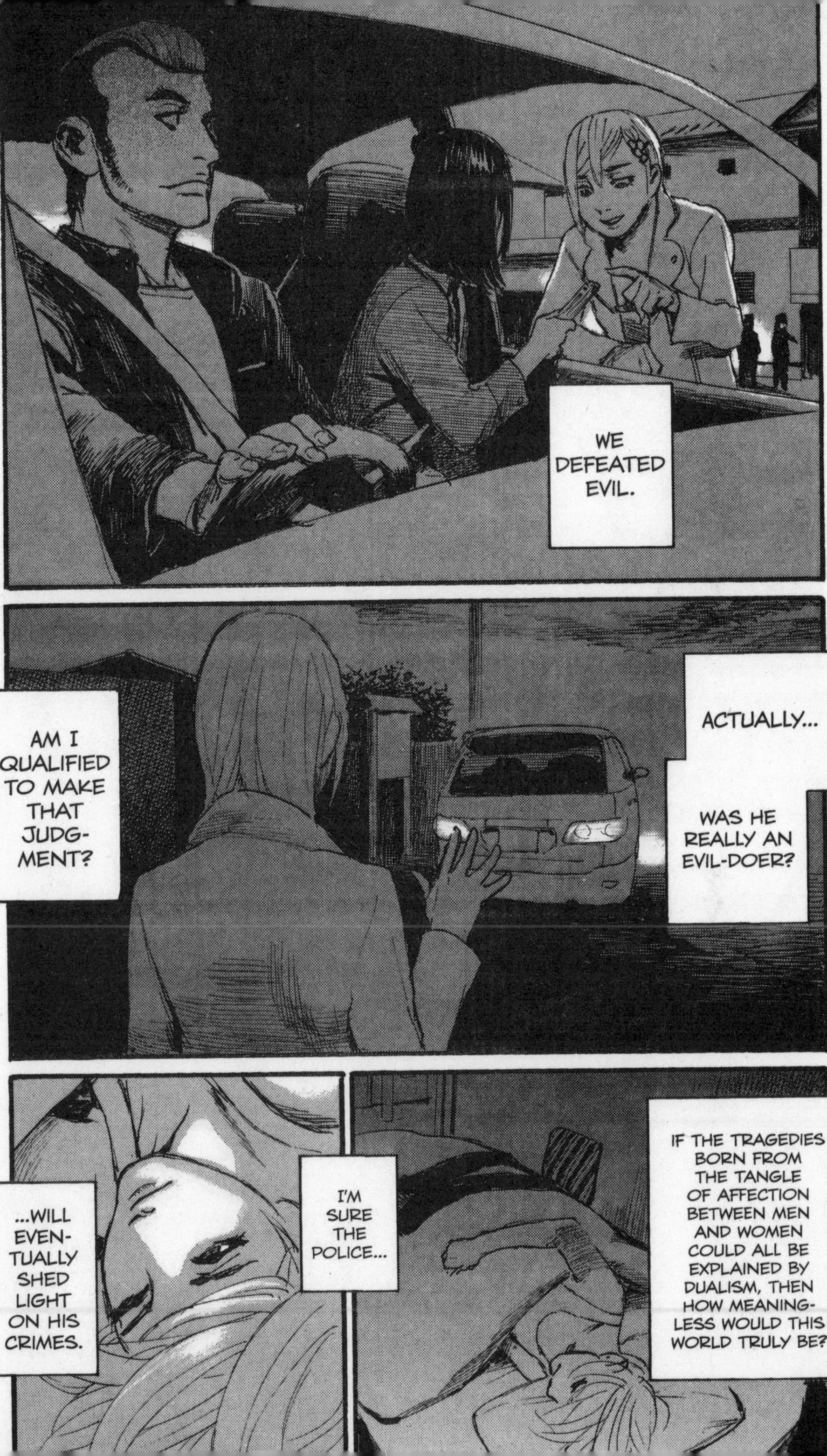
WE DEFEATED EVIL.
ACTUALLY...
WAS HE REALLY AN EVIL-DOER?
AM I QUALIFIED TO MAKE THAT JUDGMENT?
IF THE TRAGEDIES BORN FROM THE TANGLE OF AFFECTION BETWEEN MEN AND WOMEN COULD ALL BE EXPLAINED BY DUALISM, THEN HOW MEANINGLESS WOULD THIS WORLD TRULY BE?
I'M SURE THE POLICE...
...WILL EVENTUALLY SHED LIGHT ON HIS CRIMES.

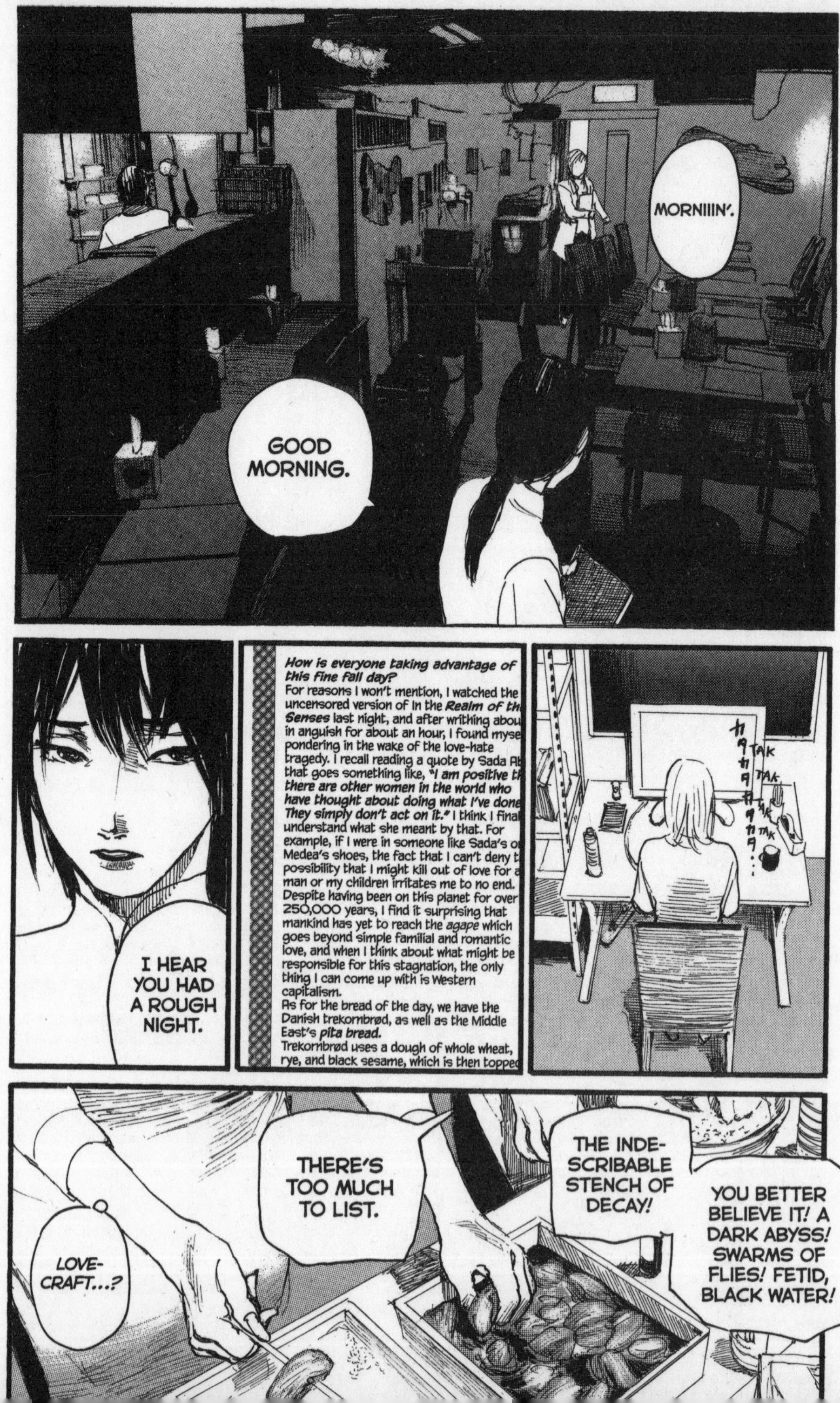
MORNIIIN'.
GOOD MORNING.
カタ TAK
カタ TAK
カタ TAK
カタ TAK
カタ...
How is everyone taking advantage of this fine fall day?
For reasons I won't mention, I watched the uncensored version of In the Realm of th Senses last night, and after writing abou in anguish for about an hour, I found myse pondering in the wake of the love-hate tragedy. I recall reading a quote by Sada Ab that goes something like, "I am positive th there are other women in the world who have thought about doing what I've done They simply don't act on it." I think I fina understand what she meant by that. For example, if I were in someone like Sada's o Medea's shoes, the fact that I can't deny t possibility that I might kill out of love for a man or my children irritates me to no end. Despite having been on this planet for over 250,000 years, I find it surprising that mankind has yet to reach the agape which goes beyond simple familial and romantic love, and when I think about what might be responsible for this stagnation, the only thing I can come up with is Western capitalism.
As for the bread of the day, we have the Danish trekornbrød, as well as the Middle East's pita bread.
Trekornbrød uses a dough of whole wheat, rye, and black sesame, which is then toppe
I HEAR YOU HAD A ROUGH NIGHT.
YOU BETTER BELIEVE IT! A DARK ABYSS! SWARMS OF FLIES! FETID, BLACK WATER!
THE INDE-SCRIBABLE STENCH OF DECAY!
THERE'S TOO MUCH TO LIST.
LOVE-CRAFT...?

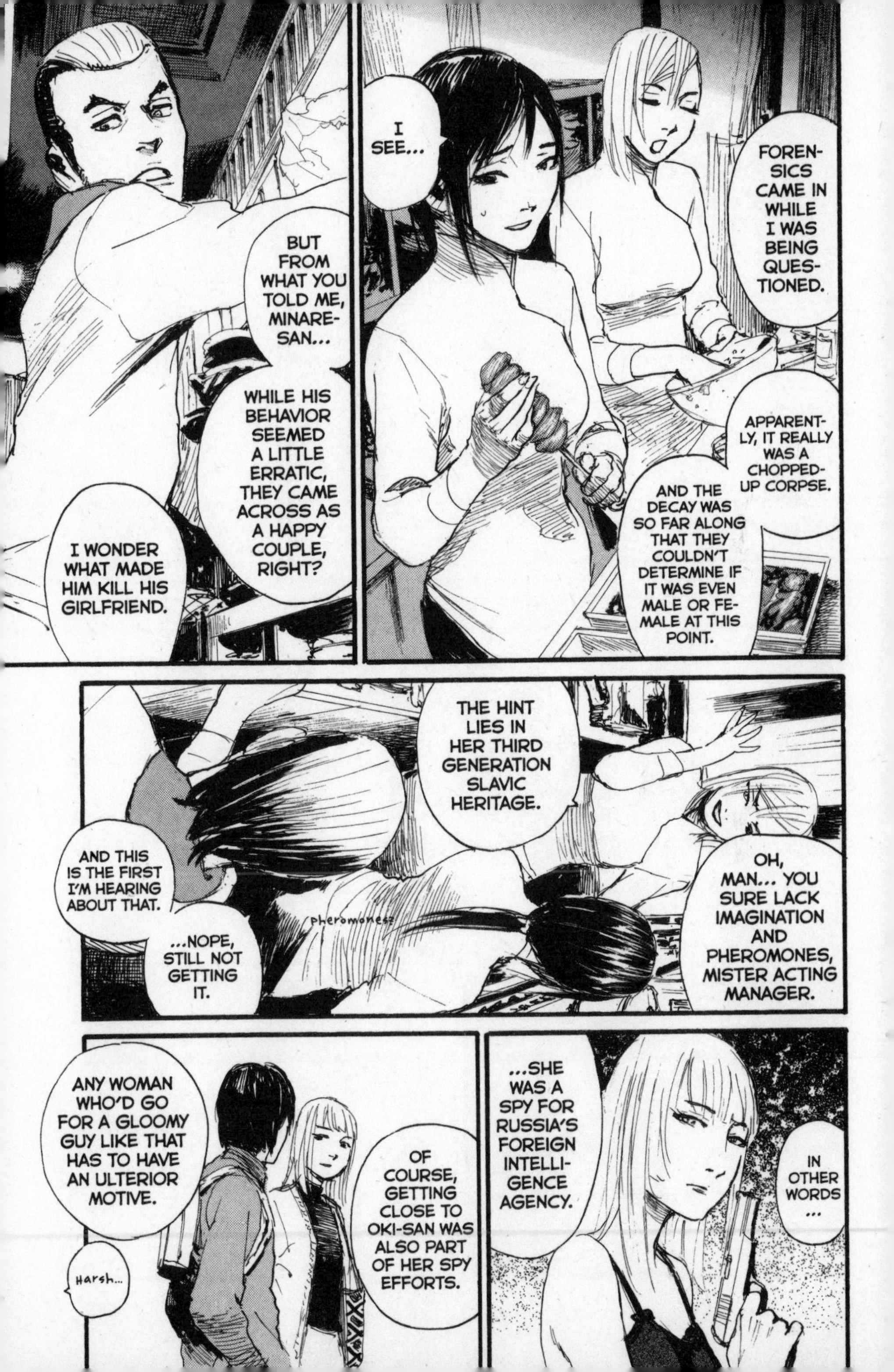
FORENSICS CAME IN WHILE I WAS BEING QUESTIONED.
I SEE...
APPARENTLY, IT REALLY WAS A CHOPPED-UP CORPSE.
AND THE DECAY WAS SO FAR ALONG THAT THEY COULDN'T DETERMINE IF IT WAS EVEN MALE OR FEMALE AT THIS POINT.
BUT FROM WHAT YOU TOLD ME, MINARE-SAN...
WHILE HIS BEHAVIOR SEEMED A LITTLE ERRATIC, THEY CAME ACROSS AS A HAPPY COUPLE, RIGHT?
I WONDER WHAT MADE HIM KILL HIS GIRLFRIEND.
THE HINT LIES IN HER THIRD GENERATION SLAVIC HERITAGE.
OH, MAN... YOU SURE LACK IMAGINATION AND PHEROMONES, MISTER ACTING MANAGER.
AND THIS IS THE FIRST I'M HEARING ABOUT THAT.
pheromones?
...NOPE, STILL NOT GETTING IT.
IN OTHER WORDS...
...SHE WAS A SPY FOR RUSSIA'S FOREIGN INTELLIGENCE AGENCY.
OF COURSE, GETTING CLOSE TO OKI-SAN WAS ALSO PART OF HER SPY EFFORTS.
ANY WOMAN WHO'D GO FOR A GLOOMY GUY LIKE THAT HAS TO HAVE AN ULTERIOR MOTIVE.
Harsh...

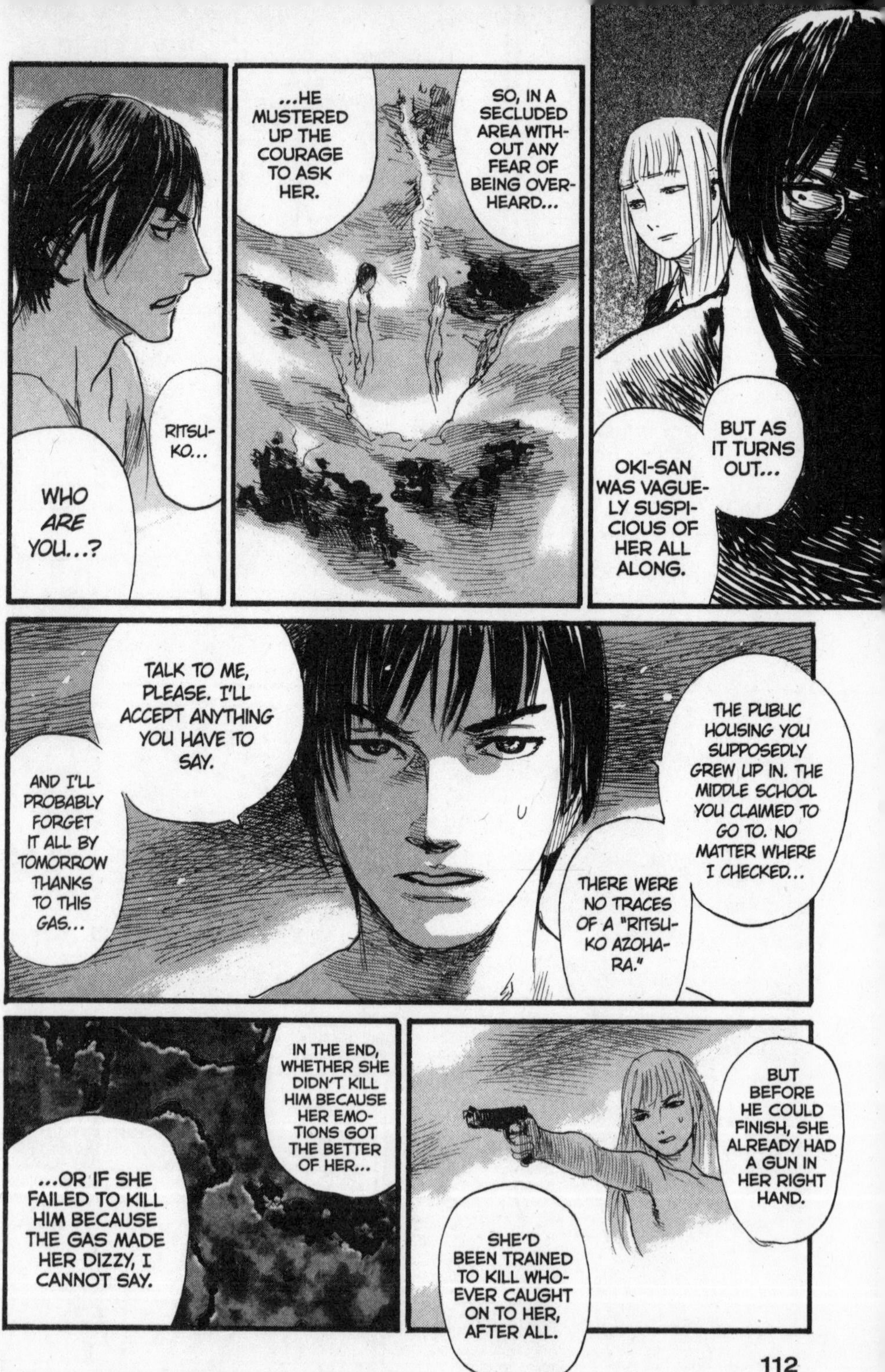

BUT AS IT TURNS OUT...
OKI-SAN WAS VAGUELY SUSPICIOUS OF HER ALL ALONG.
SO, IN A SECLUDED AREA WITHOUT ANY FEAR OF BEING OVERHEARD...
...HE MUSTERED UP THE COURAGE TO ASK HER.
RITSUKO...
WHO *ARE* YOU...?
THE PUBLIC HOUSING YOU SUPPOSEDLY GREW UP IN. THE MIDDLE SCHOOL YOU CLAIMED TO GO TO. NO MATTER WHERE I CHECKED...
THERE WERE NO TRACES OF A "RITSUKO AZOHARA."
TALK TO ME, PLEASE. I'LL ACCEPT ANYTHING YOU HAVE TO SAY.
AND I'LL PROBABLY FORGET IT ALL BY TOMORROW THANKS TO THIS GAS...
BUT BEFORE HE COULD FINISH, SHE ALREADY HAD A GUN IN HER RIGHT HAND.
SHE'D BEEN TRAINED TO KILL WHOEVER CAUGHT ON TO HER, AFTER ALL.
IN THE END, WHETHER SHE DIDN'T KILL HIM BECAUSE HER EMOTIONS GOT THE BETTER OF HER...
...OR IF SHE FAILED TO KILL HIM BECAUSE THE GAS MADE HER DIZZY, I CANNOT SAY.

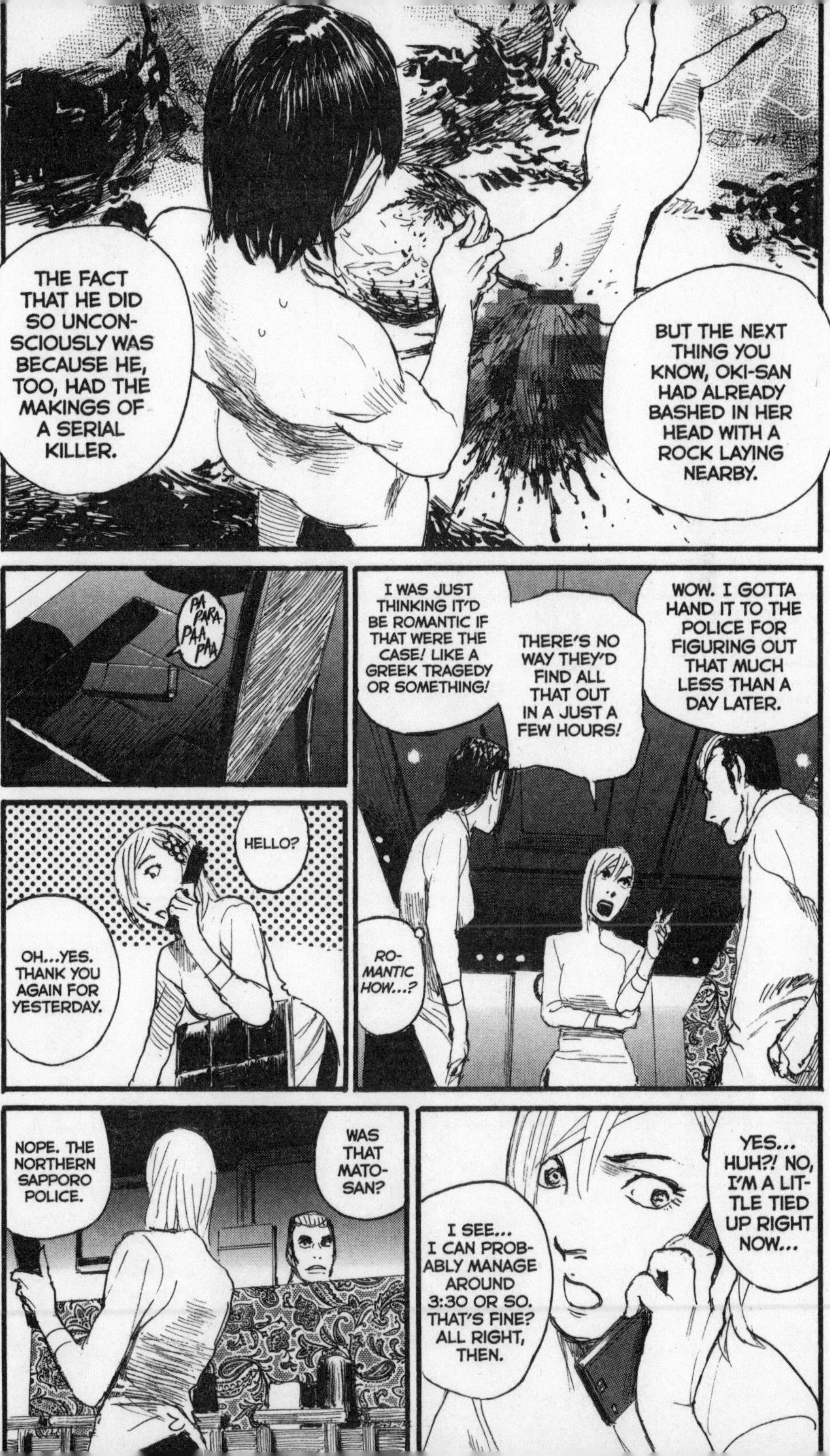
BUT THE NEXT THING YOU KNOW, OKI-SAN HAD ALREADY BASHED IN HER HEAD WITH A ROCK LAYING NEARBY.
THE FACT THAT HE DID SO UNCON-SCIOUSLY WAS BECAUSE HE, TOO, HAD THE MAKINGS OF A SERIAL KILLER.
WOW. I GOTTA HAND IT TO THE POLICE FOR FIGURING OUT THAT MUCH LESS THAN A DAY LATER.
THERE'S NO WAY THEY'D FIND ALL THAT OUT IN A JUST A FEW HOURS!
I WAS JUST THINKING IT'D BE ROMANTIC IF THAT WERE THE CASE! LIKE A GREEK TRAGEDY OR SOMETHING!
RO-MANTIC HOW...?
PA PARA PAA PAA
HELLO?
OH...YES. THANK YOU AGAIN FOR YESTERDAY.
YES... HUH?! NO, I'M A LIT-TLE TIED UP RIGHT NOW...
I SEE... I CAN PROB-ABLY MANAGE AROUND 3:30 OR SO. THAT'S FINE? ALL RIGHT, THEN.
WAS THAT MATO-SAN?
NOPE. THE NORTHERN SAPPORO POLICE.

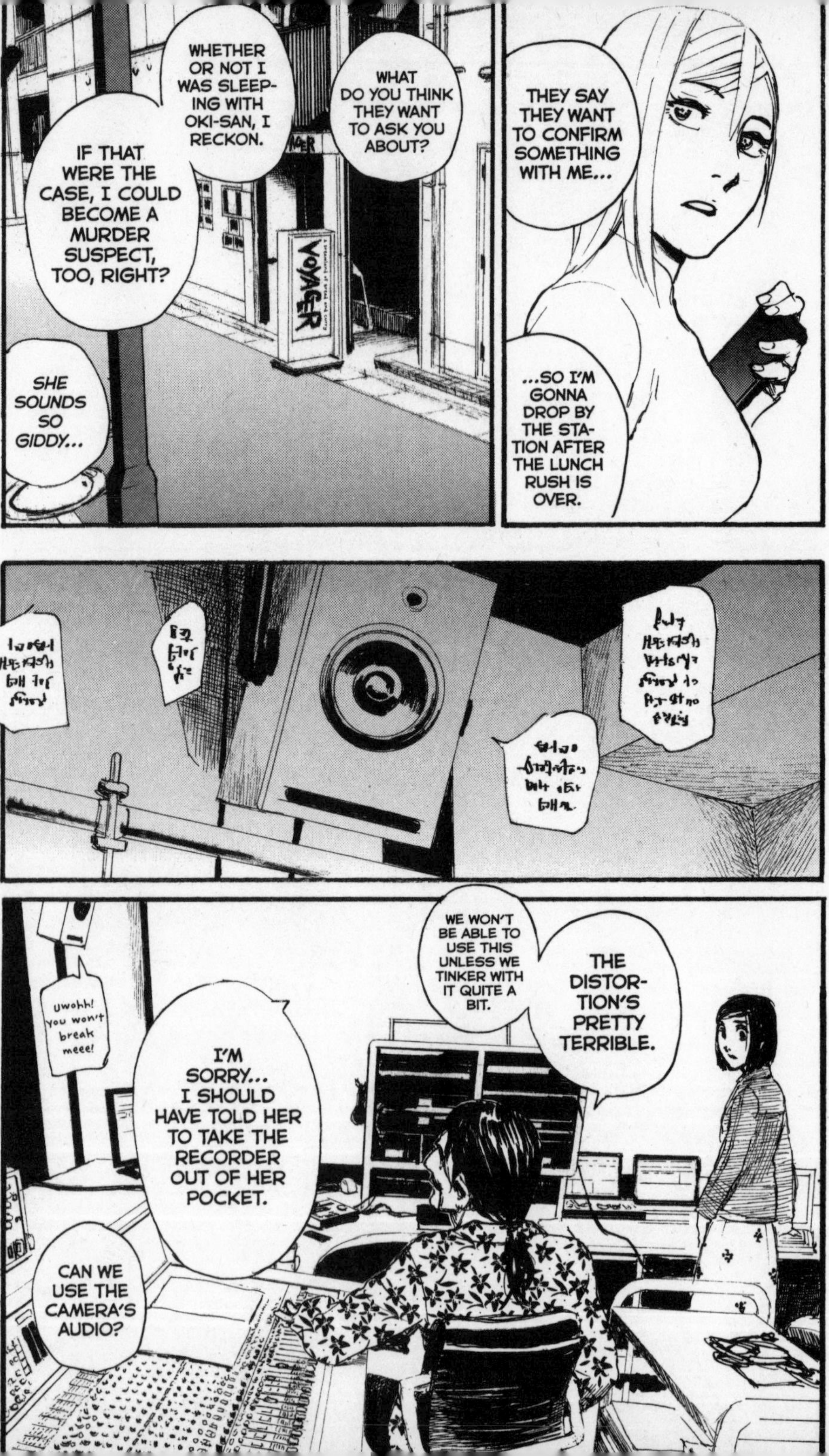
THEY SAY THEY WANT TO CONFIRM SOMETHING WITH ME...
...SO I'M GONNA DROP BY THE STATION AFTER THE LUNCH RUSH IS OVER.
WHAT DO YOU THINK THEY WANT TO ASK YOU ABOUT?
WHETHER OR NOT I WAS SLEEPING WITH OKI-SAN, I RECKON.
IF THAT WERE THE CASE, I COULD BECOME A MURDER SUSPECT, TOO, RIGHT?
VOYAGER
SHE SOUNDS SO GIDDY...
THE DISTORTION'S PRETTY TERRIBLE.
WE WON'T BE ABLE TO USE THIS UNLESS WE TINKER WITH IT QUITE A BIT.
I'M SORRY... I SHOULD HAVE TOLD HER TO TAKE THE RECORDER OUT OF HER POCKET.
Uwohh! You won't break meee!
CAN WE USE THE CAMERA'S AUDIO?

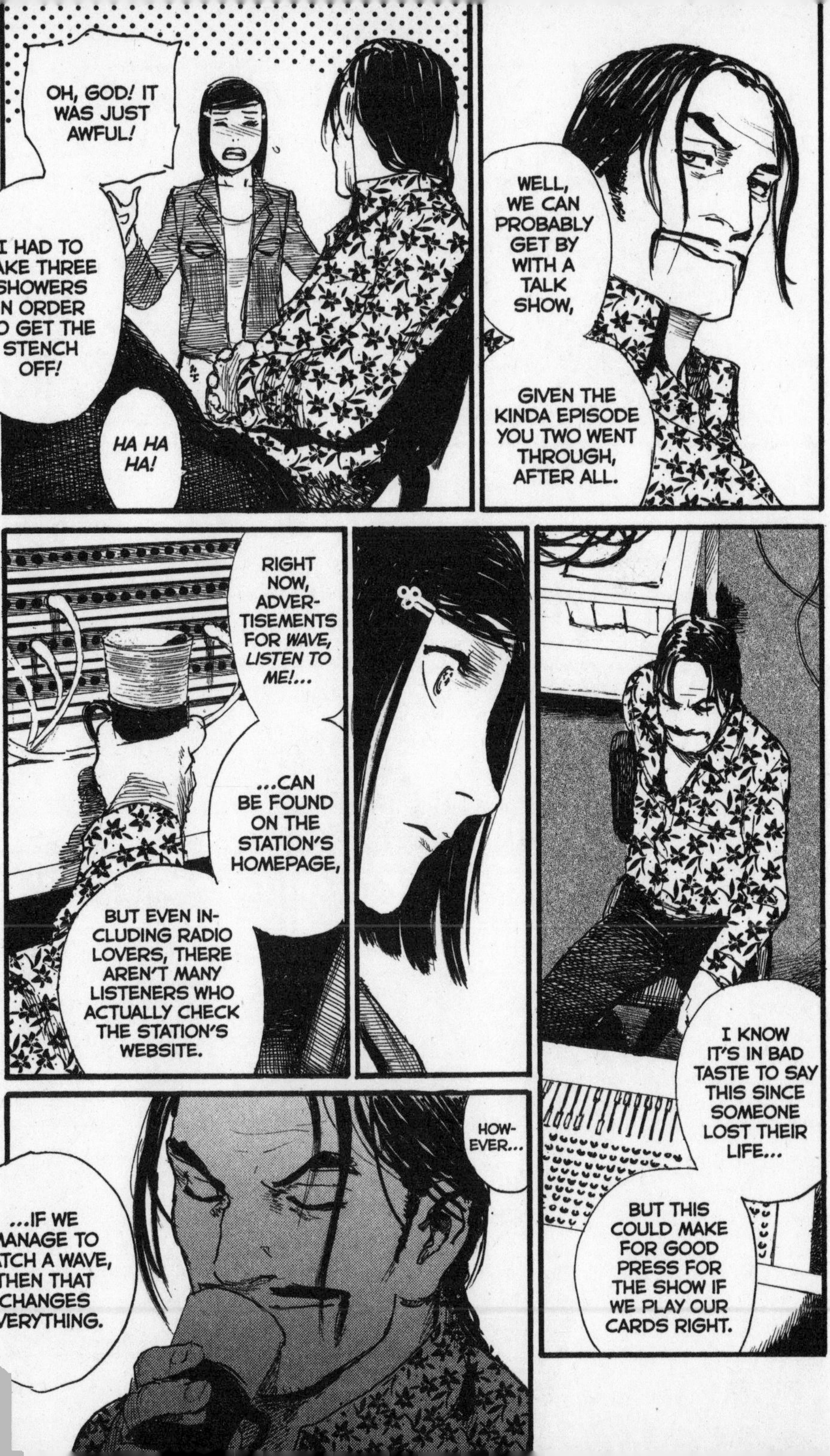
WELL, WE CAN PROBABLY GET BY WITH A TALK SHOW,
GIVEN THE KINDA EPISODE YOU TWO WENT THROUGH, AFTER ALL.
OH, GOD! IT WAS JUST AWFUL!
I HAD TO TAKE THREE SHOWERS IN ORDER TO GET THE STENCH OFF!
HA HA HA!
I KNOW IT'S IN BAD TASTE TO SAY THIS SINCE SOMEONE LOST THEIR LIFE...
BUT THIS COULD MAKE FOR GOOD PRESS FOR THE SHOW IF WE PLAY OUR CARDS RIGHT.
RIGHT NOW, ADVERTISEMENTS FOR *WAVE, LISTEN TO ME!*...
...CAN BE FOUND ON THE STATION'S HOMEPAGE,
BUT EVEN INCLUDING RADIO LOVERS, THERE AREN'T MANY LISTENERS WHO ACTUALLY CHECK THE STATION'S WEBSITE.
HOW-EVER...
...IF WE MANAGE TO CATCH A WAVE, THEN THAT CHANGES EVERYTHING.

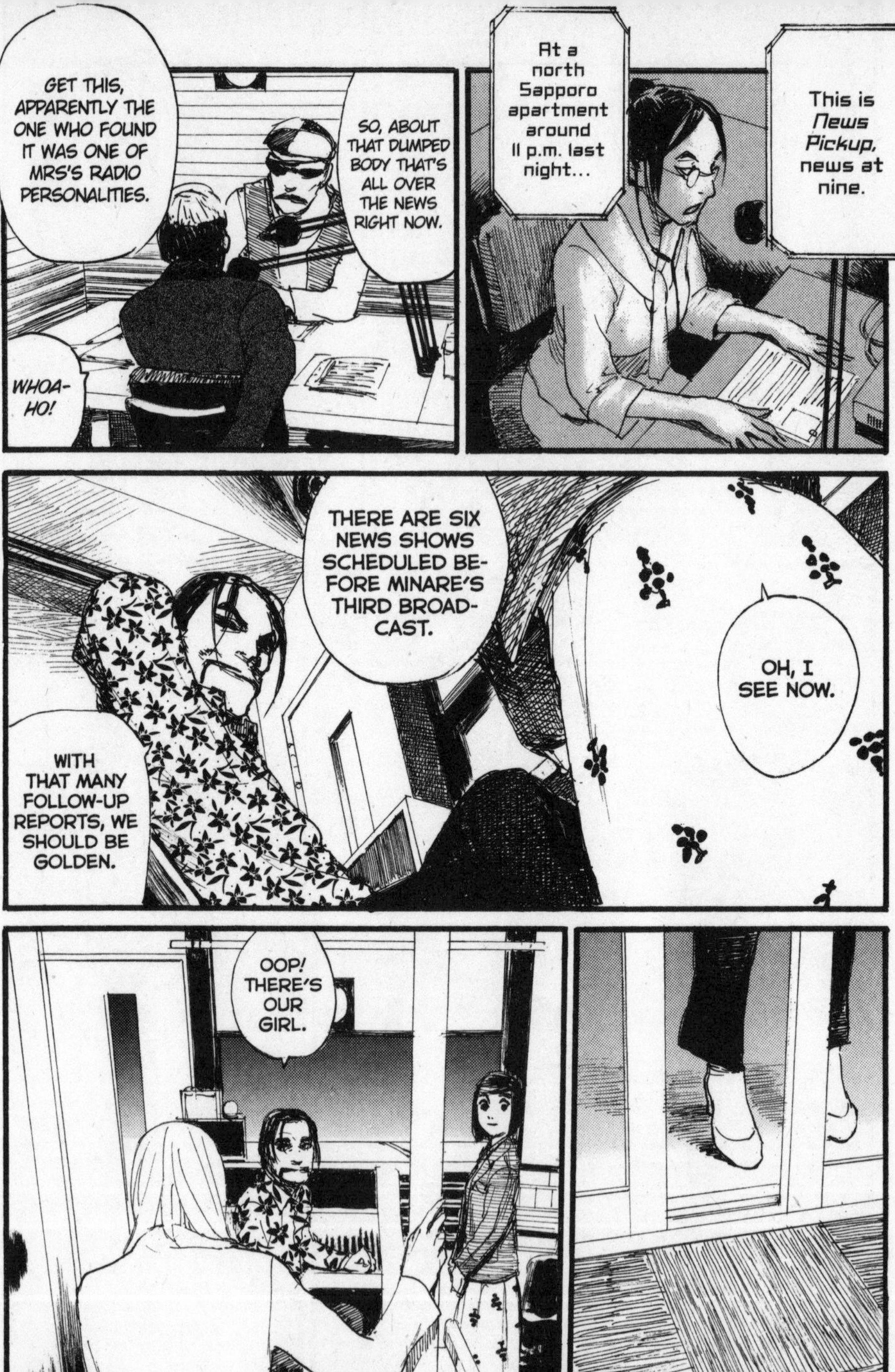
This is *News Pickup,* news at nine.
At a north Sapporo apartment around 11 p.m. last night…
SO, ABOUT THAT DUMPED BODY THAT'S ALL OVER THE NEWS RIGHT NOW.
GET THIS, APPARENTLY THE ONE WHO FOUND IT WAS ONE OF MRS'S RADIO PERSONALITIES.
WHOA-HO!
OH, I SEE NOW.
THERE ARE SIX NEWS SHOWS SCHEDULED BEFORE MINARE'S THIRD BROADCAST.
WITH THAT MANY FOLLOW-UP REPORTS, WE SHOULD BE GOLDEN.
OOP! THERE'S OUR GIRL.

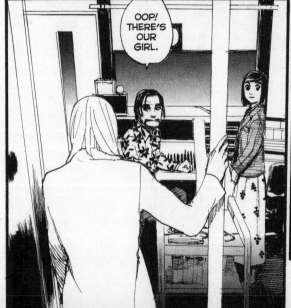

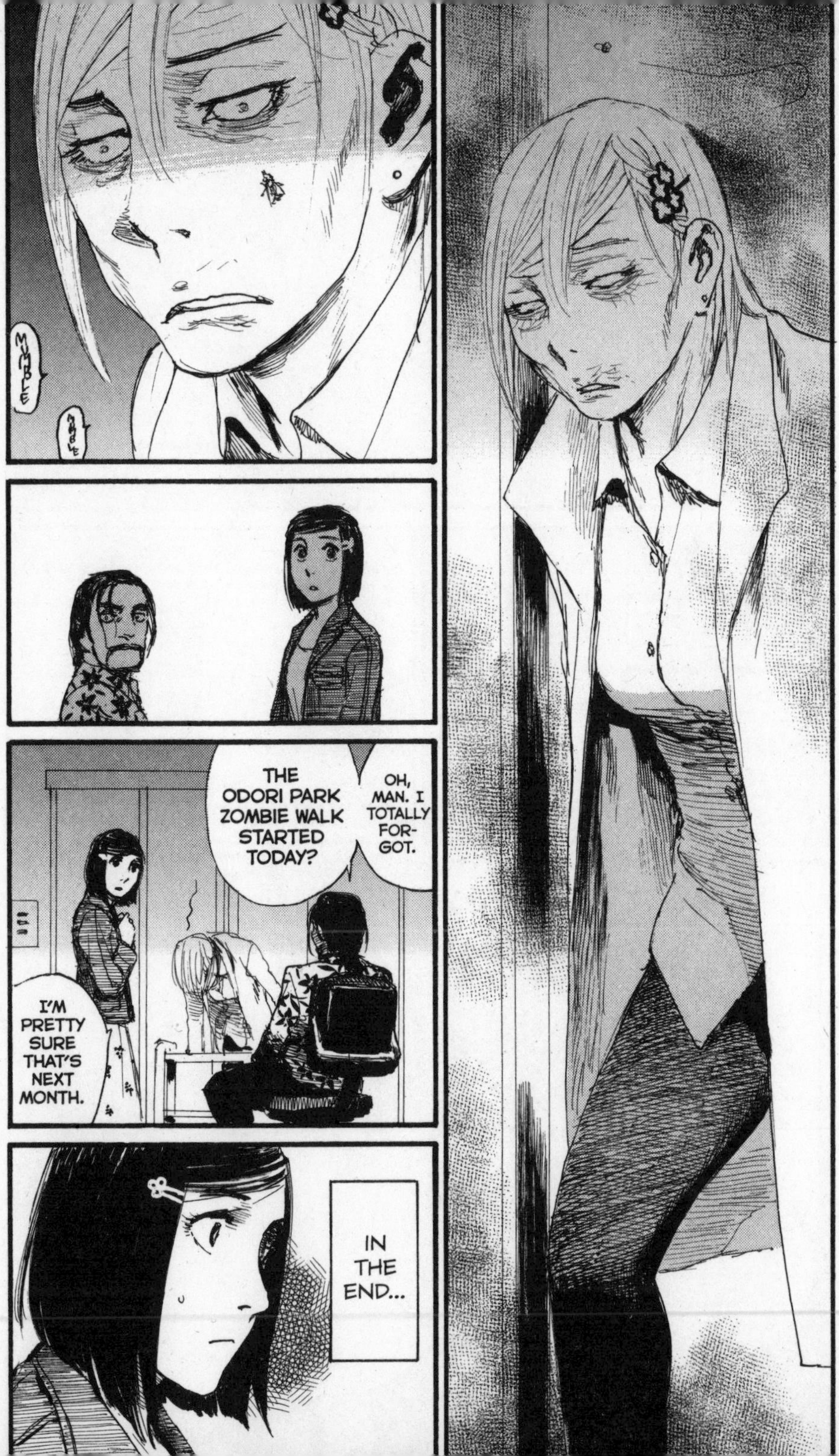
MUMBLE
MUMBLE
OH, MAN. I TOTALLY FORGOT.
THE ODORI PARK ZOMBIE WALK STARTED TODAY?
I'M PRETTY SURE THAT'S NEXT MONTH.
IN THE END...

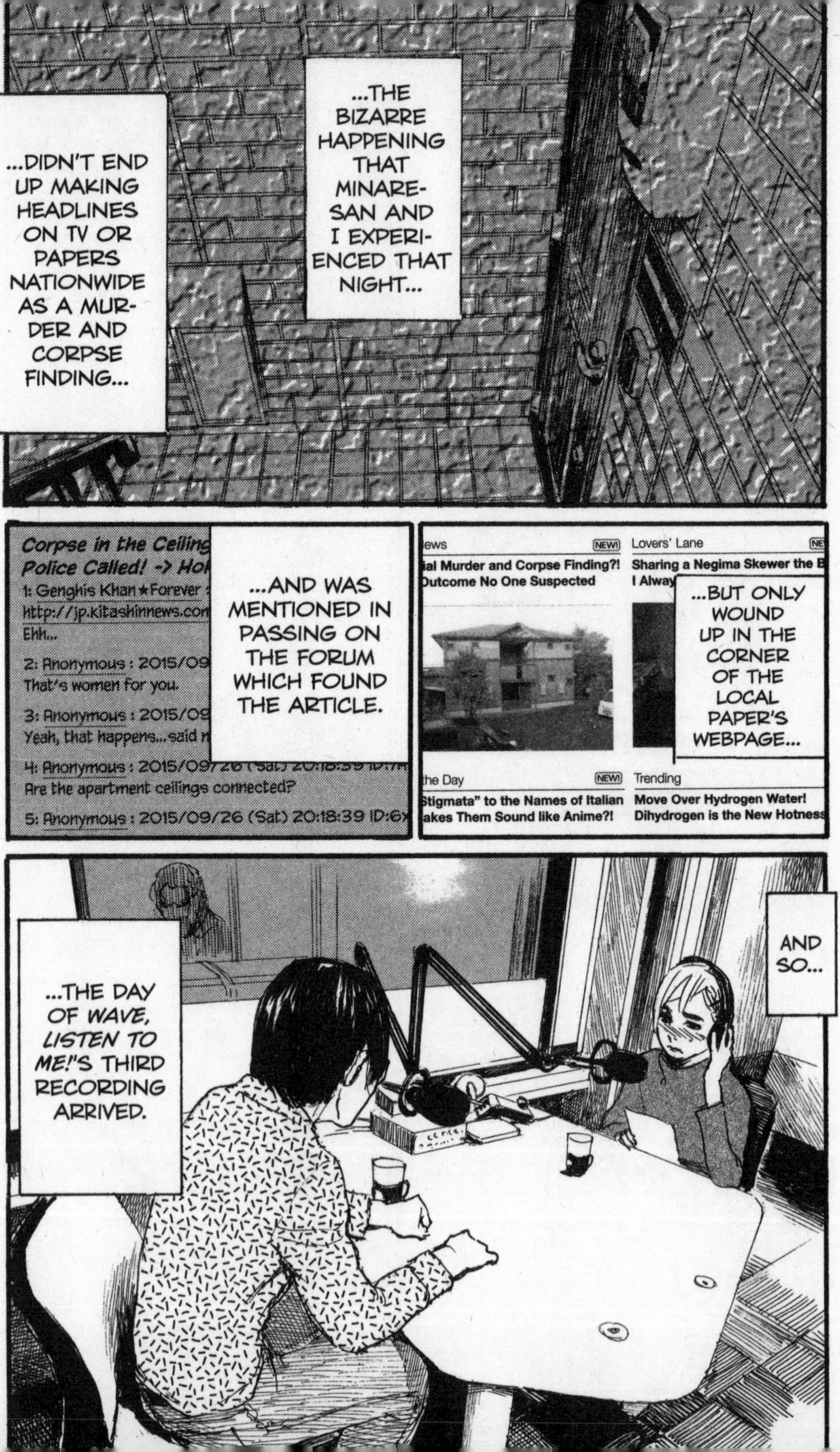
...THE BIZARRE HAPPENING THAT MINARE-SAN AND I EXPERIENCED THAT NIGHT...
...DIDN'T END UP MAKING HEADLINES ON TV OR PAPERS NATIONWIDE AS A MURDER AND CORPSE FINDING...
...BUT ONLY WOUND UP IN THE CORNER OF THE LOCAL PAPER'S WEBPAGE...
ews NEW!
ial Murder and Corpse Finding?!
Outcome No One Suspected
Lovers' Lane
Sharing a Negima Skewer the B
I Alway
the Day NEW!
Stigmata" to the Names of Italian
akes Them Sound like Anime?!
Trending
Move Over Hydrogen Water!
Dihydrogen is the New Hotness
...AND WAS MENTIONED IN PASSING ON THE FORUM WHICH FOUND THE ARTICLE.
Corpse in the Ceiling
Police Called! -> Ho
1: Genghis Khan★Forever
http://jp.kitashinnews.com
Ehh...
2: Anonymous : 2015/09
That's women for you.
3: Anonymous : 2015/09
Yeah, that happens...said
4: Anonymous : 2015/09/26 (Sat) 20:18:39
Are the apartment ceilings connected?
5: Anonymous : 2015/09/26 (Sat) 20:18:39 ID:6
AND SO...
...THE DAY OF WAVE, LISTEN TO ME!'S THIRD RECORDING ARRIVED.

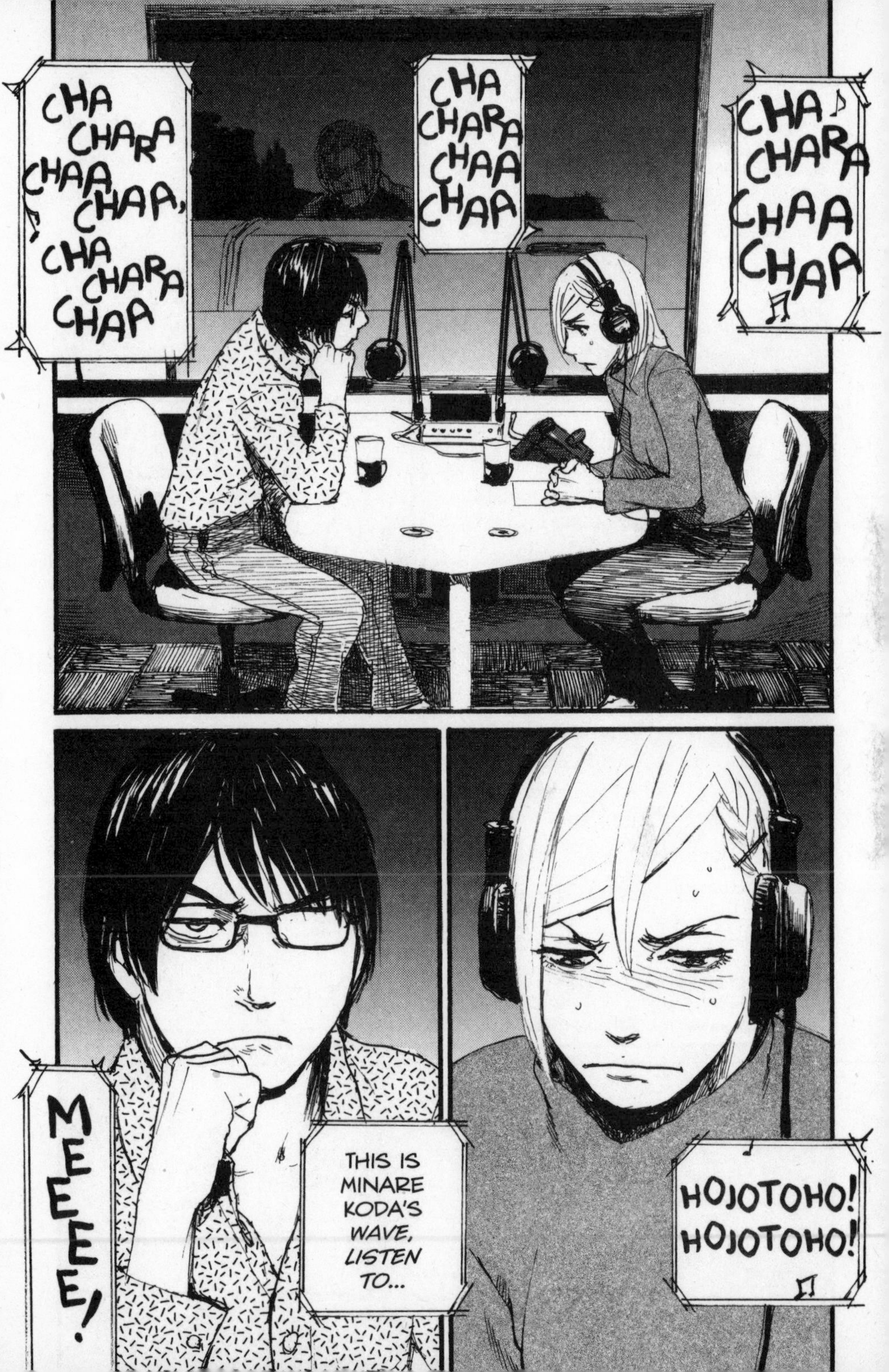
CHA CHARA CHAA CHAA
CHA CHARA CHAA CHAA
CHA CHARA CHAA CHAA, CHA CHARA CHAA
HOJOTOHO! HOJOTOHO!
THIS IS MINARE KODA'S WAVE, LISTEN TO...
MEEEEE!

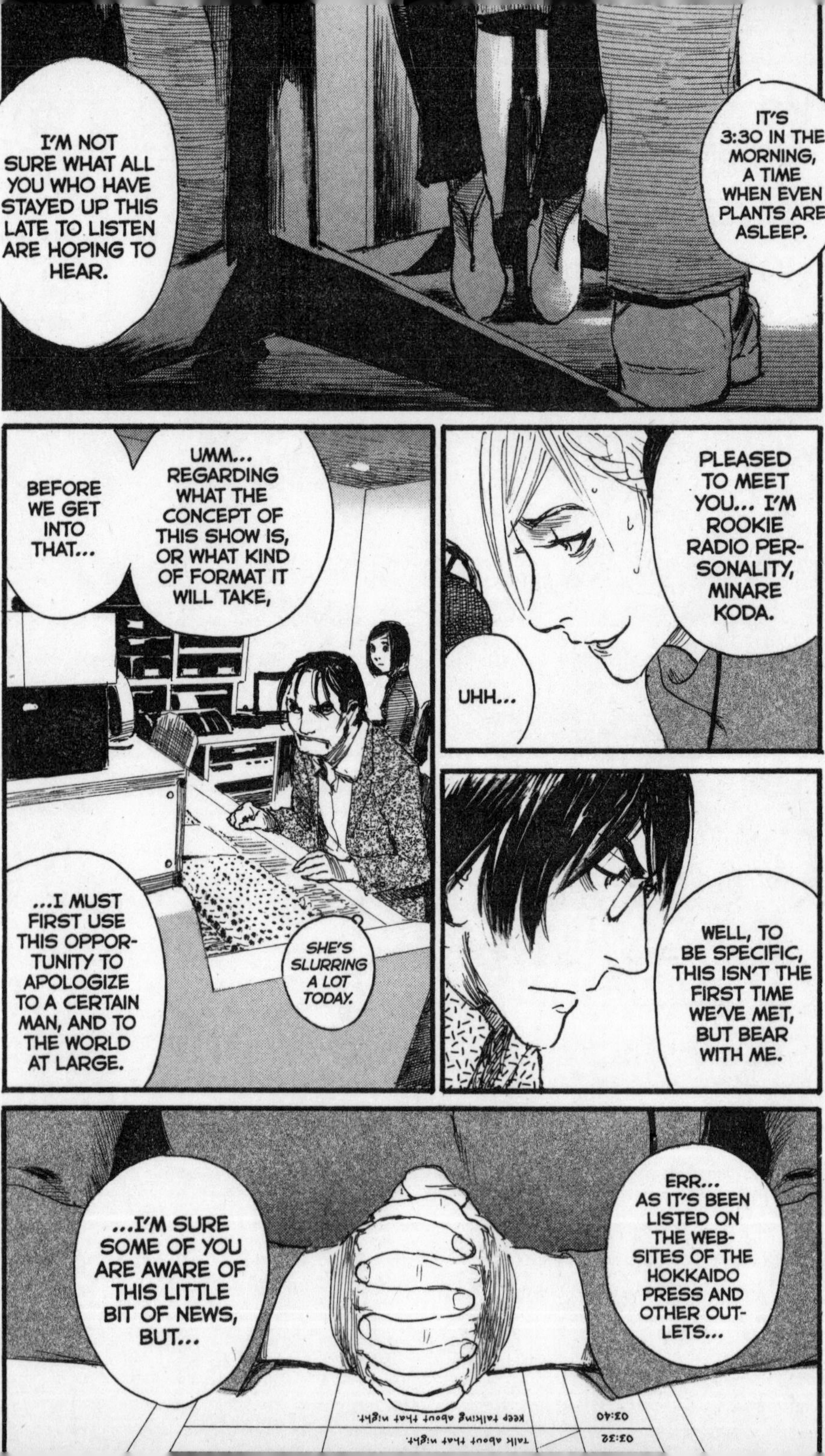
IT'S 3:30 IN THE MORNING, A TIME WHEN EVEN PLANTS ARE ASLEEP.
I'M NOT SURE WHAT ALL YOU WHO HAVE STAYED UP THIS LATE TO LISTEN ARE HOPING TO HEAR.
PLEASED TO MEET YOU... I'M ROOKIE RADIO PER-SONALITY, MINARE KODA.
UHH...
WELL, TO BE SPECIFIC, THIS ISN'T THE FIRST TIME WE'VE MET, BUT BEAR WITH ME.
UMM... REGARDING WHAT THE CONCEPT OF THIS SHOW IS, OR WHAT KIND OF FORMAT IT WILL TAKE,
BEFORE WE GET INTO THAT...
...I MUST FIRST USE THIS OPPOR-TUNITY TO APOLOGIZE TO A CERTAIN MAN, AND TO THE WORLD AT LARGE.
SHE'S SLURRING A LOT TODAY.
ERR... AS IT'S BEEN LISTED ON THE WEB-SITES OF THE HOKKAIDO PRESS AND OTHER OUT-LETS...
...I'M SURE SOME OF YOU ARE AWARE OF THIS LITTLE BIT OF NEWS, BUT...

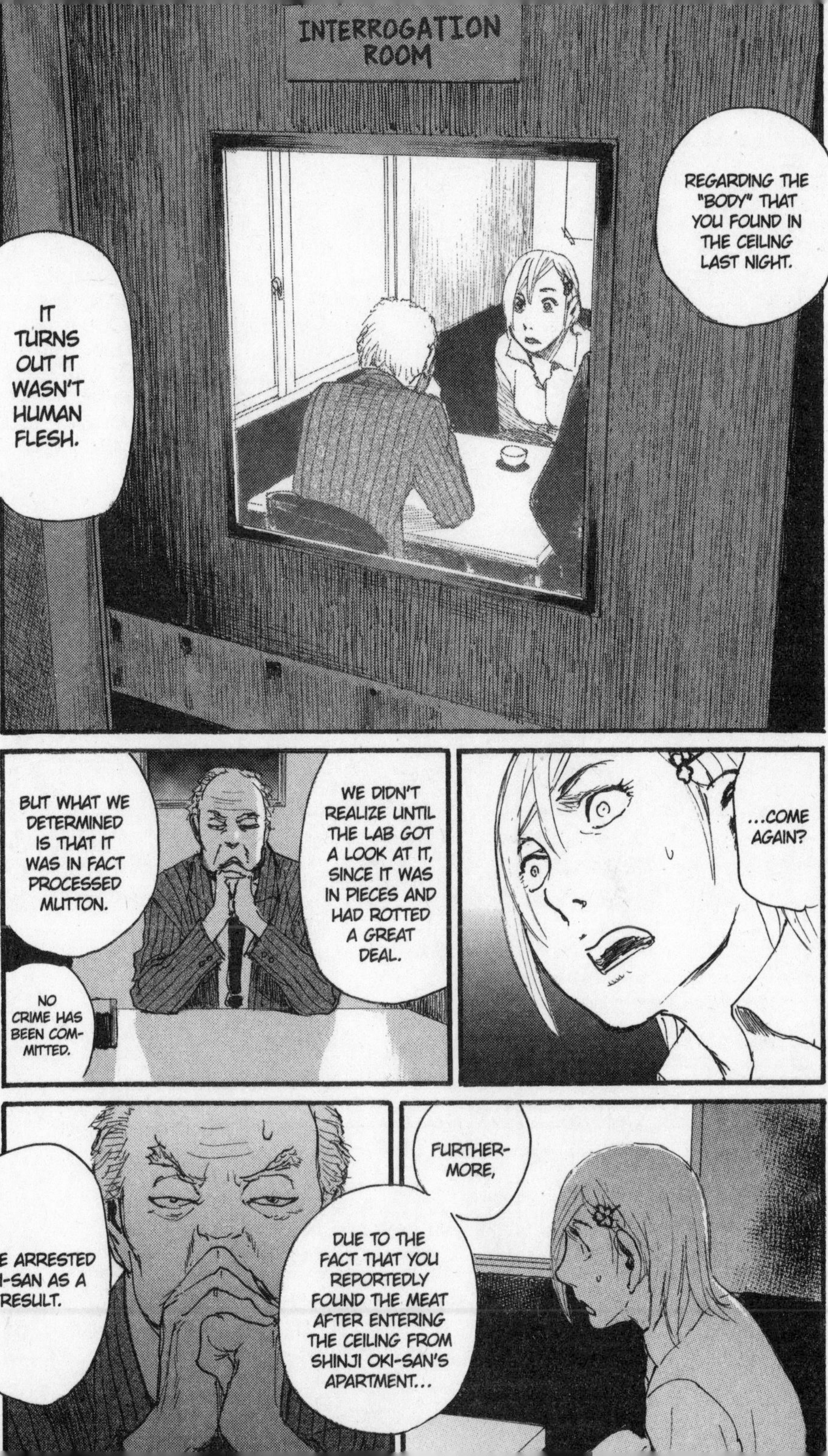
INTERROGATION ROOM
REGARDING THE "BODY" THAT YOU FOUND IN THE CEILING LAST NIGHT.
IT TURNS OUT IT WASN'T HUMAN FLESH.
...COME AGAIN?
WE DIDN'T REALIZE UNTIL THE LAB GOT A LOOK AT IT, SINCE IT WAS IN PIECES AND HAD ROTTED A GREAT DEAL.
BUT WHAT WE DETERMINED IS THAT IT WAS IN FACT PROCESSED MUTTON.
NO CRIME HAS BEEN COM-MITTED.
FURTHER-MORE,
DUE TO THE FACT THAT YOU REPORTEDLY FOUND THE MEAT AFTER ENTERING THE CEILING FROM SHINJI OKI-SAN'S APARTMENT...
...WE ARRESTED OKI-SAN AS A RESULT.

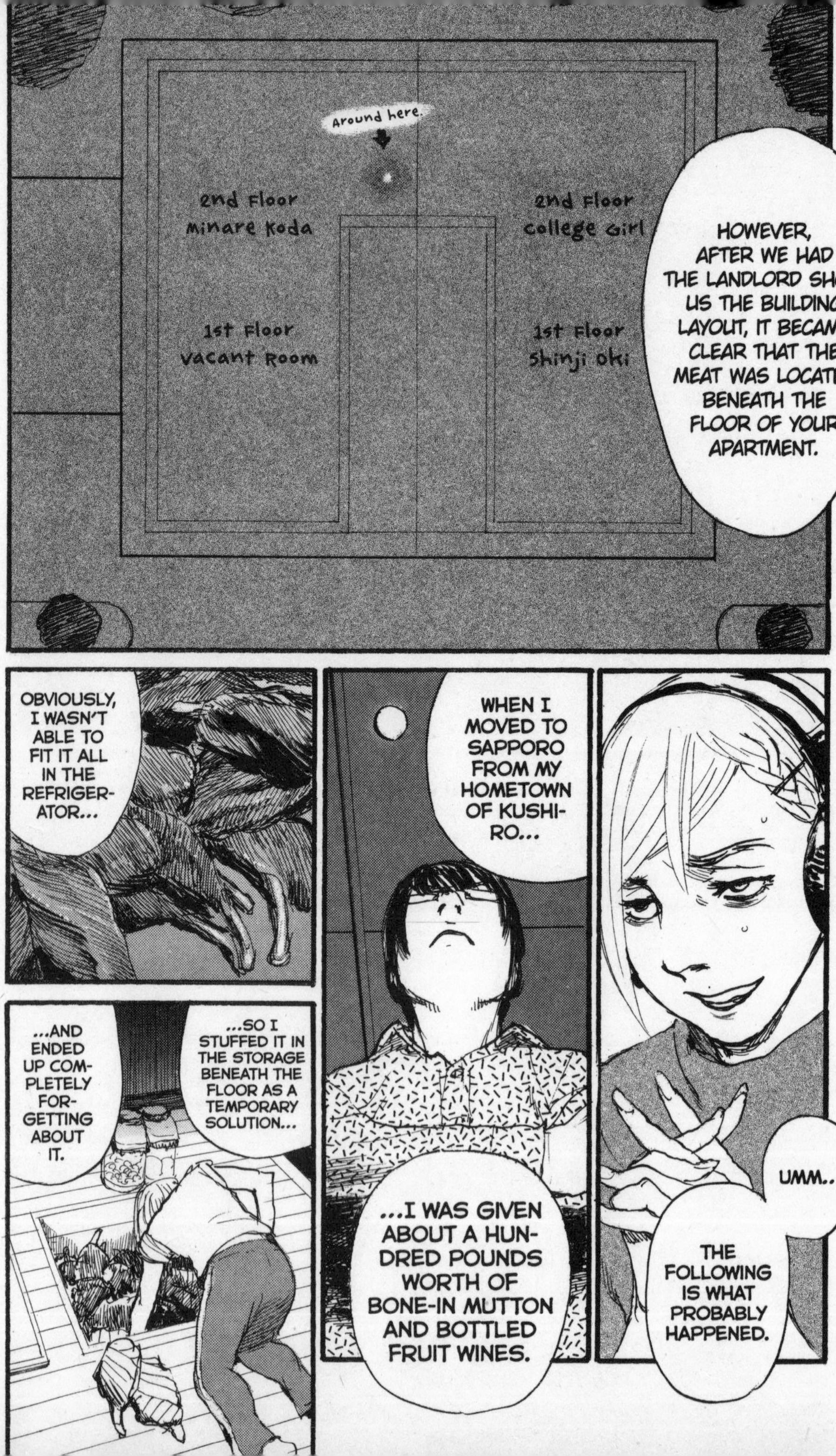

HOWEVER, AFTER WE HAD THE LANDLORD SHOW US THE BUILDING LAYOUT, IT BECAME CLEAR THAT THE MEAT WAS LOCATED BENEATH THE FLOOR OF YOUR APARTMENT.
Around here.
2nd Floor College Girl
2nd Floor Minare Koda
1st Floor Shinji Oki
1st Floor Vacant Room
UMM...
THE FOLLOWING IS WHAT PROBABLY HAPPENED.
WHEN I MOVED TO SAPPORO FROM MY HOMETOWN OF KUSHI-RO...
...I WAS GIVEN ABOUT A HUN-DRED POUNDS WORTH OF BONE-IN MUTTON AND BOTTLED FRUIT WINES.
OBVIOUSLY, I WASN'T ABLE TO FIT IT ALL IN THE REFRIGER-ATOR...
...SO I STUFFED IT IN THE STORAGE BENEATH THE FLOOR AS A TEMPORARY SOLUTION...
...AND ENDED UP COM-PLETELY FOR-GETTING ABOUT IT.

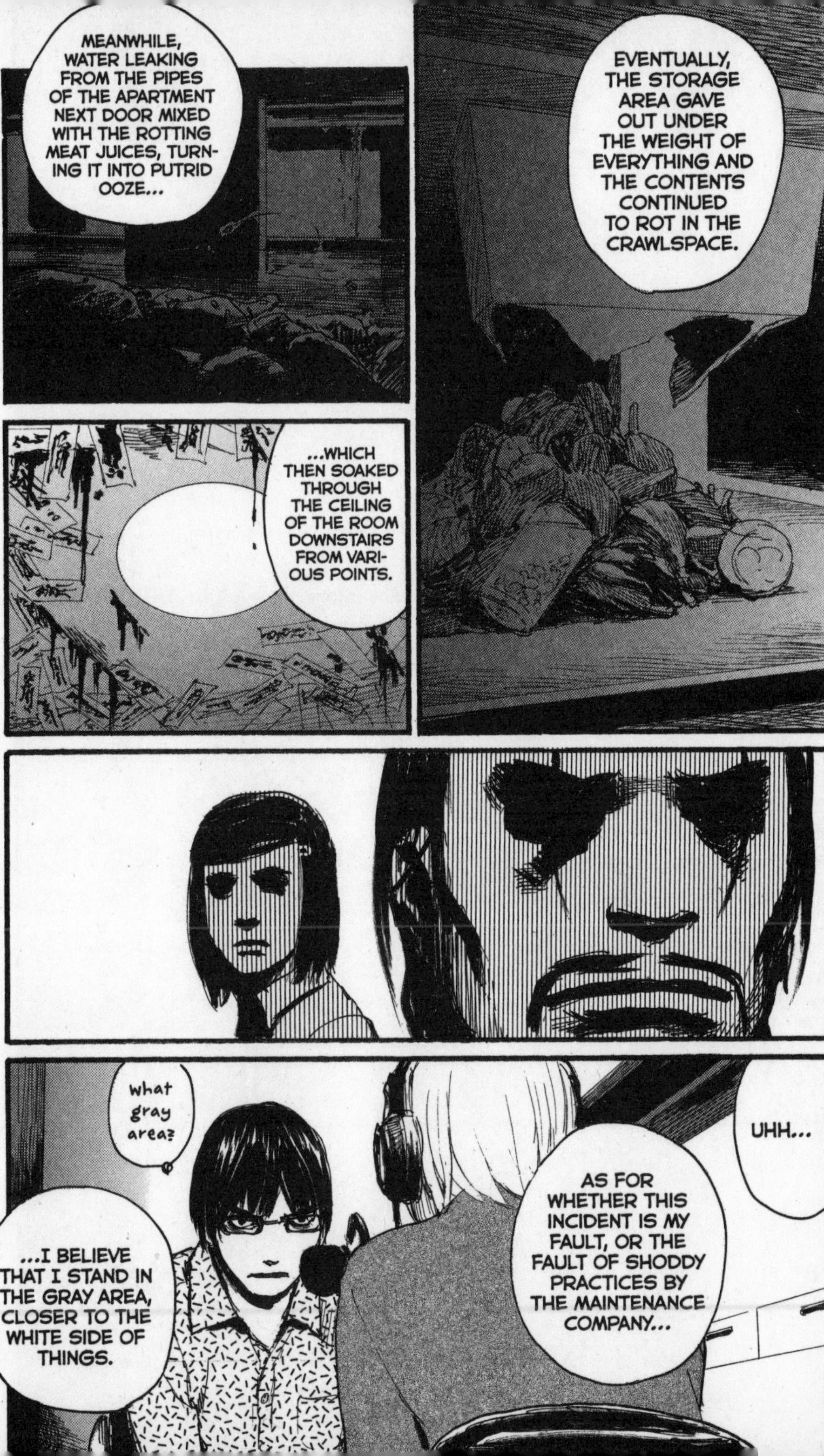
EVENTUALLY, THE STORAGE AREA GAVE OUT UNDER THE WEIGHT OF EVERYTHING AND THE CONTENTS CONTINUED TO ROT IN THE CRAWLSPACE.
MEANWHILE, WATER LEAKING FROM THE PIPES OF THE APARTMENT NEXT DOOR MIXED WITH THE ROTTING MEAT JUICES, TURNING IT INTO PUTRID OOZE...
...WHICH THEN SOAKED THROUGH THE CEILING OF THE ROOM DOWNSTAIRS FROM VARIOUS POINTS.
UHH...
AS FOR WHETHER THIS INCIDENT IS MY FAULT, OR THE FAULT OF SHODDY PRACTICES BY THE MAINTENANCE COMPANY...
...I BELIEVE THAT I STAND IN THE GRAY AREA, CLOSER TO THE WHITE SIDE OF THINGS.
what gray area?

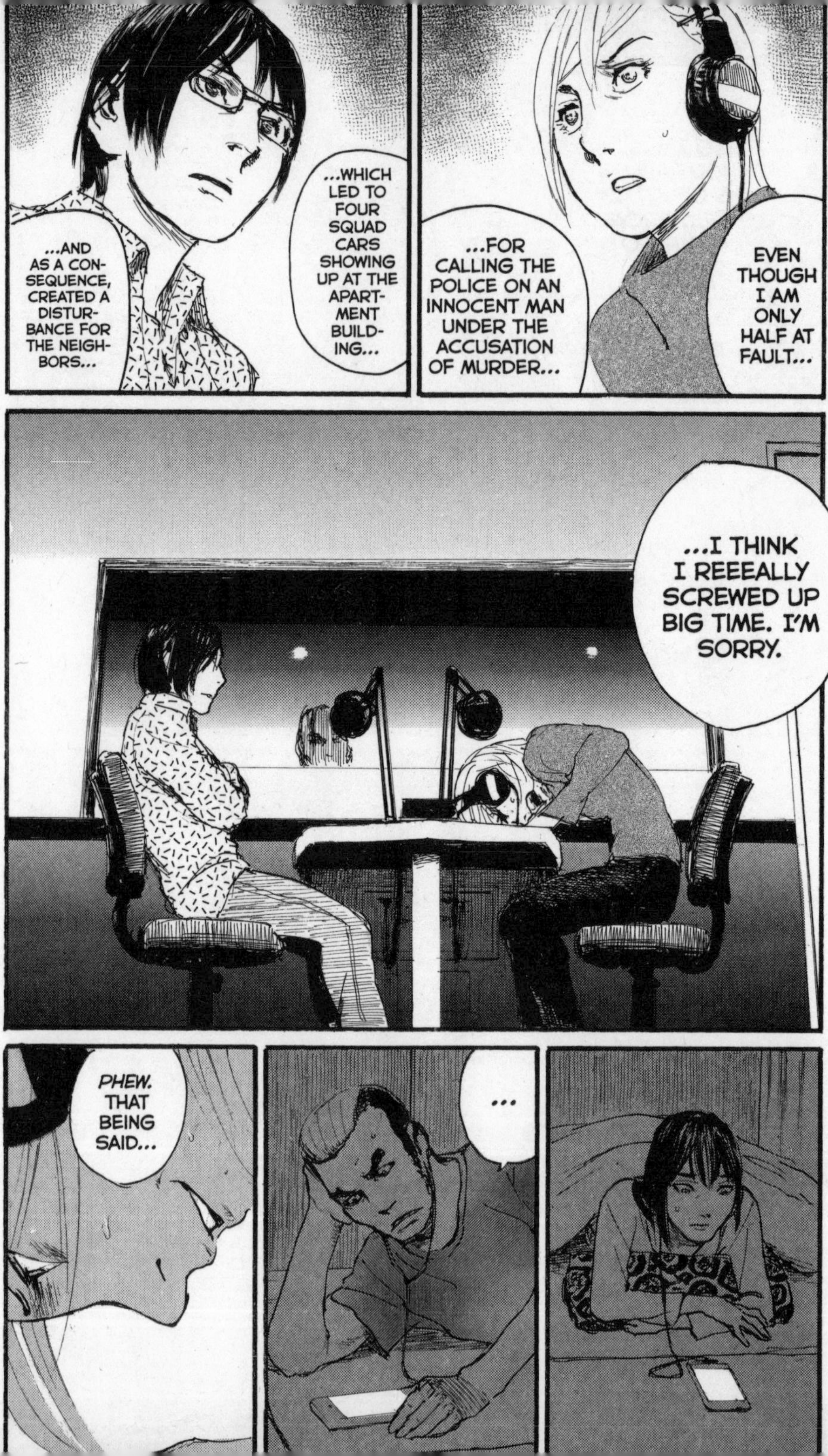
EVEN THOUGH I AM ONLY HALF AT FAULT...
...FOR CALLING THE POLICE ON AN INNOCENT MAN UNDER THE ACCUSATION OF MURDER...
...WHICH LED TO FOUR SQUAD CARS SHOWING UP AT THE APARTMENT BUILDING...
...AND AS A CONSEQUENCE, CREATED A DISTURBANCE FOR THE NEIGHBORS...
...I THINK I REEEALLY SCREWED UP BIG TIME. I'M SORRY.
...
PHEW. THAT BEING SAID...

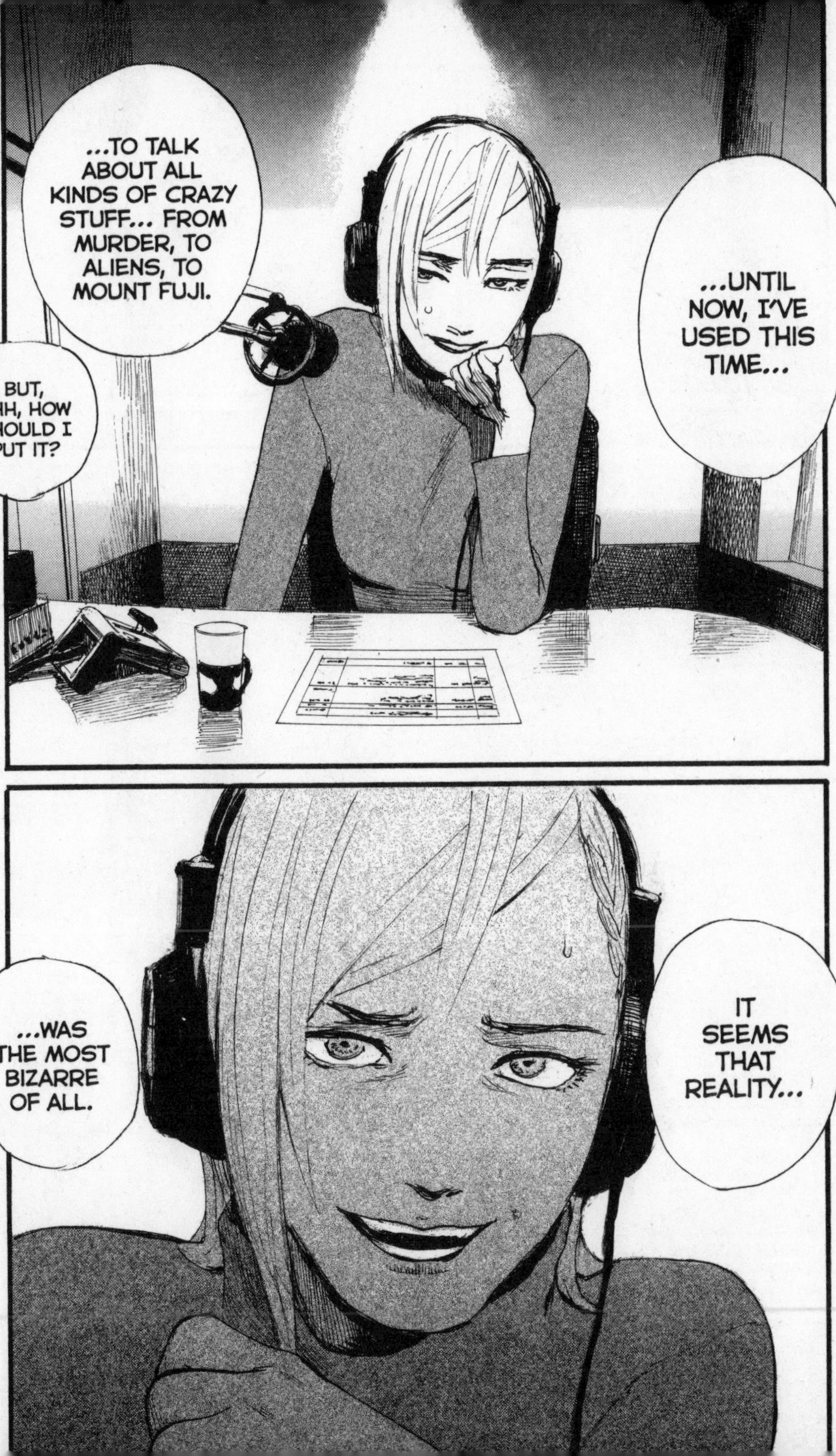
...UNTIL NOW, I'VE USED THIS TIME...
...TO TALK ABOUT ALL KINDS OF CRAZY STUFF... FROM MURDER, TO ALIENS, TO MOUNT FUJI.
BUT, UHH, HOW SHOULD I PUT IT?
IT SEEMS THAT REALITY...
...WAS THE MOST BIZARRE OF ALL.

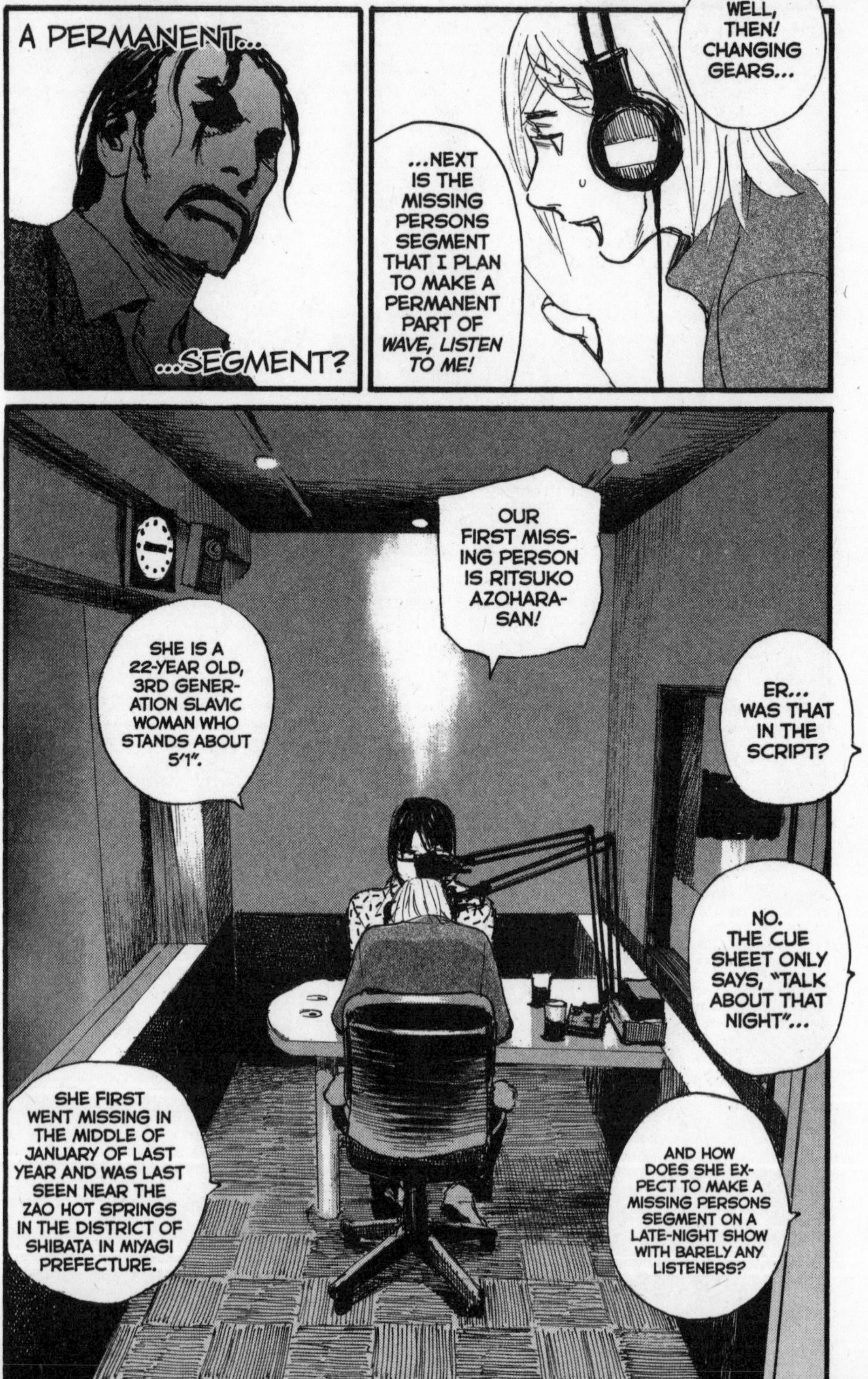
WELL, THEN! CHANGING GEARS...
...NEXT IS THE MISSING PERSONS SEGMENT THAT I PLAN TO MAKE A PERMANENT PART OF *WAVE, LISTEN TO ME!*
A PERMANENT...
...SEGMENT?
OUR FIRST MISSING PERSON IS RITSUKO AZOHARA-SAN!
ER... WAS THAT IN THE SCRIPT?
SHE IS A 22-YEAR OLD, 3RD GENERATION SLAVIC WOMAN WHO STANDS ABOUT 5'1".
NO. THE CUE SHEET ONLY SAYS, "TALK ABOUT THAT NIGHT"...
AND HOW DOES SHE EXPECT TO MAKE A MISSING PERSONS SEGMENT ON A LATE-NIGHT SHOW WITH BARELY ANY LISTENERS?
SHE FIRST WENT MISSING IN THE MIDDLE OF JANUARY OF LAST YEAR AND WAS LAST SEEN NEAR THE ZAO HOT SPRINGS IN THE DISTRICT OF SHIBATA IN MIYAGI PREFECTURE.

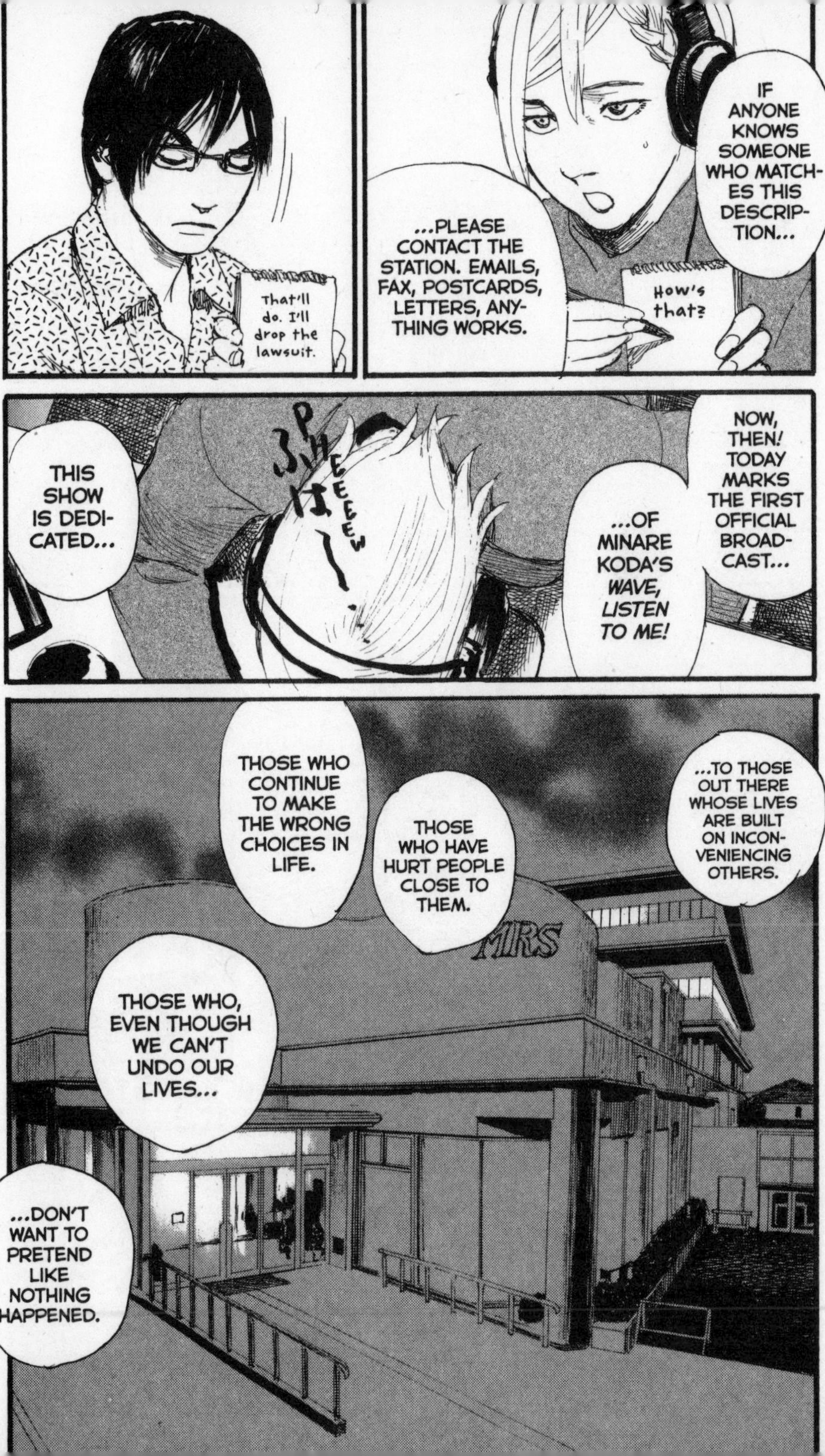
IF ANYONE KNOWS SOMEONE WHO MATCHES THIS DESCRIPTION...
...PLEASE CONTACT THE STATION. EMAILS, FAX, POSTCARDS, LETTERS, ANYTHING WORKS.
How's that?
That'll do. I'll drop the lawsuit.
NOW, THEN! TODAY MARKS THE FIRST OFFICIAL BROADCAST...
...OF MINARE KODA'S *WAVE, LISTEN TO ME!*
PHEEEEW
ふはー
THIS SHOW IS DEDICATED...
...TO THOSE OUT THERE WHOSE LIVES ARE BUILT ON INCONVENIENCING OTHERS.
THOSE WHO HAVE HURT PEOPLE CLOSE TO THEM.
THOSE WHO CONTINUE TO MAKE THE WRONG CHOICES IN LIFE.
MRS
THOSE WHO, EVEN THOUGH WE CAN'T UNDO OUR LIVES...
...DON'T WANT TO PRETEND LIKE NOTHING HAPPENED.

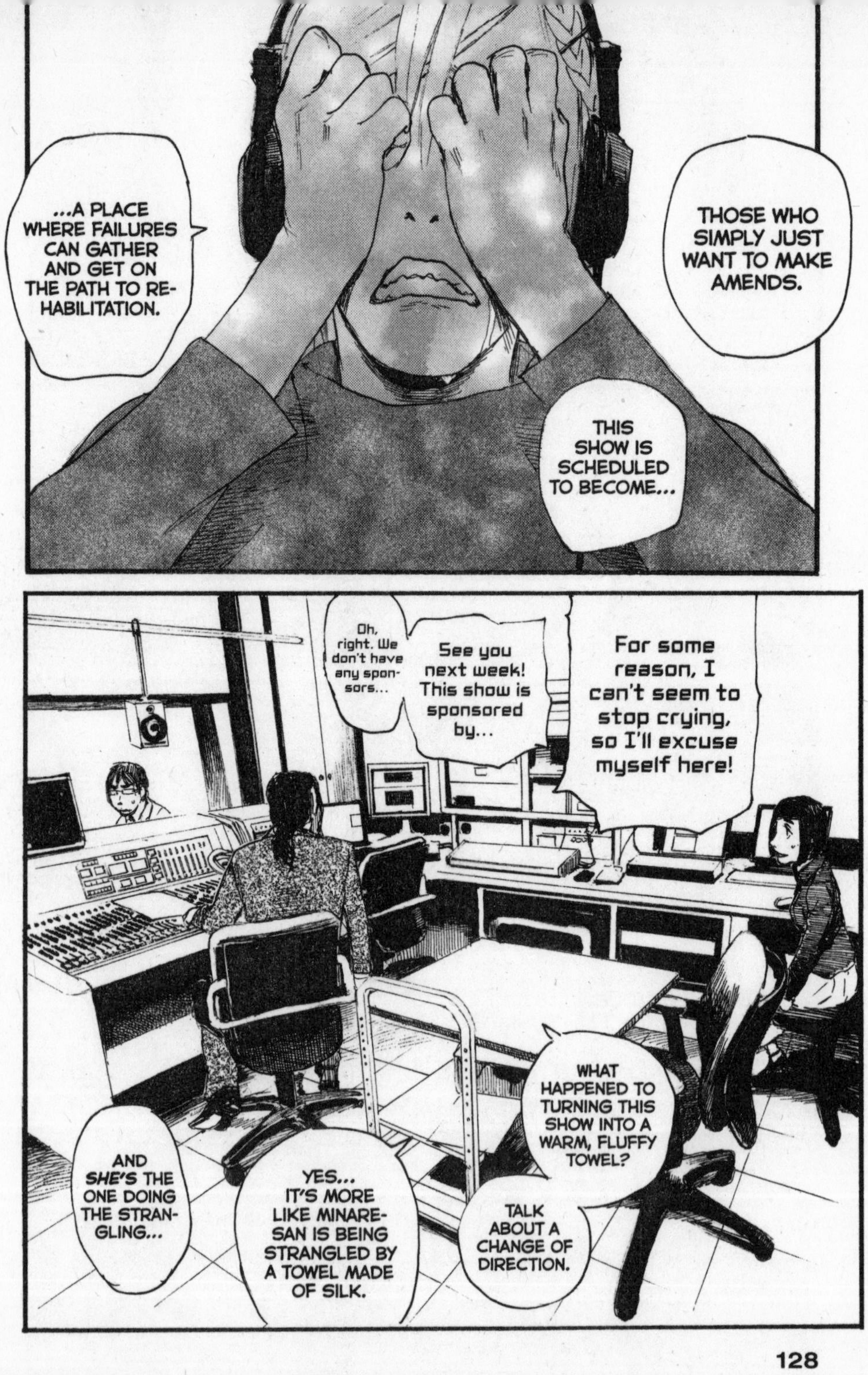
THOSE WHO SIMPLY JUST WANT TO MAKE AMENDS.
THIS SHOW IS SCHEDULED TO BECOME...
...A PLACE WHERE FAILURES CAN GATHER AND GET ON THE PATH TO RE-HABILITATION.
For some reason, I can't seem to stop crying, so I'll excuse myself here!
See you next week! This show is sponsored by...
Oh, right. We don't have any spon-sors...
WHAT HAPPENED TO TURNING THIS SHOW INTO A WARM, FLUFFY TOWEL?
TALK ABOUT A CHANGE OF DIRECTION.
YES... IT'S MORE LIKE MINARE-SAN IS BEING STRANGLED BY A TOWEL MADE OF SILK.
AND *SHE'S* THE ONE DOING THE STRAN-GLING...

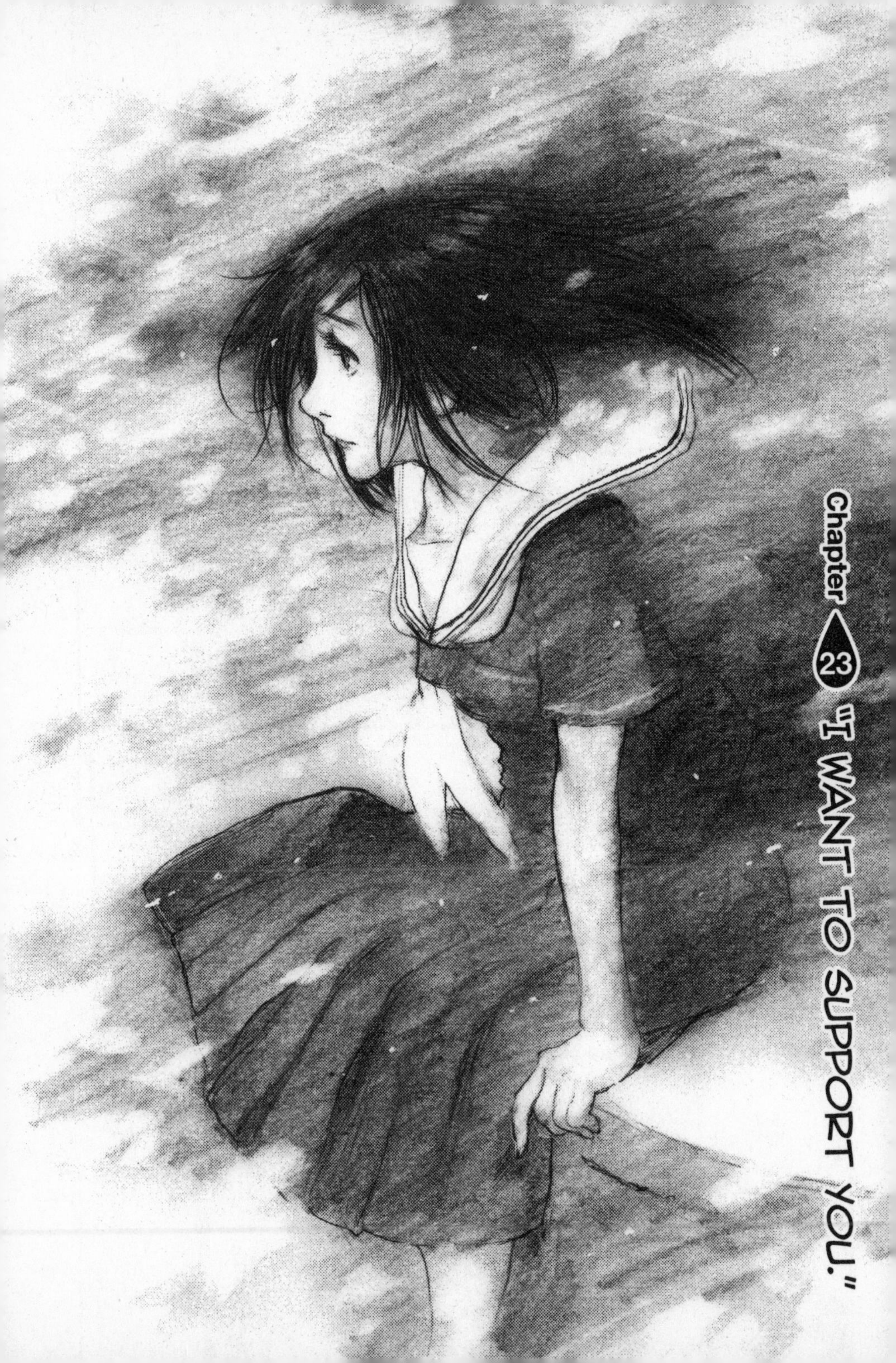
Chapter 23 "I WANT TO SUPPORT YOU."

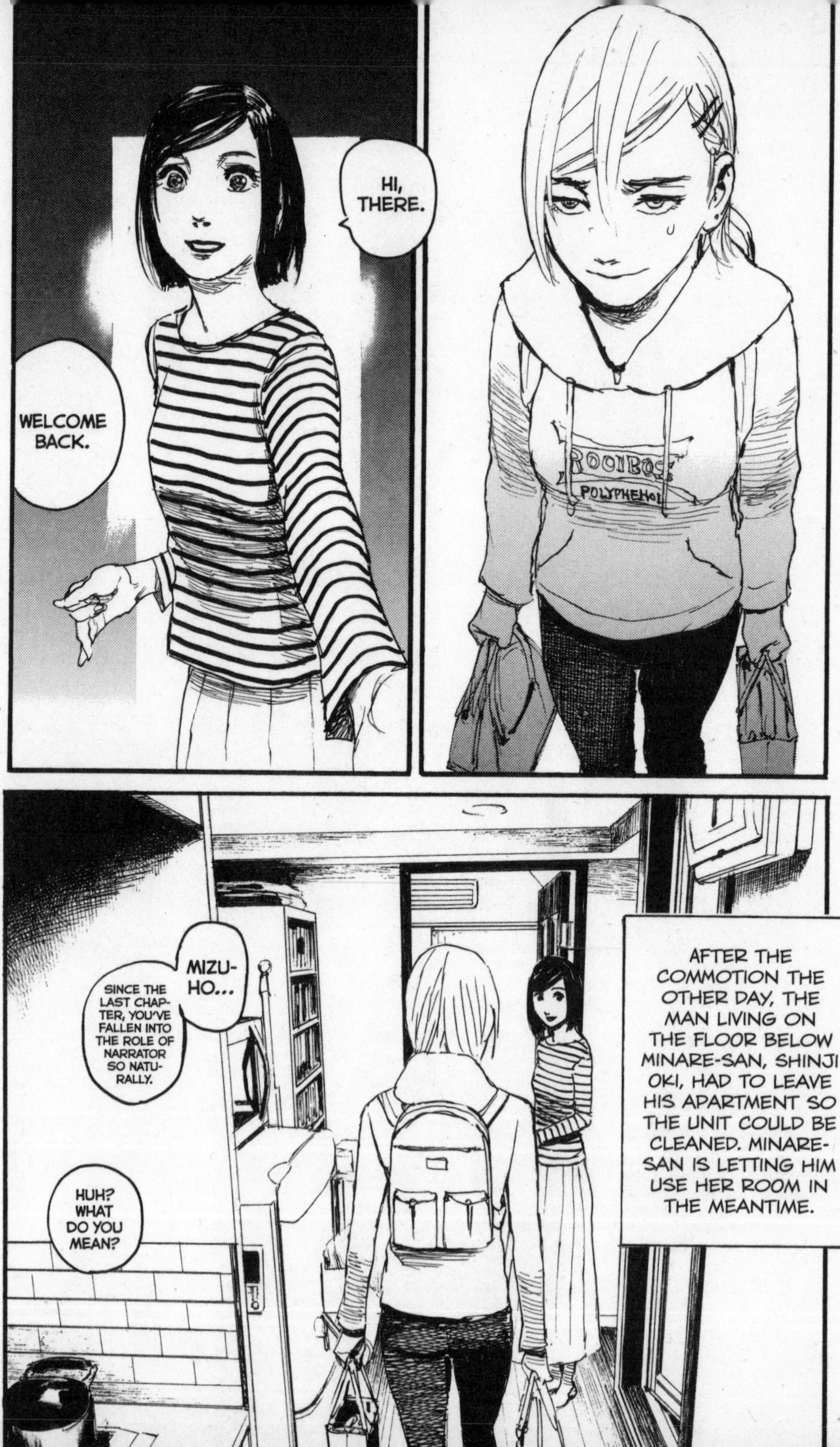
HI, THERE.
WELCOME BACK.
AFTER THE COMMOTION THE OTHER DAY, THE MAN LIVING ON THE FLOOR BELOW MINARE-SAN, SHINJI OKI, HAD TO LEAVE HIS APARTMENT SO THE UNIT COULD BE CLEANED. MINARE-SAN IS LETTING HIM USE HER ROOM IN THE MEANTIME.
MIZU-HO...
SINCE THE LAST CHAPTER, YOU'VE FALLEN INTO THE ROLE OF NARRATOR SO NATU-RALLY.
HUH? WHAT DO YOU MEAN?

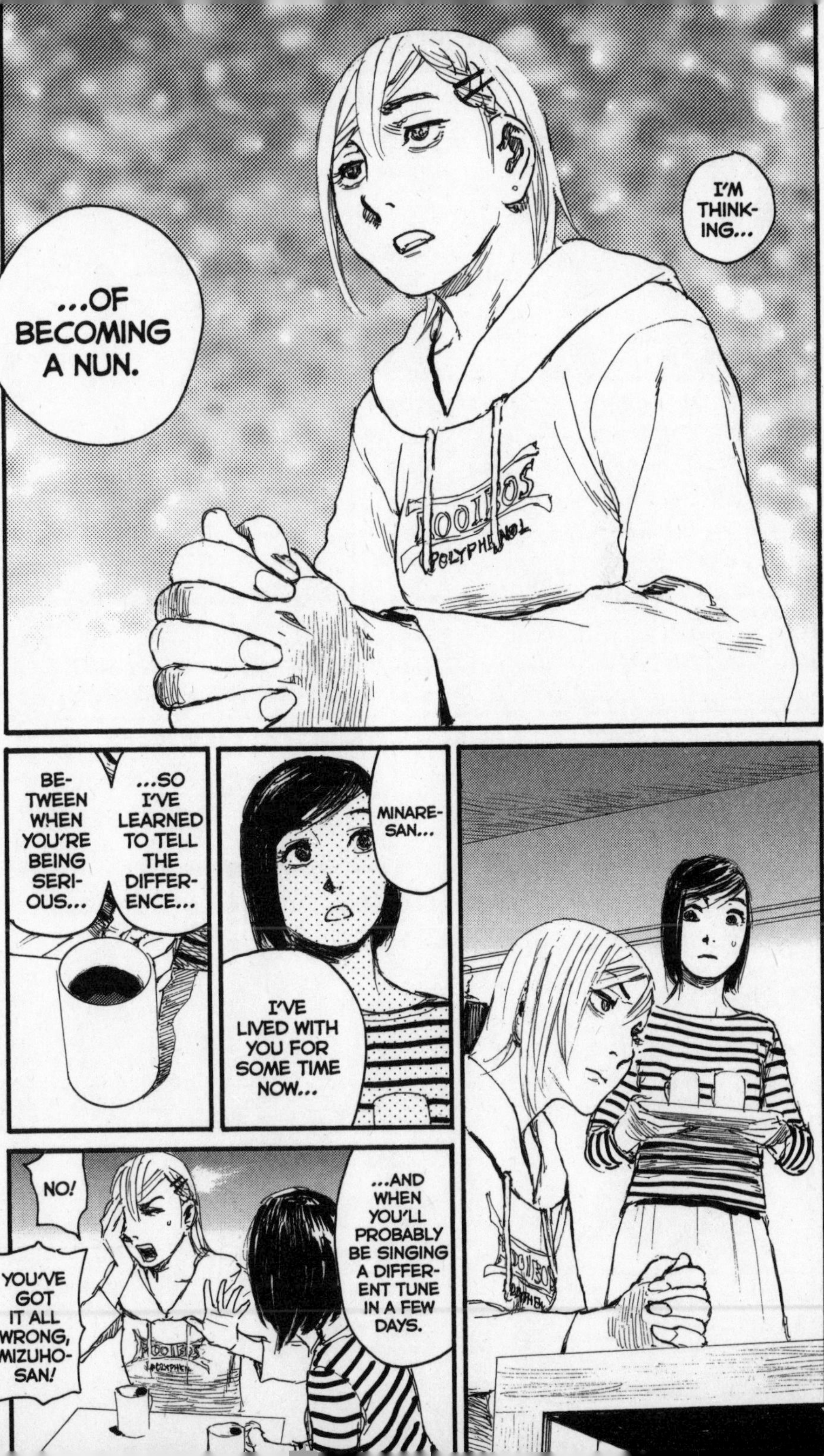
I'M THINK-ING...
...OF BECOMING A NUN.
MINARE-SAN...
I'VE LIVED WITH YOU FOR SOME TIME NOW...
...SO I'VE LEARNED TO TELL THE DIFFER-ENCE...
BE-TWEEN WHEN YOU'RE BEING SERI-OUS...
...AND WHEN YOU'LL PROBABLY BE SINGING A DIFFER-ENT TUNE IN A FEW DAYS.
NO!
YOU'VE GOT IT ALL WRONG, MIZUHO-SAN!

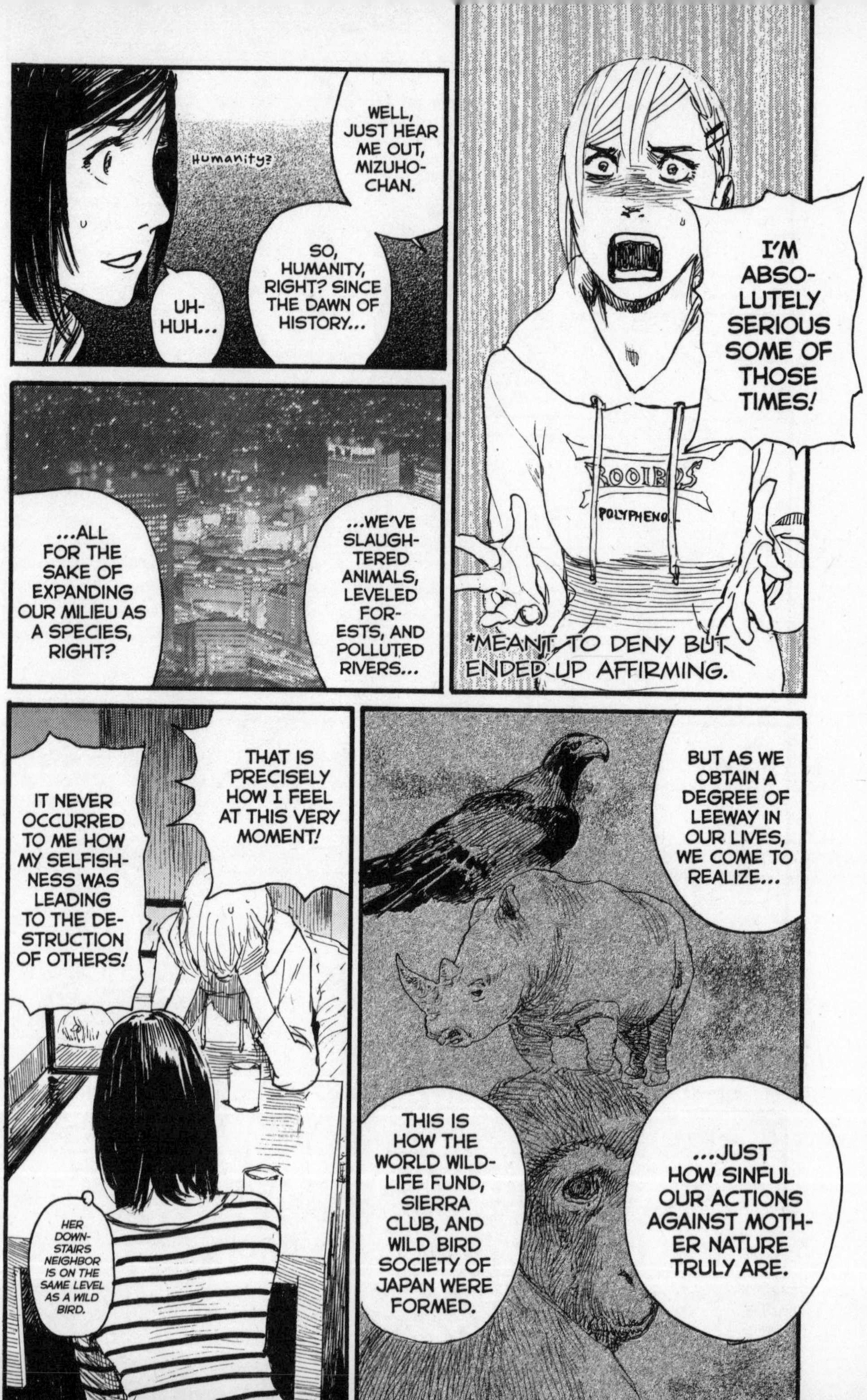
I'M ABSOLUTELY SERIOUS SOME OF THOSE TIMES!
*MEANT TO DENY BUT ENDED UP AFFIRMING.
ROOIBOS
POLYPHENOL
WELL, JUST HEAR ME OUT, MIZUHO-CHAN.
Humanity?
SO, HUMANITY, RIGHT? SINCE THE DAWN OF HISTORY...
UH-HUH...
...WE'VE SLAUGHTERED ANIMALS, LEVELED FORESTS, AND POLLUTED RIVERS...
...ALL FOR THE SAKE OF EXPANDING OUR MILIEU AS A SPECIES, RIGHT?
BUT AS WE OBTAIN A DEGREE OF LEEWAY IN OUR LIVES, WE COME TO REALIZE...
...JUST HOW SINFUL OUR ACTIONS AGAINST MOTHER NATURE TRULY ARE.
THIS IS HOW THE WORLD WILDLIFE FUND, SIERRA CLUB, AND WILD BIRD SOCIETY OF JAPAN WERE FORMED.
THAT IS PRECISELY HOW I FEEL AT THIS VERY MOMENT!
IT NEVER OCCURRED TO ME HOW MY SELFISHNESS WAS LEADING TO THE DESTRUCTION OF OTHERS!
HER DOWNSTAIRS NEIGHBOR IS ON THE SAME LEVEL AS A WILD BIRD.

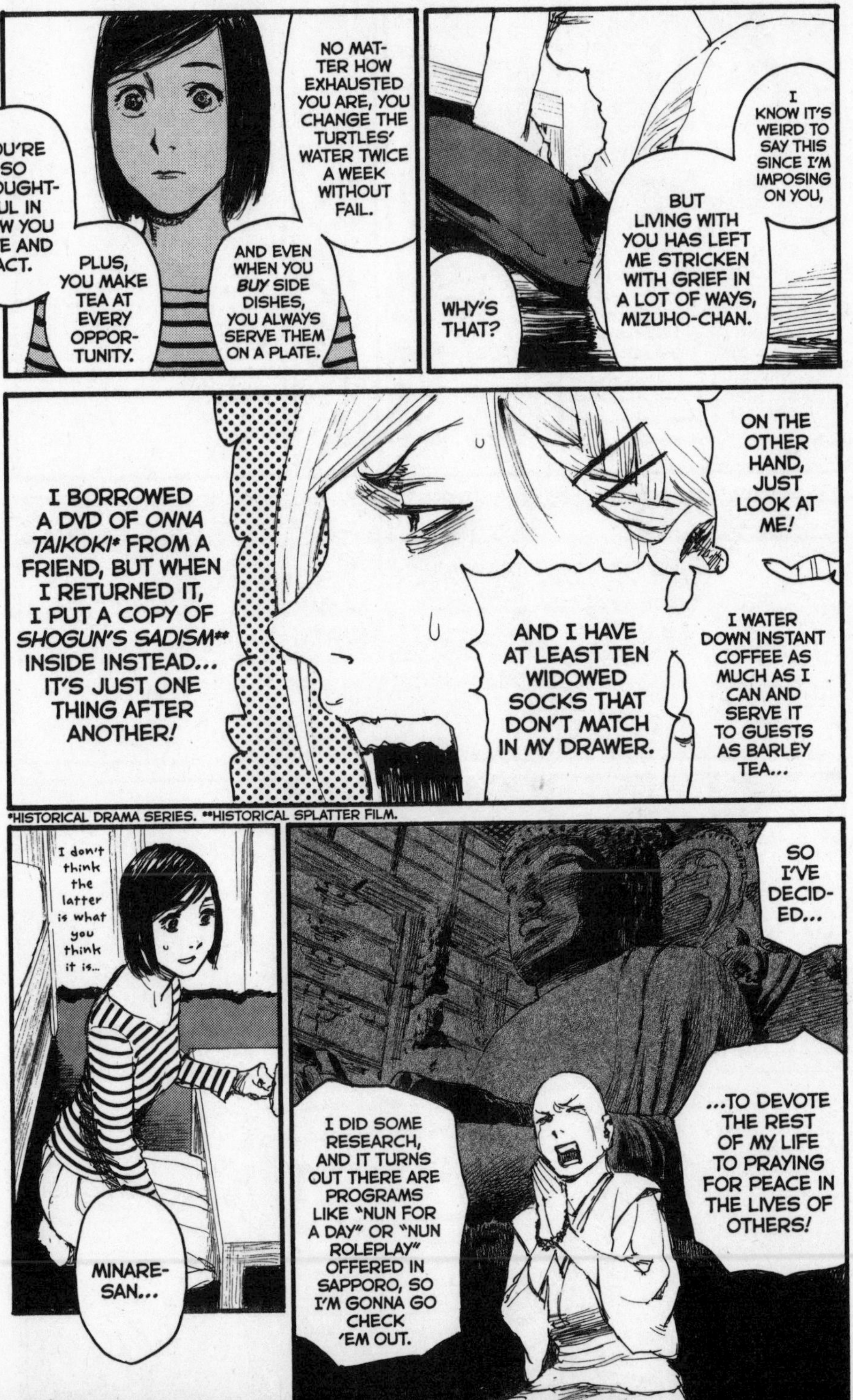
I KNOW IT'S WEIRD TO SAY THIS SINCE I'M IMPOSING ON YOU,
BUT LIVING WITH YOU HAS LEFT ME STRICKEN WITH GRIEF IN A LOT OF WAYS, MIZUHO-CHAN.
WHY'S THAT?
NO MATTER HOW EXHAUSTED YOU ARE, YOU CHANGE THE TURTLES' WATER TWICE A WEEK WITHOUT FAIL.
AND EVEN WHEN YOU *BUY* SIDE DISHES, YOU ALWAYS SERVE THEM ON A PLATE.
PLUS, YOU MAKE TEA AT EVERY OPPORTUNITY.
YOU'RE SO THOUGHTFUL IN HOW YOU LIVE AND ACT.
ON THE OTHER HAND, JUST LOOK AT ME!
I WATER DOWN INSTANT COFFEE AS MUCH AS I CAN AND SERVE IT TO GUESTS AS BARLEY TEA...
AND I HAVE AT LEAST TEN WIDOWED SOCKS THAT DON'T MATCH IN MY DRAWER.
I BORROWED A DVD OF *ONNA TAIKOKI** FROM A FRIEND, BUT WHEN I RETURNED IT, I PUT A COPY OF *SHOGUN'S SADISM*** INSIDE INSTEAD... IT'S JUST ONE THING AFTER ANOTHER!
*HISTORICAL DRAMA SERIES. **HISTORICAL SPLATTER FILM.
SO I'VE DECIDED...
...TO DEVOTE THE REST OF MY LIFE TO PRAYING FOR PEACE IN THE LIVES OF OTHERS!
I DID SOME RESEARCH, AND IT TURNS OUT THERE ARE PROGRAMS LIKE "NUN FOR A DAY" OR "NUN ROLEPLAY" OFFERED IN SAPPORO, SO I'M GONNA GO CHECK 'EM OUT.
I don't think the latter is what you think it is...
MINARE-SAN...

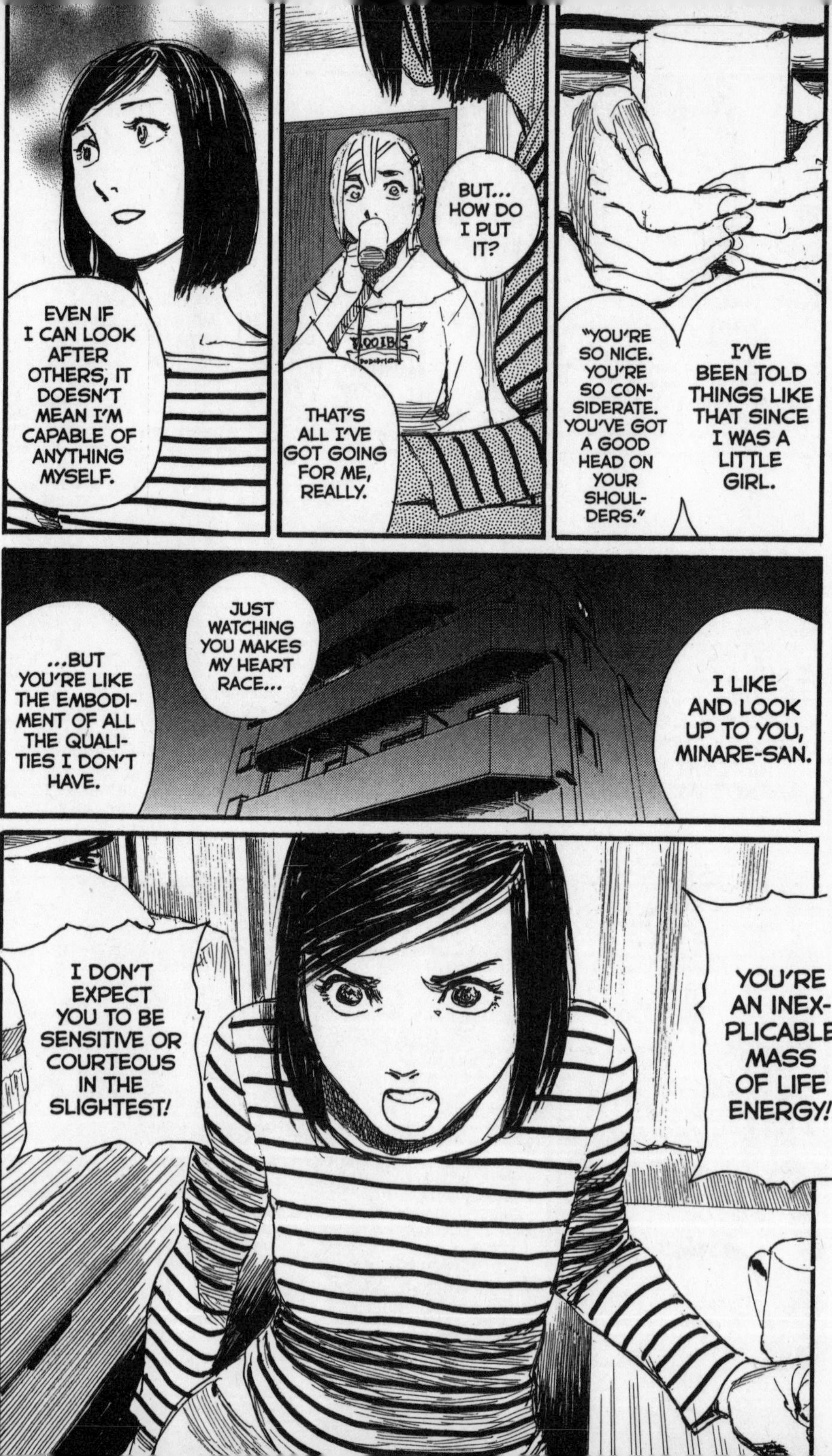
I'VE BEEN TOLD THINGS LIKE THAT SINCE I WAS A LITTLE GIRL.
"YOU'RE SO NICE. YOU'RE SO CONSIDERATE. YOU'VE GOT A GOOD HEAD ON YOUR SHOULDERS."
BUT... HOW DO I PUT IT?
THAT'S ALL I'VE GOT GOING FOR ME, REALLY.
EVEN IF I CAN LOOK AFTER OTHERS, IT DOESN'T MEAN I'M CAPABLE OF ANYTHING MYSELF.
I LIKE AND LOOK UP TO YOU, MINARE-SAN.
JUST WATCHING YOU MAKES MY HEART RACE...
...BUT YOU'RE LIKE THE EMBODIMENT OF ALL THE QUALITIES I DON'T HAVE.
YOU'RE AN INEXPLICABLE MASS OF LIFE ENERGY!
I DON'T EXPECT YOU TO BE SENSITIVE OR COURTEOUS IN THE SLIGHTEST!

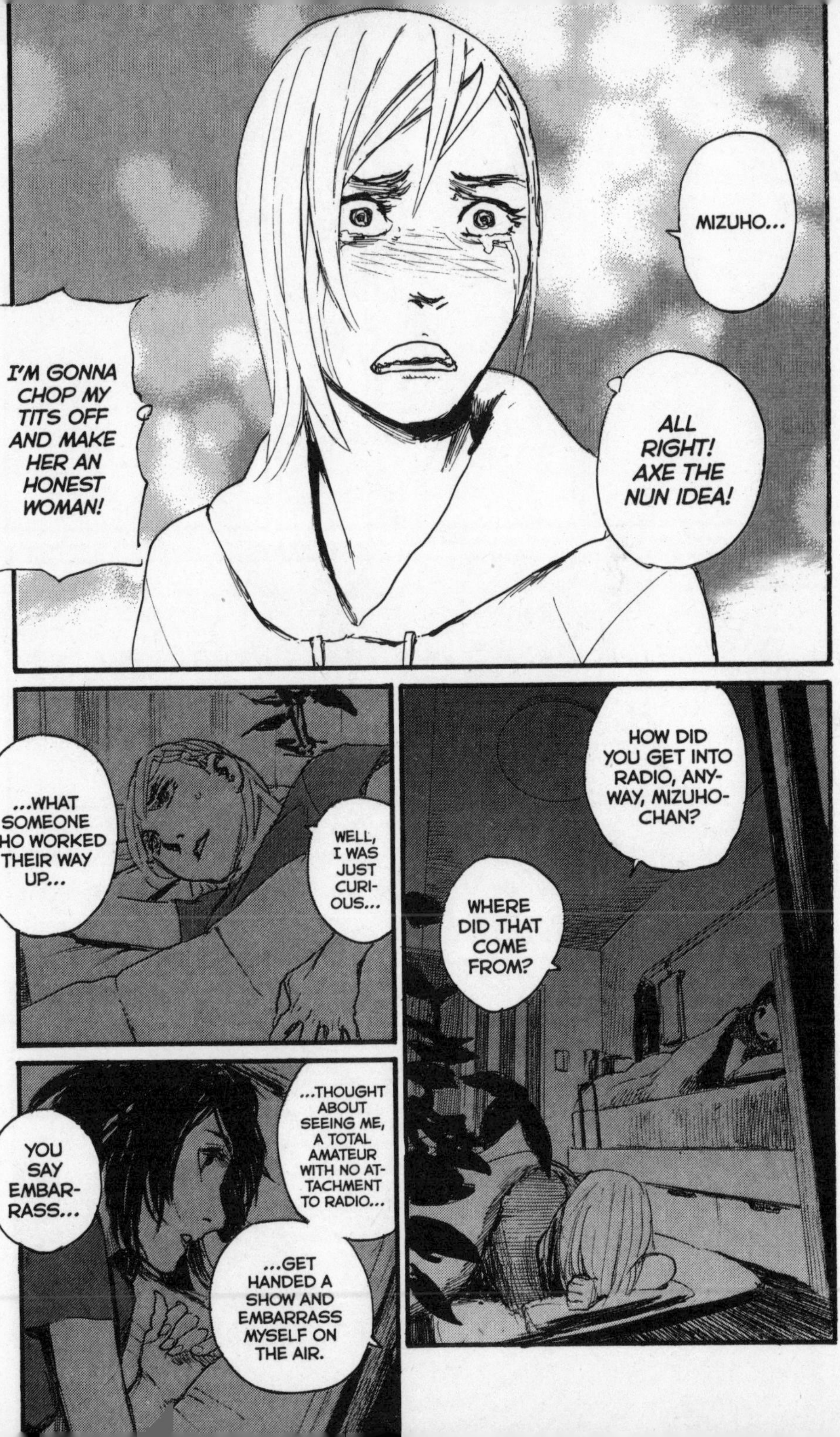
MIZUHO...
ALL RIGHT! AXE THE NUN IDEA!
I'M GONNA CHOP MY TITS OFF AND MAKE HER AN HONEST WOMAN!
HOW DID YOU GET INTO RADIO, ANYWAY, MIZUHO-CHAN?
WHERE DID THAT COME FROM?
WELL, I WAS JUST CURIOUS...
...WHAT SOMEONE WHO WORKED THEIR WAY UP...
...THOUGHT ABOUT SEEING ME, A TOTAL AMATEUR WITH NO ATTACHMENT TO RADIO...
YOU SAY EMBARRASS...
...GET HANDED A SHOW AND EMBARRASS MYSELF ON THE AIR.

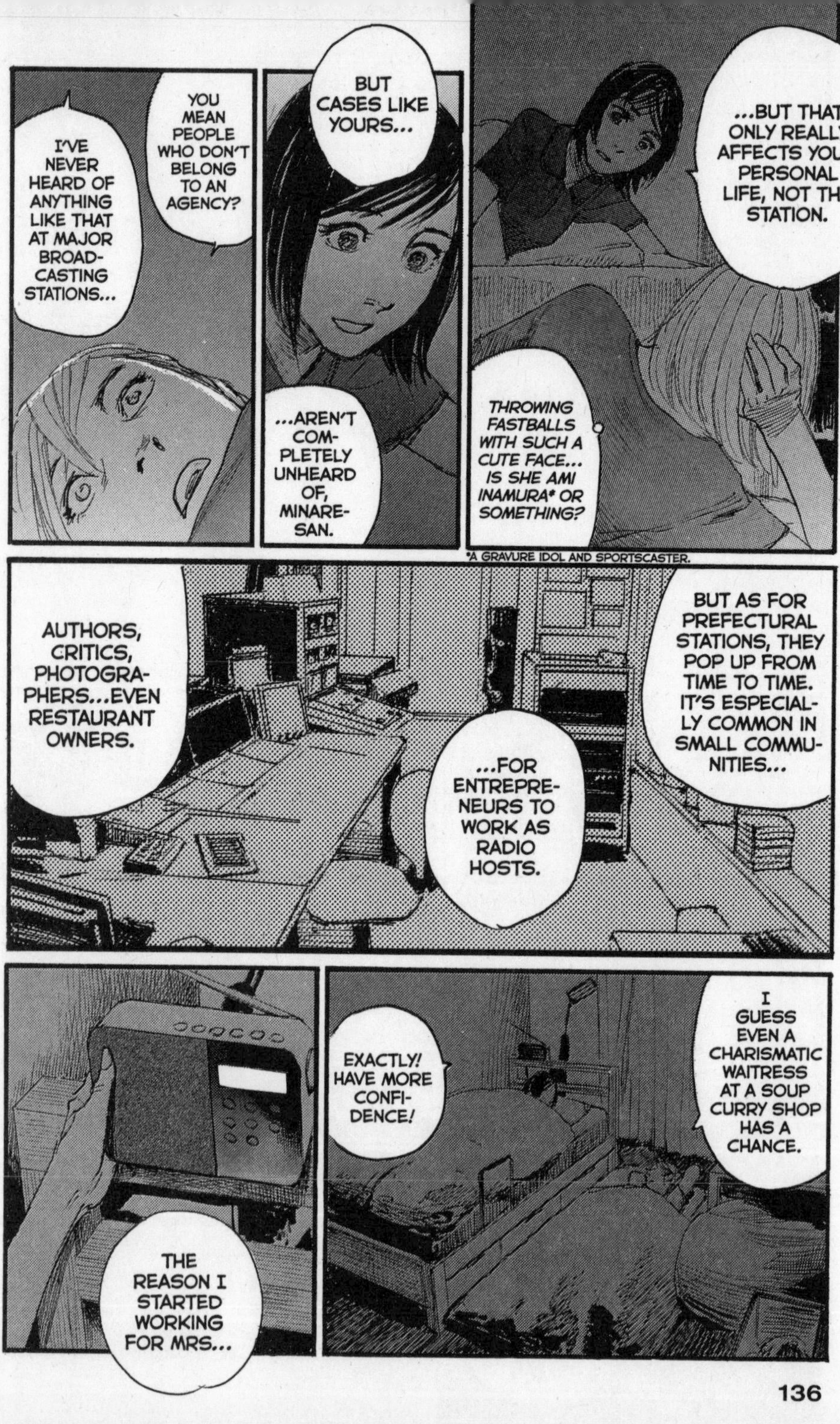
...BUT THAT ONLY REALLY AFFECTS YOUR PERSONAL LIFE, NOT THE STATION.
THROWING FASTBALLS WITH SUCH A CUTE FACE... IS SHE AMI INAMURA* OR SOMETHING?
BUT CASES LIKE YOURS...
...AREN'T COMPLETELY UNHEARD OF, MINARE-SAN.
YOU MEAN PEOPLE WHO DON'T BELONG TO AN AGENCY?
I'VE NEVER HEARD OF ANYTHING LIKE THAT AT MAJOR BROAD-CASTING STATIONS...
BUT AS FOR PREFECTURAL STATIONS, THEY POP UP FROM TIME TO TIME. IT'S ESPECIALLY COMMON IN SMALL COMMUNITIES...
...FOR ENTREPRENEURS TO WORK AS RADIO HOSTS.
AUTHORS, CRITICS, PHOTOGRAPHERS...EVEN RESTAURANT OWNERS.
I GUESS EVEN A CHARISMATIC WAITRESS AT A SOUP CURRY SHOP HAS A CHANCE.
EXACTLY! HAVE MORE CONFIDENCE!
THE REASON I STARTED WORKING FOR MRS...

*A GRAVURE IDOL AND SPORTSCASTER.

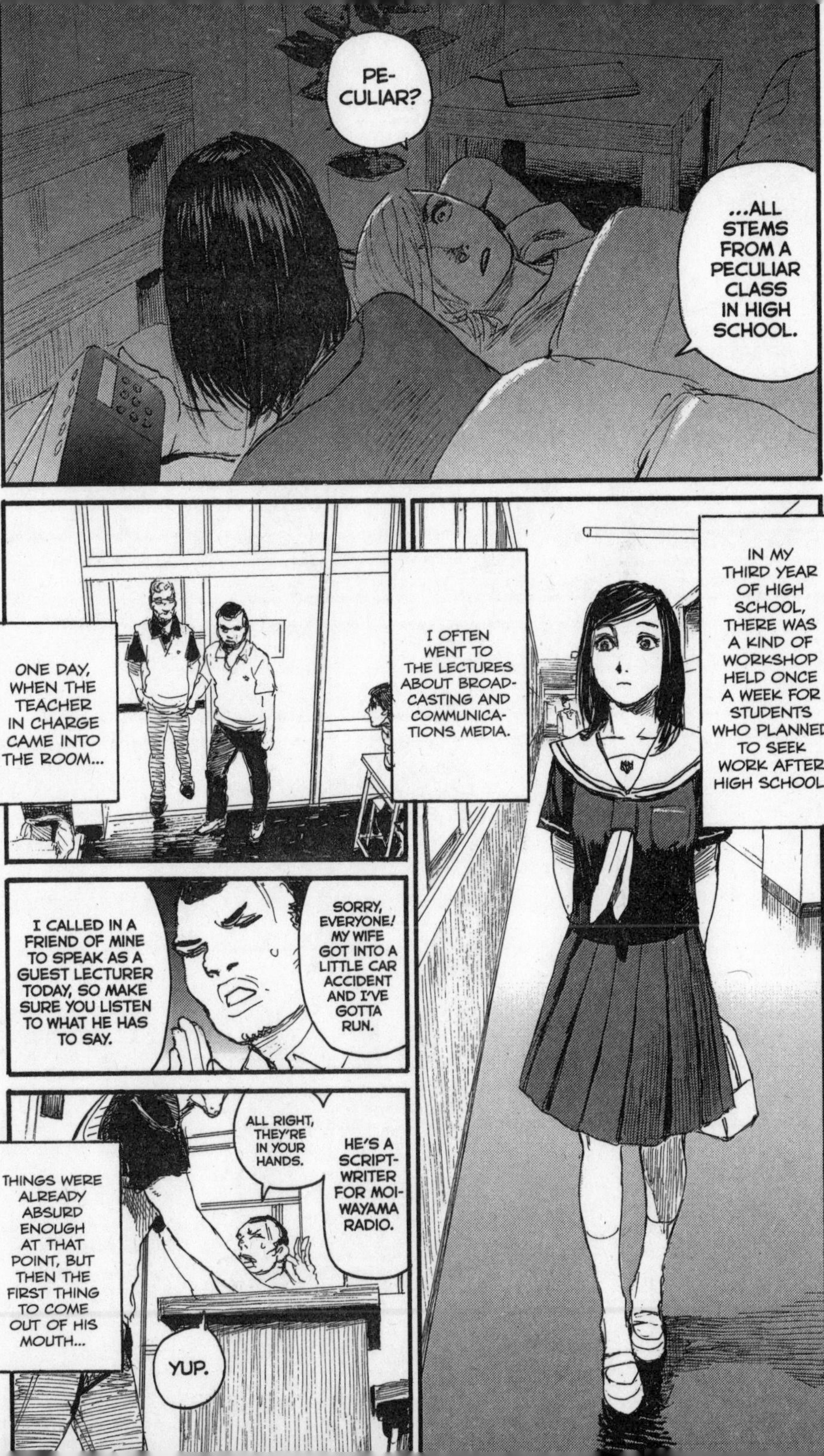
...ALL STEMS FROM A PECULIAR CLASS IN HIGH SCHOOL.
PE-CULIAR?
IN MY THIRD YEAR OF HIGH SCHOOL, THERE WAS A KIND OF WORKSHOP HELD ONCE A WEEK FOR STUDENTS WHO PLANNED TO SEEK WORK AFTER HIGH SCHOOL.
I OFTEN WENT TO THE LECTURES ABOUT BROAD-CASTING AND COMMUNICA-TIONS MEDIA.
ONE DAY, WHEN THE TEACHER IN CHARGE CAME INTO THE ROOM...
SORRY, EVERYONE! MY WIFE GOT INTO A LITTLE CAR ACCIDENT AND I'VE GOTTA RUN.
I CALLED IN A FRIEND OF MINE TO SPEAK AS A GUEST LECTURER TODAY, SO MAKE SURE YOU LISTEN TO WHAT HE HAS TO SAY.
HE'S A SCRIPT-WRITER FOR MOI-WAYAMA RADIO.
ALL RIGHT, THEY'RE IN YOUR HANDS.
YUP.
THINGS WERE ALREADY ABSURD ENOUGH AT THAT POINT, BUT THEN THE FIRST THING TO COME OUT OF HIS MOUTH...

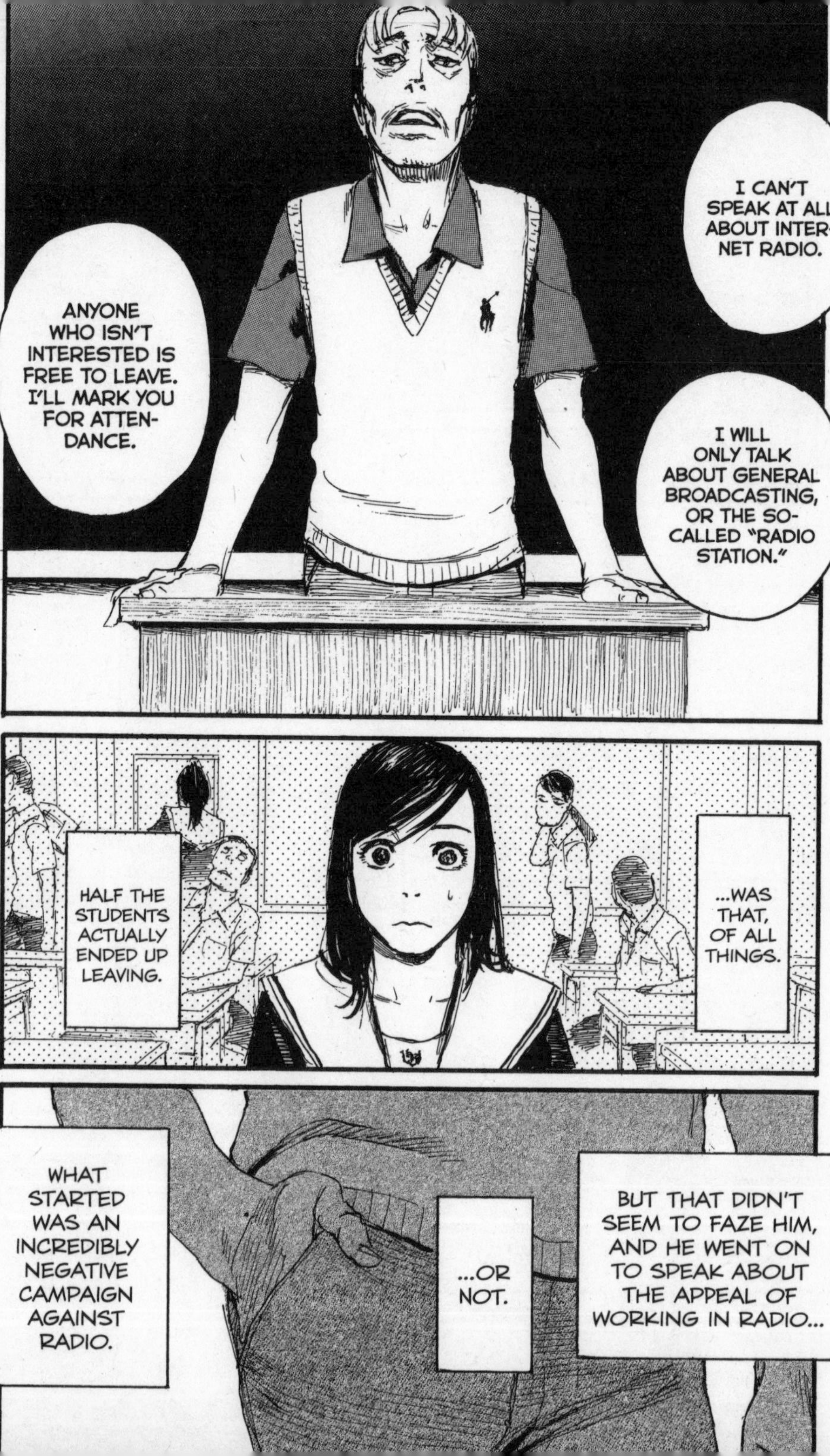
I CAN'T SPEAK AT ALL ABOUT INTER-NET RADIO.
I WILL ONLY TALK ABOUT GENERAL BROADCASTING, OR THE SO-CALLED "RADIO STATION."
ANYONE WHO ISN'T INTERESTED IS FREE TO LEAVE. I'LL MARK YOU FOR ATTEN-DANCE.
...WAS THAT, OF ALL THINGS.
HALF THE STUDENTS ACTUALLY ENDED UP LEAVING.
BUT THAT DIDN'T SEEM TO FAZE HIM, AND HE WENT ON TO SPEAK ABOUT THE APPEAL OF WORKING IN RADIO...
...OR NOT.
WHAT STARTED WAS AN INCREDIBLY NEGATIVE CAMPAIGN AGAINST RADIO.

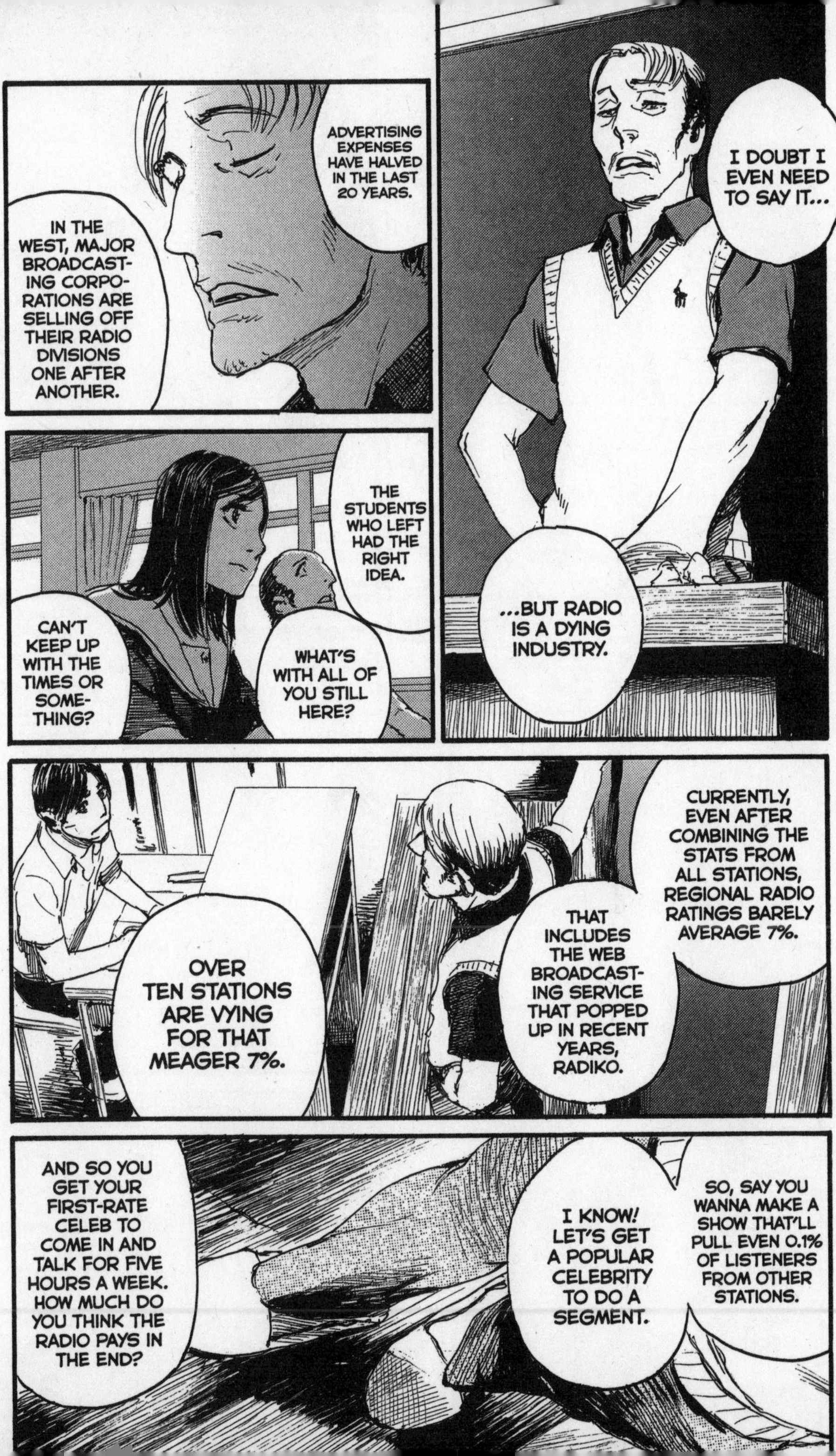
I DOUBT I EVEN NEED TO SAY IT...
...BUT RADIO IS A DYING INDUSTRY.
ADVERTISING EXPENSES HAVE HALVED IN THE LAST 20 YEARS.
IN THE WEST, MAJOR BROADCASTING CORPORATIONS ARE SELLING OFF THEIR RADIO DIVISIONS ONE AFTER ANOTHER.
THE STUDENTS WHO LEFT HAD THE RIGHT IDEA.
WHAT'S WITH ALL OF YOU STILL HERE?
CAN'T KEEP UP WITH THE TIMES OR SOMETHING?
CURRENTLY, EVEN AFTER COMBINING THE STATS FROM ALL STATIONS, REGIONAL RADIO RATINGS BARELY AVERAGE 7%.
THAT INCLUDES THE WEB BROADCASTING SERVICE THAT POPPED UP IN RECENT YEARS, RADIKO.
OVER TEN STATIONS ARE VYING FOR THAT MEAGER 7%.
SO, SAY YOU WANNA MAKE A SHOW THAT'LL PULL EVEN 0.1% OF LISTENERS FROM OTHER STATIONS.
I KNOW! LET'S GET A POPULAR CELEBRITY TO DO A SEGMENT.
AND SO YOU GET YOUR FIRST-RATE CELEB TO COME IN AND TALK FOR FIVE HOURS A WEEK. HOW MUCH DO YOU THINK THE RADIO PAYS IN THE END?

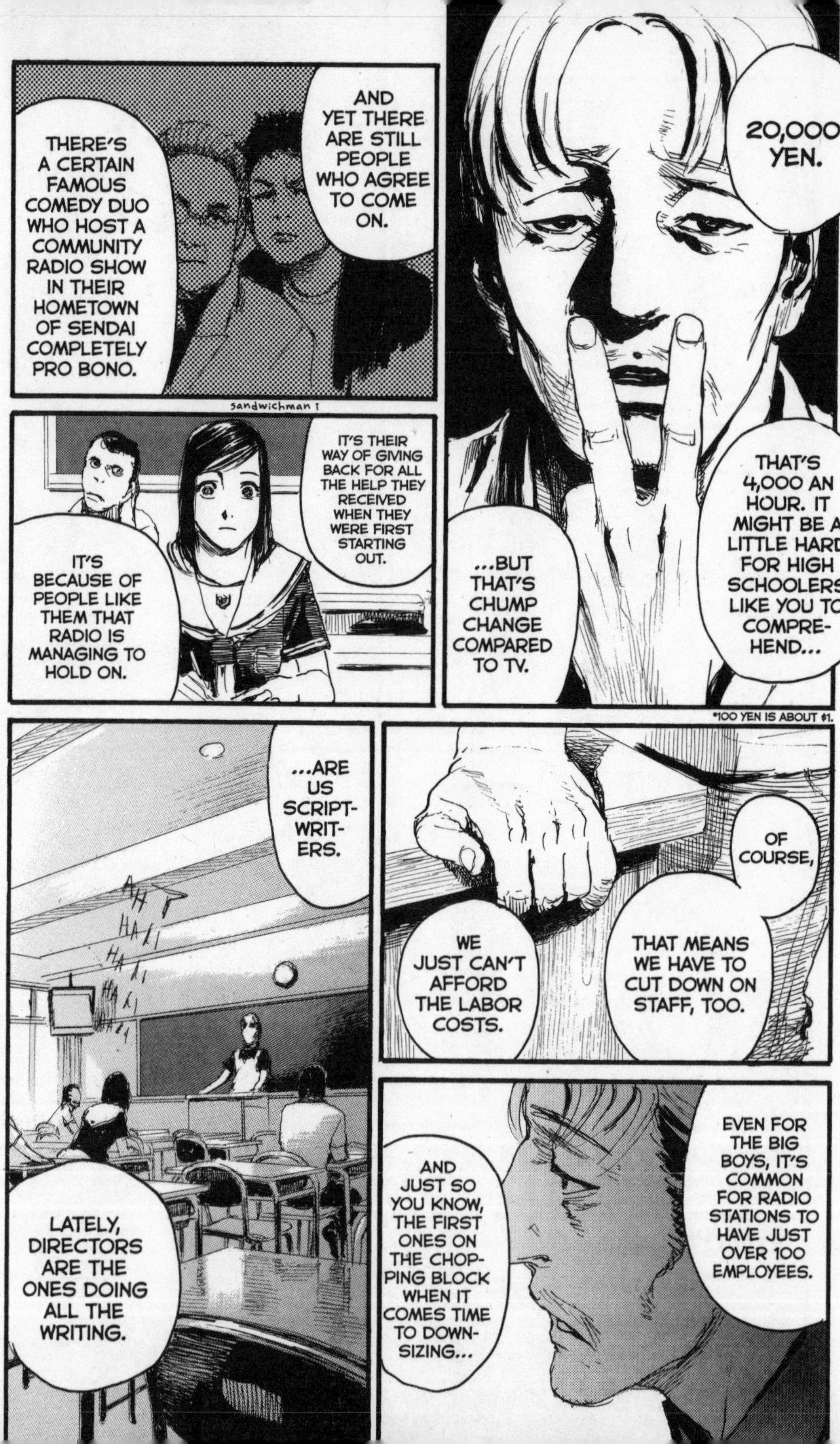
20,000* YEN.
THAT'S 4,000 AN HOUR. IT MIGHT BE A LITTLE HARD FOR HIGH SCHOOLERS LIKE YOU TO COMPRE-HEND...
...BUT THAT'S CHUMP CHANGE COMPARED TO TV.
AND YET THERE ARE STILL PEOPLE WHO AGREE TO COME ON.
THERE'S A CERTAIN FAMOUS COMEDY DUO WHO HOST A COMMUNITY RADIO SHOW IN THEIR HOMETOWN OF SENDAI COMPLETELY PRO BONO.
sandwichman!
IT'S THEIR WAY OF GIVING BACK FOR ALL THE HELP THEY RECEIVED WHEN THEY WERE FIRST STARTING OUT.
IT'S BECAUSE OF PEOPLE LIKE THEM THAT RADIO IS MANAGING TO HOLD ON.
*100 YEN IS ABOUT $1.
OF COURSE,
THAT MEANS WE HAVE TO CUT DOWN ON STAFF, TOO.
WE JUST CAN'T AFFORD THE LABOR COSTS.
EVEN FOR THE BIG BOYS, IT'S COMMON FOR RADIO STATIONS TO HAVE JUST OVER 100 EMPLOYEES.
AND JUST SO YOU KNOW, THE FIRST ONES ON THE CHOP-PING BLOCK WHEN IT COMES TIME TO DOWN-SIZING...
...ARE US SCRIPT-WRIT-ERS.
LATELY, DIRECTORS ARE THE ONES DOING ALL THE WRITING.

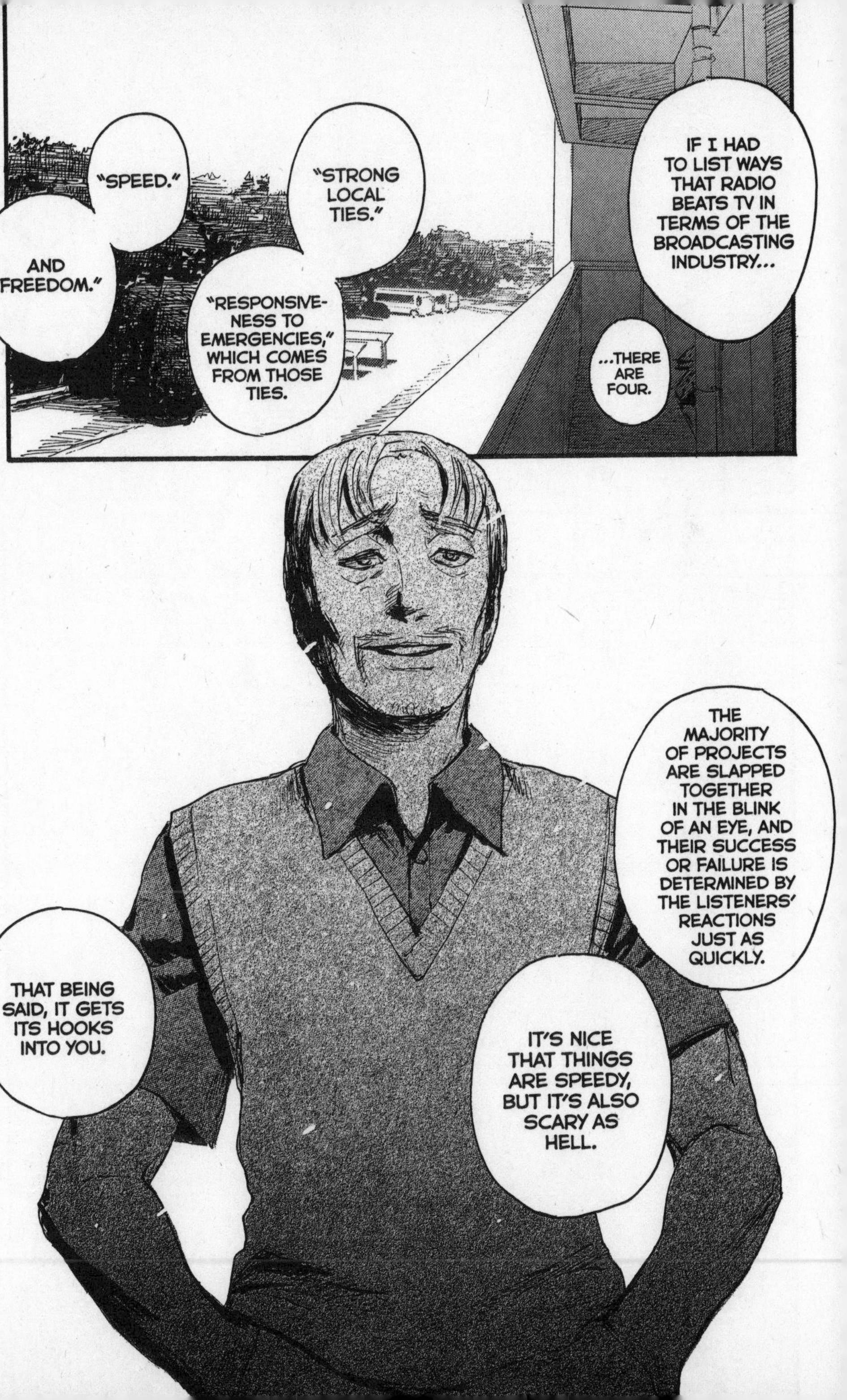
IF I HAD TO LIST WAYS THAT RADIO BEATS TV IN TERMS OF THE BROADCASTING INDUSTRY...
...THERE ARE FOUR.
"STRONG LOCAL TIES."
"RESPONSIVENESS TO EMERGENCIES," WHICH COMES FROM THOSE TIES.
"SPEED."
AND "FREEDOM."
THE MAJORITY OF PROJECTS ARE SLAPPED TOGETHER IN THE BLINK OF AN EYE, AND THEIR SUCCESS OR FAILURE IS DETERMINED BY THE LISTENERS' REACTIONS JUST AS QUICKLY.
IT'S NICE THAT THINGS ARE SPEEDY, BUT IT'S ALSO SCARY AS HELL.
THAT BEING SAID, IT GETS ITS HOOKS INTO YOU.

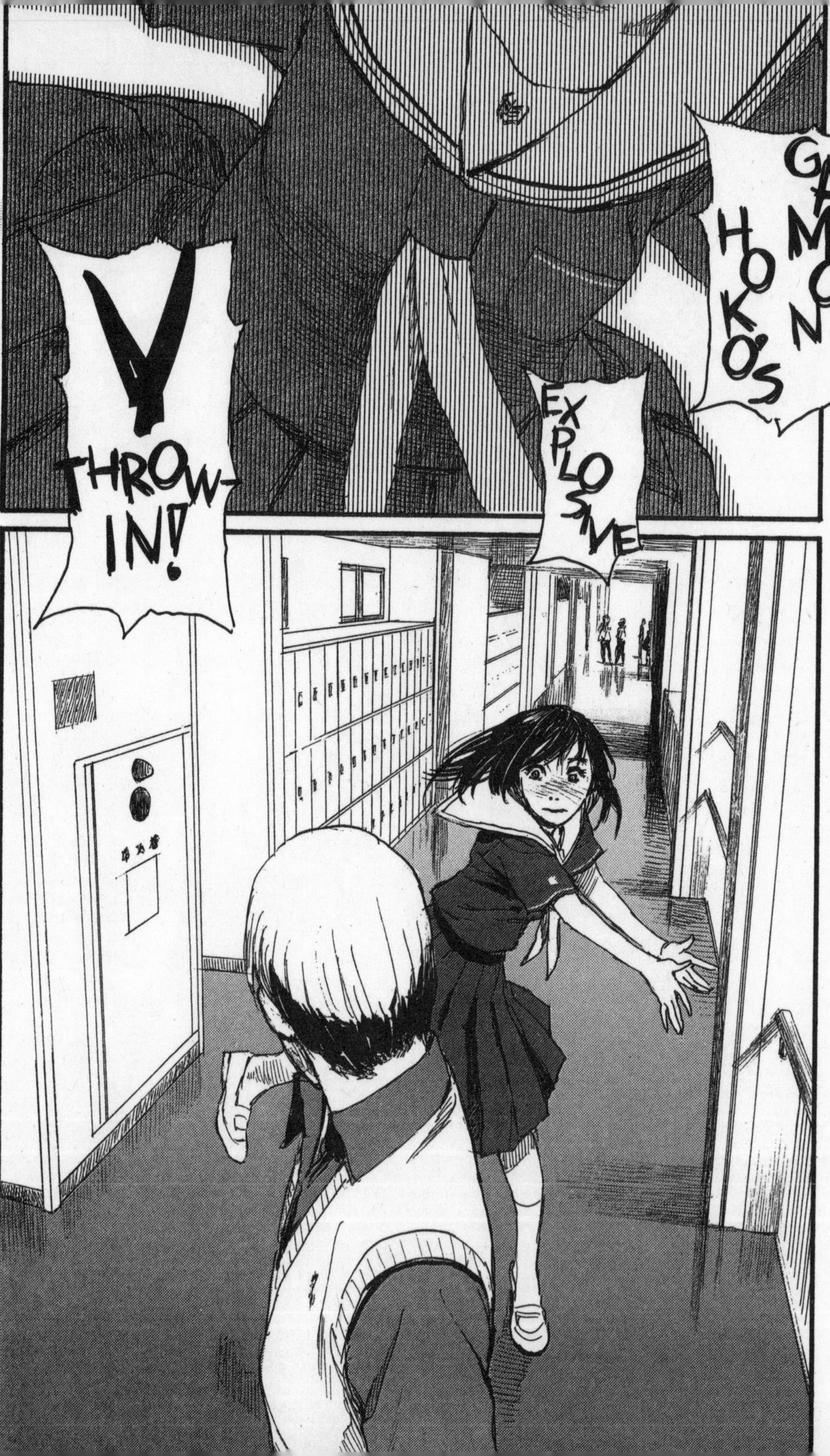
GAMON HOKO'S
EXPLOSIVE
THROW-IN!

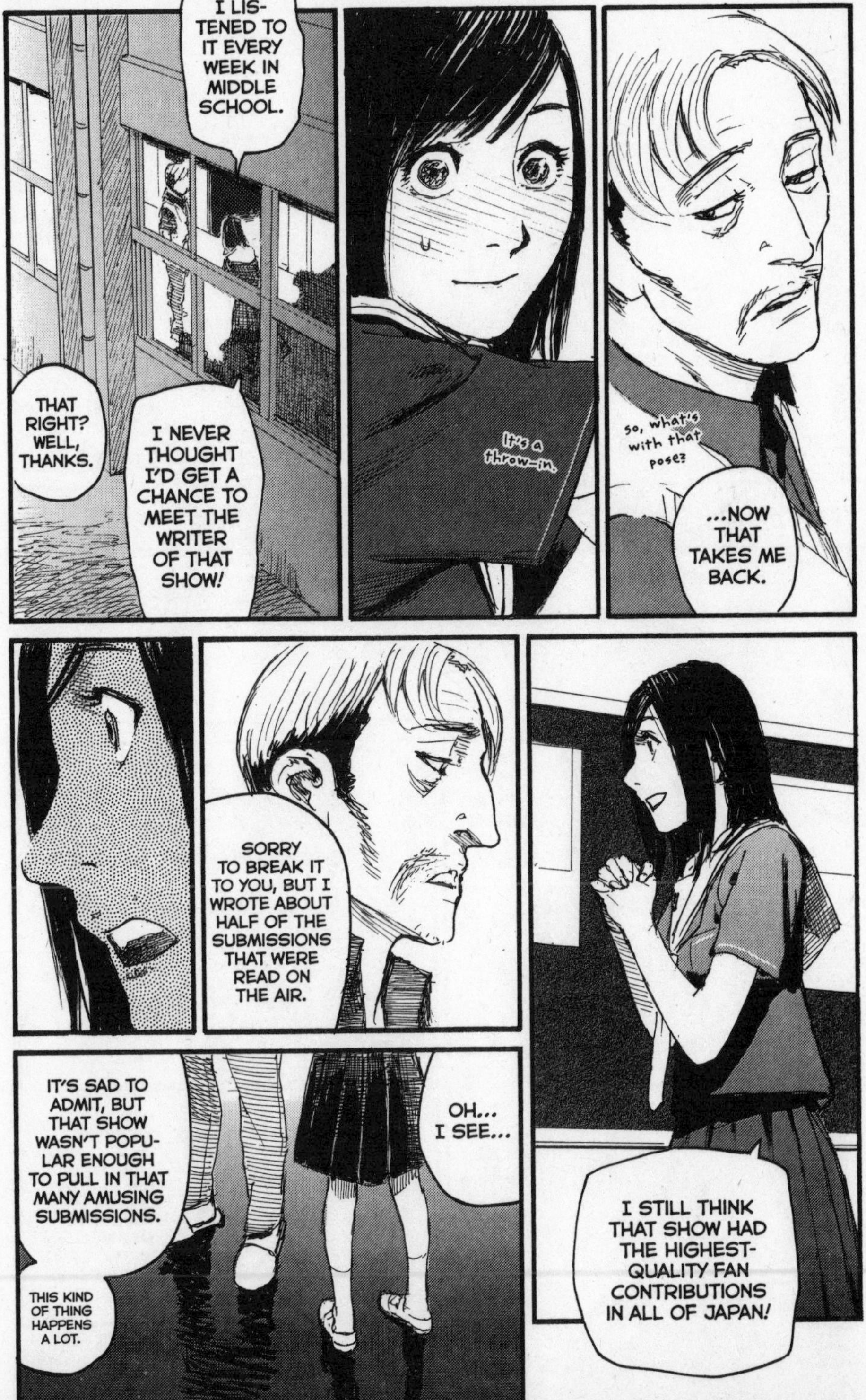
...NOW THAT TAKES ME BACK.
so, what's with that pose?
It's a throw-in.
I LIS-TENED TO IT EVERY WEEK IN MIDDLE SCHOOL.
I NEVER THOUGHT I'D GET A CHANCE TO MEET THE WRITER OF THAT SHOW!
THAT RIGHT? WELL, THANKS.
I STILL THINK THAT SHOW HAD THE HIGHEST-QUALITY FAN CONTRIBUTIONS IN ALL OF JAPAN!
SORRY TO BREAK IT TO YOU, BUT I WROTE ABOUT HALF OF THE SUBMISSIONS THAT WERE READ ON THE AIR.
OH... I SEE...
IT'S SAD TO ADMIT, BUT THAT SHOW WASN'T POPU-LAR ENOUGH TO PULL IN THAT MANY AMUSING SUBMISSIONS.
THIS KIND OF THING HAPPENS A LOT.

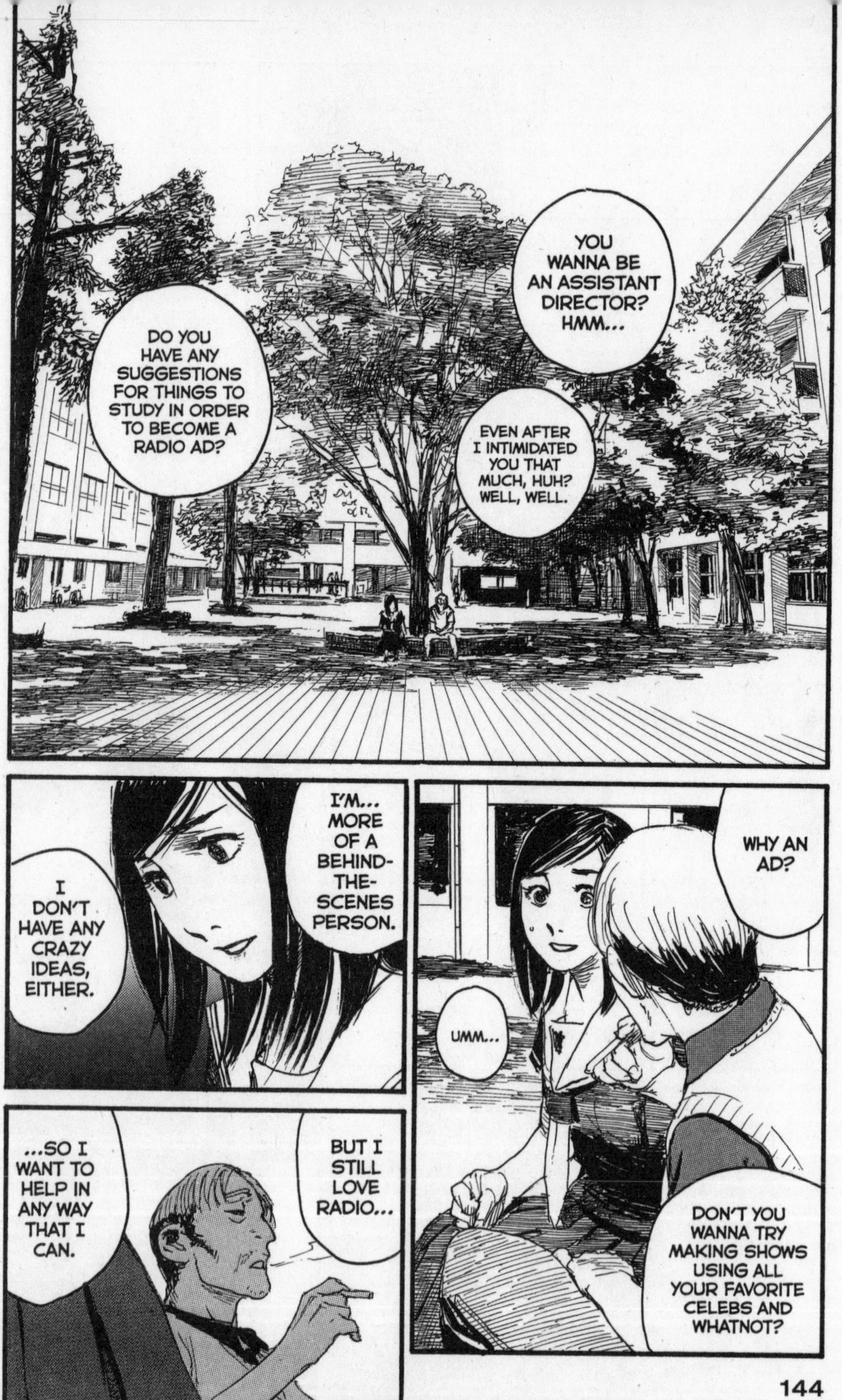
YOU WANNA BE AN ASSISTANT DIRECTOR? HMM...
EVEN AFTER I INTIMIDATED YOU THAT MUCH, HUH? WELL, WELL.
DO YOU HAVE ANY SUGGESTIONS FOR THINGS TO STUDY IN ORDER TO BECOME A RADIO AD?
WHY AN AD?
UMM...
DON'T YOU WANNA TRY MAKING SHOWS USING ALL YOUR FAVORITE CELEBS AND WHATNOT?
I'M... MORE OF A BEHIND-THE-SCENES PERSON.
I DON'T HAVE ANY CRAZY IDEAS, EITHER.
BUT I STILL LOVE RADIO...
...SO I WANT TO HELP IN ANY WAY THAT I CAN.

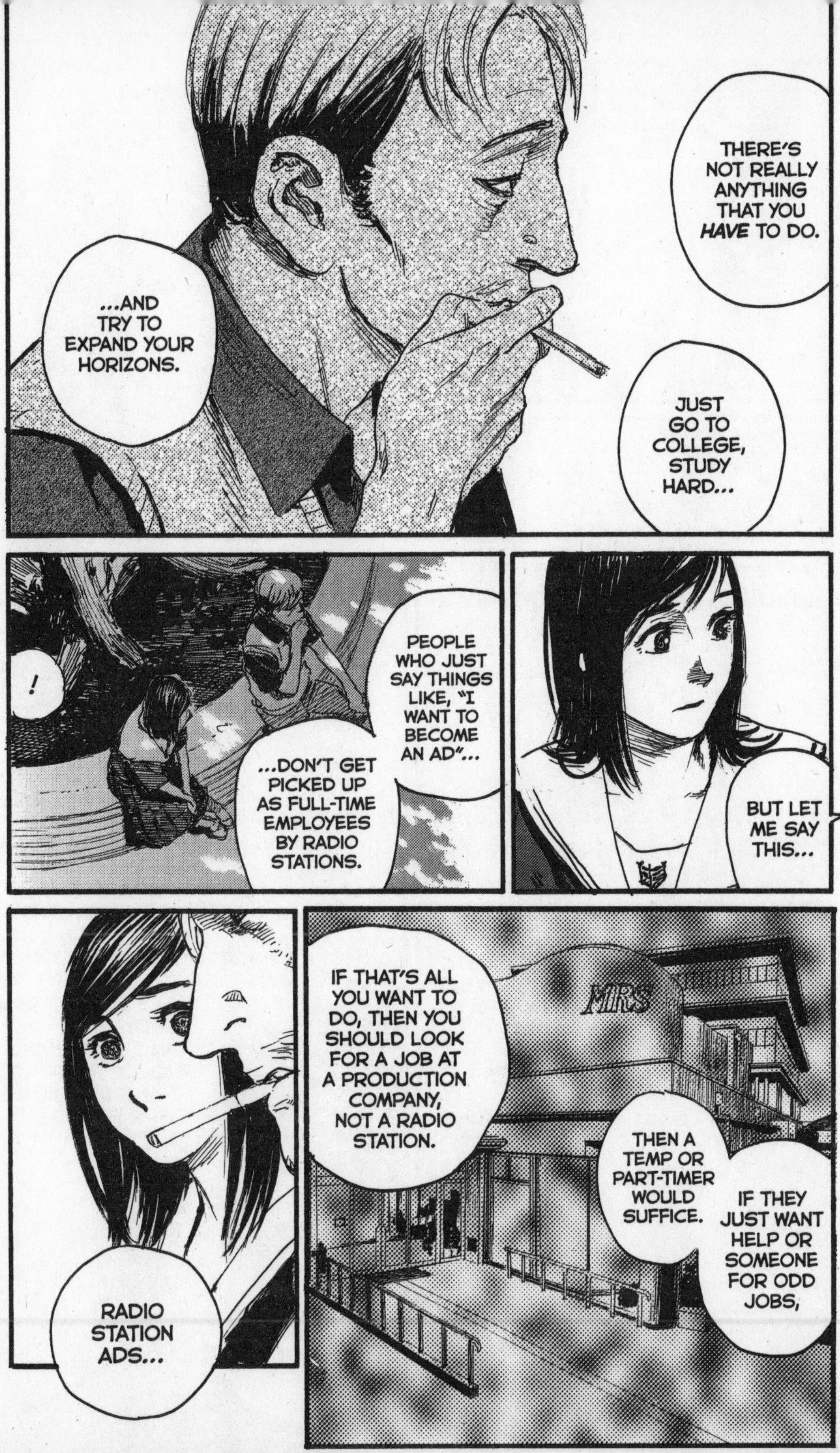
THERE'S NOT REALLY ANYTHING THAT YOU *HAVE* TO DO.
JUST GO TO COLLEGE, STUDY HARD...
...AND TRY TO EXPAND YOUR HORIZONS.
BUT LET ME SAY THIS...
PEOPLE WHO JUST SAY THINGS LIKE, "I WANT TO BECOME AN AD"...
...DON'T GET PICKED UP AS FULL-TIME EMPLOYEES BY RADIO STATIONS.
!
MRS
IF THEY JUST WANT HELP OR SOMEONE FOR ODD JOBS,
THEN A TEMP OR PART-TIMER WOULD SUFFICE.
IF THAT'S ALL YOU WANT TO DO, THEN YOU SHOULD LOOK FOR A JOB AT A PRODUCTION COMPANY, NOT A RADIO STATION.
RADIO STATION ADS...

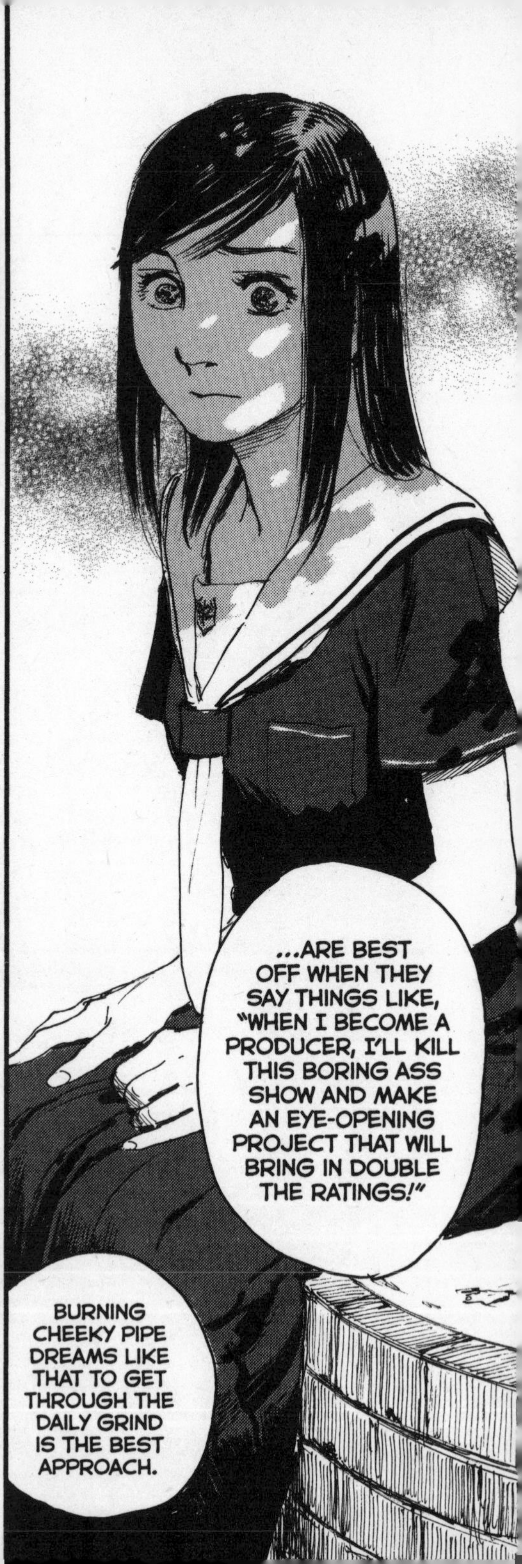
...ARE BEST OFF WHEN THEY SAY THINGS LIKE, "WHEN I BECOME A PRODUCER, I'LL KILL THIS BORING ASS SHOW AND MAKE AN EYE-OPENING PROJECT THAT WILL BRING IN DOUBLE THE RATINGS!"
BURNING CHEEKY PIPE DREAMS LIKE THAT TO GET THROUGH THE DAILY GRIND IS THE BEST APPROACH.
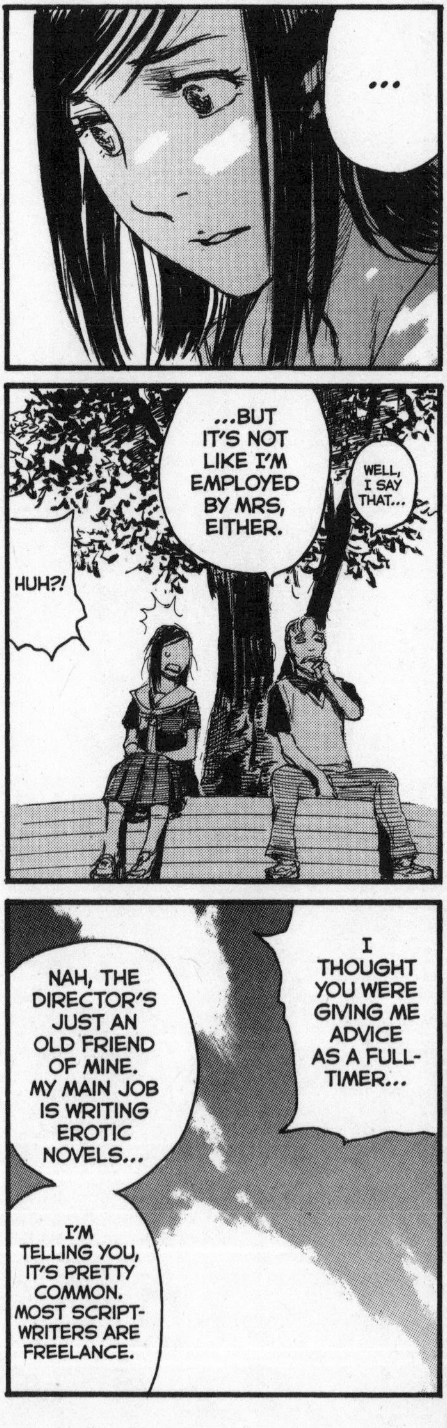
...
WELL, I SAY THAT...
...BUT IT'S NOT LIKE I'M EMPLOYED BY MRS, EITHER.
HUH?!
I THOUGHT YOU WERE GIVING ME ADVICE AS A FULL-TIMER...
NAH, THE DIRECTOR'S JUST AN OLD FRIEND OF MINE. MY MAIN JOB IS WRITING EROTIC NOVELS...
I'M TELLING YOU, IT'S PRETTY COMMON. MOST SCRIPT-WRITERS ARE FREELANCE.

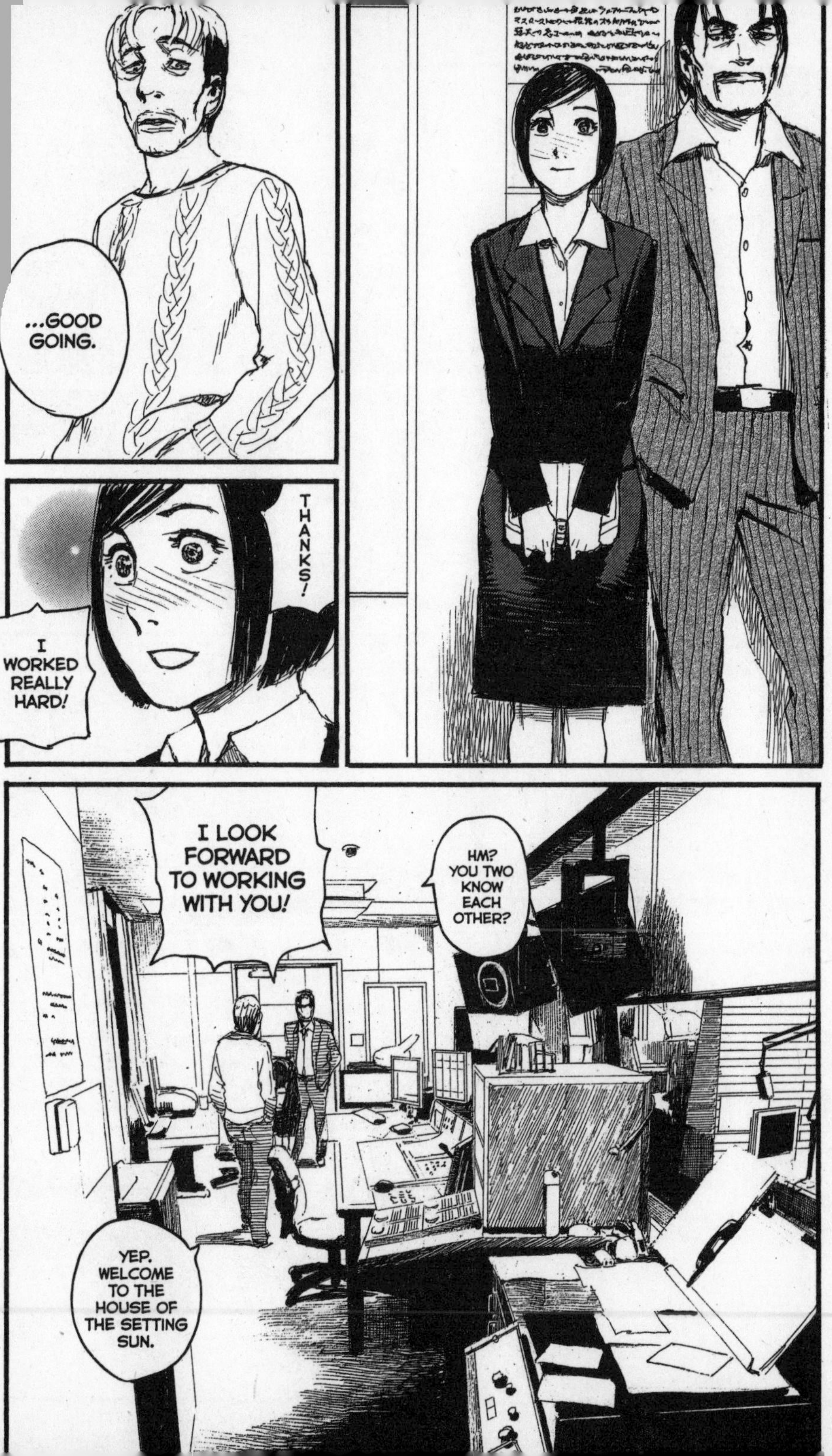
...GOOD GOING.
THANKS!
I WORKED REALLY HARD!
I LOOK FORWARD TO WORKING WITH YOU!
HM? YOU TWO KNOW EACH OTHER?
YEP. WELCOME TO THE HOUSE OF THE SETTING SUN.

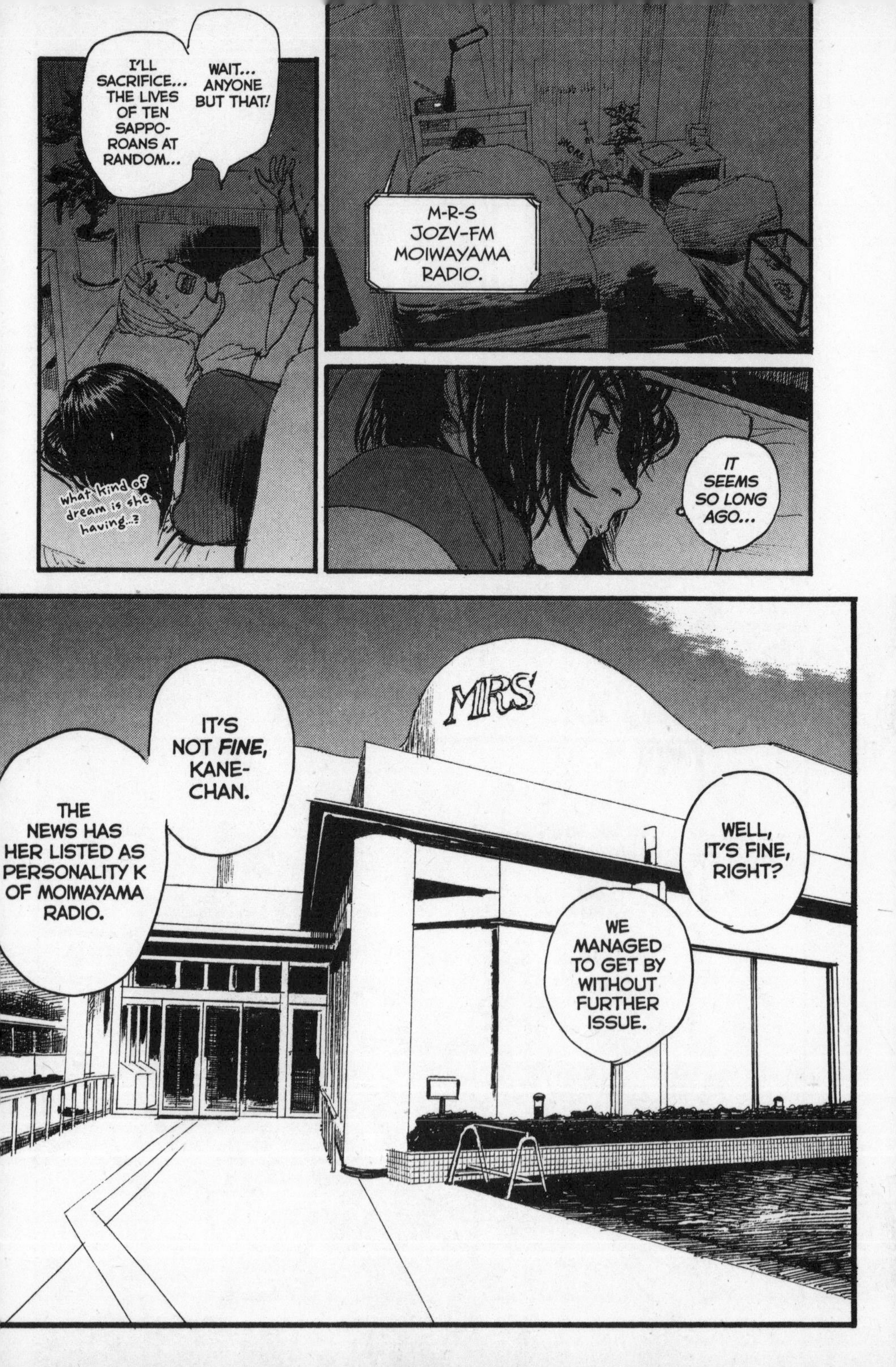
M-R-S
JOZV-FM
MOIWAYAMA
RADIO.
IT SEEMS SO LONG AGO...
WAIT... ANYONE BUT THAT!
I'LL SACRIFICE... THE LIVES OF TEN SAPPO-ROANS AT RANDOM...
what kind of dream is she having...?
MRS
WELL, IT'S FINE, RIGHT?
WE MANAGED TO GET BY WITHOUT FURTHER ISSUE.
IT'S NOT *FINE*, KANE-CHAN.
THE NEWS HAS HER LISTED AS PERSONALITY K OF MOIWAYAMA RADIO.

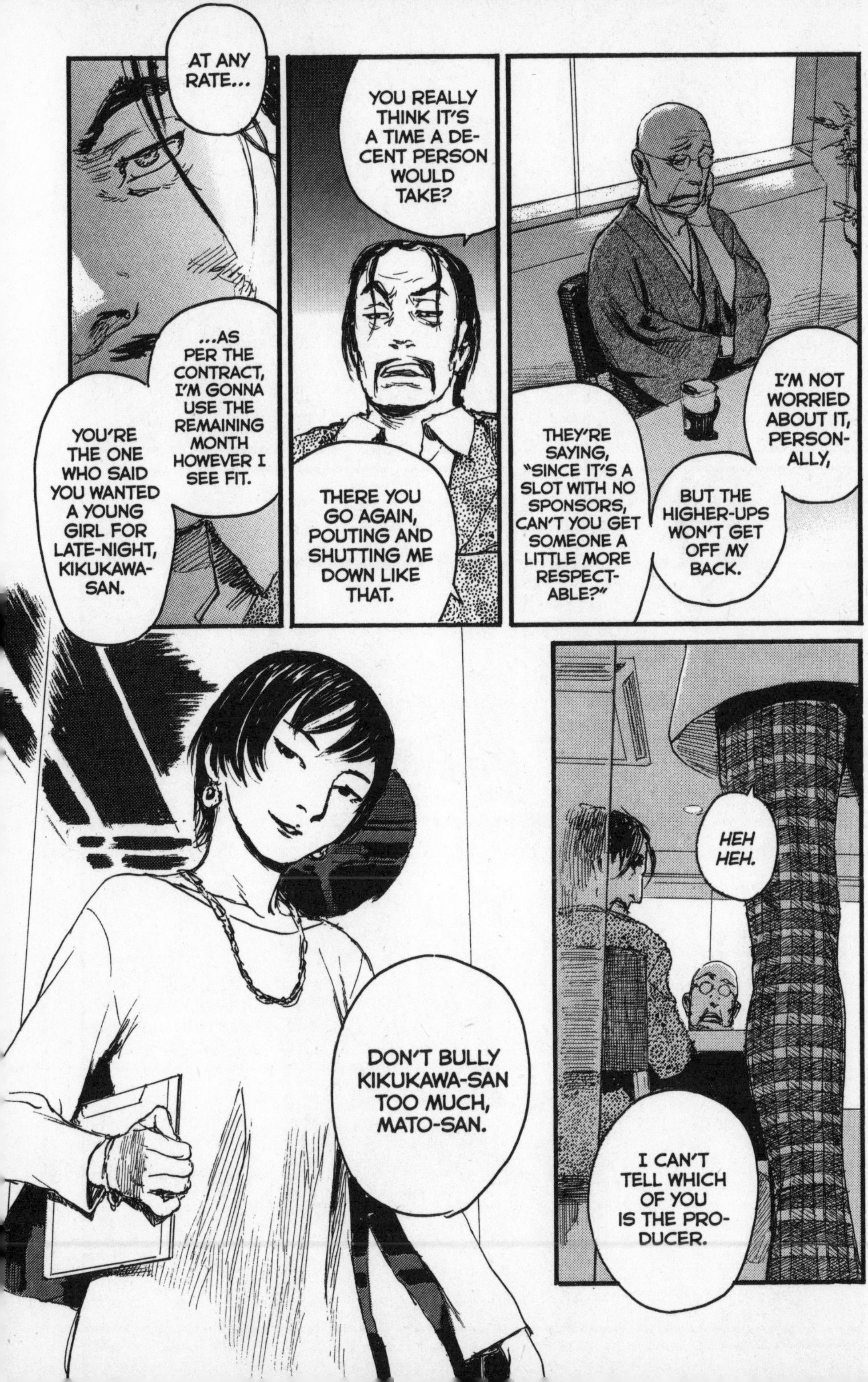
I'M NOT WORRIED ABOUT IT, PERSONALLY,
BUT THE HIGHER-UPS WON'T GET OFF MY BACK.
THEY'RE SAYING, "SINCE IT'S A SLOT WITH NO SPONSORS, CAN'T YOU GET SOMEONE A LITTLE MORE RESPECTABLE?"
YOU REALLY THINK IT'S A TIME A DECENT PERSON WOULD TAKE?
THERE YOU GO AGAIN, POUTING AND SHUTTING ME DOWN LIKE THAT.
AT ANY RATE...
...AS PER THE CONTRACT, I'M GONNA USE THE REMAINING MONTH HOWEVER I SEE FIT.
YOU'RE THE ONE WHO SAID YOU WANTED A YOUNG GIRL FOR LATE-NIGHT, KIKUKAWA-SAN.
HEH HEH.
I CAN'T TELL WHICH OF YOU IS THE PRODUCER.
DON'T BULLY KIKUKAWA-SAN TOO MUCH, MATO-SAN.

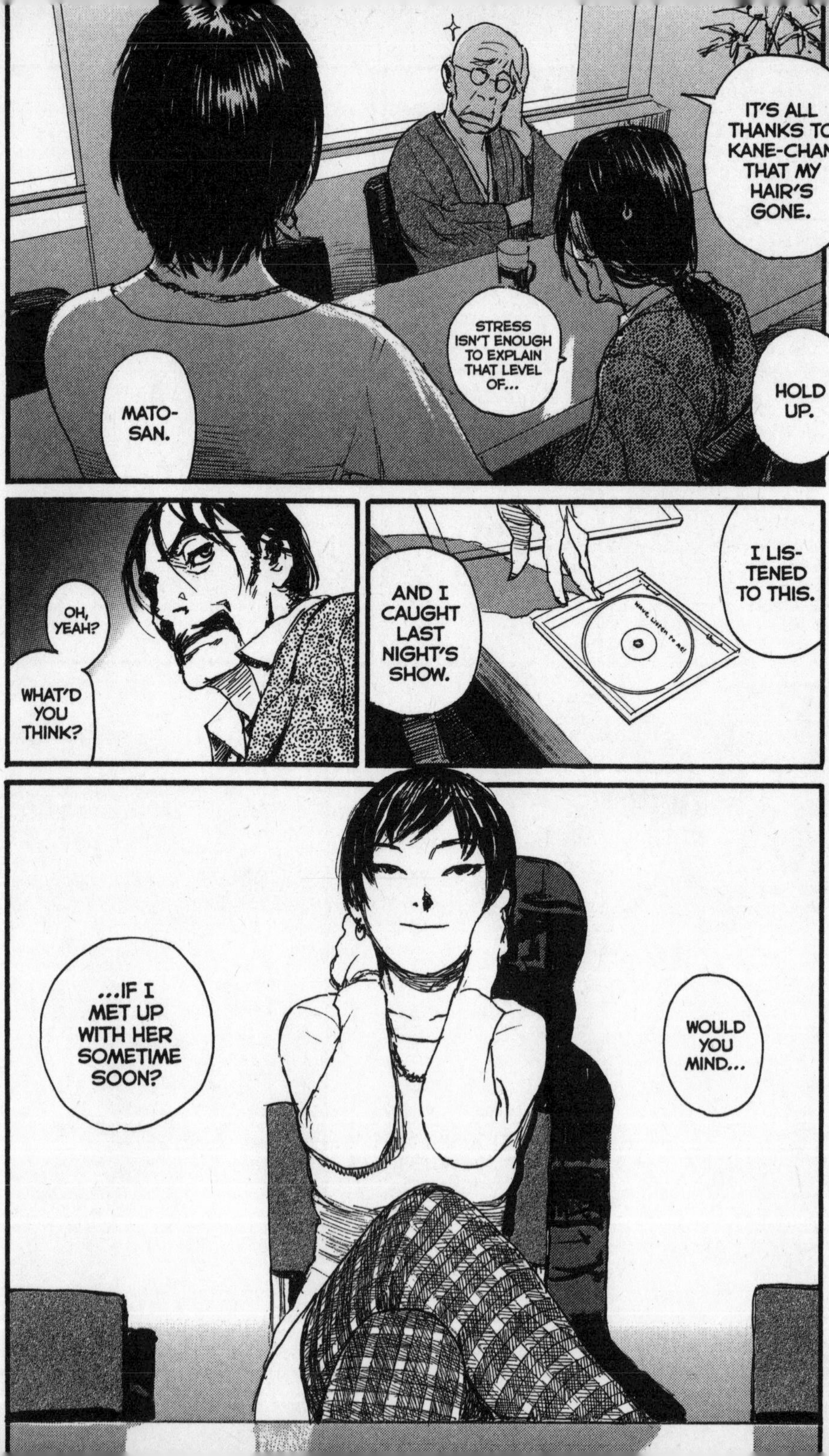
IT'S ALL THANKS TO KANE-CHAN THAT MY HAIR'S GONE.
STRESS ISN'T ENOUGH TO EXPLAIN THAT LEVEL OF...
HOLD UP.
MATO-SAN.
I LISTENED TO THIS.
AND I CAUGHT LAST NIGHT'S SHOW.
OH, YEAH?
WHAT'D YOU THINK?
WOULD YOU MIND...
...IF I MET UP WITH HER SOMETIME SOON?

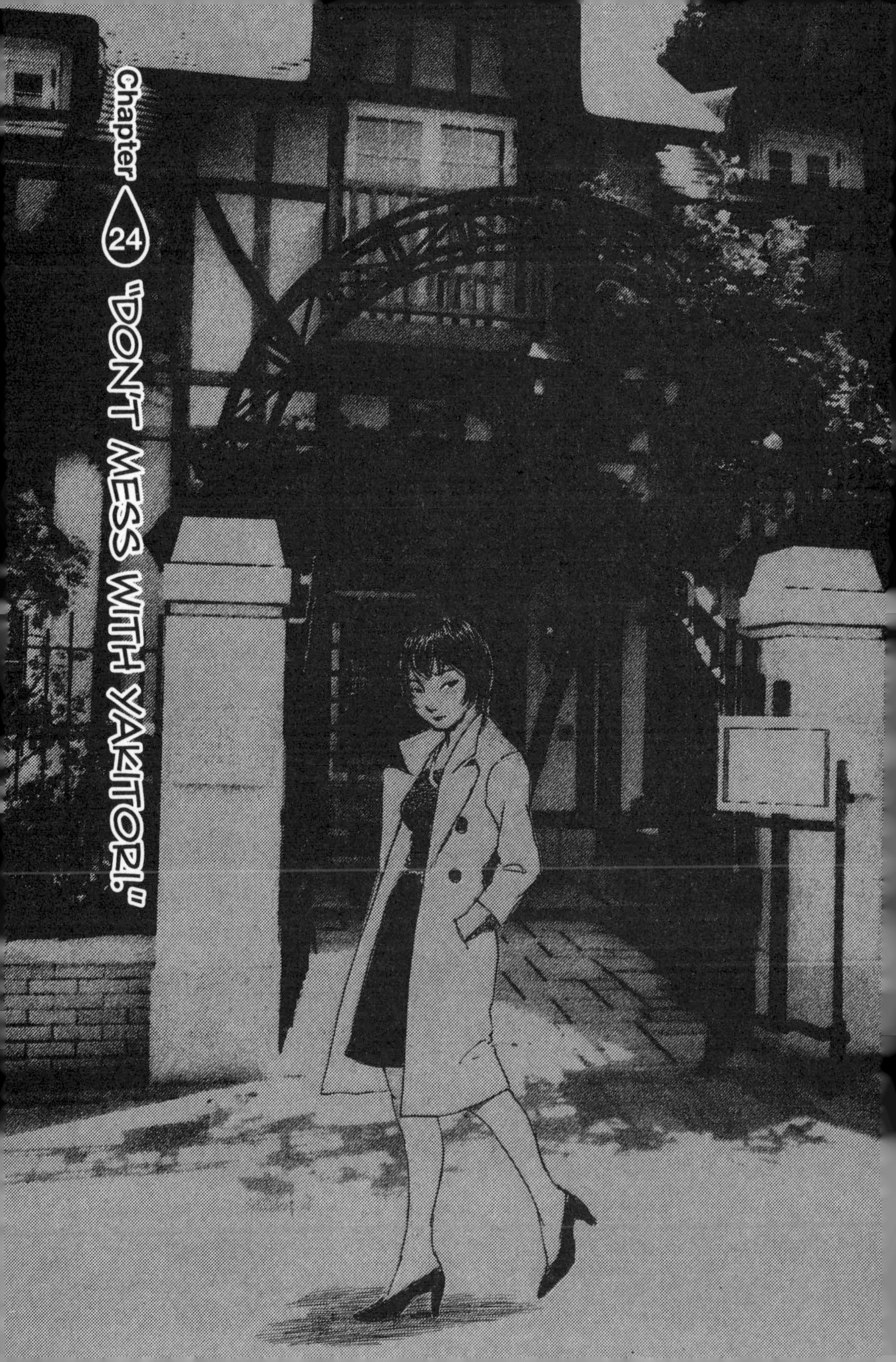
Chapter 24 "DON'T MESS WITH YAKITORI."

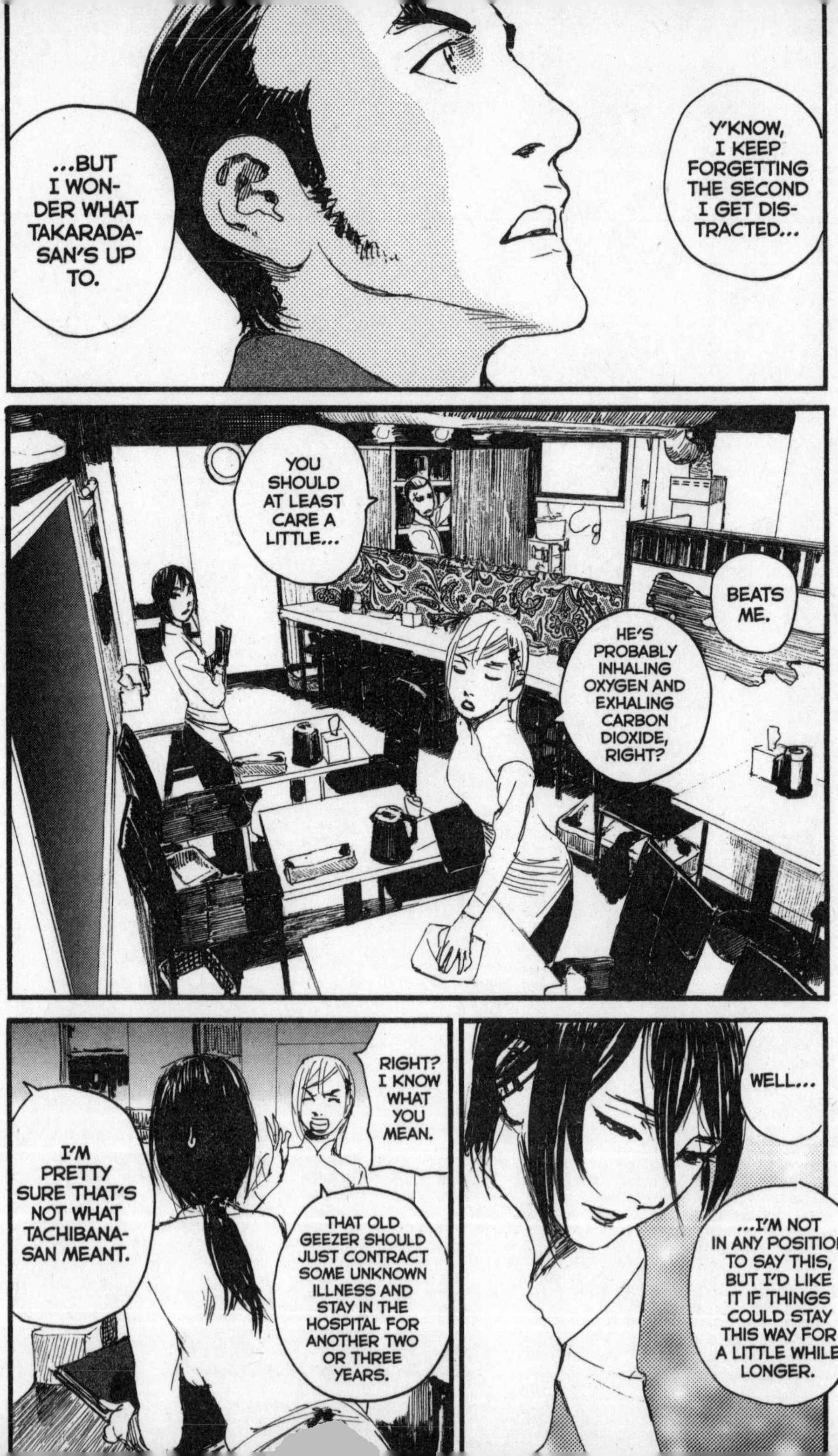
Y'KNOW, I KEEP FORGETTING THE SECOND I GET DIS-TRACTED...
...BUT I WONDER WHAT TAKARADA-SAN'S UP TO.
BEATS ME.
HE'S PROBABLY INHALING OXYGEN AND EXHALING CARBON DIOXIDE, RIGHT?
YOU SHOULD AT LEAST CARE A LITTLE...
WELL...
...I'M NOT IN ANY POSITION TO SAY THIS, BUT I'D LIKE IT IF THINGS COULD STAY THIS WAY FOR A LITTLE WHILE LONGER.
RIGHT? I KNOW WHAT YOU MEAN.
THAT OLD GEEZER SHOULD JUST CONTRACT SOME UNKNOWN ILLNESS AND STAY IN THE HOSPITAL FOR ANOTHER TWO OR THREE YEARS.
I'M PRETTY SURE THAT'S NOT WHAT TACHIBANA-SAN MEANT.

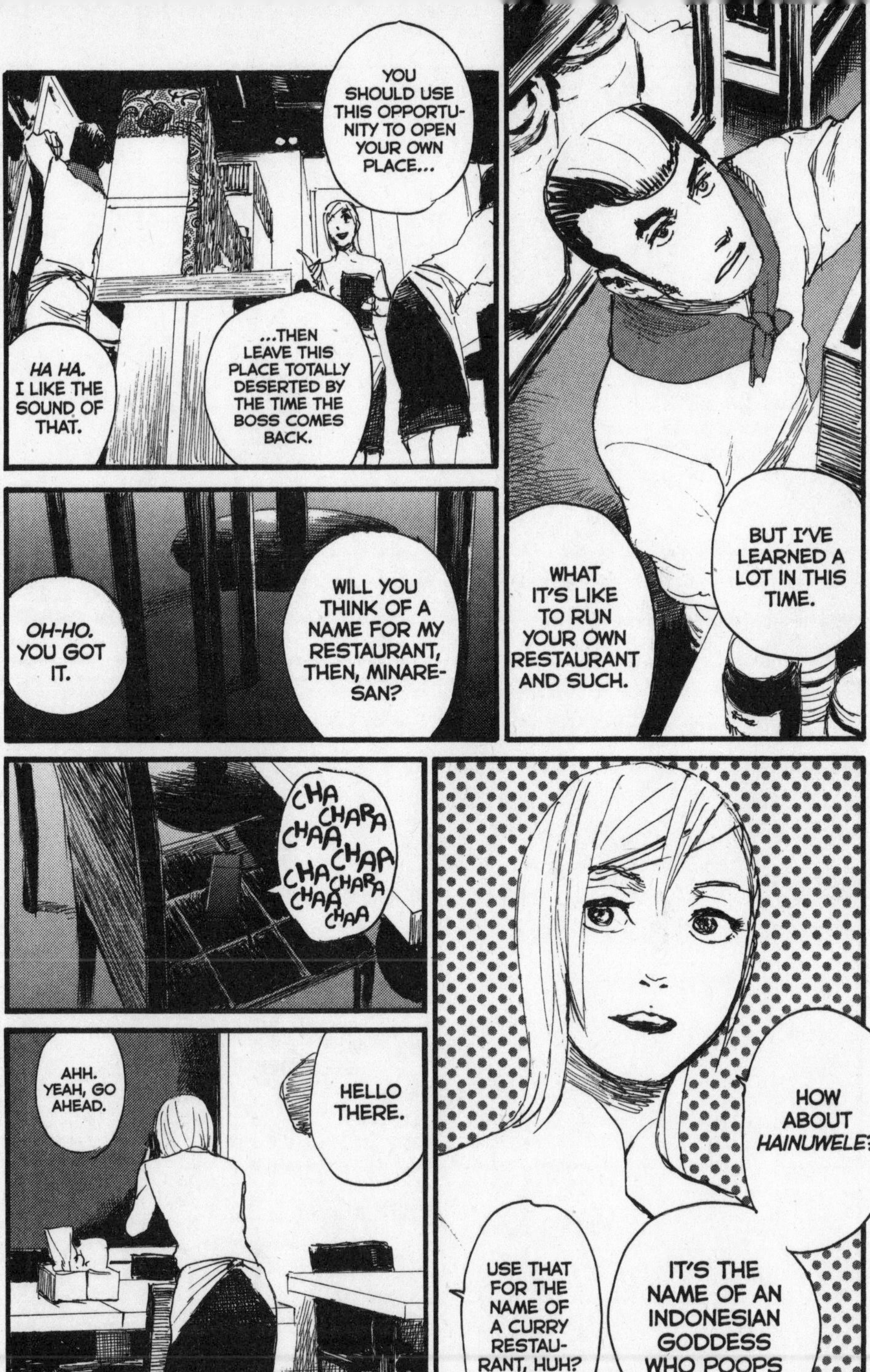
BUT I'VE LEARNED A LOT IN THIS TIME.
WHAT IT'S LIKE TO RUN YOUR OWN RESTAURANT AND SUCH.
YOU SHOULD USE THIS OPPORTUNITY TO OPEN YOUR OWN PLACE...
...THEN LEAVE THIS PLACE TOTALLY DESERTED BY THE TIME THE BOSS COMES BACK.
HA HA. I LIKE THE SOUND OF THAT.
WILL YOU THINK OF A NAME FOR MY RESTAURANT, THEN, MINARE-SAN?
OH-HO. YOU GOT IT.
HOW ABOUT *HAINUWELE?*
IT'S THE NAME OF AN INDONESIAN GODDESS WHO POOPS GOLD.
USE THAT FOR THE NAME OF A CURRY RESTAURANT, HUH? I GET YA...
CHA CHARA CHAA CHAA CHA CHARA CHAA CHAA
HELLO THERE.
AHH. YEAH, GO AHEAD.

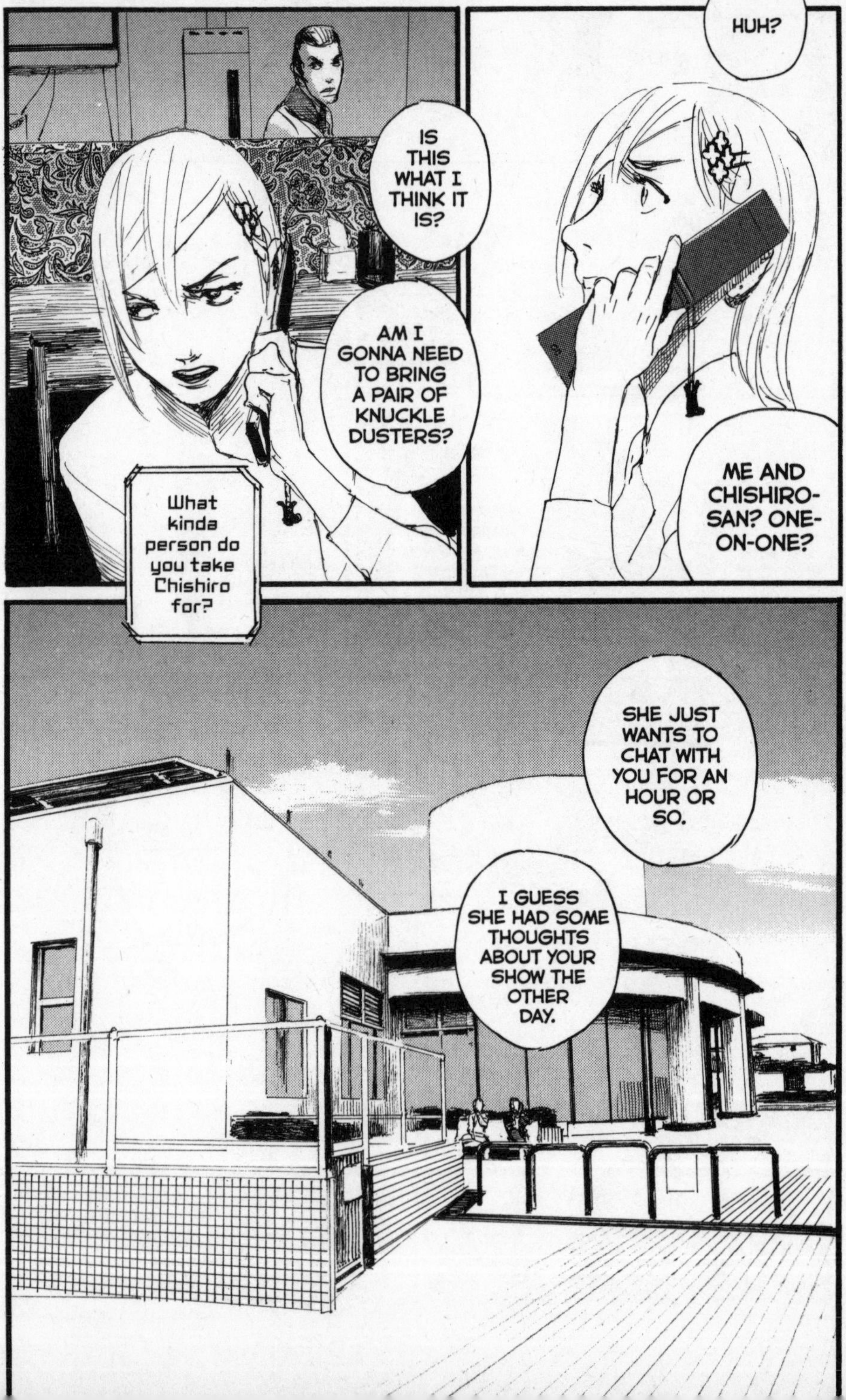
HUH?
ME AND CHISHIRO-SAN? ONE-ON-ONE?
IS THIS WHAT I THINK IT IS?
AM I GONNA NEED TO BRING A PAIR OF KNUCKLE DUSTERS?
What kinda person do you take Chishiro for?
SHE JUST WANTS TO CHAT WITH YOU FOR AN HOUR OR SO.
I GUESS SHE HAD SOME THOUGHTS ABOUT YOUR SHOW THE OTHER DAY.

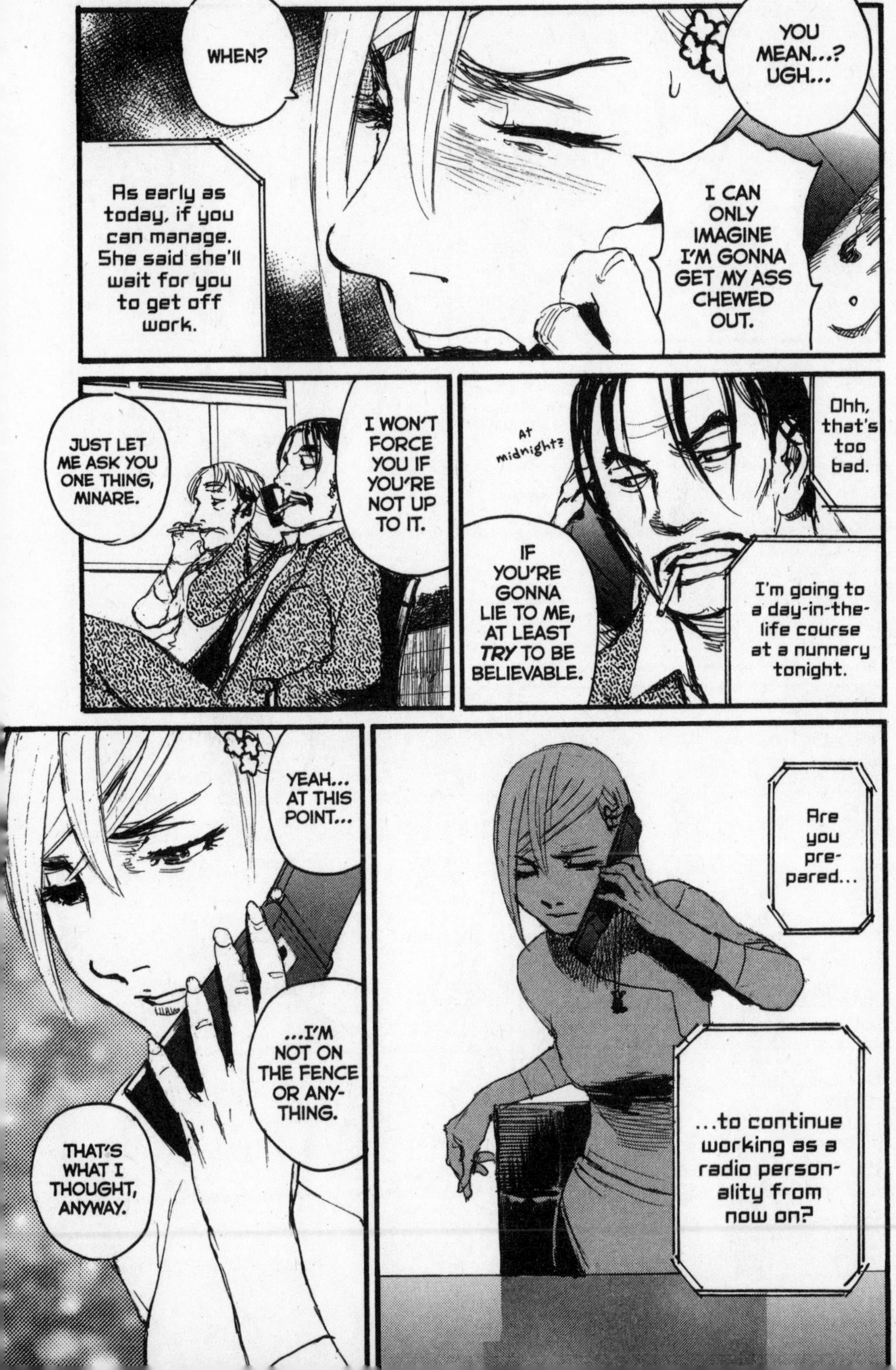
YOU MEAN...? UGH...
WHEN?
I CAN ONLY IMAGINE I'M GONNA GET MY ASS CHEWED OUT.
As early as today, if you can manage. She said she'll wait for you to get off work.
Ohh, that's too bad.
At midnight?
I'm going to a day-in-the-life course at a nunnery tonight.
IF YOU'RE GONNA LIE TO ME, AT LEAST *TRY* TO BE BELIEVABLE.
I WON'T FORCE YOU IF YOU'RE NOT UP TO IT.
JUST LET ME ASK YOU ONE THING, MINARE.
Are you pre-pared...
...to continue working as a radio person-ality from now on?
YEAH... AT THIS POINT...
...I'M NOT ON THE FENCE OR ANY-THING.
THAT'S WHAT I THOUGHT, ANYWAY.

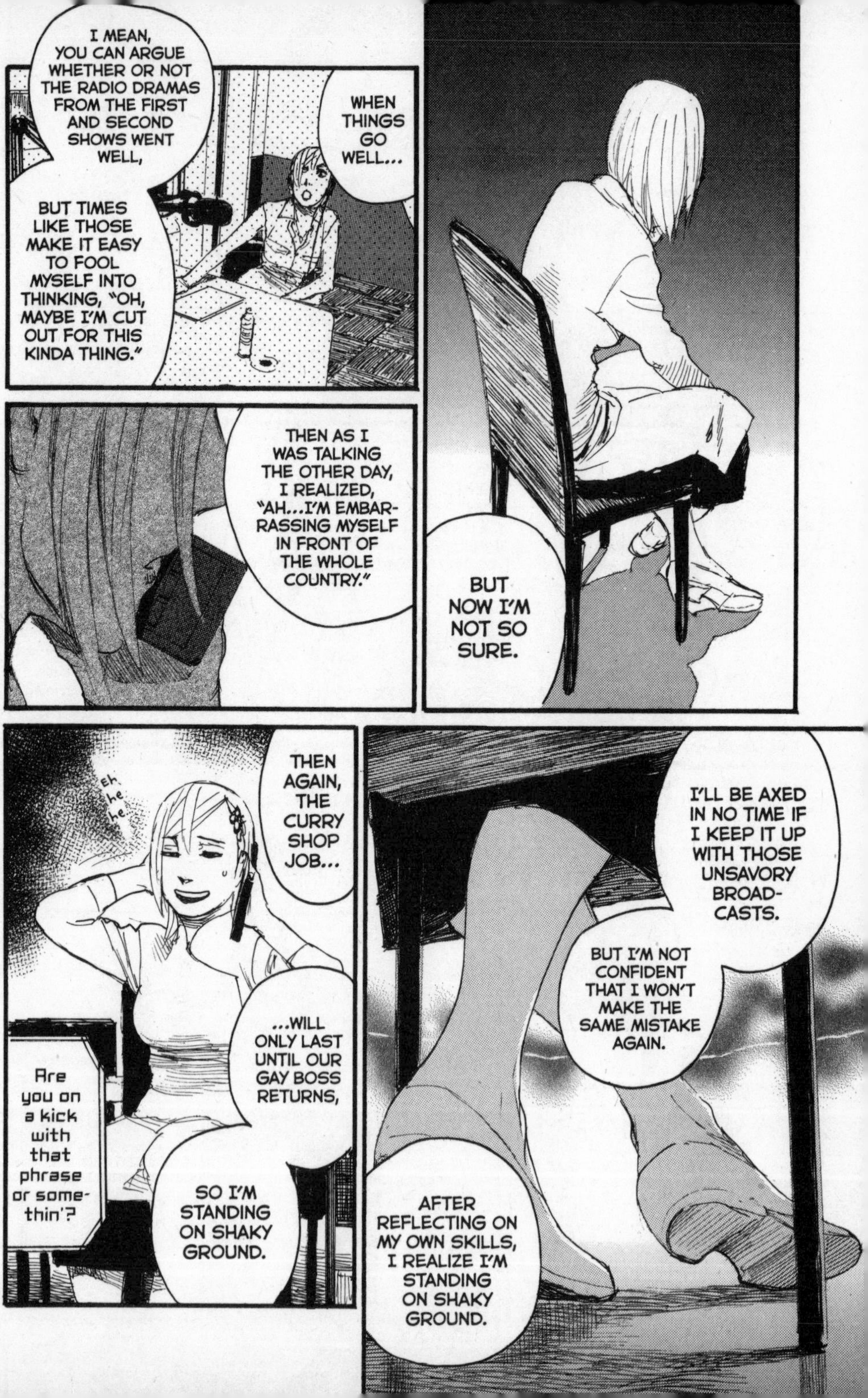
BUT NOW I'M NOT SO SURE.
I MEAN, YOU CAN ARGUE WHETHER OR NOT THE RADIO DRAMAS FROM THE FIRST AND SECOND SHOWS WENT WELL,
WHEN THINGS GO WELL...
BUT TIMES LIKE THOSE MAKE IT EASY TO FOOL MYSELF INTO THINKING, "OH, MAYBE I'M CUT OUT FOR THIS KINDA THING."
THEN AS I WAS TALKING THE OTHER DAY, I REALIZED, "AH...I'M EMBARRASSING MYSELF IN FRONT OF THE WHOLE COUNTRY."
I'LL BE AXED IN NO TIME IF I KEEP IT UP WITH THOSE UNSAVORY BROADCASTS.
BUT I'M NOT CONFIDENT THAT I WON'T MAKE THE SAME MISTAKE AGAIN.
AFTER REFLECTING ON MY OWN SKILLS, I REALIZE I'M STANDING ON SHAKY GROUND.
THEN AGAIN, THE CURRY SHOP JOB...
Eh he he
...WILL ONLY LAST UNTIL OUR GAY BOSS RETURNS,
SO I'M STANDING ON SHAKY GROUND.
Are you on a kick with that phrase or somethin'?

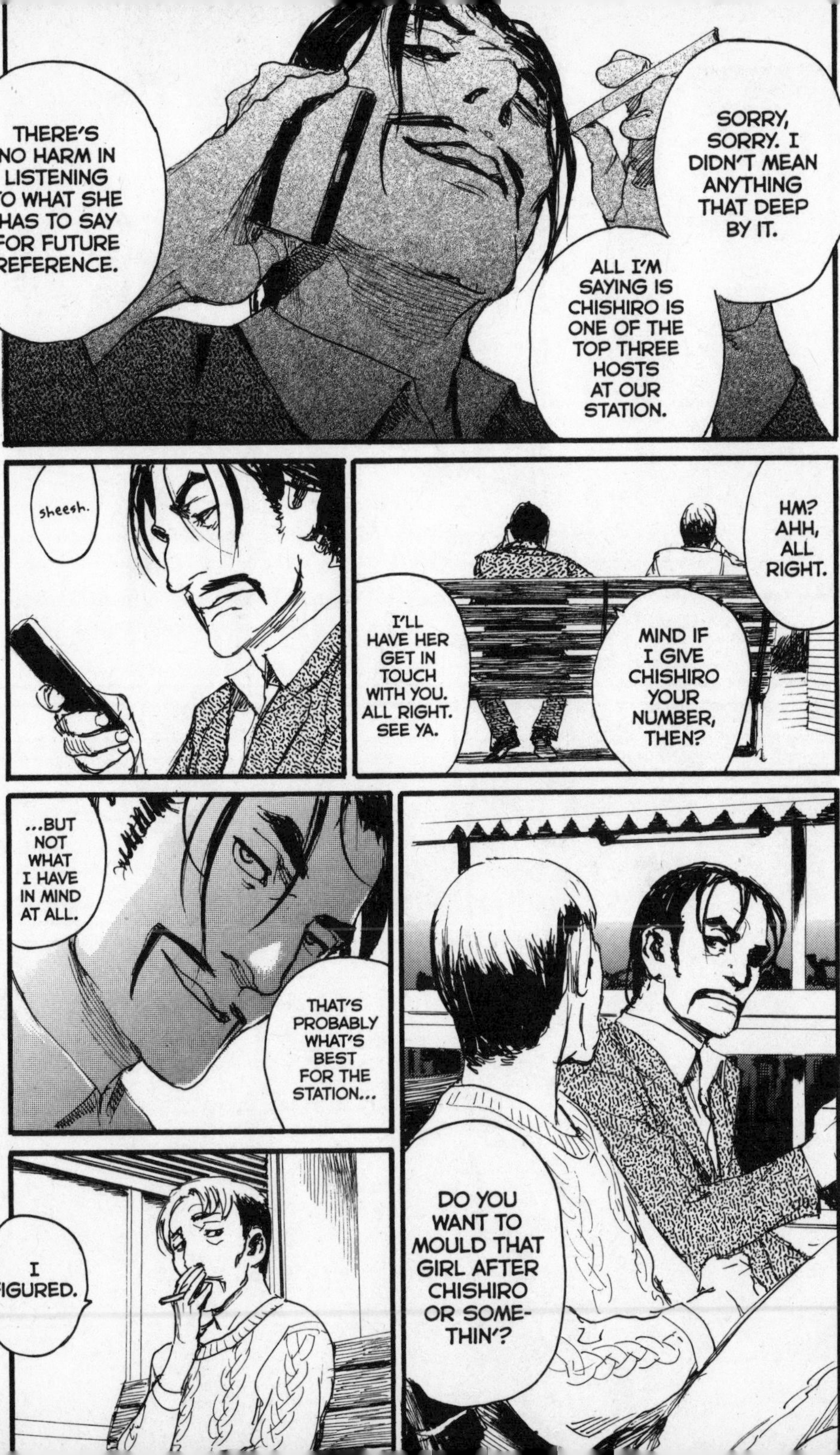
SORRY, SORRY. I DIDN'T MEAN ANYTHING THAT DEEP BY IT.
ALL I'M SAYING IS CHISHIRO IS ONE OF THE TOP THREE HOSTS AT OUR STATION.
THERE'S NO HARM IN LISTENING TO WHAT SHE HAS TO SAY FOR FUTURE REFERENCE.
HM? AHH, ALL RIGHT.
MIND IF I GIVE CHISHIRO YOUR NUMBER, THEN?
I'LL HAVE HER GET IN TOUCH WITH YOU. ALL RIGHT. SEE YA.
sheesh.
DO YOU WANT TO MOULD THAT GIRL AFTER CHISHIRO OR SOME-THIN'?
THAT'S PROBABLY WHAT'S BEST FOR THE STATION...
...BUT NOT WHAT I HAVE IN MIND AT ALL.
I FIGURED.

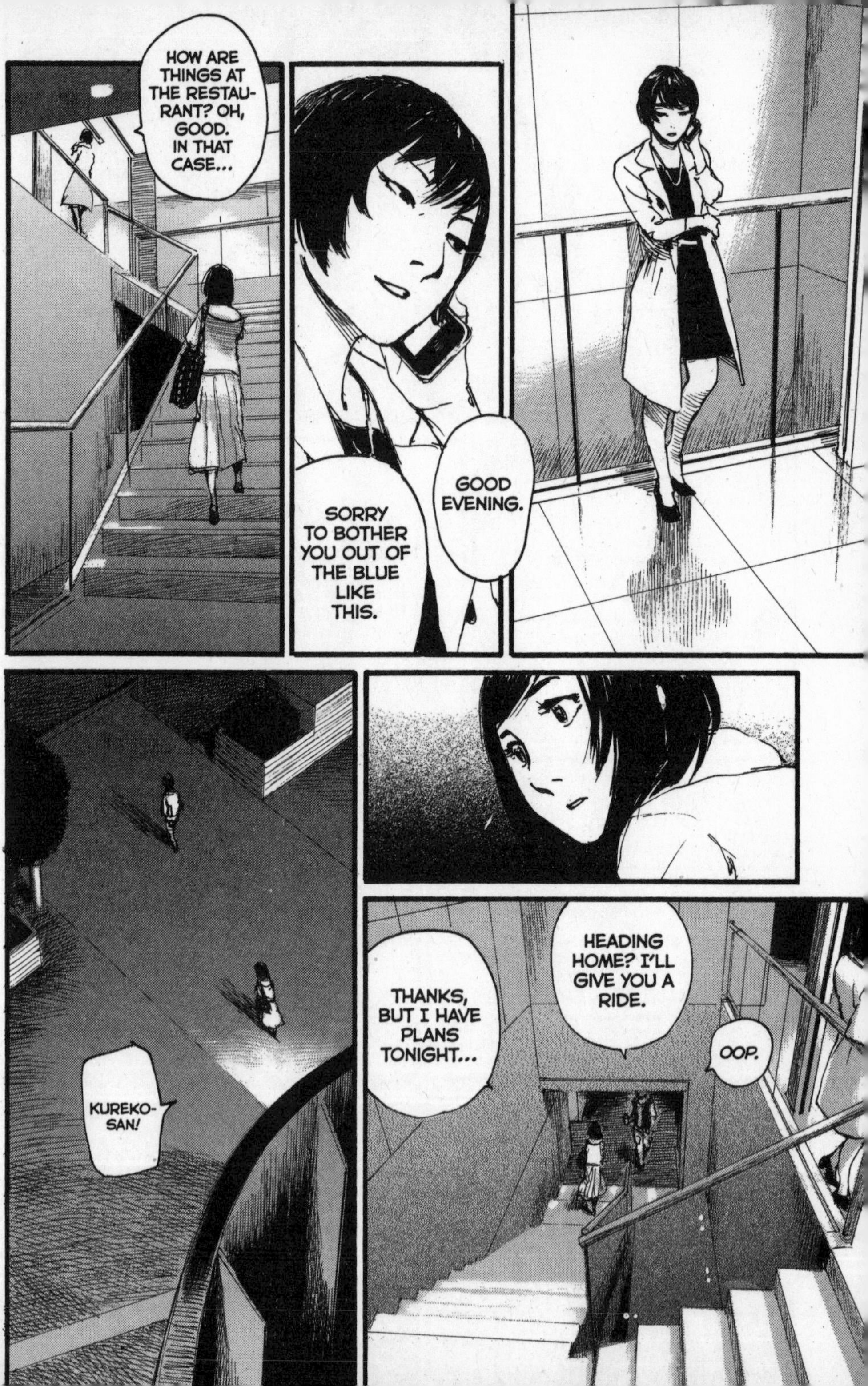
GOOD EVENING.
SORRY TO BOTHER YOU OUT OF THE BLUE LIKE THIS.
HOW ARE THINGS AT THE RESTAU-RANT? OH, GOOD. IN THAT CASE...
HEADING HOME? I'LL GIVE YOU A RIDE.
OOP.
THANKS, BUT I HAVE PLANS TONIGHT...
KUREKO-SAN!

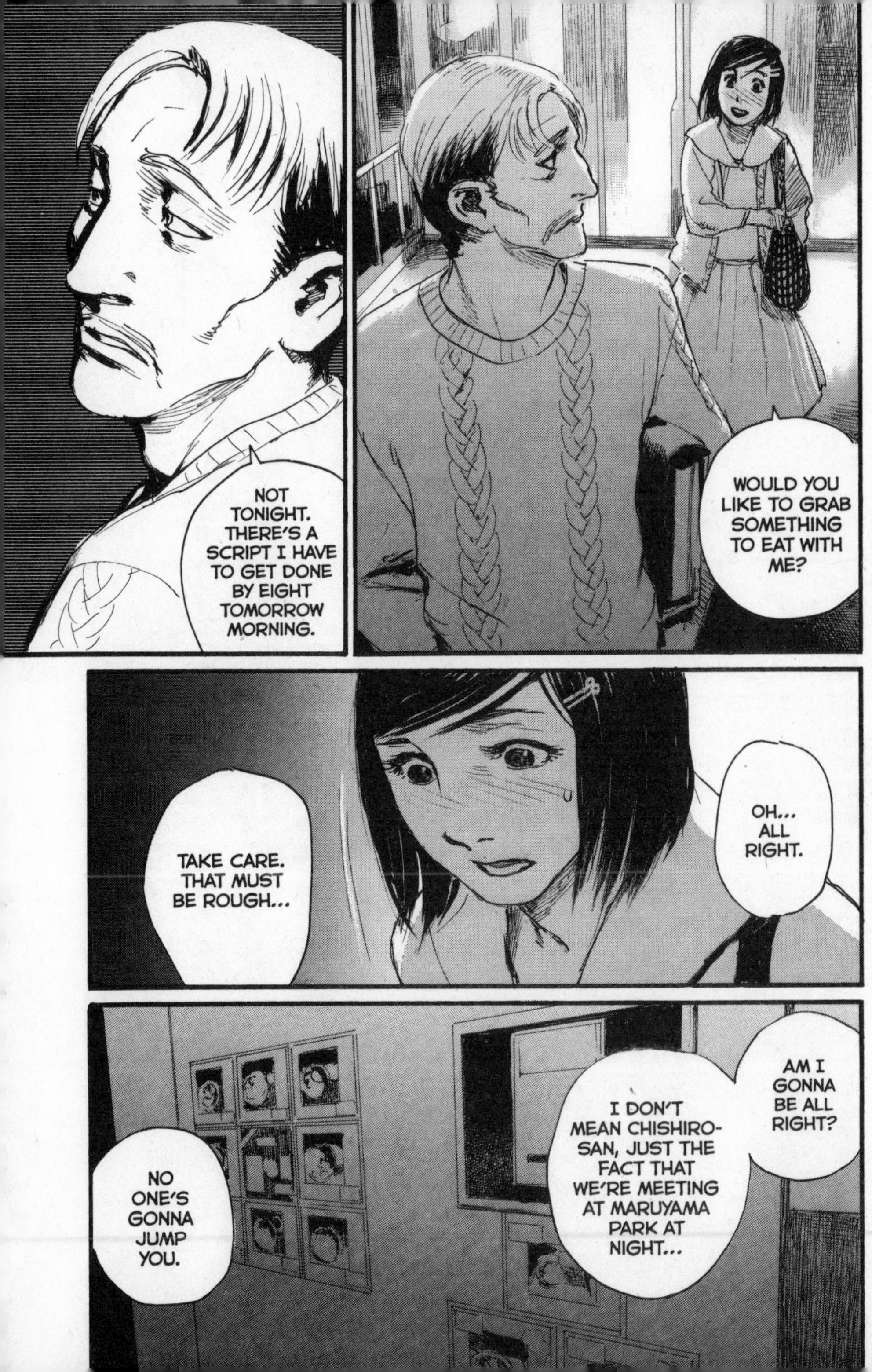
WOULD YOU LIKE TO GRAB SOMETHING TO EAT WITH ME?
NOT TONIGHT. THERE'S A SCRIPT I HAVE TO GET DONE BY EIGHT TOMORROW MORNING.
OH... ALL RIGHT.
TAKE CARE. THAT MUST BE ROUGH...
AM I GONNA BE ALL RIGHT?
I DON'T MEAN CHISHIRO-SAN, JUST THE FACT THAT WE'RE MEETING AT MARUYAMA PARK AT NIGHT...
NO ONE'S GONNA JUMP YOU.

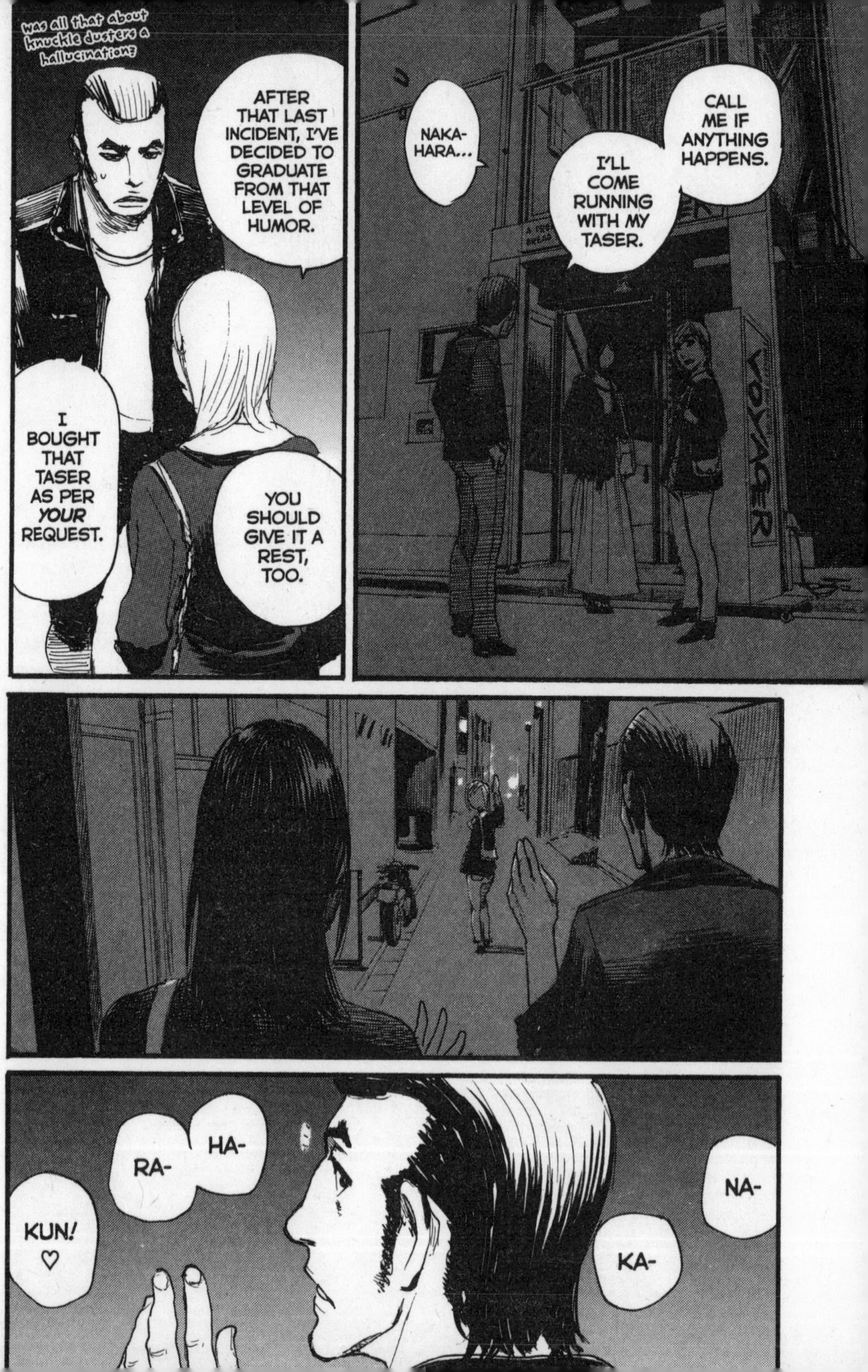
CALL ME IF ANYTHING HAPPENS.
I'LL COME RUNNING WITH MY TASER.
NAKA-HARA...
VOYAGER
was all that about knuckle dusters a hallucination?
AFTER THAT LAST INCIDENT, I'VE DECIDED TO GRADUATE FROM THAT LEVEL OF HUMOR.
I BOUGHT THAT TASER AS PER *YOUR* REQUEST.
YOU SHOULD GIVE IT A REST, TOO.
NA-
KA-
HA-
RA-
KUN! ♡

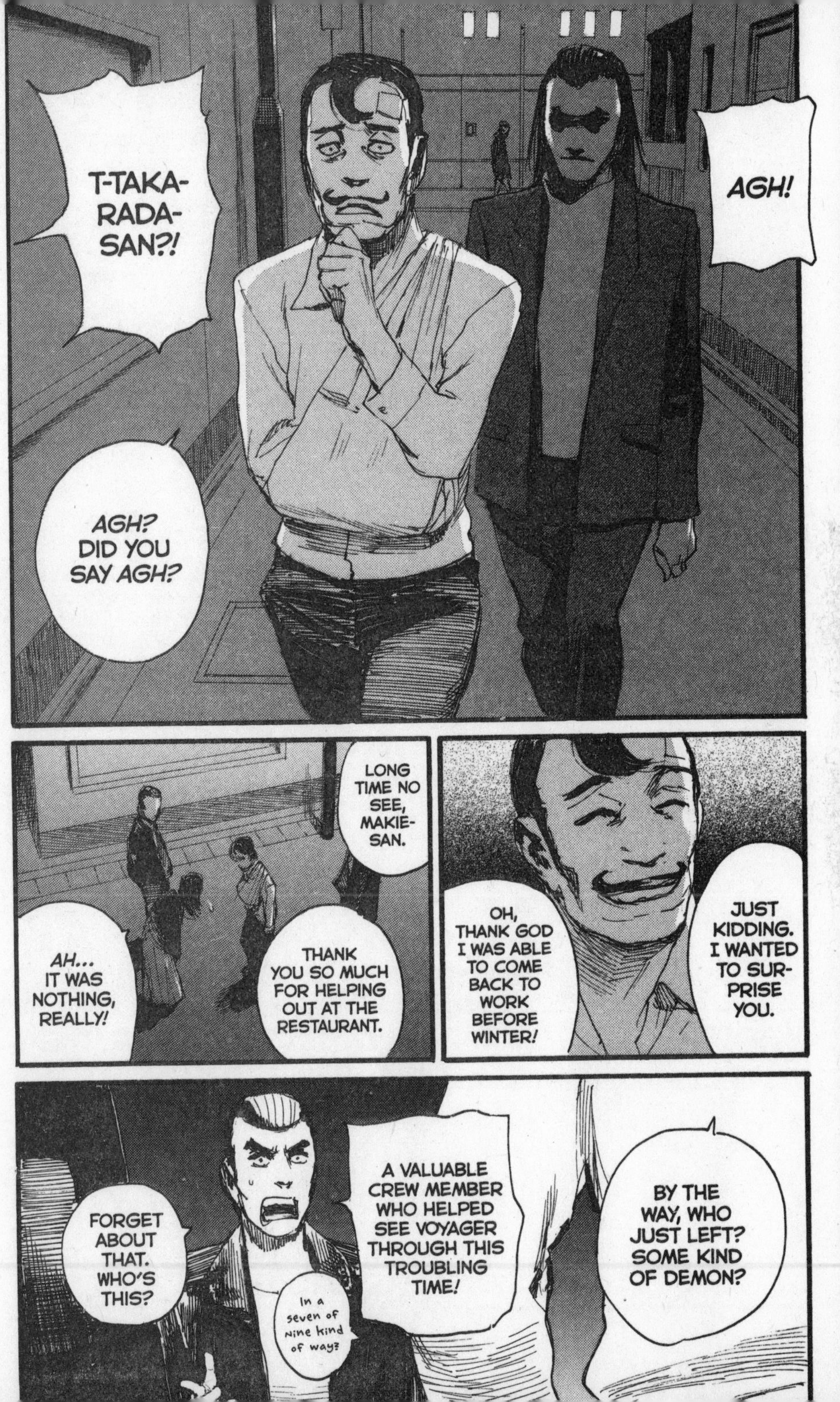
AGH!
T-TAKA-RADA-SAN?!
AGH? DID YOU SAY AGH?
JUST KIDDING. I WANTED TO SUR-PRISE YOU.
OH, THANK GOD I WAS ABLE TO COME BACK TO WORK BEFORE WINTER!
LONG TIME NO SEE, MAKIE-SAN.
THANK YOU SO MUCH FOR HELPING OUT AT THE RESTAURANT.
AH... IT WAS NOTHING, REALLY!
BY THE WAY, WHO JUST LEFT? SOME KIND OF DEMON?
A VALUABLE CREW MEMBER WHO HELPED SEE VOYAGER THROUGH THIS TROUBLING TIME!
In a seven of Nine kind of way?
FORGET ABOUT THAT. WHO'S THIS?

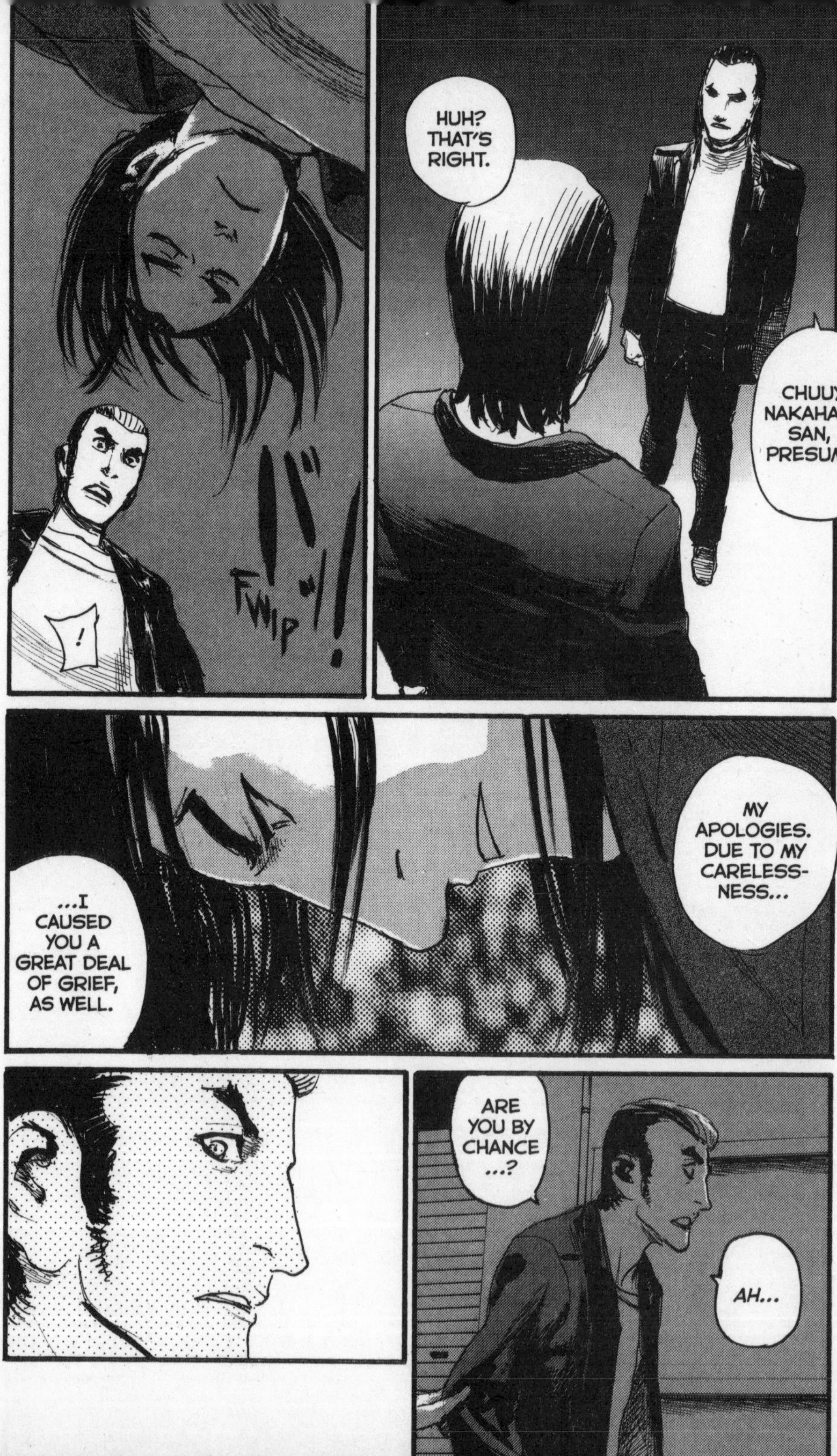
HUH? THAT'S RIGHT.
CHUUYA NAKAHARA-SAN, I PRESUME?
FWIP
!
MY APOLOGIES. DUE TO MY CARELESS-NESS...
...I CAUSED YOU A GREAT DEAL OF GRIEF, AS WELL.
ARE YOU BY CHANCE ...?
AH...

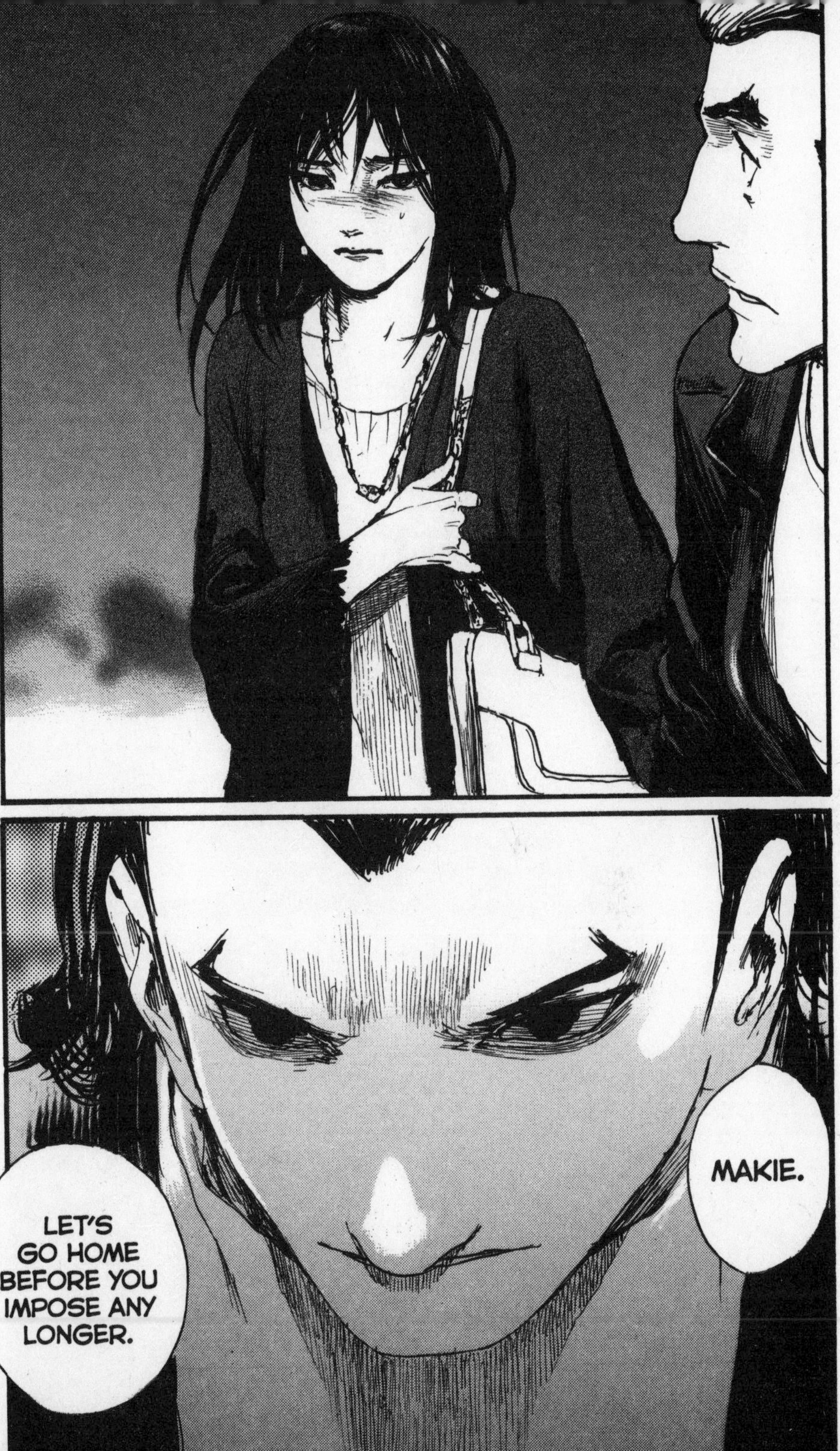
MAKIE.
LET'S GO HOME BEFORE YOU IMPOSE ANY LONGER.

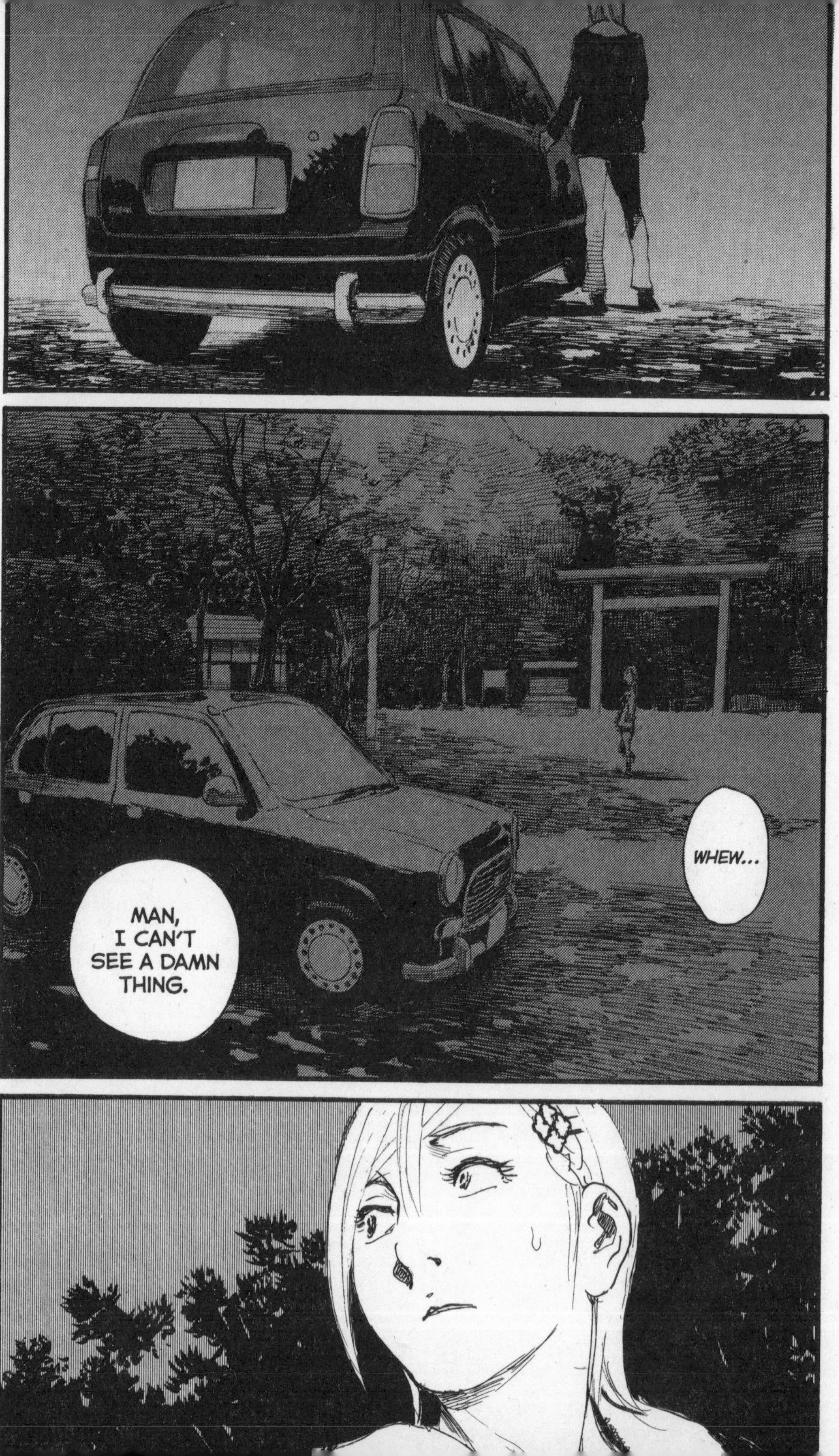
WHEW...
MAN, I CAN'T SEE A DAMN THING.

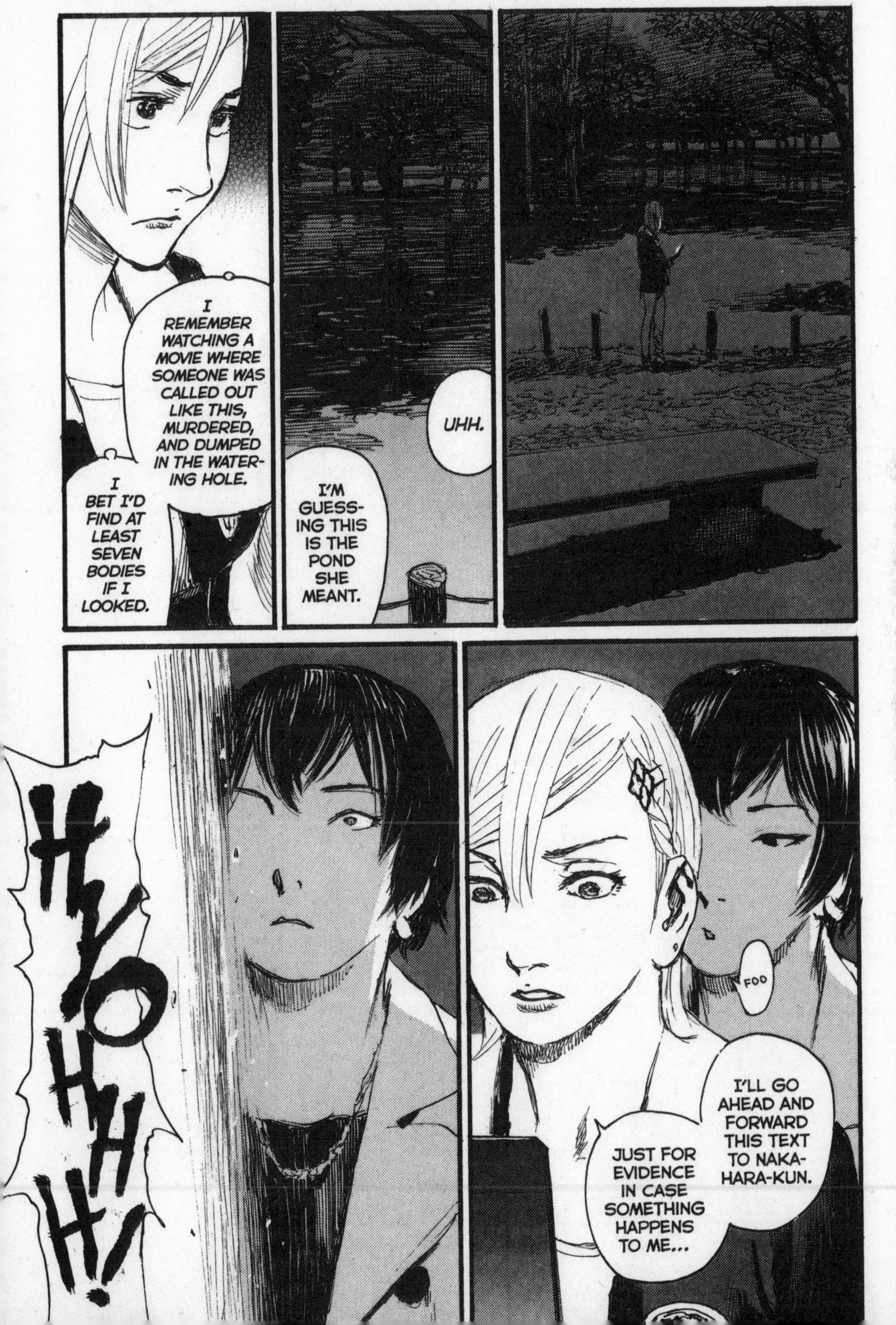
UHH.
I'M GUESSING THIS IS THE POND SHE MEANT.
I REMEMBER WATCHING A MOVIE WHERE SOMEONE WAS CALLED OUT LIKE THIS, MURDERED, AND DUMPED IN THE WATERING HOLE.
I BET I'D FIND AT LEAST SEVEN BODIES IF I LOOKED.
FOO
I'LL GO AHEAD AND FORWARD THIS TEXT TO NAKAHARA-KUN.
JUST FOR EVIDENCE IN CASE SOMETHING HAPPENS TO ME...
HYOHHHH!

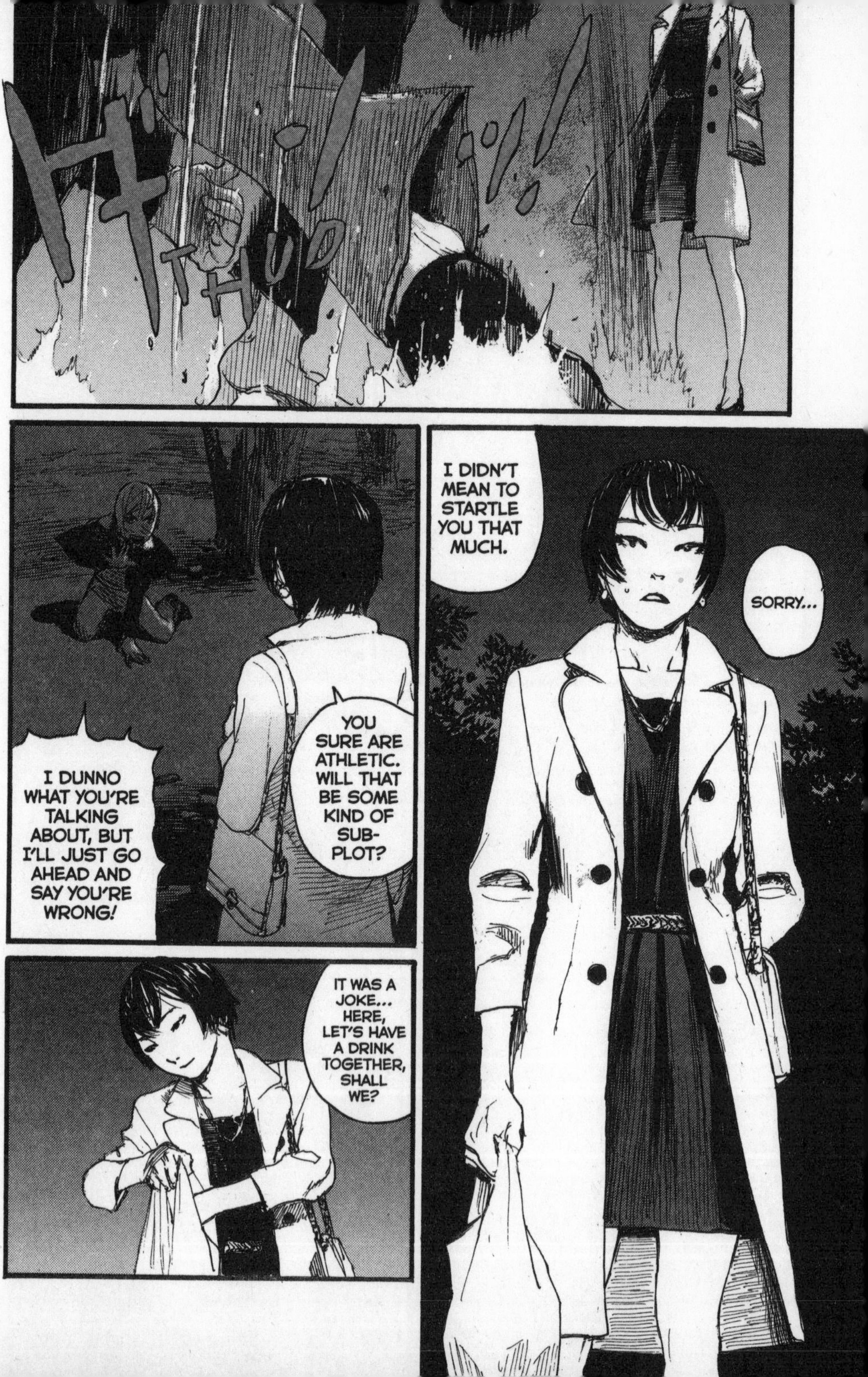
THUD
I DIDN'T MEAN TO STARTLE YOU THAT MUCH.
SORRY...
YOU SURE ARE ATHLETIC. WILL THAT BE SOME KIND OF SUB-PLOT?
I DUNNO WHAT YOU'RE TALKING ABOUT, BUT I'LL JUST GO AHEAD AND SAY YOU'RE WRONG!
IT WAS A JOKE... HERE, LET'S HAVE A DRINK TOGETHER, SHALL WE?

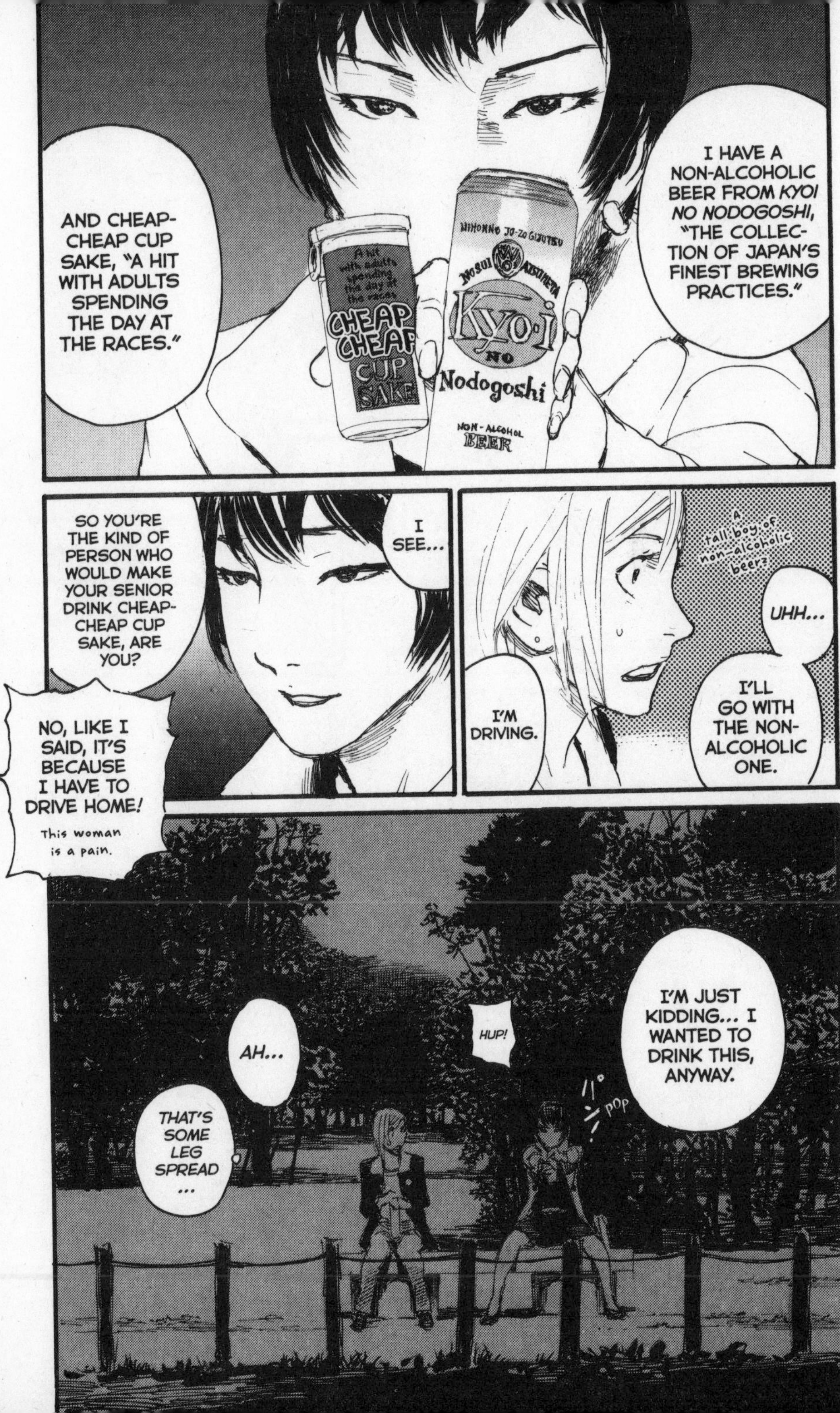
I HAVE A NON-ALCOHOLIC BEER FROM *KYOI NO NODOGOSHI*, "THE COLLECTION OF JAPAN'S FINEST BREWING PRACTICES."
Kyo-i NO Nodogoshi
NON-ALCOHOL BEER
A hit with adults spending the day at the races
CHEAP CHEAP CUP SAKE
AND CHEAP-CHEAP CUP SAKE, "A HIT WITH ADULTS SPENDING THE DAY AT THE RACES."
A tall boy of non-alcoholic beer?
UHH...
I'LL GO WITH THE NON-ALCOHOLIC ONE.
I'M DRIVING.
I SEE...
SO YOU'RE THE KIND OF PERSON WHO WOULD MAKE YOUR SENIOR DRINK CHEAP-CHEAP CUP SAKE, ARE YOU?
NO, LIKE I SAID, IT'S BECAUSE I HAVE TO DRIVE HOME!
This woman is a pain.
I'M JUST KIDDING... I WANTED TO DRINK THIS, ANYWAY.
POP
HUP!
AH...
THAT'S SOME LEG SPREAD ...

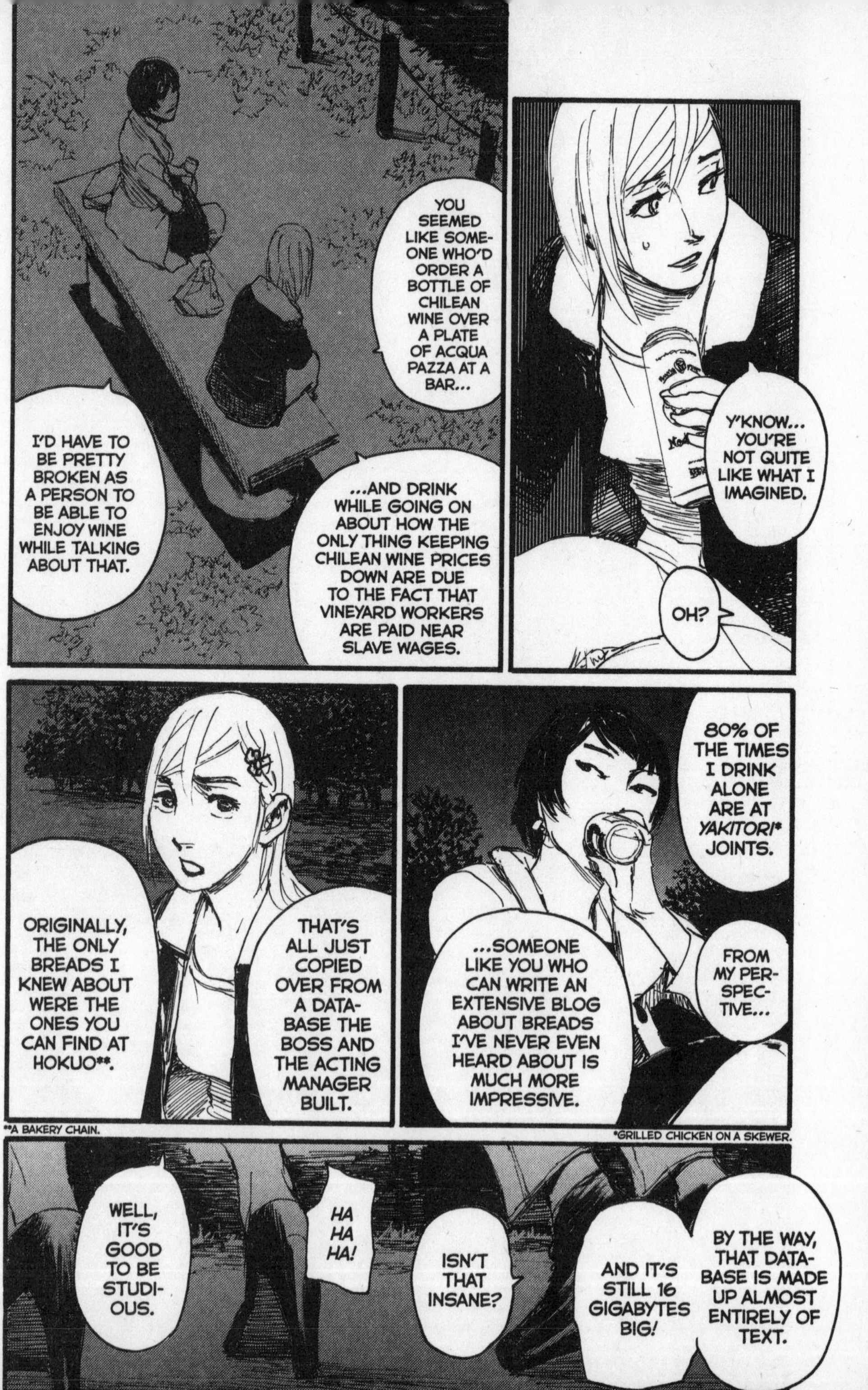
Y'KNOW... YOU'RE NOT QUITE LIKE WHAT I IMAGINED.
OH?
YOU SEEMED LIKE SOME-ONE WHO'D ORDER A BOTTLE OF CHILEAN WINE OVER A PLATE OF ACQUA PAZZA AT A BAR...
...AND DRINK WHILE GOING ON ABOUT HOW THE ONLY THING KEEPING CHILEAN WINE PRICES DOWN ARE DUE TO THE FACT THAT VINEYARD WORKERS ARE PAID NEAR SLAVE WAGES.
I'D HAVE TO BE PRETTY BROKEN AS A PERSON TO BE ABLE TO ENJOY WINE WHILE TALKING ABOUT THAT.
80% OF THE TIMES I DRINK ALONE ARE AT *YAKITORI** JOINTS.
FROM MY PER-SPEC-TIVE...
...SOMEONE LIKE YOU WHO CAN WRITE AN EXTENSIVE BLOG ABOUT BREADS I'VE NEVER EVEN HEARD ABOUT IS MUCH MORE IMPRESSIVE.
THAT'S ALL JUST COPIED OVER FROM A DATA-BASE THE BOSS AND THE ACTING MANAGER BUILT.
ORIGINALLY, THE ONLY BREADS I KNEW ABOUT WERE THE ONES YOU CAN FIND AT HOKUO**.
BY THE WAY, THAT DATA-BASE IS MADE UP ALMOST ENTIRELY OF TEXT.
AND IT'S STILL 16 GIGABYTES BIG!
ISN'T THAT INSANE?
HA HA HA!
WELL, IT'S GOOD TO BE STUDI-OUS.
*GRILLED CHICKEN ON A SKEWER.
**A BAKERY CHAIN.

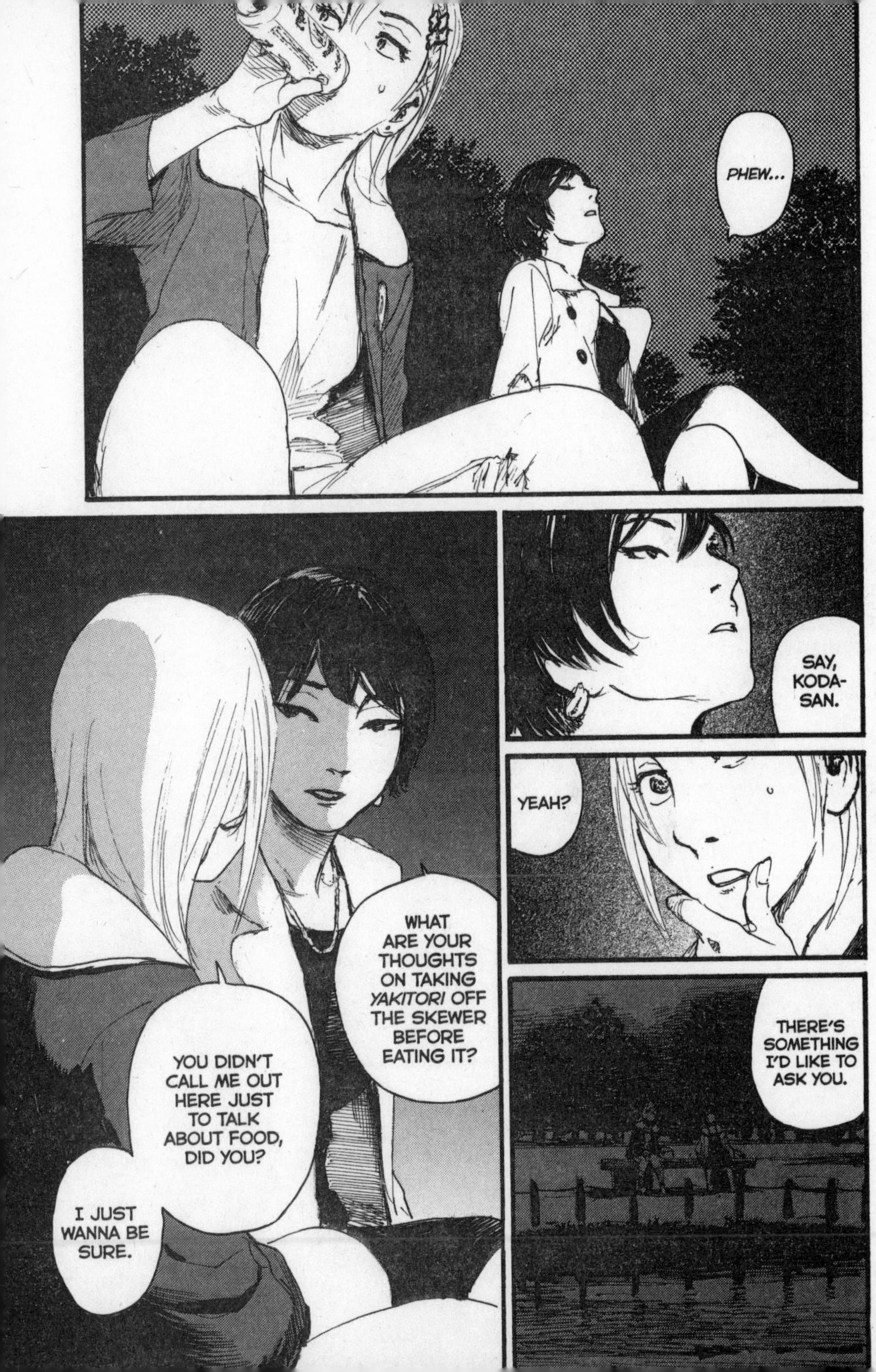
PHEW...
SAY, KODA-SAN.
YEAH?
THERE'S SOMETHING I'D LIKE TO ASK YOU.
WHAT ARE YOUR THOUGHTS ON TAKING *YAKITORI* OFF THE SKEWER BEFORE EATING IT?
YOU DIDN'T CALL ME OUT HERE JUST TO TALK ABOUT FOOD, DID YOU?
I JUST WANNA BE SURE.

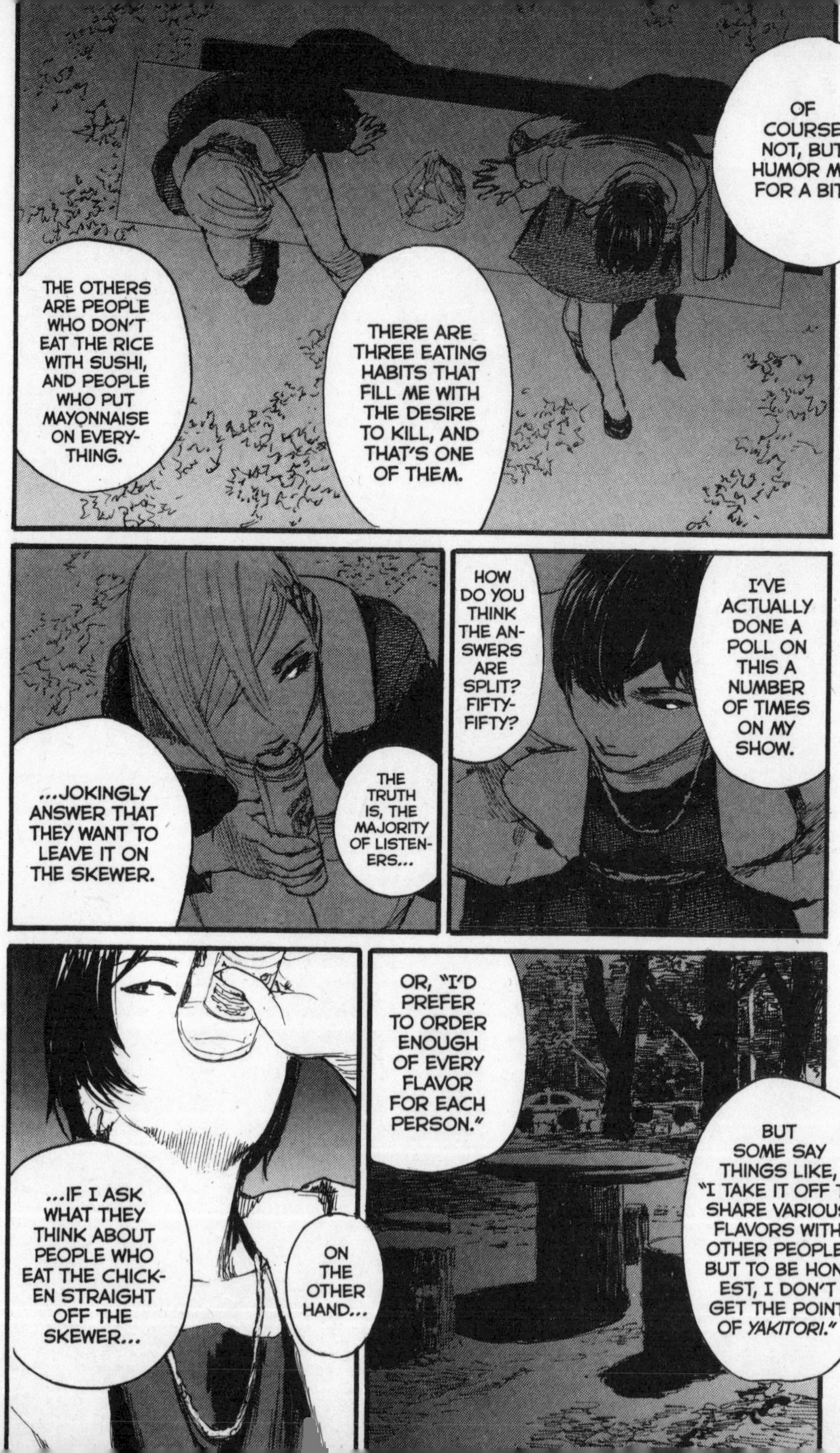
OF COURSE NOT, BUT HUMOR ME FOR A BIT.
THERE ARE THREE EATING HABITS THAT FILL ME WITH THE DESIRE TO KILL, AND THAT'S ONE OF THEM.
THE OTHERS ARE PEOPLE WHO DON'T EAT THE RICE WITH SUSHI, AND PEOPLE WHO PUT MAYONNAISE ON EVERY-THING.
I'VE ACTUALLY DONE A POLL ON THIS A NUMBER OF TIMES ON MY SHOW.
HOW DO YOU THINK THE AN-SWERS ARE SPLIT? FIFTY-FIFTY?
THE TRUTH IS, THE MAJORITY OF LISTEN-ERS...
...JOKINGLY ANSWER THAT THEY WANT TO LEAVE IT ON THE SKEWER.
BUT SOME SAY THINGS LIKE, "I TAKE IT OFF TO SHARE VARIOUS FLAVORS WITH OTHER PEOPLE, BUT TO BE HON-EST, I DON'T GET THE POINT OF *YAKITORI*."
OR, "I'D PREFER TO ORDER ENOUGH OF EVERY FLAVOR FOR EACH PERSON."
ON THE OTHER HAND...
...IF I ASK WHAT THEY THINK ABOUT PEOPLE WHO EAT THE CHICK-EN STRAIGHT OFF THE SKEWER...

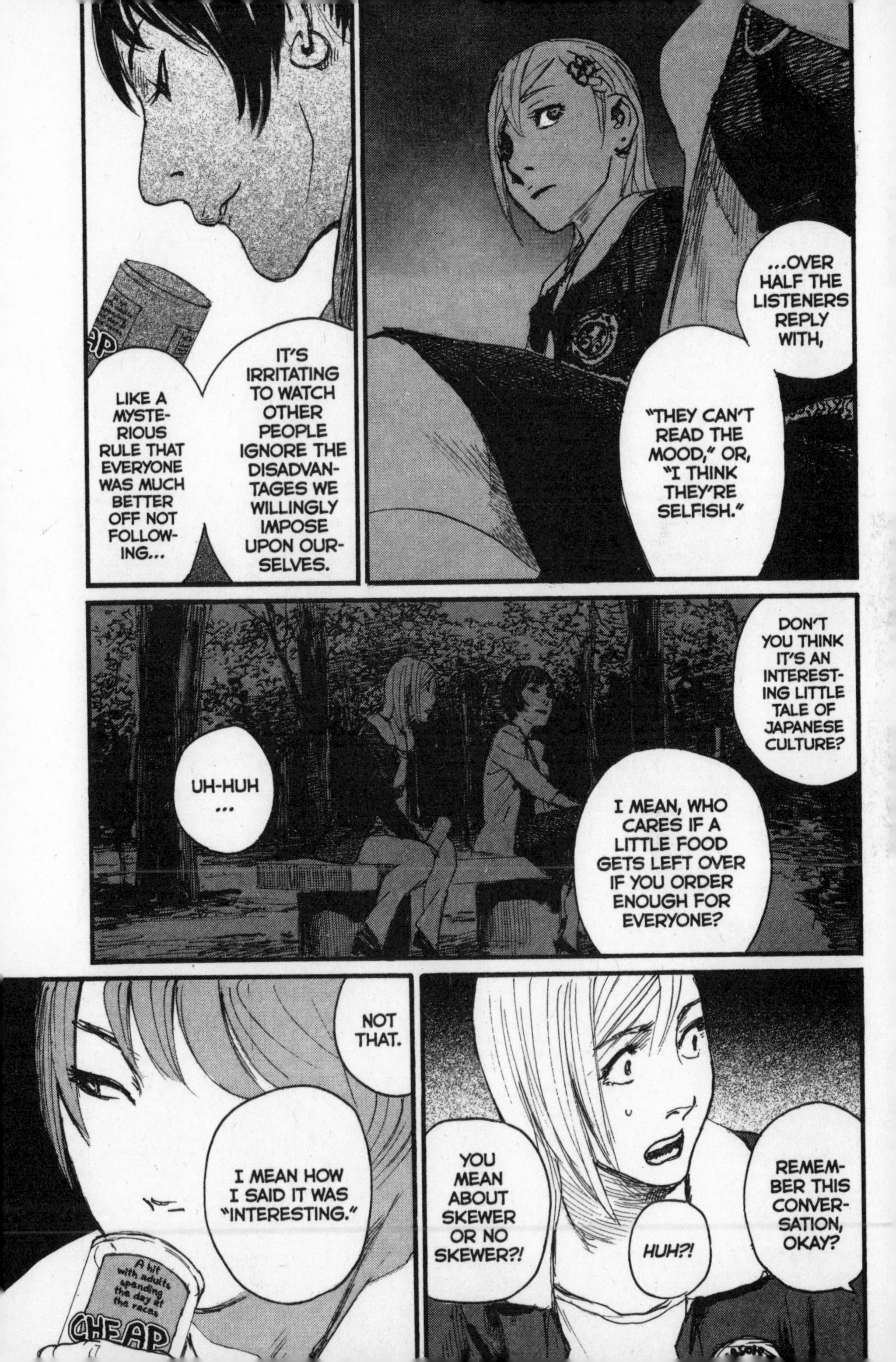
...OVER HALF THE LISTENERS REPLY WITH,
"THEY CAN'T READ THE MOOD," OR, "I THINK THEY'RE SELFISH."
IT'S IRRITATING TO WATCH OTHER PEOPLE IGNORE THE DISADVANTAGES WE WILLINGLY IMPOSE UPON OURSELVES.
LIKE A MYSTERIOUS RULE THAT EVERYONE WAS MUCH BETTER OFF NOT FOLLOWING...
DON'T YOU THINK IT'S AN INTERESTING LITTLE TALE OF JAPANESE CULTURE?
I MEAN, WHO CARES IF A LITTLE FOOD GETS LEFT OVER IF YOU ORDER ENOUGH FOR EVERYONE?
UH-HUH...
REMEMBER THIS CONVERSATION, OKAY?
HUH?!
YOU MEAN ABOUT SKEWER OR NO SKEWER?!
NOT THAT.
I MEAN HOW I SAID IT WAS "INTERESTING."
A hit with adults spending the day at the races
CHEAP

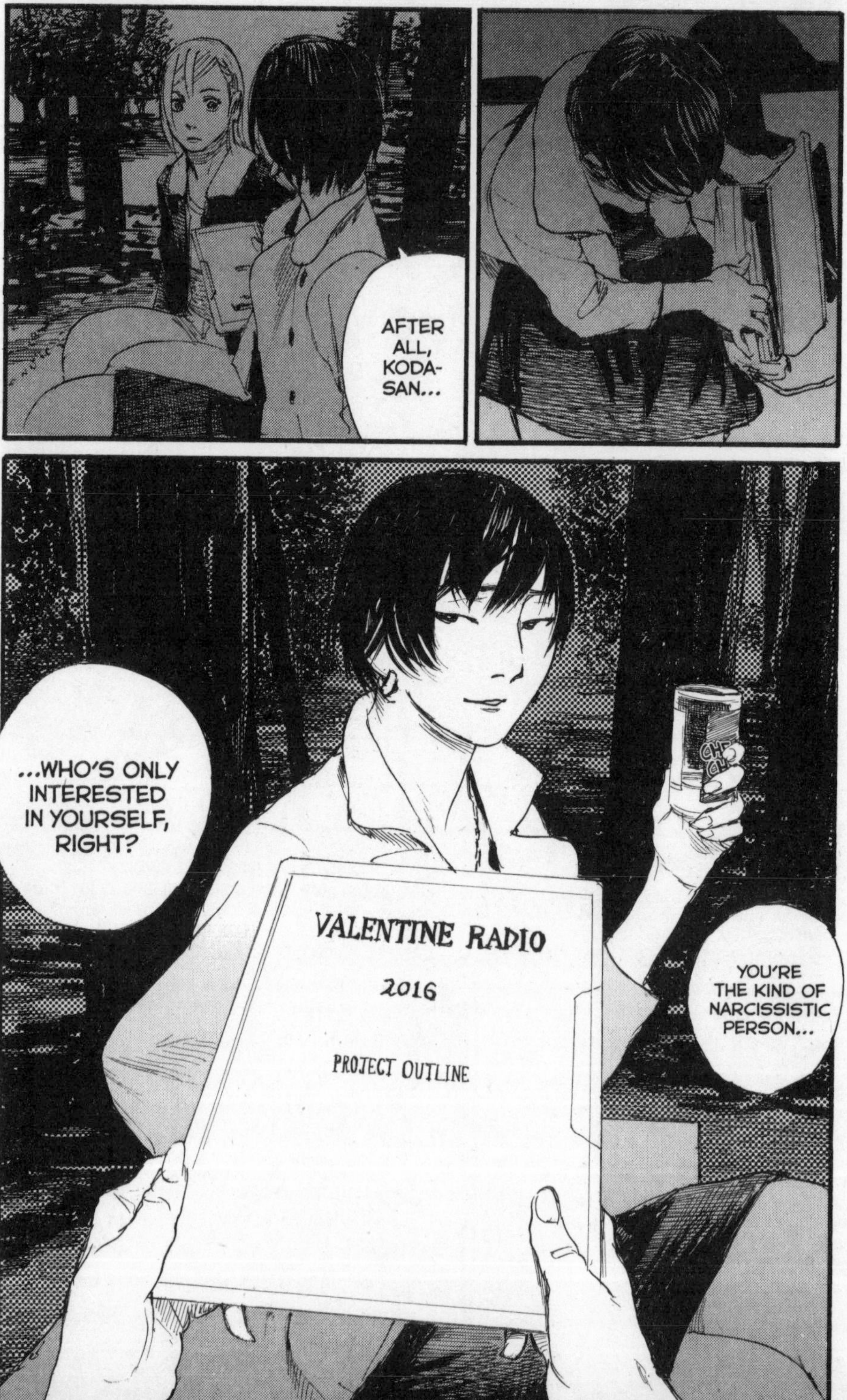
AFTER ALL, KODA-SAN...
YOU'RE THE KIND OF NARCISSISTIC PERSON...
VALENTINE RADIO
2016
PROJECT OUTLINE
...WHO'S ONLY INTERESTED IN YOURSELF, RIGHT?

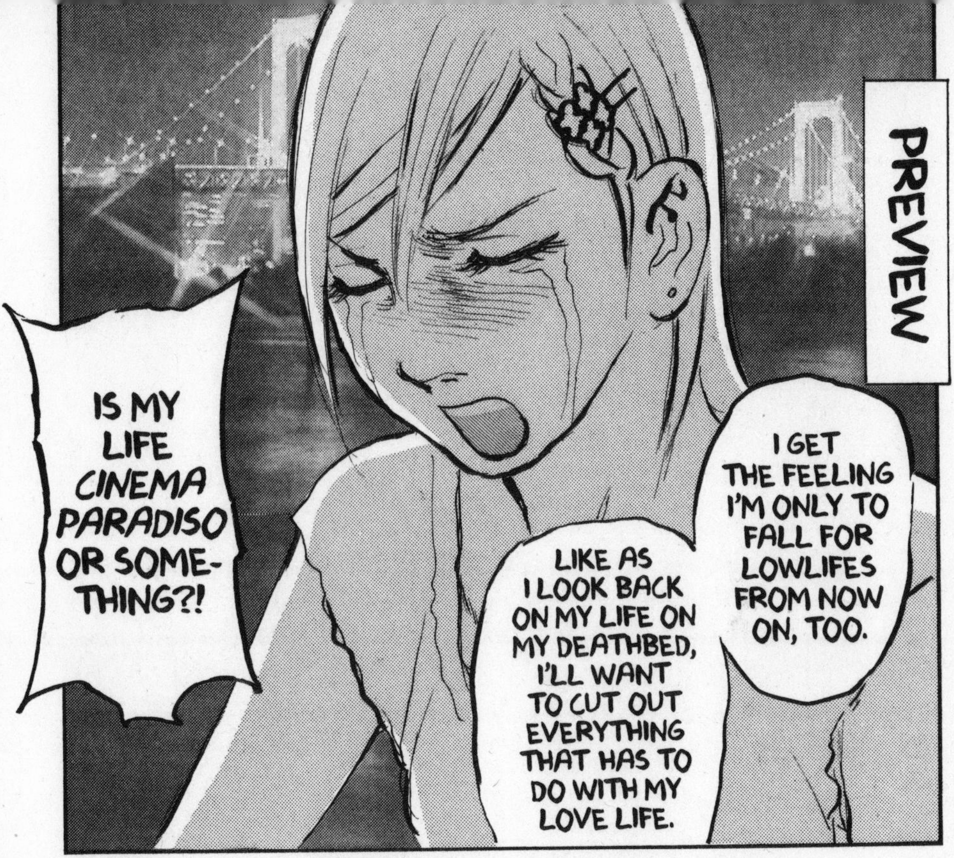
PREVIEW
I GET THE FEELING I'M ONLY TO FALL FOR LOWLIFES FROM NOW ON, TOO.
LIKE AS I LOOK BACK ON MY LIFE ON MY DEATHBED, I'LL WANT TO CUT OUT EVERYTHING THAT HAS TO DO WITH MY LOVE LIFE.
IS MY LIFE CINEMA PARADISO OR SOME-THING?!

AFTERWORD

Greetings, everyone. How did you like this third volume of the off-the-rails occult curry radio manga *Wave, Listen to Me!*? Hm? Romance? That's got nothing to do with me. Am I really obligated to pump every volume full of love affairs? Think about Japan's birth rate. It's the lowest of any developed country, right? That makes me think you're all not as interested in love as you say you are! ...So, I checked Google, and while it appears birth rate numbers continue to drop, the total fertility rate (number of children a woman gives birth to in her life) has been slowly rising since 2005. Hmm. By the way, Hokkaido is #45 out of 47 on the list of prefectural fertility rates. The lowest being, of course, Tokyo. I see...well, what I'm trying to say, everyone, is "Wikipedia sure is neat, huh?" Oh, yes. Speaking of Hokkaido, you might remember how in the last volume's afterword I mentioned that I changed my abbreviation of Seico Mart from Seico to Seicoma after being corrected by readers, then received mail from other readers saying it's actually Secoma. Well, apparently, the parent company of Seico Mart officially made the abbreviation Secoma recently. Upon further research, in addition to Seicoma and Secoma, I found other uncommon abbreviations including "Seima" and "Mart." Mart, huh? Well, see you again in volume four. Hiroaki Samura

Tanshihuai > Helian > Xuanman

↘ Kuitou

Q&A w/ Kureko

- What's your salary? → Secret

Bigwigs at key stations in Tokyo can make into the millions.

- How are ratings measured? → Surveys (Video Research) → Cancelations happen, but it's not as cutthroat as TV.
- Shows are occasionally funded by talent agencies as well.
- What goes into a radio show?
  - Production costs → Acquired through an agency.
  - Electric fees → Same as above.
  - Commercials → Materials provided for by the station or made in-house (by commission).
  - → Can be negotiated even without an agency, depending on station

☆ Lightning Round Question

- Innovative sumo clinchers?

→ Selecting the right mawashi (loincloth)

- What shows have you worked on in the past?

↙ Spelling... ()

Sakura ~~Kusakabe's~~ SOUND MIRAGE

◎ Gamon Hoko's Explosive V Throw-in!

Main writer

Biggest upset of the first half of the year.

Woooo!

Whaaaaa?!

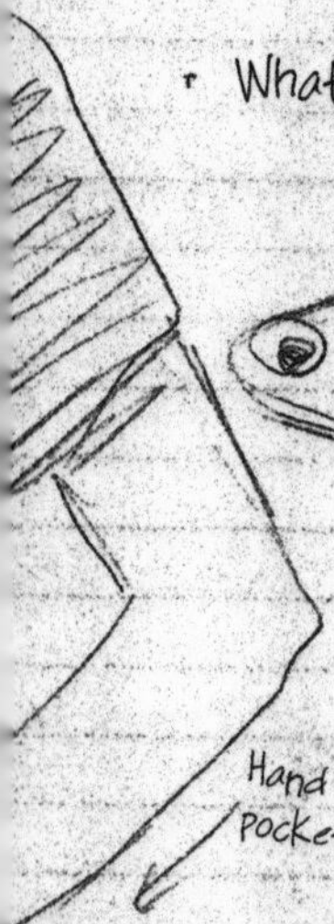

Hand in pocket.

☆ Lightning Round Question

- Give us your best pickup line.

→ "I wanna explore your southern hemisphere."

☆ Lightning Round Question

- What part of the cow is used to make the "hoba" dish served at BBQ restaurants?

→ Pit sweat

→ Teardrop moles.

☆ Lightning Round Question

Sandwich ingredients that just barely don't make the cut?

→ Cicada husks

→ Tree sap

6/8 Broadcasting - Telecom.

(Lecturer / MRS Employee) → This guy

RADIO'S DYING

- Advertising spending halved in 20 years
- Radio departments being sold off (in the States).
- Regional ratings PLUMMETING!
  ^ Uh-oh... 6

POLO

- Rate for hiring first-rate entertainers as hosts:
  5h/wk. → ¥20,000 (~$200 USD)
  Perfectly realistic.
  Specific comic duos? Sandwichman?

Even major stations only employ ~100 people.

(Radio's Strengths)

Kureko-san
^ Spelling?

- Strong local ties.

- Responsiveness in emergencies

- Speed (?)

- **FREEDOM!**

☆ Lightning Round Question

- What sort of group is MMMM?
- → Meeting for Measuring up to your Manager's ambitions

Translation Notes

Asama, page 8
A branch of the Shinto religion centered on the worship of gods of volcanos, primarily Mount Fuji.

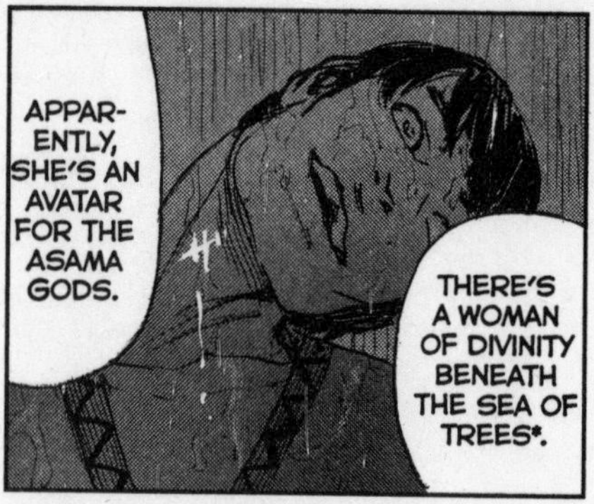
THERE'S A WOMAN OF DIVINITY BENEATH THE SEA OF TREES*.
APPARENTLY, SHE'S AN AVATAR FOR THE ASAMA GODS.

Mito-chan, Matsuko, page 9
Asami Miura (Mito-chan) is a television announcer who was ranked most popular in her field by Oricon Style in 2013 and 2014. Matsuko (Matsuko Deluxe) is a television personality known for the talk show "The World Unknown to Matsuko." Though Mitsuo draws a similarity based on their face shapes, the two have different body types.

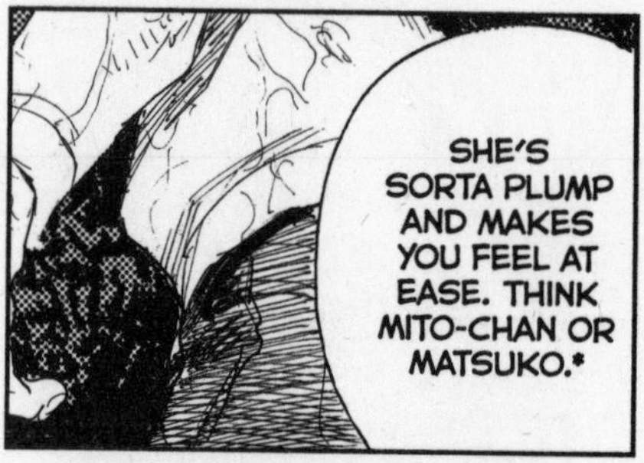
SHE'S SORTA PLUMP AND MAKES YOU FEEL AT EASE. THINK MITO-CHAN OR MATSUKO.*

Taka and Toshi, Downtown, page 24
Taka and Toshi is a stand-up comedy duo from Sapporo consisting of Takahiro Suzuki and Toshikazu Miura. Downtown is also a comedy duo consisting of Masatoshi Hamada and Hitoshi Matsumoto, who both hail from Hyogo prefecture. Downtown is particularly prolific and among the most influential comedians in Japan since their 1982 debut.

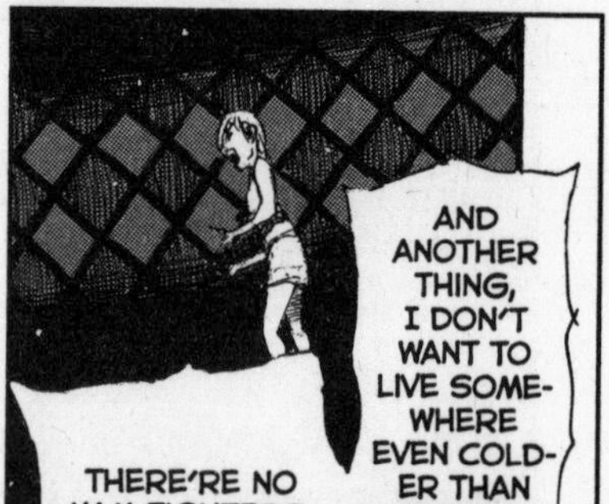
AND ANOTHER THING, I DON'T WANT TO LIVE SOME-WHERE EVEN COLD-ER THAN KUSHIRO!
THERE'RE NO HAM FIGHTERS, TAKA AND TOSHI, OR DOWNTOWN THERE, RIGHT?!

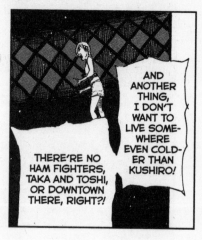

Masayuki Shuno's *Black Buddha*, page 29
The second novel in a series centering on an obscure detective named Gisaku Isurugi. Gisaku is requested to seek a hidden treasure in a temple in Fukuoka, where the object of worship is a bodhisattva figure with its face cut out…

AND THE STORY IS ALWAYS SO SLAPDASH AND TAKES AN OCCULT TURN EVERY TIME FOR SOME REA-SON.
IS THIS MASAYUKI SHUNO'S BLACK BUDDHA OR SOME-THING?!

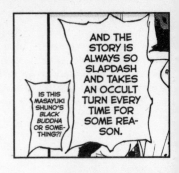

***Year One in the North*, page 39**
This film, with a star-studded cast including Ken Watanabe, paints the story of exiled loyalists struggling to begin life anew in Hokkaido following the fall of the shogunate in the late 19th century. Though the film itself wasn't very good, Hokkaido folks could probably find the setting relatable…?

That's the kinda impression I'd expect from some-one who just watched Year One in the North*...

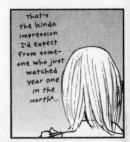

Samurai pudding, page 66
A Sapporo delicacy that boasts the freshness of local ingredients, with prices for single servings starting at about $5 and going as high as $7 for the premium variety.

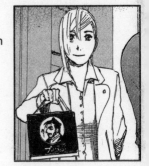

Imabari towel, page 67
A towel brand originating from the city of Imabari in Ehime prefecture. With more than a century of history, Imabari towels are considered luxury items for their premium quality, softness, and drying efficiency.

NO!
SOME-ONE, PLEASE LEAD ME OUT OF THIS LAB-YRINTH!
WITH AN IMABARI TOWEL-LIKE IDEA!

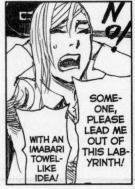

Obon, page 74

A festival in Japan, rooted in Buddhist tradition, that is considered a time for honoring the spirits of a family's deceased, including ancestors. As Mizuho's statement suggests, it is common to return to one's ancestral home and pay respects to a family grave or household altar. The holiday lasts 3 days, but the start date varies by region.

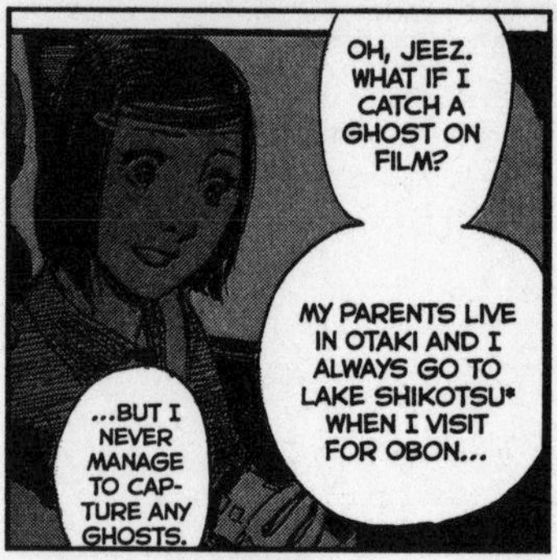
OH, JEEZ. WHAT IF I CATCH A GHOST ON FILM?
MY PARENTS LIVE IN OTAKI AND I ALWAYS GO TO LAKE SHIKOTSU* WHEN I VISIT FOR OBON...
...BUT I NEVER MANAGE TO CAPTURE ANY GHOSTS.

Third time's the charm, page 74

These are the silhouettes of the idol group Momoiro Clover Z in their rehearsal gear for the 2014 NHK Red and White Song Battle, an annual New Year's Eve television special in Japan. Aside from celebrating their third consecutive appearance on the show, the adage on their shirts commemorated achieving their dream of "appearing" with their fans at the event via special voice recordings and costumes with fan messages written on them.

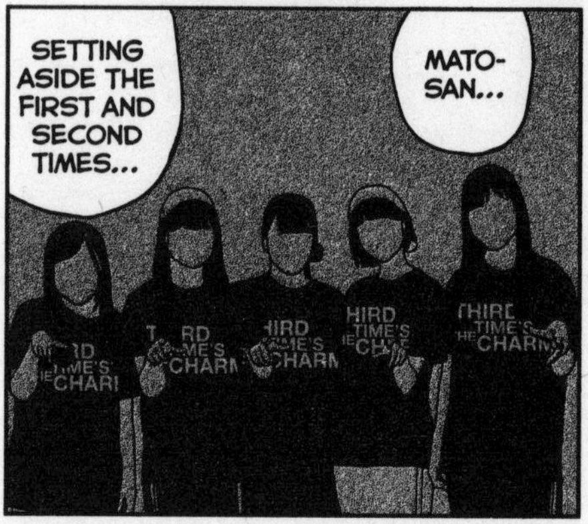
MATO-SAN...
SETTING ASIDE THE FIRST AND SECOND TIMES...

***Onna Taikoki* and *Shogun's Sadism,* page 133**

The *Taikoki* is a biography of Hideyoshi Toyotomi, one of the major personalities during the Warring States period of Japan that gave rise to the Tokugawa shogunate. *Onna Taikoki* is a typical period drama that recounts the events of that era from the perspective of Hideyoshi's wife, Nene. *Shogun's Sadism,* or *Tokugawa onna keibatsu emaki: Ushizaki no kei,* is a splatter film set in the subsequent Edo period that involves torture and other gruesome acts.

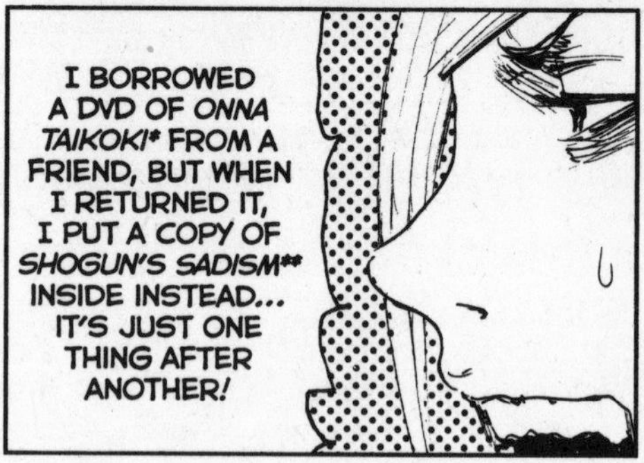
I BORROWED A DVD OF *ONNA TAIKOKI** FROM A FRIEND, BUT WHEN I RETURNED IT, I PUT A COPY OF *SHOGUN'S SADISM*** INSIDE INSTEAD... IT'S JUST ONE THING AFTER ANOTHER!

Tanshihuai, Helian, Xuanman, Kuitou, page 174

All four names belong to personalities from around the Three Kingdoms period in China. Tanshihuai was a chieftain of the Xianbei tribe, and Helian was his second son. Helian's son Xuanman was his grandson. Kuitou was Helian's nephew, making him and his brothers Fuluohan and Budugen (Mizuho's turtles' namesakes) Tanshihuai's grandsons as well.

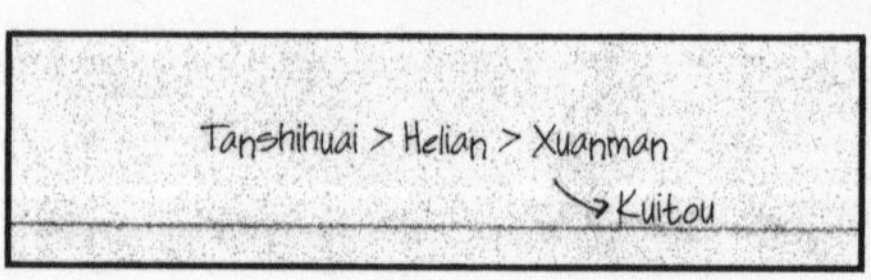
Tanshihuai > Helian > Xuanman
Kuitou

wave

LISTEN TO ME!

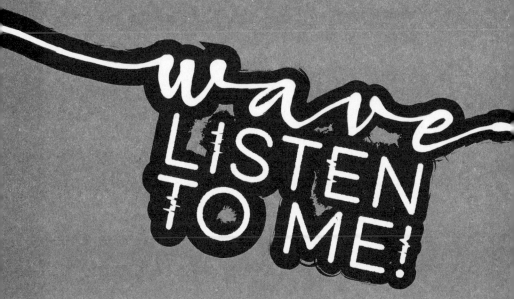

Young characters and steampunk setting, like *Howl's Moving Castle* and *Battle Angel Alita*

A boy with a talent for machines and a mysterious girl whose wings he's fixed will take you beyond the clouds! In the tradition of the high-flying, resonant adventure stories of Studio Ghibli comes a gorgeous tale about the longing of young hearts for adventure and friendship!

A dark and sexy body-horror action manga perfect for fans of *Prison School* and *High School of the Dead*!

Shuichi Kagaya is a smart kid, and most smart kids his age would be thinking about college. Shuichi is also a monster, and he's smart enough to know that monsters don't go to college. But after he uses his monstrous form to save his classmate Claire Aoki, it doesn't matter what his plans for the future were, because he's not the one making the decisions anymore. Now that the seductive, sadistic Claire knows Shuichi's secret, she's got her own ideas about what a monster is good for—because he's not the first monster she's met...

KC/
KODANSHA
COMICS

GLEIPNIR

"You and me together...we would be unstoppable."

PERFECT WORLD

Rie Aruga

A TOUCHING NEW SERIES ABOUT LOVE AND COPING WITH DISABILITY

An office party reunites Tsugumi with her high school crush Itsuki. He's realized his dream of becoming an architect, but along the way, he experienced a spinal injury that put him in a wheelchair. Now Tsugumi's rekindled feelings will butt up against prejudices she never considered — and Itsuki will have to decide if he's ready to let someone into his heart...

"Depicts with great delicacy and courage the difficulties some with disabilities experience getting involved in romantic relationships... Rie Aruga refuses to romanticize, pushing her heroine to face the reality of disability. She invites her readers to the same tasks of empathy, knowledge and recognition."
—Slate.fr

"An important entry [in manga romance]... The emotional core of both plot and characters indicates thoughtfulness... [Aruga's] research is readily apparent in the text and artwork, making this feel like a real story."
—Anime News Network

KC KODANSHA COMICS

Knight of the Ice ©Yayoi Ogawa/Kodansha Ltd.

SKATING THRILLS AND ICY CHILLS WITH THIS NEW TINGLY ROMANCE SERIES!

A rom-com on ice, perfect for fans of *Princess Jellyfish* and *Wotakoi*. Kokoro is the talk of the figure-skating world, winning trophies and hearts. But little do they know... he's actually a huge nerd! From the beloved creator of *You're My Pet* (*Tramps Like Us*).

Chitose is a serious young woman, working for the health magazine *SASSO*. Or at least, she would be, if she wasn't constantly getting distracted by her childhood friend, international figure skating star Kokoro Kijinami! In the public eye and on the ice, Kokoro is a gallant, flawless knight, but behind his glittery costumes and breathtaking spins lies a secret: He's actually a hopelessly romantic otaku, who can only land his quad jumps when Chitose is on hand to recite a spell from his favorite magical girl anime!

KC
KODANSHA
COMICS

Magus of the Library

Mitsu Izumi

MITSU IZUMI'S STUNNING ARTWORK BRINGS A FANTASTICAL LITERARY ADVENTURE TO LUSH, THRILLING LIFE!

Young Theo adores books, but the prejudice and hatred of his village keeps them ever out of his reach. Then one day, he chances to meet Sedona, a traveling librarian who works for the great library of Aftzaak, City of Books, and his life changes forever...

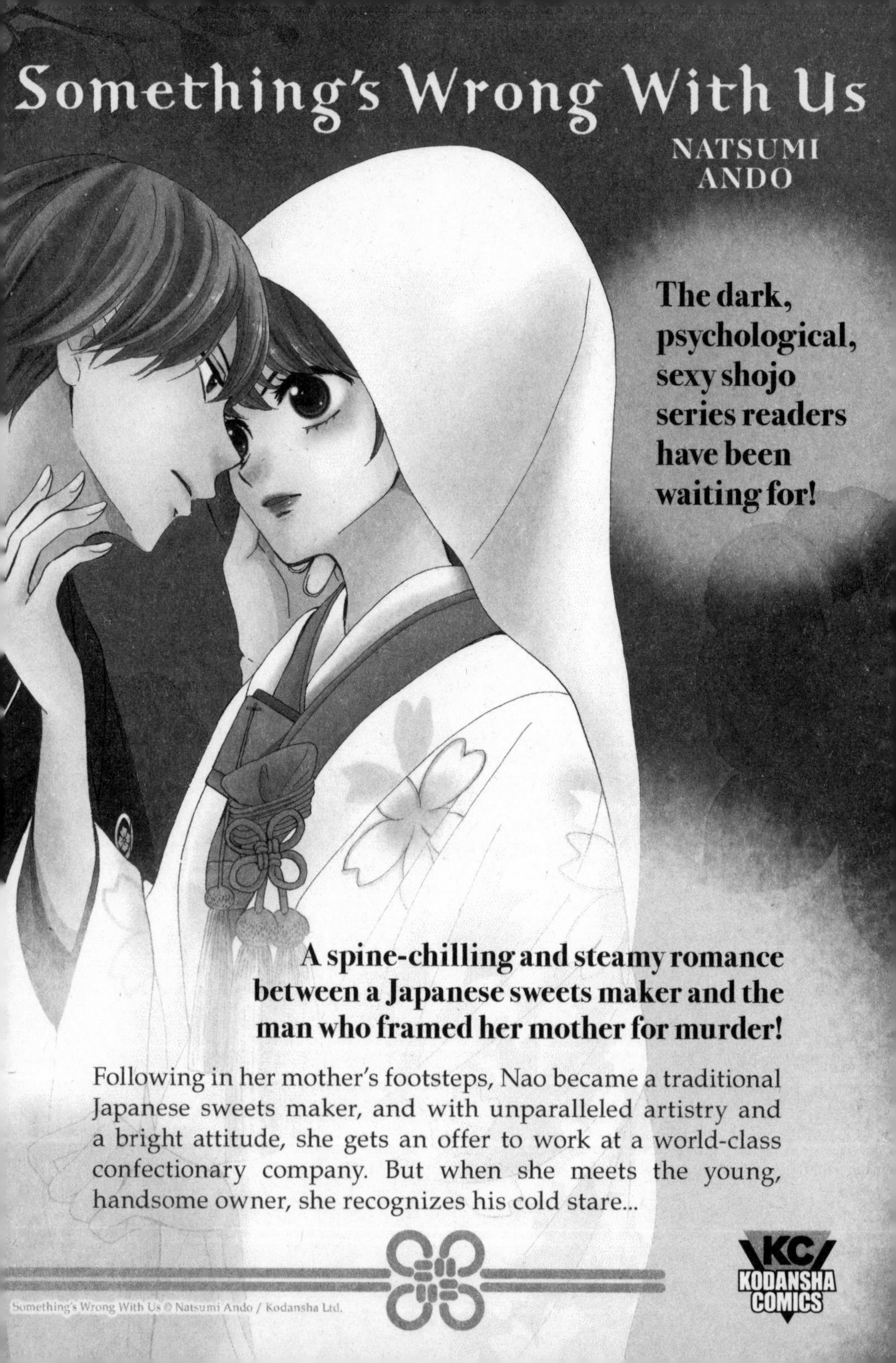
Something's Wrong With Us
NATSUMI ANDO
The dark, psychological, sexy shojo series readers have been waiting for!
A spine-chilling and steamy romance between a Japanese sweets maker and the man who framed her mother for murder!
Following in her mother's footsteps, Nao became a traditional Japanese sweets maker, and with unparalleled artistry and a bright attitude, she gets an offer to work at a world-class confectionary company. But when she meets the young, handsome owner, she recognizes his cold stare...
KC KODANSHA COMICS
Something's Wrong With Us © Natsumi Ando / Kodansha Ltd.

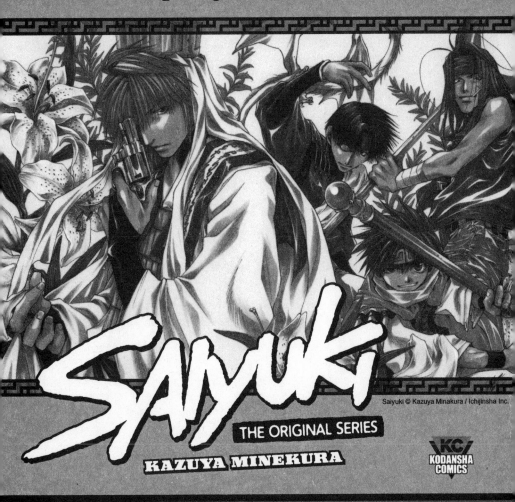

The adorable new odd-couple cat comedy manga from the creator of the beloved *Chi's Sweet Home*, in full color!

Praise for Chi's Sweet Home

"Nearly impossible to turn away... a true all-ages title that anyone, young or old, cat lover or not, will enjoy. The stories will bring a smile to your face and warm your heart."

—School Library Journal

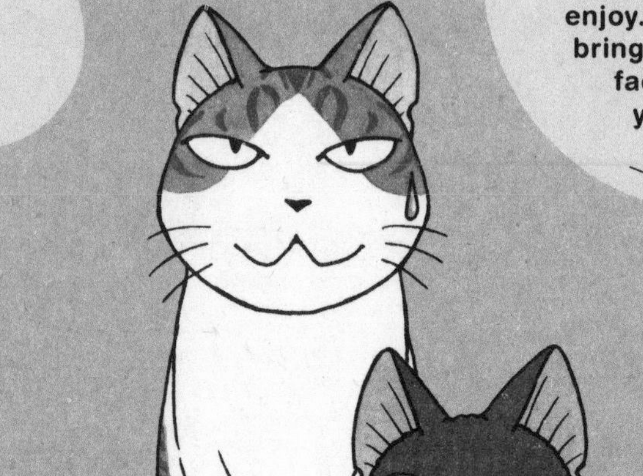

Sue & Tai-chan

Konami Kanata

Sue is an aging housecat who's looking forward to living out her life in peace... but her plans change when the mischievous black tomcat Tai-chan enters the picture! Hey! Sue never signed up to be a catsitter! *Sue & Tai-chan* is the latest from the reigning meow-narch of cute kitty comics, Konami Kanata.

KC KODANSHA COMICS

CUTE ANIMALS AND LIFE LESSONS, PERFECT FOR ASPIRING PET VETS OF ALL AGES!

YUZU THE PET VET

1

BY
MINGO ITO

In collaboration with
NIPPON COLUMBIA CO., LTD.

Yuzu the Pet Vet © Mingo Ito / NIPPON COLUMBIA CO., LTD./ Kodansha Ltd.

For an 11-year-old, Yuzu has a lot on her plate. When her mom gets sick and has to be hospitalized, Yuzu goes to live with her uncle who runs the local veterinary clinic. Yuzu's always been scared of animals, but she tries to help out. Through all the tough moments in her life, Yuzu realizes that she can help make things all right with a little help from her animal pals, peers, and kind grown-ups.

Every new patient is a furry friend in the making!

A SMART, NEW ROMANTIC COMEDY FOR FANS OF *SHORTCAKE CAKE* AND *TERRACE HOUSE*!

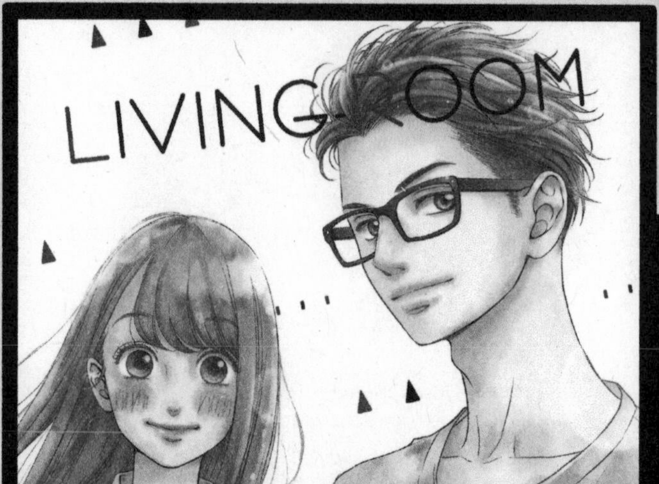
LIVING-ROOM
MATSUNAGA-SAN
1
Keiko Iwashita

A romance manga starring high school girl Meeko, who learns to live on her own in a boarding house whose living room is home to the odd (but handsome) Matsunaga-san. She begins to adjust to her new life away from her parents, but Meeko soon learns that no matter how far away from home she is, she's still a young girl at heart — especially when she finds herself falling for Matsunaga-san.

KC KODANSHA COMICS

THE SWEET SCENT OF LOVE IS IN THE AIR! FOR FANS OF OFFBEAT ROMANCES LIKE *WOTAKOI*

Sweat and Soap © Kintetsu Yamada / Kodansha Ltd

In an office romance, there's a fine line between sexy and awkward... and that line is where Asako — a woman who sweats copiously — meets Koutarou — a perfume developer who can't get enough of Asako's, er, scent. Don't miss a romcom manga like no other!

A Kodansha Comics Trade Paperback Original
Wave, Listen to Me! 3 copyright © 2016 Hiroaki Samura
English translation copyright © 2020 Hiroaki Samura

Published in the United States by Kodansha Comics, an imprint of
Kodansha USA Publishing, LLC, New York.

Publication rights for this English edition arranged through
Kodansha Ltd., Tokyo.

First published in Japan in 2016 by Kodansha Ltd., Tokyo
as Nami yo kiitekure, volume 3.

ISBN 978-1-63236-869-0

Original cover design by Tadashi Hisamochi (hive&co.,ltd.)

Printed in the United States of America.

www.kodanshacomics.com

9 8 7 6 5 4 3 2 1
Translation: Adam Hirsch
Lettering: Darren Smith
Additional lettering and layout: Michael Martin
Editing: Alexandra Swanson, Vanessa Tenazas
YKS Services LLC/SKY Japan, INC.
Kodansha Comics edition cover design by Adam Del Re

Publisher: Kiichiro Sugawara

Director of publishing services: Ben Applegate
Associate director of operations: Stephen Pakula
Publishing services managing editor: Noelle Webster
Assistant production manager: Emi Lotto, Angela Zurlo
Logo and character art ©Kodansha USA Publishing, LLC